FAIR PLAY AND FOUL?

By the same author

Who cares about the health victim?
1998

FAIR PLAY AND FOUL?

A book of revelations about
patients' rights, complaints
handling and compensation
in the United Kingdom and
elsewhere in Europe

John Elder

 BOOKS

Published by

K⸱LAXON BOOKS

PO Box 24, Chepstow NP16 6XS, United Kingdom

© John Elder 2005

British Library Cataloguing-in-Publication Data
A catalogue record for this book is available from the British Library

ISBN 0 9534604 1 X

First published in the United Kingdom 2005

Typesetting (in Sabon) and cover design by
Alan Rutherford, Cheltenham, Gloucestershire

Printed and bound in Great Britain by
Antony Rowe Limited, Chippenham, Wiltshire

The author has tried very hard to ensure that the contents of this book are essentially accurate. Nonetheless, being a fairly complex and multi-faceted work, the odd error – especially in items obtained from its many sources – may have escaped his eagle eye. Should this have happened, he apologizes in advance and hopes that any of these is inconsequential and that those concerned will overlook his slip in the circumstances.

To the memory of my adorable Kay,
and of Margaret who gave me encouragement

Contents

*Statutory patient insurance and compensation schemes in Europe,
and their effect*

Note for readers
The third full paragraph on page 31 and the second complete paragraph
on page 55 are verbatim extracts from the source publications and should
have appeared in a form to indicate the fact.

Acknowledgements

When I finally got round to start writing this book, I did not imagine the true proportions of what I was taking on – even second time around. Nor could I have foreseen the particularly unfortunate event that was to add to these daunting factors. Still, the book was eventually finished. But it was due less to my perseverance than the sustained help I was given by the many forbearing and expert contacts of mine representing organizations in Britain and elsewhere in Europe. Put more accurately, it was these terrific people who made everything achieveable. They must surely have been heartily sick of my constant approaches for additional information, or (being the novice I am) clarification of details they already had specially put together and supplied to me. Yet they never showed it, and always responded graciously.

Indeed, many of them produced much of this work for me at home as they were unable to find the time to compile it in the course of their busy occupations. Not only that, they even set aside time to then check and correct the relevant (and usually the best) part of completed draft chapters I had sent to them. All this was on top of the invariably long telephone conversations between us in the process. My telephone bills (and theirs to a lesser extent, thank goodness) are a testimony to these lengthy events. It has to be said, however, that helping me would have been easier (and probably less costly) for these good people had I been set up with an e-mail address. The problem was that, unfortunately, I could not afford the time to arrange for and also absorb high-tech matters I knew absolutely nothing about. My fax machine was the best other means of communication on offer to my contributors – apart, of course, from the mail which, although obviously slower, was as useful as ever.

The important thing is that, between us, we seem to have got there in the end, and this book of approaching 170,000 words is pretty well the result. Therefore my gratitude is expressed to each and every one of the large number of experts who so generously helped me achieve this most daunting end. I had thought of individually naming them, but then felt that doing so might not be practical (for instance, some may have moved to other employment) or appropriate for other reasons. The answer appeared to lie in providing a record of the institutions and other organizations in which they were represented at the time I was in contact with them. This I have done.

Austria
Volksanwaltshaft (Ombudsman Board), Vienna

Belgium
Dr Thierry Vansweevelt, professor in tort and medical law, University of Antwerp, Belgium

Denmark
Patientforsakringen (Patient Insurance), Copenhagen
Sundhedsstyrelsen (National Board of Health), Copenhagen
Sundshedsvæsenets Patientklagenævn (Patients' Board of Complaints), Copenhagen
Copenhagen Hospital Corporation

Finland
Ministry of Social Affairs and Health, Helsinki
Finnish Patient Insurance Centre, Helsinki
Federation of Finnish Insurance Companies, Helsinki

Iceland
Heilbrigdis – OG Tryggingamálaráduneytid (Ministry of Health and Social Security),
    Reykjavik

Ireland (Republic of)
Eastern Regional Health Authority, Dublin
Mid-Western Health Board, Limerick
North Eastern Health Board, Kells
Office of the Ombudsman, Dublin
South Eastern Health Board, Kilkenny
The Stationery Office, Dublin
Western Health Board, Galway

Norway
Norsk Pasientskadeerstatning (Norwegian Patient Compensation System), Oslo
Sosial – OG Helsedepartementet (Ministry of Health and Social Affairs), Oslo
Statens Helsetilsyn (Norwegian Board of Health), Oslo

Sweden
Hälso-och sjukvärdens ansvarsnämnd (Medical Responsibility Board), Stockholm
Patientförsäkringsforeningen (Patient Insurance Association), Stockholm
Socialstyrelsen (The National Board of Health and Welfare), Stockholm

United Kingdom
Common Services Agency for NHS Scotland (Information and Statistics Division),
    Edinburgh
Council for Healthcare Regulatory Excellence, London
Criminal Injuries Compensation Authority, Glasgow
Department of Health, Leeds
Department of Health, Social Services and Public Safety (Information and Analysis
    Unit), Belfast
Department for Work and Pensions, Preston
Eastern Health and Social Services Board, Belfast
Healthcare Commission, London
Health Service Ombudsman for England and Wales (Office of the), London and
    Cardiff

Her Majesty's Stationery Office, Norwich
Independent Review Secretariat, Brecon
ISD (Information and Statistics Division) Scotland National Statistics, Edinburgh
The Law Society of Northern Ireland Legal Aid Department, Belfast
Legal Services Commission, London
Legal Services Ombudsman (Office of the), Manchester
The National Assembly for Wales (Statistical Directorate), Cardiff
National Audit Office, London
National Institute for Health and Clinical Excellence
NHS Litigation Authority, London
NHS National Services Scotland (Information Services), Edinburgh
Northern Health and Social Services Board, Ballymena
Northern Ireland Ombudsman (Office of the), Belfast
Office of the Parliamentary Commissioner for Standards, House of Commons, London
Scottish Health Service Central Legal Office, Edinburgh
Scottish Legal Aid Board, Edinburgh
Scottish Public Services Ombudsman (Health Service Ombudsman for Scotland), Edinburgh
Southern Health and Social Services Board, Armagh
Vaccine Damage Payments Unit of the Department for Work and Pensions, Preston
Welsh Risk Pool, St Asaph
Western Health and Social Services Board, Londonderry

There were many others who inspired me and contributed towards the writing of this sequel. Among them was my charming and valued friend Margaret whose enduring support buoyed me up no end – especially in my most flagging moments. She was a member of that special breed who always put the difficulties of others before those of their own. I recall this marvellous characteristic of hers still coming to the fore when I talked to her while she was terminally ill in hospital early in 2003. Tragically, in the spring of that year, Margaret lost her fight against the illness that had suddenly recurred. I can only imagine how much her husband, Christopher, and daughters must miss her. The year before, Margaret had allowed me to recount briefly the events in the health service that had badly damaged her health (unconnected with her final illness) and permanently affected the rest of her life. It will always be a source of deep regret to me that this book did not come out (as it should have done) while she was still part of this life. I, too, miss her greatly.

Gillian, Margaret's friend and mine, likewise provided much inspiration and told me about her own lasting injuries following health care. She, too, gave me an account of her unresolved battle to get due restitution. Nor will I forget the support that Maureen and Joan gave me. They also are serious casualties of faulty health care and, similarly, have not received just redress from those responsible for their dreadful predicament.

It amazes me how all these women have carried on so well with their lives regardless of the tough burdens that have so cruelly been placed upon them. One would have thought that achieving this end was daunting enough in itself. Yet these admirable people went further and took on the causes of others who were similarly affected. They were, indeed, an inspiration to me. I hope that they and others like them will look upon this book as a modest contribution in the long haul along the road to equitable redress.

My gratitude also goes to Pinky and Colin who fortified me in other ways. They gave me a computer to replace my very limited and otherwise unsatisfactory word processor. (Its makers added the word 'computer' – more for effect than anything else, I imagine.) Not only that, they provided me with the necessary know-how to set it up and get things going properly. Thus, I could not only knock out drafts with comparative ease, but was also able to convert what I had written to the different process that was needed for editing purposes.

Many are the times when I have taken instruction from Pinky and Colin on the telephone to get myself out of trouble with the advanced piece of equipment they had gifted to me. They should have been fed up with these countless calls for help. But they did not complain – the good people that they are. Their help came in other welcome forms too numerous to recount here. In truth, writing the book would have been much more of a formidable and time-consuming commitment without their intervention. I shall not forget it.

In addition I am grateful to my editor Susannah Wight for her advice and expert attention to my copy in the most trying of circumstances. She has been incredibly patient with me.

Finally, I have to apologize to all my friends and contributors for the huge delay in publication of this book. The hold-up was connected with me and nobody else. There must have been times when even these patient people had doubted that it would be coming out at all; and believed that all the help they had given me was to be in vain. Perhaps they may now consider that the finished product has been worth the extra wait.

John Elder
July 2005

PREFACE

Background to this book

This book was not supposed to be written. There was to be no sequel to my first, much lesser, effort on the same subject, which was published in 1998.[1] I had planned to get stuck into something lighter and less brain-taxing, that would still bring me some satisfaction. But by accident in the summer of the following year I picked up a surprising snippet of information connected with the investigation of complaints about health care in Britain that seemed to be worth looking into.

I carried out some follow-up work on this unexpected disclosure and discovered that it had wider implications than I had thought at first. Indeed, enough to warrant a couple of thousand words in the press or, alternatively, a short documentary on radio or television – but nothing much more. However, despite trying to persuade numerous contacts in the media over the next 12 months or so, I could not find a taker for my researched and written-up piece. It was not that I wanted payment, or kudos in any other way, for this offering. I was simply looking for the right kind of editor in the press or broadcasting media to develop what I had already uncovered about an issue against which there seemed to be a serious question mark, and get it out into the open. (Yeah, pure, unadulterated altruistic motives on my part.)

With failure on this scale, I gave up on my cause. Shortly afterwards, I began work on a book proposal promised to a truly accessible and responsive literary agent. He was also high-powered and the breed of top-ranking professional that is harder to get hold of than gold dust – unless one has impressive credentials. My proposal concerned the less demanding undertaking mentioned earlier. That was in 2001, and the agent has still not seen my proposition. Doubtless, he has long given up on receiving the said item, and on its author. And who would blame him?

During the 1990s major medical negligence scandals had been coming to light at an alarming rate in Britain. News stories were running almost *ad nauseum* in the press and on the air waves. Additionally, surveys and other studies were picking out flaws in the regulation of the medical profession and inadequacies in Britain's National Health Service (NHS) complaints procedure. The government commissioned an evaluation of the NHS complaints mechanism[2] and became involved in a host of other initiatives connected with the health service and medical profession. So did the House of Commons Health Committee with its own investigation into the subject and subsequent publication of its report and findings.[3] Remedial action was required and the omens seemed to be good for meaningful change to the complaints handling system as a whole. The prevailing mood was also a cause for some satisfaction, especially by those who had either personally or indirectly been at the receiving end of alleged medical error.

These events and the accounts a number of complainants I had come across during this period gave of their own experiences persuaded me to look at the prospect of a sequel to my first book. But to say that the rest is history would be too simplistic a remark. In a nutshell, the first full draft of the book (and a rough one of my lighter tome, and the proposal for it I had promised the literary agent) lodged in my original, somewhat elementary, computer was 'corrupted' and rendered useless by a lightning strike. Who would believe such a calamity could happen to them? I most certainly did not expect to be a casualty of that order. Worst of all, I had very little disk or hardcopy back-up. So it was pretty well back to square one. Except that my motivation had taken a nose-dive and was hard to correct. Still, it did eventually return and, long behind schedule, this book (more than twice as long as the 'lost' version) is the result.

But this second stab at the book may never have happened had I foreseen the extra headaches that it would bring. In the first place, I had not reckoned with a book anywhere near this size. Nor did I anticipate the extent of its mind-boggling complexities – especially tricky for an amateur like me. A result of this was that I kept having to back-track on already written material to make way for additional items of relevance that I had either missed or had arisen in some other way. For example, 2004 in particular had been a year of much continuing change to procedures relating to health care in the UK. So I took it on myself (perhaps unwisely) to carry on updating and rewriting tracts of previously completed work – even into 2005.

For another thing, it was a nightmare trying to decipher and paraphrase large tracts of atrocious, repetitive legal phraseology to get to the bottom of legislation concerning many of the issues I was writing about. This frustrating difficulty applied not only to Britain but even more to some of the other European countries involved. I cursed this aspect of my country's apparent lasting legacy in international affairs and the universality of its language that had made it possible. Why, I thought, had the Plain English Campaign not intervened long ago to teach the British legal profession how to write understandable English and, by this means, influence change from the ridiculously antiquated style of wording in acts of parliament – to mention but one such likely outcome? But there could be more to it than that.

Observations about the book
It can be concluded, then, that it would be better to have left writing this book to a suitable academic or other professional (neither category applies to me) who possessed the necessary wherewithal to do the job. Small wonder, therefore, that putting it together has been so problematical for me. My loss of hair (from the little that existed in the first place) and other not quite so mundane casualties are testimony to this contention. But in mitigation of taking on the task myself, I feel that it may have been a long time waiting for some appropriate, free-thinking literary heavyweight to enter the frame and tackle the key issues addressed in the pages that follow.

The book is sure to have some flaws. I hope that the errors are not of fact, or significant in any other way. A few aspects of the book should be introduced for the purposes of clarity. First, the volume of original information readily available about the United Kingdom (chapters 1 to 9 are the result) was generally greater than that obtainable (in English) about the other European countries featured in the book. This factor is reflected in and largely explains the greater proportion of the book's content accounting for the UK's comparable practices and procedures relating to health care. As a consequence of this, and on other grounds, the comparisons drawn may not be entirely perfect. Nonetheless, the crucial differences that exist are clear and, I believe, meet a primary objective of the book: to show how far behind the thinking and practice in one country is when compared with others in an advanced society. There may be those who wonder why comparisons have been drawn almost exclusively with the Nordic countries. Why not with other European societies? The reason is simple. I considered that likening the way things are done in the United Kingdom with what appear to be generally the best practices and entitlements of their kind on offer to citizens elsewhere on the Continent would be the most useful approach. Obviously, one learn's more from one's betters.

It should further be made clear that the account given of the UK's NHS complaints procedures, its supporting organizations and statistical data (Chapter 1) is not meant to be complete in all respects. Similarly, the national evaluation of this health service complaints system, its findings and the resulting recommendations (Chapter 2) are not intended to be a full illustration of the original data. In each case only those aspects that, generally, are relevant for the purposes of this book's focus have been included. In the same way, the accounts of the reforms to this country's General Medical Council and the Nursing and Midwifery Council (chapters 5 and 6) are not intended to be complete descriptions of the changes to these two regulatory bodies. Again, only directly applicable or other important elements of the improvements to their structures and procedures are included. Similarly, the account of the report, recommendations and resulting consultation paper produced by England's Chief Medical Officer concerning a patient redress and compensation scheme (Chapter 9) is not complete in all ways. But it is sufficiently detailed for its purpose.

Likewise, the portrayal in chapters 3, 4, 7 and 8 of the other elements in the complaints system and additional practices relating to health care in the United Kingdom are not paraphrased replicas of the original and additional information upon which they are based. Nevertheless, the accounts presented are inclusive enough to provide a clear picture of all the relevant aspects of these matters. It should also be appreciated that, occasionally, information provided in some of these chapters might be a little dated. To illustrate, financial help (and qualifying for it) from the Legal Services Commission (Chapter 8) can be subject to periodic change. Indeed, there are instances in certain chapters throughout the book where statistics are a year or two (and occasionally more) behind what they might have been, although this does not affect any issues that are raised or commented on. (Also, in the case of certain statistics shown about complaints lodged with the NHS in Scotland for the period 2002–03, published information that was supposedly correct in late 2004 seems to have been altered six months later at source.)

Therefore I am aware that the annual statistical data provided in words or tabulated form in certain chapters to demonstrate the various complaints and additional procedures in action do not always refer to identical sets of periods for each country. Nevertheless, this information remains useful both for straightforward comparison purposes and in its other more specific implications. I realize, too, that the near complete reforms to the Nursing and Midwifery Council may have developed further since I described the then current position in late 2004 in Chapter 6. Also, since I put together chapters 12 to 19, in particular, there has been the odd important development concerning matters decribed in this part of the book. However, I later established (in early 2004) that apart from the Republic of Ireland, none had – or would – materially affect the existing situation in the countries to which these changes apply.

The explanations I have given thus far to aspects of this book make dull reading – especially in these opening pages. Nevertheless, if the observations have succeeded in clearing up any significant uncertainties that otherwise may have arisen in the course of reading this book, the exercise has done its job.

My hopes

I cannot deny my broad approval for the relevant entitlements and practices relating to health care that are on offer to citizens in the Nordic countries, and this is apparent from the tone of what I have written. Indeed, the tenor of certain references and comments I have made might lead some to suggest that the book is also something of a polemic on the way that the British health system handles these procedures. They may be right. But as long as they concede that my censure, where it is applied, is not without foundation, I have no problem with the description. It is one's motives that should count for most. For my part, I would like to think that the essential message in this book will be well received by citizens in Britain (and elsewhere) whose cause it seeks to champion. Equally, I hope it will be recognized by those wielding the power who still seem reluctant to relinquish control.

J.E.

INTRODUCTION

Imagine a legal system where the defence for the accused decides whether its client has a case to answer. Visualize, also, the defence then going on to appoint the judge and jury (some of whom are connected with the defence) who will preside over the proceedings, examine the allegation(s) and pass judgement. Now that *would* truly be a daft state of affairs by any stretch of the imagination.

Yet this unlikely scenario resembles the way in which Britain's NHS complaints procedure (including its *independent* component) established in 1996 was conducted. It was also the primary reason why this internally managed mechanism for addressing complainants' grievances attracted more or less sustained public excoriation following its introduction. As a consequence, the government commissioned an evaluation of how the system had worked and been received by those concerned. The appraisal was carried out in 1999 and 2000 and the outcome became a blueprint for remedial change with a key focus on providing greater independence in the investigation of complaints about health care.[1]

Wales was first off the mark and put its own interpretation of the survey's results into action when it launched its reformed health service complaints system in April 2003. The local resolution first stage of the procedure remains essentially unchanged from that in the previous arrangement. In contrast – and unlike that in the earlier procedure – the review process is now the responsibility of a body and panels that are independent of the health service.

The reforms in England began to take effect in August 2004, with the review phase similarly in the hands of an autonomous organization that is independent of the NHS. However, other unavoidable priorities mean that a re-shaped local resolution structure will not be in place until an unspecified point in 2005. Decisions on the changes to the procedures in Scotland and Northern Ireland were still outstanding in late 2004, but the reforms that arise are scheduled to be in place during 2005.

Nevertheless, the changes to the complaints systems do not alter the fact that complainants have a statutory obligation to lodge their grievances with the health service at local level before they are allowed access to a possible independent review – similar to the position in the previous procedures. It is conceivable that the reforms will improve the internal investigation of complaints at this initial stage of the process. The question is, will the desire of the public for an equitable complaints mechanism be met by the changes as a whole?

The overall reforms to the NHS complaints procedure for each of the four countries (with the possible future exception of Scotland) generally do not affect the role of the next and final complaints adjudicator for complainants who consider that their grievances had not been properly investigated earlier. As in the mechanism in its previous form, complainants can refer their cases (or these complaints may be referred in another way) to one of the three health service ombudsmen in the United

Kingdom provided they have completed what is required of them up to or following the review phase of the NHS procedure, and are still dissatisfied. Otherwise the Ombudsman will refuse to investigate their grievances. Nevertheless, even when accepted, complaints must first be screened before proceeding to a full investigation. The result is that only a very small proportion progress to this final point. What is the reason for this phenomenon, and what other issues arise? Who are the people in the Ombudsman's organization responsible for deciding the progress and outcome of complaints referred to them and how impartial is the Ombudsman's intervention?

Britain's medical regulatory bodies also came under intense fire by the public and the media in the late 1990s, except the attack seemed to be more sustained and it spilled over into the new century. The revelations about the Bristol Royal Infirmary babies' heart surgery cases and the repeated misconduct of gynaecological surgeon Rodney Ledward are among a long list of high-profile scandals that led to this national uproar. The uncovering of the deliberate killings by Dr Harold Shipman underscored the fact that something seemed to be seriously wrong with the regulation and discipline of the medical profession.

In July 2000 the government presented *The NHS Plan: a plan for investment, a plan for reform*, a detailed scheme to reshape the health service and improve the delivery of health care and associated provision. The Plan called for reforms to the General Medical Council (GMC) and what was then the United Kingdom Central Council for Nursing, Midwifery and Health Visiting (UKCC). It stated that these regulatory bodies must mend their ways, 'develop meaningful accountability to the public and health service' and provide greater patient and public representation in the bodies' respective councils. Another requirement was that complaints procedures must be faster and more transparent. The changes that resulted have been fully implemented in the UKCC, now called the Nursing and Midwifery Council, and those concerned with the GMC are also in place apart from the latest reforms in progress as a result of the Shipman Inquiry report in December 2004.

Notwithstanding, the comparison with the imaginary and implausible judicial arrangement already alluded to of the previous NHS complaints procedure can, perhaps, still be applied in some measure to the way allegations against health care practitioners are scrutinized by these medical regulatory institutions. Even in their apparent greatly reformed state these bodies continue to be generally self-regulated and, accordingly, a kind of conflict of interest might be suspected by some on the outside. In such circumstances, will the reforms be enough to avoid past flaws in their operation and gain public confidence?

By contrast, the same analogy cannot be made about the corresponding health service complaints and medical regulatory systems operating in the Nordic countries. Here, almost uniquely, the bodies concerned are entirely detached from those whose actions they are authorized to investigate and, therefore, the question of suspicion about the judgements they make is less likely to arise. It is a distinction that will probably come across as being the most compelling issue in the reasoning of this book, but there are other crucial differences that are placed under the spotlight.

So far, the British public has not been conferred with sweeping legal patients' rights, nor is there a set of similarly comprehensive statutory rights, that account for the interests of the health care practitioners who attend them. Instead these joint entitlements are covered by a combination of legislation, case law, ethical criteria and health service policy rules. Although the arrangement is in keeping with the high standards expected of any advanced nation, would it not be more appropriate in the 21st century to have these entitlements more firmly established?

Britain has no mechanism that will automatically compensate victims of medical error. The only recourse for claimants is civil litigation, a potentially risky and expensive way of seeking financial redress. Public legal aid is in short supply and available usually for cases with a strong chance of success, and the process of claiming damages can be long and arduous. In June 2003 the government's chief medical officer put forward a patient redress and compensation scheme that is intended to combat this unsatisfactory state of affairs. He announced his recommendations in *Making Amends* – a consultation paper that set out proposals for reforming the approach to clinical negligence in the NHS. What is the potential value of the new scheme to claimants, and to what extent will it affect the status quo when it is in operation?

All these and other matters, together with the questions posed in each case, are set out and addressed in the first section of this book. The second part of the book describes the entitlements that are enjoyed by citizens of certain other European countries, and demonstrates the continuing disparities between these prerogatives and those on offer to Britons. For example, in contrast with the position in Britain, self-regulation has no real place in the investigation of complaints about the health service and medical profession in any of the five Nordic countries. Also, there are key differences over patients' statutory rights and access to compensation when injury has been caused to them while in the care of the health service.

The Nordic nations are generous in their provision of patients' legal entitlements. Finland was the first among the five to legislate for a set of comprehensive rights for patients. The legislation took effect in early 1993, with Iceland, Denmark and Norway (in that order) following with their own versions during the next eight years. These countries are part of a small, select group – virtually unique to Europe – that have conferred upon their citizens the benefit of statutory patients' rights in this all-encompassing way.

Patient insurance and no-fault compensation for health care is another area where the Nordic countries excel above most others. Sweden, the prime mover in patient insurance and compensation in their most radical forms, made its debut in no-fault compensation as far back as 1975. Finland and Norway followed in the late 1980s, Denmark in 1992 and Iceland in January 2001. A consequence of this is that civil litigation plays little or no part in claims for damages connected with health care in these countries. (Austria has long had its own form of alternative compensation for patients but has also made inroads into no-fault compensation. Belgium may be the latest candidate for this system.

So how much better does their public fare with the corresponding health care rights and procedures on offer in Denmark, Finland, Iceland, Norway and Sweden and, in part, with those in Austria? To what extent will the apparent disparities be reduced between the evenhandedness that the arrangements in these countries seem to provide and what may be available in the new structures that have been introduced in Britain? (And what will the reforms to Ireland's existing health service complaints procedures mean in practice for its citizens?)

This book tries to shed some light on a range of important issues, some of which have already surfaced in Britain but which have not adequately been addressed and responded to. Nevertheless, it does not claim to provide an entirely exhaustive account of the facts, nor that all its conclusions are the right ones. But it has tried to present the most important facts, and many of its deductions might find approval where it matters most.

CHAPTER 1

A flawed mechanism delivered flawed results

That was the legacy of Britain's erstwhile health service complaints system

Although only one half of the picture, it is well documented that, almost since its inception in April 1996, the erstwhile NHS complaints mechanism attracted widespread public excoriation of the way it worked, its component parts and the suspect decisions that emerged from it. Between them, complainants, the media, consumer organizations and other agencies began spreading their own particular messages about the state of affairs.

The focus was specifically on the numerous cases of patients who had suffered injury or died in apparently questionable circumstances while in the care of health service practitioners. Yet the internal investigations that followed seemed unduly to exonerate the NHS and the medical professionals involved. There appeared to be little justice and accountability from a patient's perspective.

Practically from the outset it has been accepted that this severe censure was justified. The vital flaw lay in a mechanism through which all incoming complaints were being managed and examined by the health service during the initial stage and, to a large extent, in the selective final, review phase of investigations. In a nutshell there was no real independence in the way that the statutory complaints system was being operated. A closer examination of the precise character and component parts of this mechanism – and its far-reaching effects in practice – may provide a clearer picture and illustrate the extent of the problem facing complainants.

The NHS complaints procedure established in 1996

A two-stage, effectively self-regulated system, the mechanism initially involved a mandatory 'local resolution' process following which dissatisfied complainants were eligible to take their cases forward to be considered for 'independent review'. Nevertheless, this second step in the procedure was open only for those complaints that a health service official (usually) judged to be acceptable for investigation by a panel that the same person played a key role in subsequently setting up and managing for the purpose.

Complainants whose cases had completed local resolution but were then rejected for review, and those who disagreed with the outcome of an investigation by a review panel, could refer their grievances to one of the nation's three health service ombudsmen. Their complaints bodies have greater powers to examine cases (following assessment) brought before them and serve as an independent, though hard-to-come-by extension of the NHS complaints procedure (see Chapter 3).

Any person who was receiving, or had previously been provided with, treatment or services by the NHS could complain to the health service establishment concerned. A complaint could also be made on behalf of a patient by anyone – usually a relative or close friend – who had the patient's consent, or if the latter was unable to do so. The complaints mechanism additionally covered complaints about staff or facilities relating to patients receiving private medical treatment in a NHS hospital, but not the consultant involved.[1]

The 1996 models of the complaints system in the UK had four common aspects:
- When a complaint was lodged there was a local inquiry by the body being complained about.
- If the matter was not resolved, a decision was made on whether to convene a review panel for a further examination.
- If it had been agreed to examine the case further, the complaint was investigated by the review panel.
- If still not settled, the case could be referred to the Health Service Ombudsman.[2]

The Patients' Advice and Liaison Services[3]
In 2001 the first series of Patients' Advice and Liaison Services (PALS) units was set up for complainants to obtain on-the-spot advice about their grievances. One of the purposes of the service was to assist in resolving complainants' grievances and so avoid the need, in most cases, for complainants to lodge a formal complaint. However, it was not part of the NHS complaints procedures and its responsibilities go beyond issues simply involving complaints (see Chapter 7). In 2005 there are PALS units in all NHS trusts (hospital establishments) and primary care trusts (PCTs) in the country.

PALS units had replaced community health councils (CHCs) in their role of advising complainants. CHCs were units of an independent national advisory body, the Association of Community Health Councils for England and Wales (ACHCEW), which was established by act of parliament in 1974. Included in its legal powers was the right of access to NHS premises. The organization ceased to function from 1 December 2003. (Scotland, Wales and Northern Ireland did not follow England's example and have kept their existing health councils, community health councils and health and social services councils.) Unlike community health councils, PALS staff are employed by and are responsible to health service trusts. The quality and effectiveness of each PALS unit is monitored by a local 'patients' forum'.

The Independent Complaints and Advocacy Service[4]
The PALS could also act as (and continue to be) an opening to the Independent Complaints and Advocacy Service (ICAS), which provides additional assistance to individuals lodging or intending to make a formal complaint about a health service body in England. Introduced under the Health and Social Care Act 2001, the service is independent ('so far as practicable') of anyone who is the subject of a complaint about which it is concerned and of any others who are involved in the investigation or adjudication of that matter.

The service that ICAS provided included advice (if that was all a complainant wanted), advocacy, or both, in proceeding with a complaint. Its duties could also extend to letter writing and attending meetings to speak on behalf of those who had asked for representation. Since it was set up in September 2003, four voluntary sector providers had been operating an interim system of ICAS outlets in each of the country's regions. The pilot operation was to continue for 12 or 18 months from this date before being fully established regionally – which it is in 2005.

The time to complain
Complaints about the health service were required to be made as soon as possible – normally within six months of the event that had prompted the complaint. Alternatively, grievances should have been lodged within six months of a complainant believing that there were grounds for doing so, although this should not have been more than one year since the incident occurred. These deadlines could be waived if good reasons were given explaining why the complaints were not made earlier.[5]

When the complaints procedure could not be used
However, there were circumstances in which the NHS complaints mechanism could not deal with cases referred to it for examination. It could not consider matters that were the responsibility of a professional regulatory body, nor cases that had gone to litigation. Similarly, it was not authorized to handle complaints about the private health care sector, nor those involving local authority social services.[6]

Local resolution[7]
A complaint could initially be referred to a health service employee close to its cause such as a doctor, nurse, receptionist or practice manager. Alternatively, in the case of NHS trusts, complainants could speak or write to the complaints manager or approach the local PALS unit. The chief executive of either a trust or health authority was required to provide a full written response to any written complaint, where possible within 20 working days of its being received. If there were good reasons why this time limit could not be met, complainants had to be advised about progress.

Complaints about a family health services (FHS) professional – a general practitioner (GP), dentist, pharmacist or optician – could be lodged directly. In this case, a reply was required to be given to the complainant within 10 working days. The alternative to this direct approach was to contact the complaints manager at the health authority who would act as a kind of intermediary in this initial process. There were also instances where the health authority would provide a lay conciliator for the purpose. This individual was not permitted to report the details of the case to the health authority because the complaint might later be investigated at 'independent review' – the next stage in the procedure.

Independent review[8]
Complainants who were dissatisfied with the outcome of a complaint at local resolution could ask the health service body involved to consider referring their case for investigation by a review panel. Requests had to be made within 28 days of complainants being sent the local resolution report. These appeals were considered by a 'convener', a person who was normally a non-executive board member of the health service establishment concerned in the complaint.

The convener would ask complainants to describe in writing the reasons for their continuing dissatisfaction, assuming that this account had not already been given. In considering the request for independent review, the convener approached an independent lay person (enlisted by the health service and who would become the chairman of a panel that subsequently might be set up) to assist in the matter. The convener arrived at any one of three decisions: to refer the case back to local resolution for further action, to reject the request, or to accept the complaint for investigation by a review panel.

Whichever way the decision went, the convener would inform the complainant in writing about the verdict, normally within the set time-frame of 20 working days since receiving the request. Thus, a complainant had no automatic right to an independent review. The convener may have considered that a case had been properly looked into and a satisfactory explanation given at local resolution, so that nothing further could be gained – even if the complainant continued to be dissatisfied.

In instances where a convener decided to set up an independent review panel, complainants were given a written account (the terms of reference) of the matters that would be investigated. Each panel consisted of three members: the chairman, convener and another person connected with the health service, such as a non-executive board member of a health authority or some other similar representative. In cases that involved clinical issues, independent review panels were supported by assessors who were normally based outside the area where a complaint had been lodged. These assessors were usually selected from lists held by the health service.

The panel and the appointed assessors interviewed all the parties involved in a complaint. It would then examine all aspects of the case and prepared a report of its investigations and gave its recommendations and conclusions. Once this process had been completed, the panel's chairman sent a copy of the signed report to the complainant. Simultaneously, the latter would also be advised of the right to refer the complaint to the Health Service Ombudsman. Later, the chief executive of the health service body concerned in the case would write to tell the complainant of any action that was being taken following the panel's recommendations. An independent review panel had no executive authority over any action by a trust, health authority or family health services practitioner. Nor was it permitted to suggest in its report that any person being complained against should be disciplined or referred to one of the professional regulatory bodies.

The 1996 model NHS complaints system in practice

Probably the most noticeable characteristic of this previous health service complaints procedure was the consistently low proportion of cases that proceeded further through the system following the 'local resolution' first stage. A similarly small percentage of these complaints going forward to the next step in the process – 'independent review' – was given the green light for a more detailed investigation. And, by the time these accepted cases had passed through the internally regulated review process, the picture arising of their authenticity appeared even less flattering. At this stage, too, most cases were deemed to be flawed and got rejected. The statistics tell the story.

England

As an example, the NHS in England received a total of 140,436 written complaints during 2000–01 (see tables 1.1a, 1.1b, 1.2a and 1.2b). There were 95,994 (68.4 per cent) complaints concerning hospital and community health services and 44,442 (31.6 per cent) complaints about family health services – general medical practitioners, dentists and health authority administration. Only 3,585 complaints (2.6 per cent) out of the combined total were subsequently put forward for prospective investigation at independent review. Out of the 3,022 cases considered during the year, 611 (20.2 per cent) were approved for review. Presumably, therefore, the balance of 2,411 cases (79.8 per cent of those considered) were rejected, including some that may have been referred back to local resolution for further inquiry.[9]

Of the 95,994 complaints about hospital and community health services in 2000–01, there were 89,945 (93.7 per cent) relating to hospital and community trusts, 3,637 (3.8 per cent) involving ambulance trusts, 2,152 (2.2 per cent) about health authorities and 260 about primary care trusts. Nearly all (98 per cent) of these complaints were concerned with the provision of health care services, with the remaining 2 per cent about commissioning them.[10]

Table 1.1a Written complaints about hospital and community health services in England, 1996–97 to 2002–03[a]

	1996–97	1997–98	1998–99	1999–2000	2000–01[b]	2002–03
Local resolution						
completed within year	88,999	85,212	82,106	81,717	89,761	85.867
unfinished by end of year	3,975	3,545	3,907	4,819	6,233	5,166
Total	*92,974*	*88,757*	*86,013*	*86,536*	*95,994*	*91,023*
Independent review						
seeking	1,612	1,871	1,838	2,061	2,243	2,380
approved for	373	348	285	296	312	255
rejected	283	370	336	394	446	582
completed within year	198	184	176	179	192	122
unfinished by end of year	175	164	109	117	120	133

Source: Department of Health, *Written Complaints About Hospital and Community Health Services by Service Area, England, 2002–03*[11]
[a] Figures for 2001–02 are not available.
[b] The figures for 2000–01 include written complaints about the 40 primary care trusts, which had become operational during the year.

Table 1.1b Percentage complaints about hospital and community health services in England, 1996–97 to 2002–03[a]

	1996–97	1997–98	1998–99	1999–2000	2000–01[b]	2002–03
Local resolution						
completed within year	95.7	96.0	95.5	94.4	93.5	94.3
unfinished by end of year	4.3	4.0	4.5	5.6	6.5	5.7
Independent review						
seeking	1.8	2.2	2.2	2.5	2.5	2.8
approved for	28.0	23.2	19.0	17.8	17.4	14.2
rejected	17.6	19.8	18.3	19.1	19.9	24.4
completed within year	53.1	52.9	61.8	60.5	61.5	47.8
unfinished by end of year	46.9	47.1	38.2	39.5	38.5	52.2

Source: Department of Health, *Written Complaints About Hospital and Community Health Services by Service Area, England, 2002–03*[11]
[a] Figures for 2001–02 are not available.

ᵇ The figures for 2000–01 include written complaints about the 40 primary care trusts, which had become operational during the year.

This pattern of there being a high number of incoming complaints and a very low proportion successfully progressing through the complaints system (whether for hospital and community health services or family health services) in 2000–01 was similar in the preceding four years. There seems to be no detailed information available about the passage of complaints at local resolution during this period or, for that matter, in each of the previous years shown in tables 1.1 and 1.2. In the case of hospital and community health services, only the number of complaints that were dealt with or ongoing up to the end of each 12-month period can be provided. But no data at all appears to exist for family health services about this first stage of the process, other than the total numbers of complaints that were received. The position relating to independent review, in either case, is similarly incomplete. No information can be provided on the outcome of cases that were actually investigated at this second phase of the procedure.

Table 1.2a Written complaints about family health services in England, 1996–97 to 2002–03ᵃ

	1996–97	1997–98	1998–99	1999–2000	2000–01	2002–03
Seeking independent review	1,040	1,390	1,430	1,396	1,342	1,220
Rejected for independent reviewᵇ	702	906	984	905	926	876
Still under consideration at end year	119	153	133	150	117	149
Approved for independent review	219	331	313	341	299	195
Completed within year	142	230	226	222	210	399
Unfinished by end of year	77	101	87	119	89	121
Total	*36,990*	*38,093*	*38,857*	*39,725*	*44,442*	*42,844*

Source: Department of Health, *Written Complaints About Hospital and Community Health Services by Service Area, England, 2002–03*¹²
ᵃ The figures here refer to general medical and dental services and FHS administration only, but the totals corresponding to cases seeking independent review involve all family health services. Figures for 2001–02 are not available.
ᵇ This category is not mentioned in the official statistics. The data has been compiled by simple subtraction from existing figures and is included in the table to provide greater clarity.

Table 1.2b Percentage written complaints about family health services in England, 1996–97 to 2002–03ᵃ

	1996–97	1997–98	1998–99	1999–2000	2000–01	2002–03
Rejected for independent reviewᵇ	76.2	73.2	75.9	72.6	75.6	72
Still under consideration at end year	11.4	11.0	9.3	10.8	8.7	12
Approved for independent review	23.8	26.8	24.1	27.4	24.4	16

Source: Department of Health, *Written Complaints About Hospital and Community Health Services by Service Area, England, 2002–03*¹²
ᵃ The figures here refer to general medical and dental services and FHS administration only, but the totals corresponding to cases seeking independent review involve all family health services. Figures for 2001–02 are not available.

ᵇ This category is not mentioned in the official statistics. The data has been compiled by simple subtraction from existing figures and is included in the table to provide greater clarity. Presumably these rejected cases include those on which no further action was taken because it was considered that a satisfactory response had been given at local resolution. Additionally, some could also comprise complaints that had been referred back to this first phase of the procedure because it had not been fully used.

All aspects of clinical treatment were involved in 32,809 (34.2 per cent) complaints, which represented the single highest proportion of the total received about hospital and community health services. With a combined figure of 16,550 (17.2 per cent), delays in or cancellation of in-patient and out-patient appointments accounted for the second largest number of complaints. Staff attitude was the third largest category of complaints, accounting for 12,439 (13 per cent) cases.[13]

The same pattern of a very small percentage of complaints progressing further through the system was to be seen in the figures for 2002–03 (no statistics were available for 2001–02), which showed that 133,867 written complaints were lodged with the NHS in England. Hospital and community health services accounted for 91,023 complaints (68 per cent) and 42,844 (32 per cent) were about family health services – general medical, dental, family health services (FHS) administration, pharmaceutical and opthalmic (tables 1.1a, 1.1b, 1.2a and 1.2b).[14]

Subsequently a combined total of 3,600 requests were made for independent review, of which 2,869 were considered during the year and 450 (15.7 per cent) referred to a review panel. Thus it would appear that the remaining 2,419 cases (84.3 per cent) were unsuccessful, including a proportion that may have been referred back to local resolution for further examination. There were 731 requests outstanding at the end of the year.[15]

The 91,023 complaints about hospital and community health services comprised 65,013 (71.4 per cent) that involved hospital acute services, 21,343 (23.5 per cent) concerning other health care services, 2,897 (3.2 per cent) about ambulance services and 1,770 (1.9 per cent) relating to primary care trust (PCT) commissioning.[16]

Scotland
Similar to the position in England, the statistics for Scotland covering the years 1998–99 to 2002–03 show that the vast majority of complaints received by NHS trusts go no further than local resolution level. Only a very small proportion of complainants, dissatisfied with the answers given during this first phase of the procedure, asked for their cases to be considered by an independent review panel.

Table 1.3 Complaints about hospital and community health services received by NHS trusts in Scotland, 1998–99 to 2002–03

	1998–99	1999–2000	2000–01	2001–02	2002–03
Total	7,306	7,157	7,389	7,723	7,770
Responded to at local level	7,217	7,033	7,275	7,683	7,763
Of which:					
Upheld (%)	33.7	32.8	32.0	31.2	27.4
Partially upheld (%)	27.5	28.3	30.8	33.0	35.6
Not upheld (%)	38.5	38.9	36.9	34.8	37.0
Outcome not known (%)	0.3	0.0	0.3	1.0	0.0

Source: ISD Scotland National Statistics, *NHS Trust Complaints – Outcome of Complaints 1998–1999 to 2000–03*[17]

A total of 7,770 complaints were lodged with NHS trusts in 2002–03 (Table 1.3). Out of the 7,763 complaints responded to at local resolution in 2002–03, 27.4 per cent were upheld compared with 31.2 per cent in 2001–02, 32 per cent during 2000–01, 32.8 per cent in 1999–2000 and 33.7 per cent in 1998–99. A further 35.6 per cent were partially upheld during 2002–03 with the remaining 37 per cent not upheld after this first phase of the procedure. It is not clear if the 85 requests for independent review (Table 1.4) arose wholly or partially from the proportion (more than one-third) that were not upheld. However, it is clear that nine of these cases were accepted for review (Table 1.4).[18]

Table 1.5 provides a breakdown of the subjects of complaints to NHS trusts from 1998–99 to 2002–03. Similar to the four previous years, in 2002–03 the single largest proportion of complaints (30.6 per cent) related to staff issues, including attitude or behaviour and written or oral communication, and the second largest (22.8 per cent) were about aspects of treatment. Other subjects of complaint related to environmental or domestic matters, waiting times and procedural matters.[19]

Table 1.4 Progress and outcome of complaints concerning NHS trusts in Scotland about which requests were made for independent review, 2000–01 to 2002–03

	2000–01	2001–02	2002–03
Total requests for independent review	103	127	83
Accepted for independent review	7	10	9
Referred back to local resolution	47	58	39
Rejected for independent review	32	44	28
Still under consideration	17	15	7

Source: ISD Scotland National Statistics, *NHS Trust Complaints – Status of Requests for Independent Review*[20]

Table 1.5 Subjects of complaints to NHS trusts about hospital and community health services in Scotland, 1998–99 to 2001–02[a]

	1998–99	1999–2000	2000–01	2001–02	2002–03
Staff	3,561	3,032	2,658	2,316	2,500
Treatment	2,583	2,353	2,127	2,111	1,865
Environment or domestic	1,434	1,161	961	1,141	1,075
Waiting times	887	1,065	1,217	1,370	1,618
Delay	705	570	511	506	424
Transport	206	142	96	102	92
Procedural matters	180	157	139	150	105
Other	569	446	358	368	486
Total	10,125	8,926	8,067	8,064	8,165
Not recorded	16	22	7	2	1

Source: ISD Scotland National Statistics, *NHS Trust Complaints – Summary of Issues Raised*[21]
[a] Some complaints refer to more than one subject.

Complaints about primary care include those referring to medical services, dental services and primary care administration. Responsibility for collecting this information passed from health boards to primary care trusts on 1 October 1999. The total number of complaints received during 2002–03 was 3,173, compared with 2,806, 2,677, 2,581 and 2,710 in 2001–02, 2000–01, 1999–2000 and 1998–99, respectively. In each of these years the majority of cases were about medical services (Table 1.6). Complaints relating to pharmaceutical and opthalmic services are reported only where these led to requests for independent review and, therefore, are excluded from the annual totals.[22]

Most primary care complaints were dealt with at the local resolution first phase of the procedure, as with complaints about NHS trusts and health boards (involving hospital and community health services). However, in keeping with the rest of Britain, statistics about primary care are less detailed than those collected on complaints about hospital and community health services. It appears that this modified arrangement was nationally agreed on the grounds that primary care practitioners are independent contractors to the NHS.[23]

Table 1.6 Primary care complaints by service in Scotland, 1998–99 to 2002–03[a]

	1998–99	1999–2000	2000–01	2001–02	2002–03
Medical services	2,323	2,259	2,351	2,430	2,792
Dental services	371	316	326	365	369
Primary care administration	16	6	–	11	12
Total	2,710	2,581	2,677	2,806	3,173

Source: ISD Scotland National Statistics, *Primary Care Complaints – by Service 2002–03*[24]
[a] Complaints about pharmacies and those referring to opthamology are not included in this table. Responsibility for collecting data on complaints about primary care passed from health boards to primary care trusts on 1 October 1999.</notes>

Although there is no useful picture for the outcome of complaints at local resolution, the position is much clearer about the cases that were subsequently put forward to be considered for independent review. Out of a total of 69 requests for review during 2002–03, the convener rejected 30 and referred back 29 for further inquiries at local resolution. Six cases were accepted for independent review and a decision was still to be made on four at the end of the year. Clinical issues were involved in 55 (79.7 per cent) of the 69 cases and eight concerned staff communication or attitude. The figures for all these matters for 1998–99 to 2002–03 are shown in tables 1.7 and 1.8.[25]

Table 1.7 Outcome of complaints about primary care considered for independent review in Scotland, 1998–99 to 2001–02

	1998–99[a]	1999–2000	2000–01	2001–02	2002–03
Rejected for independent review	34	36	64	60	30
Referred back to local resolution	31	22	23	29	29
Accepted for independent review	14	15	13	3	6
Decisions outstanding at end of year	7	5	3	–	4
Total	87	78	103	92	69

Cases for which a panel was convened	12	11	11	1	–
Complaints upheld	3	4	8	–	–
Complaints partially upheld	4	2	1	–	–
Complaints not upheld	5	5	2	1	–

Source: ISD Scotland National Statistics, *Primary Care Complaints – Independent Review Requests 2000–01 to 2002–03*[26]
[a] The decision of the convener was not recorded in one of the cases under consideration for independent review during 1998–99.

Table 1.8 Subjects of complaints about primary care considered for independent review in Scotland, 1998–99 to 2002–03

	1998–99	1999–2000	2000–01	2001–02	2002–03
Clinical matters	49	49	71	55	55
Staff communication or attitude	16	14	15	19	8
Practice, surgery or management	4	4	2	3	–
Premises	1	1	1	–	–
Delay in doctor attending	2	1	2	1	1
Administration	–	–	1	–	–
Other	7	4	7	5	1
Not recorded	8	5	4	9	4
Total	87	78	103	92	69

Source: ISD Scotland National Statistics, *Primary Care Complaints – by Service 2002–03*[27]

In 2002–03, 121 written complaints were received by non-island NHS boards (Table 1.9) compared with 138 in 2001–02 and 56 during 2000–01. Of the complaints received and dealt with in full in 2002–03, 16 per cent were fully upheld, 43 per cent upheld in part and 41 per cent not upheld. (The proportion upheld in 2001–02 and 2000–01 was 9 per cent in each case, while those for partially upheld cases were 49 and 38 per cent and 43 and 54 per cent that were not upheld.) Out of the total number responded to, only one resulted in a request for independent review compared with four in 2001–02 and one in 2000–01. Accounting for one-third of all issues raised, procedural matters were the single most common subject of complaint to non-island NHS boards during 2002–03, but still substantially less than in the two previous years (Table 1.10). The Scottish Ambulance Service received 393 complaints and 150 were lodged with the State Hospital Unit during 2002–03 (Table 1.9).[28]

Table 1.9 Outcome at local resolution of complaints made to NHS boards, island boards, the Scottish Ambulance Service and the State Hospital Unit, 2000–01 to 2002–03

NHS boards[a]	2000–01	2001–02	2002–03
Total received	56	138	121
Not yet responded to	–	–	–
Responded to	56	138	121
Of which:			
Upheld (%)	9	9	16
Upheld in part (%)	38	49	43
Not upheld (%)	54	43	41

Island boards	Orkney			Shetland			Western Isles		
	2000–01	2001–02	2002–03	2000–01	2001–02	2002–03	2000–01	2001–02	2002–03
Total received	21	7	16	13	20	17	18	26	37
Not yet responded to	2	–	–	–	–	–	2	3	2
Responded to	19	7	16	13	20	17	16	23	35
Of which:									
Upheld (%)	21	29	38	69	45	29	6	13	17
Upheld in part (%)	37	43	37	15	40	65	31	39	40
Not upheld (%)	42	29	25	15	15	6	63	48	43

Scottish Ambulance Service	2000–01	2001–02	2002–03
Total received	460	465	393
Not yet responded to	–	11	–
Responded to	460	454	393
Of which:			
Upheld (%)	40	36	48
Upheld in part (%)	23	23	20
Not upheld (%)	37	40	32

State Hospital Unit	2000–01	2001–02	2002–03
Total received	145	111	150
Not yet responded to	–	–	–
Responded to	145	111	150
Of which:			
Upheld (%)	23	25	16
Upheld in part (%)	–	–	17
Not upheld (%)	77	75	67

Source: ISD Scotland National Statistics, *NHS Board Complaints – Issues Raised 2002–03*[29]
[a] Excludes complaints about the island boards, Scottish Ambulance Service, the State Hospital and the Scottish National Blood Transfusion Service.

The 'island boards' (covering Orkney, Shetland and the Western Isles) received 70 complaints in 2002–03 (Table 1.9) compared with 53 during 2001–02 and 52 for 2000–01. These establishments deal with health board and hospital and community health services complaints made to directly managed units. As such, the two sets of complaints are not separately identified for statistical purposes. The progress and outcome of complaints involving island boards in the years 2000–01 to 2002–03 are also shown in Table 1.9.[30] Procedural matters continued to be the most common subject of complaint to NHS boards (Table 1.10).[31]

Table 1.10 Subjects of complaints to NHS boards in Scotland, 1998–99 to 2001–02

	1998–99[a]	1999–2000	2000–01	2001–02	2002–03
Procedural matters	143	33	31	96	42
Waiting times	21	6	6	17	36
Staff	17	2	10	12	19
Treatment	10	10	2	10	3
Delay	6	1	5	1	2
Environment or domestic	7	1	2	9	5
Transport	3	–	–	–	1
Other	87	8	9	15	17
Total	294[b]	61	65	160	125

Source: ISD Scotland National Statistics, *Health Board/NHS Board Complaints – Summary of Issues Raised 1998–99 to 2001–02*[32]
[a] As previously explained, the comparatively much greater number of complaints received in 1998–99 include a large proportion that were made to Lothian Health Board about the review of opthamology services in its area.
[b] Does not include four unrecorded complaints.

Wales

In keeping with England and Scotland, the vast majority of complaints lodged with the health service in Wales go no further through the system than the 'local resolution' first stage. A total of 5,475 complaints was received by the health service in 2002–03 compared with 5,828 during the preceding year (Table 1.11). Hospital and community health services accounted for 3,581 of these cases, out of which inquiries into 3,257 were concluded at local level during the year, with 324 complaints outstanding.[33]

Table 1.11 Complaints lodged with the health service in Wales, 1996–97 to 2002–2003

	1996–97	1997–98	1998–99	1999–2000	2000–01	2001–02	2002–03
Hospital and community health services	3,899	3,915	3,981	3,673	4,125	3,979	3,581
Family health services	1,456	1,463	1,530	1,470	1,938	1,849	1,894
Total	5,355	5,378	5,511	5,143	6,063	5,828	5,475

Source: National Assembly for Wales, Health Statistics and Analysis Unit, *Complaints to the NHS in Wales*[34]

Subsequently, in 2002–03 independent review was requested for 119 cases, 74 of which were rejected and 14 accepted for investigation. The remaining 31 cases were still being considered when the year ended (Table 1.12). One in three complaints involved in-patient services and the same proportion referred to out-patient services, with one-third of cases being about clinical treatment and over half of all complaints referred to medical staff.[35]

Table 1.12 Requests for 'independent review' and their outcome in Wales, 2000–01 to 2001–02

	2000–01	2001–02	2002–03
Hospital and community health services			
Considered	97	101	88
Accepted	44	42	14
Rejected or referred back to local resolution[a]	53	59	74
Still under consideration at end of year	40	34	31
Total	137	135	119
Family health services			
Accepted – review completed or in progress	37	21	16
Position not known[b]	40	77	53
Total	77	98	69

Source: National Assembly for Wales, Health Statistics and Analysis Unit, *Complaints to the NHS in Wales*[36]
[a] Extrapoltated from source information.
[b] These cases of reqeusts for review presumably comprising those refered back, rejected or still being considered.

In 2002–03 family health services accounted for 1,894 complaints (Table 1.11) of which 1,616 (85.3 per cent) concerned medical practitioners and 263 (13.9 per cent) were about dentists. But, similar to the previous two years, no details are available about the number of cases that completed the local resolution process or were still being dealt with at the end of the year. Figures show that after this first stage independent review was requested in 69 cases, a total of 16 reviews were completed or in progress and the position of the balance of 53 cases was unclear. During 2001–02, a total of 1,849 complaints involved family health service practitioners (Table 1.11).[37]

Northern Ireland
Northern Ireland's Health and Personal Social Services (HPSS) complaints procedure was a slightly modified version of the NHS form operating on the mainland, but the distinction did not essentially affect standard rules and procedure. Similarly, complaints that remained unresolved after proceeding through the two stages of review could be referred to the Ombudsman for assessment and possible re-examination. The Northern Ireland Ombudsman carried out these duties in addition to those he undertook as Commissioner for Complaints.

The key difference that existed between the system in Northern Ireland and England and Wales was that relating to requests for independent review. Unlike England and Wales, where such applications were made to the trusts concerned, in Northern Ireland complainants had to approach the regional health and social services boards. Indeed, it was the latter who decided whether complaints about any health care establishment within the area they covered proceeded to independent review. Akin to the rest of the United Kingdom, these decisions were made by non-executive board directors acting as conveners for this purpose and performing a key role in any panel that subsequently might be set up.[38]

It was not easy to obtain statistics relating to Northern Ireland that are as detailed as those for the rest of the United Kingdom about the number and progress of complaints lodged with the health service. Nevertheless, some useful statistics were available from the Department of Health, Social Services and Public Safety. These showed that in 1998–99 health and social services trusts throughout the country received 3,395 formal complaints and 72 complainants subsequently requested an independent review. The figures for 1999–2000 were 3,679 and 60 respectively. In 2000–01, 3,702 complaints were received, but the number of requests for independent review could not be ascertained at the time of writing.[39] (The corresponding information for 2001–02 and 2002–03 had not been released up to September 2004.) Other than this, no information had been found about the progress and outcome of cases from local resolution up to and including independent review during this period. Only percentages of the total numbers of complaints lodged that were responded to within the stipulated 20-day time frame appear to have been recorded.[40]

With 19 health and social service trusts located in the region it covers, the Eastern Health and Social Services Board (EHSSB) is easily the largest of four such bodies in Northern Ireland. Nevertheless, unlike its smaller counterparts, certainly up to 2003 it did not compile detailed statistics on the numbers of complaints lodged annually with trusts in its jurisdiction, including figures on their progress and outcome at local resolution.[41] It seems that the analysis was carried out by each trust in an annual complaints report. But, short of approaching these health care establishments individually and providing information about each of them (an exercise that would not be practical – especially for reasons of space), no adequate picture can be described here of the complaints that were received and processed annually.

What can be stated, though, is that the number of complaints made about the health service in the EHSSB's jurisdiction had steadily risen since the Health and Personal Social Services complaints procedure was implemented in April 1996.[42] Covering the most densely populated region of the country, the EHSSB's authority also comprises the largest number of familly health services practitioners. There were 279 complaints made against general practitioners in 2001–02 and 93 concerned dentists, compared with 159 and 53, respectively, during the previous year. (Figures were not obligatory for complaints involving pharmacists and opticians and were not included in the EHSSB's annual report for the year.)[43]

The number of requests for independent review of complaints involving all health service bodies within the EHSSB's jurisdiction rose dramatically over those received in 2000–01. During 2001–02 the total was 51 compared with 29 the year before. Out of these requests 23 were rejected; 19 were referred back to local resolution; two were partially rejected with some aspects of the cases passed back to local level; and one was postponed because of the serious illness of the complainant. The remaining six applications were accepted for investigation by a review panel. Eight of the complainants who had requested an independent review subsequently referred their cases to the Commissioner for Complaints because they were dissatisfied with the response from the EHSSB. Seven of these complaints were then rejected and one was accepted for formal investigation by the Commissioner (see Table 1.13).[44]

Table 1.13 Progress and outcome of complaints referred for review to the EHSSB, 2000–01 and 2001–02

	2000–01	2001–02
Requests for independent review	29	51
Cases referred back to local resolution	12	19
Rejected for review	9	23
Accepted for review	6	6
Referred to the Commissioner for Complaints Of which:	1	8
Rejected for formal investigation	1[a]	7
Accepted for formal investigation	–	1

Source: Eastern Health and Social Services Board, *Fifth Annual Review of Complaints*[45]
[a] Inquiries were ceased by the Commissioner for Complaints when this case was taken to litigation.

As in previous years, the majority of complaints for which independent review was requested in 2001–02 concerned the quality of treatment and care given by trusts (28) and general medical practitioners (7). The same picture arose for the six cases subsequently accepted for investigation at this stage of the complaints procedure. Four of these approved cases related to the standard of therapy and support that had been given.[46]

During 2001–02 the EHSSB also received 45 complaints about its own functions – non-clinical matters associated with treatment or care – compared with 39 on this subject in the previous year. One request was made for independent review, but no cases were referred to the Commissioner for Complaints. In 2000–01 none of the complainants asked for their case to be considered for review. However, the Commissioner for Complaints was involved in the satisfactory resolution of one case concerning the re-imbursement of a complainant.[47]

The four trusts within the authority of Northern Ireland's Southern Health and Social Services Board received a combined total of 573 complaints in 2001–02 compared with 523 and 391, respectively, in the previous two years. The subjects that drew the greatest number of complaints were care and treatment (209), and staff attitude or behaviour (81). These subjects were also the most common cause of complaint during preceding years.[48]

General practitioners and dentists are obliged by their terms of service to provide details of the number of complaints lodged with their practices. During 2001–02, the Southern Health and Social Services Board received a total of 129 complaints: 61 concerned general practice; 19 were about GP out-of-hours service; and 49 involved dentists. In the previous year, the combined figure was 91, made up of 74 relating to general practice and 17 to dentists (see Table 1.14).[49]

Table 1.14 Complaints lodged with family health service practitioners in the jurisdiction of the Southern Health and Social Services Board, 1999–2000 to 2001–02

	1999–2000	2000–01	2001–02
General practice	57	74	61
GP out of hours service	–	–	19
Dental service	21	17	49
Total	78	91	129

Source: Southern Health and Social Services Board, *Annual Report 2000–01*[50]

The Board itself received 45 complaints directly from service users in its area of authority. With the complainants' agreement, these grievances were referred to the health care establishments concerned for investigation at local level under the terms of the complaints procedure. (Presumably some – if not all – of these redirected complaints form part of the overall totals recorded for the health service in the area during 2001–02.) By comparison, 49 direct complaints reached the Board in 2000–01 and were dealt with in the same way.[51]

According to the Southern Health and Social Services Board's annual review of complaints lodged with health service establishments in 2001–02, around 96.3 per cent of those investigated were 'resolved' at local level. The remaining 3.7 per cent that were not settled amounted to 26 cases for which independent review was requested. Trusts accounted for 21 of these complaints and five involved family health service (FHS) practitioners (see tables 1.15a and 1.15b). By far the greatest number of complaints (18) were about treatment and care.[52]

Table 1.15a Progress and outcome of complaints lodged with trusts and family health services within the jurisdiction of the Southern Health and Social Services Board, 2000–01 and 2001–02

	2000–01	2001–02
Lodged with trusts	523	573
Lodged with family health services (GPs and dentists)	91	129
Total 614	702	
Of these:		
Resolved locally	589	676
Independent review requested	25	26
Requests about trusts	23	21
Requests involving family health services	2	5
Referred back for local resolution	7	10
Rejected for review	13	9
Accepted for review	5	4
Referred for conciliation	–	1
Still under consideration	–	2

Table 1.15b Percentage complaints lodged with trusts and family health services within the jurisdiction of the Southern Health and Social Services Board, 2000–01 and 2001–02

	2000–01	2001–02
Lodged with trusts	85.2	81.6
Lodged with family health services (GPs and dentists)	14.8	18.4
Of these:		
Resolved locally	96	96.3
Independent review requested	4	3.7

Source: Southern Health and Social Services Board, *Annual Review of Complaints 2001–02*[53]

By the end of 2001–02 there were 10 cases that had been referred back to the trusts for further examination, nine were rejected and four accepted for investigation by a review panel. One of the remaining three complaints was passed on for conciliation and two were still under consideration. (The final outcome of those cases that were investigated at independent review is not given in the Southern Health and Social Services Board's annual reviews for 2000–01 and 2001–02.) Three of the complainants whose requests for independent review were rejected took their cases to the Commissioner for Complaints. In each instance the latter agreed with the earlier decisions taken and did not carry out an investigation. In 2000–01 three cases had been referred for the same reasons to the commissioner for complaints but were similarly rejected.[54]

During 2001–02 the three health service trusts operating within the Western Health and Social Services Board's area of control received 359 complaints compared with 320 the year before. Following local resolution, a total of 18 cases was referred by complainants to the Board's convener to be considered for investigation by an independent review panel. Seven were subsequently turned down for review and four were referred back to the trusts concerned for further scrutiny. Another two cases were withdrawn by complainants and the remaining five accepted for review. Two out of the eighteen cases for which independent review was requested had been referred to the commissioner for complaints by the time the Board's annual report was released. But no judgements had been made in these two instances (see Table 1.16).[55]

Table 1.16 Progress and outcome of complaints in health service trusts referred to the Western Health and Social Services Board, 2000–01 and 2001–02

	2000–01	2001–02
Total all complaints	320	359
Of which:		
Requests for independent review	24	18
Cases referred back for local resolution	10	4
Rejected for review	9	7
Accepted for review	2	5
Withdrawn by complainants	3	2
Referred to the Commissioner for Complaints	2	2
Rejected for formal investigation	2	-
Under consideration	–	2

Source: Western Health and Social Services Board, *Annual Reports*[56]

Neither of the annual reports covering the period 2000–02 provided information about the numbers of complaints that had been lodged with family health service practitioners. It appears that the available data was insufficient for practical use by the Board, including the provision of statistics on the progress and outcome of any cases that passed to the review stage of the procedure.

There were 463 complaints lodged with all health service outlets and bodies in the jurisdiction of the Northern Health and Social Services Board during 2001–02, compared with 443 the year before (Table 1.18). Health and social service trusts accounted for 219 cases and 244 (Table 1.17) referred to family health services. In 2000–01, by comparison, 203 complaints were about health and social service trusts, 231 involved family health services and nine were directly concerning the Board. Acute treatment and care accounted for 48 per cent (101) of all complaints received by trusts. Table 1.16 shows the number of complaints that were made about family health service practioners during 2000–01 to 2001–02.[57]

Table 1.17 Complaints lodged with family health service practitioners by service, involving the Northern Health and Social Services Board, 2000–01 and 2001–02

	2000–01	2001–02
General practice	155	134
Dental services	31	63
Optician services	31	33
Pharmaceutical services	14	14[a]
Total	231	244

Source: Northern Health and Social Services Board, *Complaints Monitoring Reports*[58]
[a] Information on complaints received by five pharmacies was not supplied to the Board and is not included in this total.

Following local resolution, 10 complainants asked for their cases to be considered for independent review in 2001–02. Four complaints involved health and social service trusts, one concerned the registration and inspection unit, three were about general practitioners, one against a dentist and the other related directly to the Board. But none of these cases was accepted for investigation by a review panel. In all but one instance the complaints concerned clinical assessment, treatment or care. Up to the end of the year, no cases considered for independent review had been referred by complainants to the Commissioner for Complaints (Table 1.18).[59]

Table 1.18 Progress and outcome of complaints in all health service outlets and bodies dealt with by the Northern Health and Social Services Board, 2000–01 and 2001–02

	2000–01	2001–02[a]
Total all complaints	443	463
Of which:		
Requests for independent review	20	10
Referred back to local resolution or other destination	3	5
Rejected for review	15	3
Accepted for review	0	0
Ongoing at end of year	2	0
Referred to Commissioner for Complaints	4	0
Rejected for formal investigation	–	–
Under consideration at end of year	4	–

Source: Northern Health and Social Services Board, *Complaints Monitoring Reports*[60]
[a] In 2001–02 two cases were partially closed; the remaining part of one was referred back for local resolution and that of the other drawn to the attention of the party being complained against.

Out of the 20 complaints put forward for investigation by a review panel in 2000–01, by comparison, less than half were directly connected with clinical issues. Trusts and other health service outlets were involved in 10 complaints, family health service practitioners in six and four directly concerned the Board. Four of the cases – and two from a previous period – considered for review were subsequently referred to the Commissioner for Complaints. These cases were still being considered at the end of the year.[61]

What can be concluded from the UK's 1996 version of the health service complaints system in operation?
Probably the most striking impression of this NHS complaints procedure was its lack of independence. To begin with, and judging by the occupational connections of those who conducted investigations locally, it cannot be said that what took place in any of the regions of the United Kingdom was carried out impartially. It was therefore unlikely that the complaints procedure would ever gain much public confidence and, apparently, it did not.

Indeed, it can be powerfully argued that the consistently large proportion of complaints that were either 'resolved' at an early stage in the process, or got no further, was probably a direct product of the lack of detachment that local resolution carried out by the NHS body concerned symbolizes. It is difficult to imagine that any kind of organization conducting its own investigation into a serious complaint from the outside about one of its personnel will always perform the task meticulously and impartially. For instance, will it, without exception, volunteer evidence that is likely to incriminate the staff member under scrutiny?

The complaints statistics for each of the four UK countries – especially those about England – demonstrate the extent of the problem about the health service system: they show that only a small proportion of the number of complaints that were made progressed through the system. It is a situation that might lead some uninformed people – on first glance – to form the impression that complainants about health care in the United Kingdom may be a particularly trivial or vexatious breed. But they would probably change their minds after learning more of the facts.

Even once the mammoth local resolution sifting process had been completed, the comparatively small number of complainants who decided to pursue their cases further had no automatic right to a review. The review depended on a flawed selection procedure, which determined the complaints that were to be referred for investigation by a review panel – itself a questionable group, considering its component parts. (The 'independent' tag attached to the review proceedings was clearly something of a misnomer and was perhaps introduced by design rather than accident to exaggerate the panel's status in the eyes of complainants.)

Nor were complainants entitled to an independent investigation of their grievances by the relevant ombudsman once the compulsory health service complaints mechanism had been fully used according to statutory rules. This would happen only if the Ombudsman's screeners gave their approval to a formal examination. (The position remains unchanged in 2005. Chapter 3 and – by implication – Chapter 4 suggest that there may even be underlying flaws in the complaints bodies that these ombudsmen front.)

Another apparent drawback for complainants was the limited powers invested in review panels, and even in the ombudsmen themselves. Neither set of complaints investigators could compel a health service body to act on their judgements (although what they recommended was invariably carried out, despite there being no legal requirement to do so.) Nor did review panels or any ombudsman have any disciplinary authority over health care practitioners. (In 2005 this continues to be the jurisdiction of effectively self-regulating professional bodies who are invariably involved in clinical cases when the complaints handlers within the NHS complaints mechanism or the ombudsman concerned have made their judgements.) The result was that complainants had often to endure an arduous and protracted journey in their search for answers or remedial action – quite apart from any subsequent action that might have involved a claim for compensation. (Chapters 13, 17, 18 and 19 show that there are better ways of dealing with and redressing complaints relating to health care.)

One might argue that the NHS complaints procedure model of 1996 could not (or would not) come up with any outcome other than to continue to reject a large proportion of cases that passed through its handlers. Certainly there often existed a wide chasm between complainants and the health service about what constituted a legitimate grievance. Some people maintained that, like its predecessor, this internally managed complaints system was another deliberate invention to protect the health service and medical profession. Cynical though this observation may seem, it is probably not without some foundation, all things considered.

Whatever the justification for this view, the public furore about the NHS complaints system (and other associated and similar issues) alluded to at the start of this chapter seems to have been convincing enough for the House of Commons Health Committee to hold an inquiry and produce a report and recommendations for change in 1999 (see note 3, Preface Notes). So did the government at around the same time when it commissioned a two-year national evaluation of the complaints procedure and followed up the study with an additional public exercise of its own.

What did these combined initiatives reveal? And are the consequent recommendations and resulting reforms likely to make a real difference, most of them having already been passed into law in England and Wales (and set to do the same in Scotland and Northern Ireland during 2005)? Will it be a change so notable that the complaints sytem that emerges is certain to capture public confidence? The next chapter considers the key issues that arose – particularly in the government's initiatives – and the reforms that are in place and those due to come about as a result.

CHAPTER 2

The groundwork on the NHS complaints mechanism has delivered reforms

There is a problem though – the likely benefits may be nowhere near enough

The revelations in the government-sponsored national evaluation of the NHS complaints procedure[1] and in its own follow-up survey[2] may have been an eye-opener to the uninitiated. But they must have come as no surprise to those who previously had cause to express their serious concerns about the way the mechanism was being operated. Nevertheless, what the two exercises did achieve was to confirm the crucial flaws they had identified and uncover numerous other key faults in the system.

Commissioned by the Department of Health in co-operation with its counterpart in the three devolved administrations of Scotland, Wales and Northern Ireland, the independent nationwide appraisal of the NHS complaints procedure was carried out in 1999 and 2000. Its remit was 'to provide an evaluation of how the new complaints procedures are operating across all parts of the NHS – hospital, community and family health services (FHS)…and to meet the information needs of policymakers and managers concerned with the future development of the system'.[3]

More than 4,000 questionnaires were circulated to health service chief executives, complaints managers, independent review panel (IRP) conveners, lay chairmen and panel members, conciliators and clinical assessors. The research further involved 315 interviews with complainants and health service staff complained against, and NHS personnel responsible for setting up structures and overseeing the mechanics of dealing with complaints in regions across the nation. It also included sessions with focus groups concerned with primary care and other similar actions. In addition, the research team dealt with written submissions from NHS staff and individuals with experience of the complaints procedure.[4] The group's findings and recommendations for change were reported in *NHS Complaints Procedure National Evaluation*, a government publication issued in September 2001.

Complainants generally disapprove of the system

In the questionnaires and additional interviews complainants were asked about their experience of the NHS complaints procedure. The evidence showed that easily the larger proportion of them was greatly dissatisfied with the working of the existing system. This was true for cases that did not progress beyond local resolution and for those where a request for independent review had been put forward.[5]

In one sample of 271 complainants (relating to a random group of 50 health service trusts and authorities or boards in the United Kingdom) the vast majority (96 per cent) did not advance further than local resolution with their cases, although in 11 per cent of instances they had asked for independent review. Just over 30 per cent of these complainants felt that their cases had been handled properly at local resolution, while 49 per cent did not. A little under 30 per cent were content with the time taken to deal with their complaints, but 47 per cent were not. A large majority of the complainants (65 per cent) found the process to be stressful or distressing compared with 19 per cent who did not. The responses also showed that 54 per cent considered that the complaints process was unfair, as opposed to about 26 per cent who did not. Similarly, around 51 per cent of complainants felt that the system was biased, while around 22 per cent thought otherwise. Less than 24 per cent were satisfied with the outcome of their case and 58 per cent were displeased with it.[6]

Out of another group comprising 148 complainants, with one exception – complaint handling – the satisfaction ratings for local resolution in cases concerning family health services (FHS) were lower in all respects than those given by the sample of 271 complainants of NHS services as a whole. This group had been approached via health councils (137) and practices (11). In 54 per cent of cases complainants had requested independent review. But the greater proportion (70 per cent) of those who had done so failed to progress further than local resolution.[7]

It was found that community health councils (and their equivalent) were an important source of information and support for complainants at local resolution. In 48 per cent of cases complainants had approached these agencies for assistance with their complaint, and 77 per cent stated that the agency had been helpful. Nearly 25 per cent of all respondents had contacted their health council in first pursuing their complaint.[8]

A 'very common and pervasive source of dissatisfaction' among some complainants was the poor attitudes of clinical and managerial personnel. The complainants invariably mentioned lack of respect, sympathy and understanding, and patronizing, aggressive and arrogant behaviour by these health service staff. They called for staff to listen to what they had to say, be more honest, communicate more effectively and deal quickly with their grievances.[9]

A further sample was taken of 137 complainants (including 40 per cent of whose cases concerned hospital and community health services and 33 per cent general practitioners) who had requested an independent review. A total of 73 (53 per cent) of these complaints were accepted for investigation by an independent review panel (IRP), but this batch of complainants were generally more critical of the system as a whole than those who had expressed an opinion about the local resolution process.[10]

About 65 per cent of the responding complainants believed that their cases had not been properly handled, while 23 per cent were satisfied with the service. An even greater proportion, 78 per cent, were not content with the time the complaints procedure had taken; less than 10 per cent were satisfied. Nearly three-quarters considered the process to be biased and 71 per cent thought that it was unfair, compared with about 13 per cent in each case who had the reverse view. Similarly, almost 78 per cent of respondents were dissatisfied with the outcome, while 13 per cent were not. Around 4.5 per cent of them had not been stressed at this second phase of the complaints process and 6 per cent had found it not distressing. In contrast about 89 per cent indicated that they had been either stressed or distressed as a result of the experience.

When asked about the most important changes that were needed in the existing review process, the respondents in this sample stated that there should be greater impartiality in the role of the convener and in the review process itself. They considered that a health service establishment that is the subject of complaint should have less discretion to decide whether and in what way the recommendations of the review panel involved will be implemented.[11]

Those on the receiving end of complaints are mostly content with the procedure
On the other hand, the views expressed to the study group by NHS personnel who had been the subject of complaint told a sharply different story. Most of the 144 respondents (93 per cent with trusts and the rest from health authorities and boards) to a postal questionnaire, including 39 who were interviewed, 'felt very positive about their experience of the complaints procedure'. The majority of complaints (77 per cent) had not proceeded further than local resolution and only 2 per cent reached an independent review.[12]

Table 2.1 Views of NHS staff who had complaints made against them as percentage of total

	Trust		Health Authority or Health Board	
	Yes	No	Yes	No
I was satisfied with the outcome	58.1	19.4	50.0	37.5
The complaint was handled properly	68.2	15.5	57.2	28.6
I was satisfied with the time it took	64.0	16.0	55.5	22.2
The process was fair	58.7	17.4	50.0	25.0
The process was unbiased	63.5	15.0	75.0	–
The experience was not stressful	16.1	71.0	22.2	66.7
I was given enough information	68.5	22.8	77.7	22.2
I was kept informed	38.3	44.6	44.4	33.3

Source: *NHS Complaints Procedure National Evaluation,* 2001[13]
[a] Figures for 'yes' and 'no' do not add up to 100 per cent because some respondents could not give an opinion one way or the other.

Most of these participants were content with the outcome of the complaint against them and considered that it had been handled properly. A big majority of them said that they had been given sufficient information, although a somewhat larger percentage of trust staff stated that they were not kept informed. Also, the greatest proportion of respondents acknowledged that the process was stressful and most were satisfied with the time taken to resolve the issue and believed that the 'process was both fair and unbiased'[14] (see Table 2.1). Moreover, 65.2 per cent of trust staff and 87.5 per cent in health authorities and boards felt supported by professional colleagues; while 64.9 per cent and 66.6 per cent, respectively, considered that they had been backed up by managerial associates.[15]

Health councils with experience of assisting complainants give a mixed opinion of the system
The evaluation team sent a questionnaire to all the health councils in the UK: community health councils in England and Wales; health councils in Scotland; and

health and social services councils in Northern Ireland. The content of the form centred on the councils' work in assisting complainants and asked for their opinions on the three key aspects of the complaints procedure: local resolution; request (to the convener) for independent review; and independent review itself. Out of the total circulated, 130 health councils (58 per cent) responded to the questionnaire.[16]

The views of health council respondents on the individual performance of these phases of the mechanism mostly varied according to the service involved against three defined objectives:

• meeting the reasonable expectations of complainants
• improving services as a result of complaints
• identifying serious clinical problems and/or professional misconduct.[17]

In the case of hospital and community health services most health council respondents considered local resolution to perform satisfactorily or well (or very well) – 44.2 and 16.3 per cent, 38 and 21.7 per cent and 31.7 and 20 per cent, respectively – in fulfilling these aims. The balance of respondents placed a poor or very poor rating (39.5, 40.3 and 48.3, respectively) against each objective. But the picture was reversed for primary care. Here, the majority judged that local resolution performed poorly or very poorly – 51.6 per cent, 70.4 per cent and 63.3 per cent, respectively – against each of the same goals. The remainder in each instance felt that the process functioned satisfactorily (35.9, 18.4 and 25 per cent) and well or very well (12.5, 11.2 and 11.7 per cent).[18]

A majority of respondents from health councils considered the convening aspect of the complaints procedure to function poorly or very poorly against the first and third defined objectives (the second not being relevant) in primary care and other services. Responses concerning these two goals showed that 64.1 per cent and 63.3 per cent, respectively, regarded the existing system of convening to be performing poorly or very poorly in primary care. The balance in each case thought that it worked satisfactorily (23.9 and 24.8 per cent) or well or very well (12.8 and 11.9 per cent). A similar picture emerged for hospital and community health services: more than half of the respondents considered the process to be poor or very poor – 65.6 per cent and 64.1 per cent, respectively – against each of the two aims. The remaining proportion in each instance believed that existing convening practice performed satisfactorily (27.2 and 23.9 per cent) or well or very well (7.2 and 12 per cent) against the two objectives.[19]

The views of health council respondents on the same three objectives about independent review in primary care were a little less discouraging: 48.6 per cent, 56.3 per cent and 51 per cent, respectively, considered that it functioned poorly or very poorly, but the balance felt that the process worked satisfactorily (33.3 per cent, 29.1 per cent and 30.2 per cent) or well or very well (18.1 per cent, 14.6 per cent and 18.8 per cent). Independent review involving hospital and community health services was given a higher rating: 43.6 per cent, 44.7 per cent and 36.8 per cent, respectively, judged that it operated satisfactorily and 12 per cent, 14.9 per cent and 17 per cent well or very well. The balance of respondents in each case (44.4 per cent, 40.4 per cent and 46.2 per cent) considered the process to have performed poorly or very poorly.[20]

Patient interest groups are mostly critical of the complaints mechanism
Patient interest organizations who responded to the study group's questionnaire survey were those with experience of dealing with people who had complained or wanted to complain about the health service. Most of them confirmed that complainants are usually seeking an explanation for what went wrong, an apology and a reassurance that lessons have been learned from health service errors. However, they observed that there are times when complainants expect a decision to be reversed – for instance, when it concerns the provision of services that were previously denied.[21]

The respondents strongly criticized the operation of the NHS complaints mechanism, chiefly in its failure to deal satisfactorily with these and other issues, thus causing further distress to complainants – especially when a serious incident is involved. They added that many individuals seeking their help are deterred from complaining because they are frightened that services will be withdrawn or reduced. Potential complainants were also put off by the complicated system itself. Nevertheless, the existing mechanism was seen by most respondents to have some assets – a clear procedure, fixed time objectives for dealing with complaints and a thorough approach. But they called for improved staff training, greater access to information for complainants, better checks on action taken following complaints and more independence in the system.[22]

NHS complaints handlers are found to be inadequately trained
As well as confirming widespread dissatisfaction by complainants and others about the complaints system, the evaluation team found that disquietingly low levels of training were given to staff operating complaints procedures. The sample of responding health service complaints managers showed that they received an average of 5.6 days of instruction. Conveners, on the other hand, had an average of only 15 hours of training, while review chairs and lay panel members were a little better off with three days of coaching. Indeed, the study showed that a significant minority had not received any training, and a majority in all groups would have liked additional instruction.[23]

Some key recommendations for change by the national evaluation team
Based on the evidence, the sweeping study of the complaints system concluded that 'it is not working particularly well'. The evaluation further showed that complainants and those managing the procedure agree that improvements are needed.[24] As a result of their findings, the researchers came up with a wide-ranging set of recommendations aimed at upgrading the workings of the mechanism across its two phases.

Local resolution
The national evaluation team recommended that the board of every NHS establishment should be held accountable for the way the handling of complaints is discharged. It should ensure that the personnel concerned are at all times properly trained for the purpose, and supported when being complained against. Moreover, the complaints process should be integrated into the 'clinical governance/quality framework' of each health service organization.

Every quarter, a report on the causes of complaints and on the action taken or proposed to prevent a recurrence should be given to the board in person by the complaints manager or chief executive. The document should be copied to the local health council (or equivalent) and the local patients' forum in England or any counterpart in Scotland, Wales and Northern Ireland. These agencies should be invited to monitor the implementation of the agreed plan of action responding to complaints. A 'national service framework' should be developed to manage complaints and provide clear guidance to health service establishments on the standards that are expected.

Family health services should be subject to the same principles as those that apply to the rest of public sector health care. The boards of primary care groups, local health groups in Wales and primary care trusts should replace health authorities in their responsibility over complaints against family health service contractors. They should co-operate with these contractors to ensure that an acceptable complaints procedure is in place. Practices should provide boards with a quarterly report on the causes of incoming complaints and on the action taken or proposed. Where it is relevant, boards should offer assistance to practices in dealing with complaints. They should also be responsible for introducing complainants to the nominated person charged with handling complaints involving member practices. Where no primary care organizations of the type described are in place, alternative sources will need to be considered to provide support in the handling of complaints.

Less discretion should be in the hands of individual NHS establishments to determine the duties of and resources available to complaints managers. 'More detailed guidance should be offered from the centre, based on an analysis of best practice.' Complaints managers should have a key role in making sure that front-line staff are sufficiently trained and supported when dealing with complainants. Additionally, these personnel should be given regular instruction. On an associated point, health service bodies should assess the availability of trained local conciliators, encourage a broader use of conciliation and review their policy on offering the service. [25]

Independent review
The researchers in the national study observed that existing criteria for granting an independent review are not necessarily known to complainants. Accordingly, their view was that these principles should be publicized and also applied consistently throughout the NHS. Consideration should be given in each of the four UK countries to the suggestion that, in future, both the convening decision and conduct of a review should be the responsibility of a specifically appointed regional or sub-regional panel.

Two options were put forward on where the accountability of such a panel should lie. One was that it should be answerable to the regional offices of the NHS Executive (in England) or to national or sub-national bodies in Scotland, Wales and Northern Ireland. The other suggestion was that panels should be accountable to regional or sub-regional offices of a new national complaints authority that is independent – locally and regionally – of the NHS.

Another of the study group's conclusions was that more consideration should be given to the suggestion by the House of Commons Health Committee that an independent review panel is granted formal powers to summon witnesses and take evidence. The evaluation team went on to recommend that the Health Service Commissioner (or Ombudsman) for England and Wales [and presumably counterparts in the other two countries] should be consulted about whether a 'fast-track' process for certain complaints to this officer's organization would be viable and appropriate. In particular, the reference was to instances where a convener (or complaints panel) felt that it would be better suited for cases to be referred directly to the Ombudsman for a more formal investigation, rather than to progress further through the independent review process.

The boards of NHS establishments should take more 'active' responsibility in complaints-handling affairs. They should also receive a copy of the independent review panel report relevant to their organization and accept accountability for ensuring that the agreed plan of action to meet the panel's recommendations is implemented. The regional and national bodies responsible for NHS performance (for instance, the Commission for Health Improvement in England) should also be sent the panel's report and ensure that the remedial measures to be taken are satisfactory and put into effect. Additionally, copies of all this information should be sent to the local health council and patients' forum in England or to their counterparts in the case of Scotland, Wales and Northern Ireland. These agencies should be authorized to check that the agreed course of action is being complied with by the health service organization involved.

Training relating to the independent review phase of the procedure should be reviewed for complaints handlers. In particular, conveners, chairs and other lay members may need to be given some compulsory instruction. There is also a requirement for more central guidance on the amount and type of training on offer to offset inconsistencies between NHS establishments and for lists of clinical assessors in certain regions of the UK to be updated.[26]

A 'listening document' is issued and circulated for comment

At the same time that it made public the report *NHS Complaints Procedure National Evaluation* in September 2001, the government issued *Reforming the NHS Complaints Procedure: a listening document*. The document applied to England only and was, among other things, the government's response to the independent national evaluation, and it summarised the study group's findings and recommendations. It drew on the issues raised in the report and invited a cross-section of parties to express their views on a number of 'Key Questions' and on the proposals put forward to improve the complaints system.[27]

There were 600 written responses to the document after it was circulated, including those from targeted respondents in the health service: chief executives, chairmen, complaints managers and IRP conveners in NHS establishments. Others who replied were patient representative and support groups, professional and regulatory bodies, voluntary organizations, individual patients and members of the public. The operation was completed a few weeks later in October 2001.[28]

The response to this listening exercise, reported in *NHS Complaints Reform – Making Things Right* (March 2003), apparently confirmed the key issues and priorities identified in the national evaluation report that needed to be addressed to change the complaints procedure.[29] These were to:

- regard complaints as a means of finding out why things go wrong and how the position can be improved
- get local resolution right
- make independent review fair and unbiased
- improve staff training
- staff and resource the system so that it is 'supportive, effective and time-efficient'
- 'harmonize' health and social services complaints procedures.

Responses to the follow-up action pointed to other areas that needed upgrading or change if there was to be an improved complaints system.[30] These included:

- improving access to the procedure
- improving guidance and support
- monitoring and accountability
- improving time scales for handling complaints
- improving mediation and conciliation
- providing scope for patients to complain directly to primary care trusts (PCTs) where family health service practitioners are involved
- allowing leeway for certain complaints to be refered to the Ombudsman more quickly.

NHS Complaints Reform – Making Things Right stated that the issues highlighted by respondents had helped to establish which aspects of the complaints mechanism it was best to focus on.[31] In essence the aims were to:

- encourage, enable and help health service staff to take a 'patient-focused' and more positive path to complaints and concerns
- improve the transmission of information to patients and their access to it
- provide truly independent assistance to people wishing to lodge a complaint
- raise complainants' expectations about the investigation of their grievances at local resolution, which, accordingly, will enhance the quality of such inquiries and provide the basis for judgements about suitable redress
- reform the independent review, second stage of the procedure to make it entirely independent and gain the confidence of patients and health service staff; the responsibility for managing this process to rest with the (now set up) Commission for Healthcare Audit and Inspection (CHAI) or Healthcare Commission
- introduce a new clinical assessors' database to sustain a more effective second stage
- spell out the functions and responsibilities of various individuals within and outside the NHS in order to improve accountability, monitoring standards and performance management, and learn from complainants
- encourange consistency between the mechanisms for handling complaints relating to health care and those about social services.

What the programme of change for the NHS complaints sytem means – or will mean – in practice[32]

England
Elements of the proposals in *NHS Complaints Reform – Making Things Right*, which sets out a programme of change to overhaul the NHS complaints mechanism, are contained in the Health and Social Care (Community Health and Standards)

Act 2003. The legislation was passed in November of that year. England's Department of Health considers that the plan of action as a result will open the door to:

- making the system more flexible so that there are a number of ways in which the public can express their concerns about the services they have received
- improving local resolution so that formal complaints are more likely to be resolved at this phase of the procedure
- radical reform to the review stage by placing it in the hands of the Healthcare Commission (CHAI), an independent body, which became operational as an organization in April 2004
- ensuring that information about complaints and their causes are a fundamental part of a health service whose role is to provide a safe and progressively high standard of care.

The Health and Social Care (Community Health and Standards) Act 2003 has provided for regulations to be made setting out the framework for a reformed NHS complaints procedure. Implementation of the reforms was being phased in because of the ongoing Shipman inquiry, which reported in December 2004. But the complaints process continues to consist of three facets: local resolution, independent review and the Health Service Ombudsman's involvement.

Until some point in 2005 (when changes to local resolution will be made after consideration of the Shipman inquiry report and the results of certain other such inquiries), the procedure for local resolution will remain unchanged. However, the existing directions governing complaints about NHS organizations and primary care practitioners have been combined in the NHS (Complaints) Regulations, which came into force in August 2004. At the same time these regulations placed responsibility for the independent review process in the hands of the Healthcare Commission.

Where local resolution fails, complainants can ask the Commission to review their case. In doing so the latter will have one of a number of options open to it including, for example:

- to recommend that the NHS organization involved takes further action where there are shortcomings in the way a complaint has been handled
- to carry out a detailed investigation to resolve the complaint and, if relevant, an inspection into the failures of the establishment complained against as part of a wider inquiry
- to refer complaints directly to the Ombudsman
- to refer cases to another organization such as a professional regulatory body
- to decide that no further action is needed.

If the Commission decides to investigate a case the inquiry will be conducted by its staff and they will prepare a report that may include recommendations to the health service organization concerned. This may resolve the issue successfully. Where it does not, complainants will have a right to ask for their case to be considered by an independent panel, although being granted such a request is not a statutory entitlement. The panel, comprising three lay people unconnected with the NHS, will study the investigation that has taken place and may take evidence from the complainant and others involved in the case.

Should the response from independent review be unacceptable, the complainant can refer their case to the Ombudsman. Under section 118 of the Health and Social Care (Community Health and Standards) Act 2003 amending the Health Service Commissioners Act 1993, the Ombudsman has powers to investigate complaints about maladministration against the Healthcare Commission in its role as a component of the NHS complaints procedure.

(NHS 'foundation trusts' are to have their own internal complaints handling procedures, which may differ from the 'local resolution' model in the universal NHS system. Despite this, these health service bodies will be subject to the Healthcare Commission's independent review process and the Health Service Ombudsman's involvement.)

Scotland

In September 2004 the arrangement for an amended NHS complaints procedure in Scotland was still under discussion. Nevertheless, the country's Department of Health and others involved in this plan of change were looking at introducing a more investigative local resolution process that would make unnecessary the existing review stage of the system. This would put dissatisfied complainants in a position to refer their case to the Scottish Public Services Ombudsman after a single phase of investigation by the health service instead of following two stages. The proposal had not been finalized at the time, but whatever changes were decided would, it appears, be implemented in a reformed complaints system to commence in spring 2005. On an associated issue, health councils continue to fulfill their role as complainant advice and support agencies in grievances about the health service.

Wales

A revised NHS complaints system has been in operation in Wales since April 2003. The procedure for lodging a complaint and the local resolution process that ensues remain essentially unchanged from those followed in the previous mechanism described in Chapter 1. However, after or as an alternative to first approaching the health service provider, complainants can lodge their grievances with one of the local health boards that have recently been established for when GPs, dentists, pharmacists or opticians are involved in a complaint. On the direct support side, complainants continue to have access to community health councils (these were replaced by new complainant assistance and advocacy groups in England), a group of independent agencies who provide them with help and advice in proceeding with their case through the NHS procedure.

Similar to the change in the complaints mechanism in England, the independent review stage of the system for Wales has seen radical reform. The former convener – a person who was widely considered to be inappropriately connected with the NHS (see Chapter 1) – has been replaced by a 'reviewer', an independent lay person who decides whether a complaint has been examined sufficiently at local resolution or that a panel should be set up to investigate the case further. In reaching a decision on a case the reviewer is advised by another lay individual and, where necessary, by a clinical assessor.

The reviewer, lay adviser and clinical assessors are selected by the newly formed Independent Review Secretariat (IRS) from a register that the Welsh Assembly government has developed and holds for the purpose. It is the responsibility of the IRS to allocate cases to these examiners and also to set up an independent panel to investigate complaints where a reviewer has considered that this course of action should follow. The panel of three independent lay persons and the independent clinical assessors advising it are similarly appointed from lists with the Assembly government. Unlike the Healthcare Commission in England, neither panels nor the Independent Review Secretariat have powers to refer complaints to the Health Service Ombudsman or to the professional regulatory bodies. Nonetheless, akin to the previous arrangement, the decision of a reviewer or panel is given in writing to the complainant concerned, following which the latter may take their case to the Ombudsman or to a regulatory body.

Northern Ireland
Like the position in Scotland, the precise form of a revised NHS complaints procedure for Northern Ireland was still under review in September 2004. It appears that no radical changes are expected in the new system once it is in force, although it is clear that the local resolution and independent review phases are to be strengthened. For example, training will play a more dominant role than hitherto and, in the case of the review process, panel recommendations will be more robustly enforced. The changes were expected to start being implemented from April 2005. In Northern Ireland the existing health and social services councils continue to assist complainants with their grievances about the NHS.

Will the proposed new formula work for complainants?
One thing is certain about the national evaluation report on the NHS complaints procedure that was introduced in 1996: although probably predictable in most of its findings, it puts to shame the Wilson Committee review of 1994[33] as a catalyst for equitable change – whatever its extent. The interesting outlook of the review of the Wilson Committee on impartiality in complaints handling may help to illuminate this:

Complainants want *impartial* consideration of their complaint. Impartiality is achieved by care and accuracy by the investigator. This applies whether the investigator belongs to the organisation concerned or is outside it. Investigation by someone external to the organisation may appear more impartial, but we believe this is not essential. Public confidence will be promoted if responses to complaints include information about who complainants should approach if they wish to take their complaints further.[34]

Being associated with this kind of curious logic, it may be unsurprising that the complaints system established in 1996 (effectively the product of the Wilson review) seems to have performed no better than its predecessor. However, even accepting that the later inquiry is the superior of the two, it is unfortunate from a complainant's perspective that its remit was not more meaningful. In sponsoring an inquiry with the aim of simply improving the existing system, the powers that be missed (or perhaps side-stepped) a golden opportunity to wipe the slate clean and establish the framework for a new, autonomous national complaints body for each of the four countries to replace the statutory health-service-operated mechanism together with the Ombudsman's organization. Such a body would have the authority to examine cases from the outset of the complaint – if asked to do so by the complainant – rather than be concerned merely with the many fewer cases that are referred for independent review. The effective implementation of the stronger and more radical of the study group's two proposals – making review panels accountable to a new independent national complaints authority (for example, the Healthcare Commission in England) – probably continues to address only an extremely small proportion of the total number of cases entering the system.

Interestingly, aspects of the evaluation's findings did seem to imply – if not intentionally – that an injection of independence into complaints handling at local resolution would not go amiss. For instance the review found that 'one of the most common characteristics of protracted cases' was 'the singular failure to deal adequately with the complaint from the outset'. For example, there were delays at local resolution in arranging for staff to attend meetings with complainants and in obtaining information. 'In many case it appears to be almost impossible for clinicians or managers to admit that a mistake has been made and to offer a genuine apology,' the evaluation's authors added. Other findings by them shed light on the poor state of affairs concerning local resolution in its existing form generally: the majority of complainants were dissatisfied with key aspects of this initial process.[35]

The question then arises of whether a local resolution system that is subject to the plethora of checks and balances proposed in the national evaluation report – summarized in *NHS Complaints Reform – Making Things Right*, or what actually emerges as a result[36] – will completely (or even mostly) eradicate the difficulties that have been identified while it continues to remain in health service hands. Will the reformed local resolution arrangement, for England as an instance, prevent these systematic failures when it comes in 2005? Will it be in a position to provide the same level of service as an independently run system with which complainants can lodge their grievances either as a first or final resort? The answer on each count is that it will probably not.

With the right formula a one-stop complaints mechanism should function faster than one containing more than one stage and deal with complaints more quickly than the two to three years that have invariably been involved in handling cases in the continuing phased NHS system. Equally it should be speedier than any upgraded model of a procedure that will still have two stages, with the albeit independent second stage evidently continuing to be open to the comparatively few. A detached and independently operated mechanism is also more likely to provide an efficient way of resolving complaints as it should be less disposed to being submerged in the bureacracies of the health service. There is also a greater likelihood that an independently managed procedure would be accepted by complainants as being an equitable means of dealing with their grievances.

An independent complaints authority is also unlikely to attract anywhere near the same level of criticism from complainants that the 1996 NHS-run complaints system has been receiving or, for that matter, as much as a reformed version of it that continues to be predominantly managed by the health service is likely to generate. Of course those who may be complained about may be apprehensive of change on this scale, especially after being long-accustomed to an internally managed system of investigation. Nevertheless, nobody should be fearful of a neutral body assuming the role of investigator. (As a high-ranking officer in a Nordic independent complaints and medical regulatory body recently put it to the author of this book: 'What can they be afraid of?') In any event, one would have thought that the health service should be managing health care; not also being committed to dealing with large numbers of complaints – a state of affairs in which it has been involved for years. Moreover, who knows, an externally operated complaints system might just turn out to be less expensive to manage – and more efficient.

Other questions that arise about the reforms
The authors of *NHS Complaints Reform – Making Things Right* had much to say about why, what and how changes to the present system should be made. They stated that their vision of a successful complaints procedure 'is one which meets the needs of patients and staff by making the process: open and easy to access...fair and independent...responsive...learning and developing'.[37]

Who would disagree with such ideals? The question is: how are all these principles supposed to be fulfilled in a complaints system that continues to be almost entirely in health service hands? For a start, the crucial issues of openness, fairness and independence will go on being in doubt – from a complainant's perspective – whatever the assurances.

One of the observations made in the report was that 'high among the reasons that motivate people to complain'[38] is the wish for reassurance that the same mistakes will not be repeated and affect others. Although complainants have frequently made this point, it may be naïve and reading too much into its importance to place the issue high on the list of reasons complainants have for pursuing a grievance. Obviously those who complain do not want errors to be repeated and they would no doubt expect to be given an explanation about what went wrong, and an apology when it is due. But a priority for many complainants – especially in serious cases – is the need to get justice: honesty, accountability by the health service body involved when negligence has occurred and fitting action taken against those who are responsible. Are the new procedures likely to fulfill these obligations? If not, legal proceedings by some complainants may follow as before and, accordingly, do little to reduce the build-up of claims against the NHS (although the proposed new patient compensation scheme described in Chapter 7 should alleviate this problem when it is in operation).

It was also stated in *NHS Complaints Reform – Making Things Right* that only 3,500 (2.5 per cent) out of 140,000 people who lodged a formal complaint in 2000–01 'felt the need' to request an independent review.[39] How did they arrive at this conclusion? Is this what the remaining 97.5 per cent of complainants whose cases did not proceed further tell the health service's complaints handlers? If not, it is a false premise. These findings differ from what is revealed in the report of the earlier national evaluation of the complaints procedure.

For example, in one of this review's references to local resolution, the results from two samples of cases (comprising 271 and 148 complainants respectively) showed a 'level of dissatisfaction with present procedures which is surprising in view of the fact that the vast majority of these complaints had apparently been resolved'.[40] It appears that the complainants involved were chosen broadly on the basis that their cases were no longer active. The report added that its references to a complaint being 'resolved' simply meant that the case was not being pursued further. It went on to say: 'the fact that a complaint is resolved does not imply that either party is content with the outcome'.[41]

Is it possible that an unknown proportion of complainants who did not request an independent review following local resolution simply withdrew from the system because they lost confidence in its worth? Who can tell how many of them subsequently decided to take civil action, even at this early stage of the procedure? (Perhaps those who did partly contributed to the heavy build-up of claims in the hands of the NHS Litigation Authority, the legal arm of the health service.) It is fair to assume that these litigants were not satisfied with the outcome of their cases at local resolution, nor optimistic about their prospects further in the NHS complaints procedure.

Conclusion

All these factors would seem to cast some doubt on the value ascribed to the reforms. Even considering the warm words, assurances and good intentions expressed in *NHS Complaints Reform – Making Things Right*, the likely reality is that the vast majority of complaints will still be resolved by the health service. On this pretty cast-iron assumption the reforms already in place – or in the pipeline – involving the review stage of the process, while commendable, will consequently (as previously indicated) continue to address only a tiny proportion of the complaints entering the system in the first place and are therefore unlikely to please the public at large. The numerous and bureaucratic checks and balances may alleviate some of the drawbacks of a still mostly internally managed operation, but the extent to which this is likely to occur remains to be seen and may also not impress the public or the majority of complainants.

Accordingly many will be concerned that the new arrangements in place – and those outstanding – do not go far enough and cynics may consider that this is yet another ploy by the UK's legislators, either in league with or under pressure from vested interests, to continue denying citizens a basic right – the opportunity for independent handling of their complaints relating to health care from the outset, if this is what they would prefer. Perhaps it does not help that the conduct of parliamentarians – the country's lawmakers – is also not subject to neutrally administered regulation.

A well-known television mogul made a general observation in 2001 that radical institutional change in Britain – however much it is needed – mostly continues to be anathema to those in charge. His comment certainly seems to have some resonance when it is applied to the limited reforms to the NHS complaints procedure in the nation's four countries. Some might even say that he had got it just about right.

CHAPTER 3

Where and when will the Health Service Ombudsman come in?

And what do the statistics tell us about this independent arbiter's judgements?

The three Health Service Ombudsmen in the United Kingdom (for England and Wales, Scotland and Northern Ireland) preside over an exclusive club, full entry to which is gained by the few and fortunate. They are the lucky and comparatively small number of complainants who have not only met their obligations in completing the preceding NHS complaints procedure, but whose cases then survived the Ombudsman's own initial screening test.

Only a minuscule proportion of the complaints that are lodged annually with the health service reach the Ombudsman, so nobody with a complaint about health care provided by the NHS can assume that this independent adjudicator will ultimately attempt to intervene in the matter. Even when this does happen, the chances are far more likely that the complaint will be rejected for a full and formal investigation. But will the remedies within the Ombudsman's gift to recommend always reflect the gravity of the issue being complained about when a case is upheld?

The point at which the Health Service Ombudsman will consider a complaint
The Ombudsman serving England and Wales and the Scottish Public Services Ombudsman do not normally become involved in a case unless complainants remain dissatisfied after pursuing their grievances sufficiently at local level through the NHS complaints procedure.[1] This disaffection will have arisen, for example, because:
* It had taken too long for the health service body to deal with a complainant's case.
* A complainant's request for investigation by a review panel or body had been unreasonably rejected.
* A complainant had not been given an acceptable response to the grievance(s) raised.

All other relevant or key aspects of the jurisdiction and powers of these two ombudsmen and the terms and process under which they are authorized to start considering a complaint and proceed further with it are also generally common to the three countries concerned. Where the occasional exception may exist (in Scotland for example), it does not affect the essential role of that country's Ombudsman, as it would not her England-based counterpart's in a similar situation.

Complaints can be made to the Ombudsman by patients, close relatives of patients or other representatives such as designated individuals employed by the NHS or a community health council. If the complainant is not the patient concerned, the reason for this person making the complaint on behalf of the patient must be explained and it must be established that the complaint has the support of the patient.[2] All complaints must be referred to the Ombudsman no later than one year from the date a patient became aware of the events that are the subject of complaint. Nevertheless, this time limit can be extended if there is a good reason for doing so. For instance, a case may have exceeded the deadline because of unavoidable delays during the preceding NHS complaints procedure.[3]

Complainants must describe all details about the incident and if possible name whoever was involved. The reason for complaining is also required, and it must be shown that hardship or injustice has been suffered as a result of the event leading to the complaint. Additionally, complainants need to provide all available evidence, including correspondence and background papers, and a completed standard complaints form or a letter of explanation.[4]

The Ombudsman can investigate complaints about or associated with the health care provided by the NHS at hospital and community health service levels that refer to:

- a poor service
- failure to purchase or provide a service that a complainant was entitled to receive
- administrative or operational shortcomings, including avoidable delay, incorrect procedures, not explaining decisions taken or answering a complaint fully or promptly
- care or treatment provided by medical and other trained professionals in hospitals and by family health service practitioners.[5]

Complaints about access to information on services that are available and associated NHS matters can also be referred to the Ombudsman by those who are dissatisfied with the response received locally to these concerns.[6] The Ombudsman will consider cases alleging a refusal to provide information, a delay of more than four weeks in obtaining the requested details or the extent of any charge complainants have been asked to pay.

Grievances from NHS staff about the way in which complaints about them from, or on behalf of, patients have been dealt with by the health service body involved can also be scrutinized.[7] Additionally, the Ombudsman can examine complaints relating to services provided by the private health care sector if these functions have been paid for by the NHS.[8] Complaints about commercial or contractual matters can also be investigated, but on condition that the grievances refer to services for patients contracted to the NHS.[9]

Nevertheless, the Ombudsman will not normally intervene if the establishment or practitioner concerned has done all that could be reasonably expected to redress the matter;[10] nor will the Ombudsman deal with complaints about which legal action is planned or has already begun.[11] In any event, it is the prerogative of the Ombudsman's organization to decide whether or not a complaint is to be investigated.[12]

When a complaint is received, after making initial inquiries a decision is made about whether it will be investigated. This is the screening process. If it cannot be investigated or it is decided not to do so, the complainant will be told why.[13] Where a case is accepted for formal investigation, a statement of complaint setting out the issues to be examined will be sent to the complainant and to the health service (or other) body involved in the case. The latter will be asked to provide all papers and comments, and the patient's medical records where these apply.[14]

Once this information has been received and studied, the complainant is normally asked to attend an interview, and may be accompanied by a friend. Others involved in the case may also be seen. Interviews are in private and are usually informal, although the Ombudsman has the same powers to obtain evidence as the civil courts. In cases involving clinical matters independent professional assessors will normally advise the Ombudsman's investigators in an examination process that can take several months.[15]

When the investigation is completed a report in the Ombudsman's name is forwarded to the complainant and to the health service establishment or their body involved in the case. (The Ombudsman for England and Wales has been known to give a draft report – excluding the professional assessors' opinions, in clinical cases, and the investigation's findings – to the parties concerned for reference and to correct any errors, see Chapter 11.) In instances where complaints are found to be justified, the Ombudsman will ask for an apology or some other form of remedy. This may include getting a decision changed, or a repayment of unnecessary costs incurred by the patient or that person's family. The Ombudsman cannot recommend that damages should be paid, but can call for changes to be made so that what has gone wrong should not recur. Where the health service establishment involved agrees to make these changes, the Ombudsman's organization will check that it has done so.[16]

All decisions arrived at following investigation are final and cannot be appealed against. Re-examining a case is extremely rare and occurs only if fresh evidence comes to light.[17] The only way that a decision made by the Ombudsman can be challenged is by persuading the High Court (or its equivalent in Scotland) to grant a judicial review on the grounds that the judgement was faulty in law; or should be set aside for some other reason. To date, no complainant has succeeded in obtaining such an intervention.[18]

As already stated, the role, jurisdiction and powers of the Scottish Public Services Ombudsman concerning the health service are principally the same as those in the hands of her counterpart responsible for the other two mainland countries. With certain statutory exceptions, she can also deal with complaints about the administrative actions of the Mental Welfare Commission for Scotland.[19] The office of the Scottish Public Services Ombudsman was created in October 2002 and absorbed the previous complaints body headed by the Scottish Health Service Ombudsman.[20] Before this, Scottish Health Service Ombudsman was a title used by the Health Service Ombudsman for all of mainland Britain (and its islands) to deal with complaints in Scotland.

The Health Service Ombudsman's organization in action and its outcome
What is the reality of the Ombudsman's intervention, and how is it reflected in the annual statistics? To begin with, during the term of the last Health Service Ombudsman (1996 to 2002), who had responsibility for the three mainland countries, he frequently drew attention in his annual reports to the large proportion of complaints that for jurisdictional or other reasons had to be refused consideration by his organization. Indeed, the statistics provided in these yearly reports not only show this to be the case, but also demonstrate that the majority of the remaining

complaints were rejected for full investigation (Table 3.1). The partially redeeming aspect of the statistics is that, of the low proportion of cases accepted for investigation, the greater number of grievances making up these complaints were either wholly or partially upheld (Table 3.2).

Table 3.1 Complaints and enquiries handled by the Office of the Health Service Ombudsman in the three mainland countries and their outcome, 1998–99 to 2002–03

1998–99	England	Scotland[a]	Wales	Total
Screened	2,479	238	165	2,882
Non-investigable	1,402	135	79	1,616
Investigable	1,077	103	86	1,266
Rejected	745	73	51	869
Other action[b]	197	19	24	240
For investigation	135	11	11	157
1999–2000				
Screened	2,583	234	148	2,965
Non-investigable	1,469	133	57	1,659
Investigable	1,114	101	91	1,306
Rejected	787	68	54	909
Other action[b]	115	15	13	143
For investigation	212	18	24	254
2000–01				
Screened	2,732	247	185	3,164
Non-investigable	1,870	160	101	2,131
Investigable	862	87	84	1,033
Rejected	555	49	45	649
Other action[b]	66	4	14	84
For investigation	241	34	25	300
2001–02				
Screened	2,710	250	163	3,123
Non-investigable	1,836	138	90	2,064
Investigable	874	112	73	1,059
Rejected	630	83	51	764
Other action[b]	40	2	8	50
For investigation	204	27	14	245
2002–03				
Screened	3,035	–	180	–
Non-investigable	2,112	–	116	–
Investigable	923	–	64	–
Rejected	666	–	30	–
Other action[b]	81	–	16	–
For investigation	176	–	18	–

Source: Health Service Commissioner for England, Scotland and Wales, and Health Service Ombudsman, *Annual Reports*[21]

[a] Source data not presented specifically in these categories for 2002–03.

[b] 'Other action' refers to complaints about which advice was given by the Ombudsman's office to the health service body involved, or to further action that was agreed to be taken by such an establishment

England

During 2002–03 the Health Service Ombudsman's office received 3,994 complaints about NHS bodies, establishments and practitioners in England (Table 3.3). It also handled 540 complaints and enquiries carried over from the previous year and more than 100 enquiries that arrived in the current year. Out of a total of 4,636 cases, 3,035 were screened and their progress determined.

A total of 2,112 (69.6 per cent) fell into the category of 'non-investigable' complaints and enquiries. These included 1,665 that were premature because local action through the NHS complaints procedure had not been completed, and 275 on matters outside the Ombudsman's jurisdiction. The balance comprised 49 complaints that were 'referred back and closed'; 'no action' was required on 48; a further six were 'withdrawn'; and 69 enquiries were 'answered'.[22]

Out of the remaining 923 'investigable' complaints (30.4 per cent), 'no formal action' was taken on more than two-thirds (666) of the cases. In these complaints that were dismissed, the Ombudsman's staff considered that 'further action would be unlikely to achieve any added benefit for the complainant' or 'there was no evidence that failings had led to unremedied injustice or hardship'. The screeners had taken professional advice in arriving at their judgements where clinical issues were involved. In such cases, complainants were given an explanation of the decision that had been taken and of the issues involved. 'Advice' was given to the health service body in 58 of the remaining investigable complaints, and in another 23 the establishment involved agreed to take 'further action'. These outcomes were the result of action (short of investigation) taken by the Ombudsman on behalf of complainants.[23]

The balance of 176 complaints (19.1 per cent of the 923 'investigable cases) were accepted for investigation. Of the cases referred to the Ombudsman, 192 had already been considered by a review panel during the earlier NHS complaints procedure, while the vast majority of the rest had been refused this privilege. A total of 179 investigations were completed during 2002–03, with almost 87 per cent of these cases containing some clinical element. There were 271 grievances involved, of which 205 (75.6 per cent) were upheld.[24]

Wales

In 2002–03 there were 180 complaints about the health service in Wales lodged with the Ombudsman (Table 3.3), 17 enquiries were received and 15 complaints and enquiries were brought forward from the year before. From a combined total of 212 cases screening decisions were taken on 180. Out of the 116 categorized as non-investigable 72 were deemed to be premature, having not completed local action, 14 were out of jurisdiction, no action was needed on four, six were referred back and closed, two were withdrawn and 18 enquiries were answered. The remaining 64 (35.5 per cent of all screened) investigable complaints included 30 about which no formal action was taken, 11 where advice was given to the health care body, five where further action was agreed by the establishment, and 18 that it was decided to investigate (Table 3.1). There were 23 completed investigations in the year, involving 45 grievances, two-thirds of which were upheld either wholly or in part (Table 3.2).[25]

Scotland

The Health Service Ombudsman for Scotland received 225 complaints during 2001–02 (Table 3.3). There were also 29 enquiries, and 13 complaints and enquiries brought forward from the previous year, amounting to 267 cases that required attention. Screening decisions were taken on 250 of these complaints, with 138 (55.2 per cent) being judged as non-investigable: 73 had been prematurely referred to the Ombudsman; 24 were out of jurisdiction; seven were referred back and closed; five required no action; and 29 enquiries were answered. Out of the 112 investigable cases (44.8 per cent of all screened), more than two-thirds (83 cases) were rejected; two were agreed to require further action; and less than one-third (27 cases) were accepted for investigation (Table 3.1).

Out of the 25 investigations completed during 2001–02, 19 related to aspects of clinical care and treatment. These cases covered a total of 44 grievances, more than half of which concerned clinical care and treatment; and nearly two-thirds of the latter were upheld (Table 3.2). Grievances about communication, including many about clinical matters, accounted for 20 per cent of the total; and 67 per cent of these were upheld. Another 20 per cent referred to the way complaints had been handled and 78 per cent of these grievances were judged to have been legitimate.[26]

The Scottish Public Services Ombudsman received 262 written complaints in 2002–03 and 44 cases (20 screening and 24 under investigation) were brought forward from the previous year. A total of 261 cases were completed – 236 of which did not go to formal investigation, and investigation reports were issued in 25 instances. From the cases that were rejected for investigation 81 had either not been raised with the relevant establishment or did not proceed sufficiently through the NHS complaints procedure. In 94 cases the Ombudsman considered that there were no grounds to intervene. There were an additional 35 enquiries (19 outside the Ombudsman's jurisdiction) that were dealt with under his authority.[27] (Published data in the Ombudsman's annual report about the complaints handled in 2002–03 is presented somewhat differently and in less detailed form than for previous years.)

Table 3.2 Grievances investigated and upheld in the three mainland countries, 1997–98 to 2002–03[a]

a) All countries, 1997–98 to 1999–2000			
All countries	1997–98	1998–99	1999–2000
Investigated	270	248	262
Upheld[b]	210	153	172
Upheld (%)	77.8	61.7	65.6

b) England, Scotland and Wales, 2000–01 to 2002–03			
2000–01	England	Scotland[c]	Wales
Investigated	343	37	40
Upheld[b]	236	19	18
Upheld (%)	68.8	51.4	45
2001–02			
Investigated	383	44	51
Upheld[b]	281	28	35
Upheld (%)	73.4	63.6	68.6

2002–03			
Investigated	271	25	45
Upheld[b]	205	–	30
Upheld (%)	75.6	–	67

Source: Health Service Ombudsman, *Annual Report 2002–2003*[29]
[a] The average number of grievances per investigation report for the three mainland countries as a whole for 1992–93 was 3.1. Those for 1993–94 to 1998–99 ranged between 2.1 and 2.6, but the figure dropped to 1.7 in 1999–2000. The number of grievances per report for England covering 2000–01 and 2001–02 remained constant at 1.7.[30] Although the proportions have not been given in Table 3.2, this pattern of investigation, often involving more than one grievance, also continues to apply to Scotland and Wales and is reflected in the annual figures for 2000–01 and 2001–02, and for 2002–03 (Wales).
[b] It would appear that the totals refer to grievances wholly or partially upheld.
[c] Figures for Scotland not published in 2002–03.

Table 3.3 Complaints (excluding enquiries) received by the Health Service Ombudsman in the three mainland countries, 1997–98 to 2002–03[a]

	1997–98[b]	1998–99[b]	1999–2000	2000–01	2001–02	2002–03
England	–	–	2,526	2,595	2,660	3,994
Scotland	–	–	215	224	225	262
Wales	–	–	146	162	155	180
Total	2,660	2,869	2,887	2,981	3,040	4,436

Source: Health Service Commissioner for England, Scotland and Wales, and Health Service Ombudsman, *Annual Reports*[28]
[a] Approximate populations: England – 48.9 million; Scotland – 5.1 million; Wales – 2.9 million. (Rounded off totals of estimates by the UN in 1996 – *Whitaker's Almanack 2003*)
[b] Figures for individual countries were not collected before devolution was introduced.

In 2002–03 the average time taken by the Ombudsman's team to complete clinical investigations about England was 66 weeks, compared with 65 weeks in the previous year. The non-clinical cases took 51 and 54 weeks respectively.[31] In Scotland, during 2001–02 the average investigation (76 per cent of which concerned clinical care) took 52 weeks to be completed compared with 42 weeks in 2000–01 (when 80 per cent of cases related to clinical matters).[32] Investigations about cases in Wales took an average of 81 weeks to complete in 2002–03; and there was no unfinished investigation of more than a year old remaining at the end of the year. Around half of all grievances (22 out of 45) were about clinical care. As a comparison, the average time taken to complete investigations (94 per cent of which involved clinical issues) was 70 weeks in 2001–02.[33]

When the Northern Ireland Ombudsman will decide to investigate a complaint[34]
The basis for a complaint being accepted by the Northern Ireland Ombudsman and the process of screening and any investigation that may follow is essentially the same as that used in the UK mainland. First comes an 'initial sift'. This involves checking that the issue and body being complained about are within the Ombudsman's jurisdiction. It also entails verifying that the matter has already been raised with the organization concerned through the preceding formal health service complaints procedure. Another prerequisite is that the complaint is sufficiently supported by

information and within the Ombudsman's statutory limits. These conditions apply to complainants and to any Member of the Legislative Assembly (MLA) who by necessity may have referred a complaint for scrutiny.

If one or more of these prerequisites are not met, the Ombudsman will point this out in writing to the complainant or MLA and ask for the requirements to be complied with before any further action can be taken (or he might suggest in his correspondence that the matter is referred to a more appropriate authority). Where a complaint satisfies all the necessary conditions, it will proceed to the 'preliminary investigation' second stage.

Here it will be decided whether there is evidence of maladministration in the handling of the complaint by the body concerned, and if the complainant has been unjustly treated in the process. After enquiries to and responses from the organization about which the complaint has been made, the case is handed to one of the Ombudsman's directors of investigation. This officer decides the necessary course of action, the outcome of which takes one of three forms.

- Where proof of maladministration is not found, the complainant (or the MLA involved) is given the reasons for this decision and told that the case will not be investigated.
- If maladministration has been found, but has not caused the complainant undue personal injustice, the complainant is sent a report of the preliminary investigation and an explanation of why no further examination of the case is warranted. A copy of the report, which may be critical of the body concerned, is also sent to its chief officer.
- Where there is evidence that maladministration has brought about considerable personal wrong, a complaint progresses to the 'in-depth investigation', third stage of the process. If the Ombudsman establishes from the outset of this phase that maladministration and injustice have been caused, he considers whether an early resolution to the matter is right for the purpose. In this case, he writes to the chief officer of the body being complained about outlining the maladministration and suggesting a suitable remedy. Should his findings and suggestions be unacceptable, a full and formal investigation follows.

When there is a full and formal investigation complainants and the officials involved are interviewed and all the documentary evidence is examined. In complaints about the health service professional advice is obtained from independent medical assessors – where this is relevant. Once an investigation has been completed, a draft report of the case, including a statement of the Ombudsman's likely findings, is prepared. It is reviewed with the complainant and sent to the body concerned, which has the opportunity to respond to the report and to any redress the Ombudsman proposes to recommend. When the two parties have responded, the final report of the investigation is produced and circulated to them. The objective is to complete a case involving all three stages of the process within one year of its being lodged.

The passage and outcome of health service complaints lodged with the Northern Ireland Ombudsman

The Northern Ireland Ombudsman deals with complaints relating to health care in his role of Commissioner for Complaints. (He is also the Assembly

Ombudsman.) In 2002–03 his organization received 103 written complaints about the health services (Table 3.4) and 26 cases were brought forward from the previous year.[35]

Table 3.4 Health service complaints[a] received by the Commissioner for Complaints in Northern Ireland, 1998–99 to 2002–03[b]

	1998–99	1999–2000	2000–01	2001–02	2002–03
Total	57	66	85	107	103

Source: Parliamentary Ombudsman for Northern Ireland and Northern Ireland Commissioner for Complaints, *Annual Report*, 1998–99 to 2001–02[36]
[a] Excluding oral complaints and letters related to previously cleared cases
[b] Based on the 1996 UN estimate, the population of Northern Ireland is about 1.65 million.

Out of the total of 129 complaints, action was completed in 96 cases, including 46 that were dismissed at the initial sifting stage and another 46 that were resolved without the need for a detailed investigation. Four cases were fully investigated and reported. The balance of 33 cases (30 of which were under investigation) were ongoing at the end of the year. One case was upheld in full, with an apology given, another was partially upheld and two were not upheld (tables 3.5 and 3.6).[37]

In 2002–03 the average time taken to examine a case, make enquiries and respond to the complainant at investigation stage was 21.6 weeks. Out of the four fully investigated complaints, one was about 'hospital acute – A&E', two referred to 'all aspects of care and treatment' and one was about 'hospital acute – in patient'.[38]

Table 3.5 Ongoing and processed cases dealt with by the Northern Ireland Ombudsman, 1998–99 to 2002–03

	1998–99	1999–2000	2000–01	2001–02	2002–03
Brought forward	0	9	9	17	26
Received in the year	57	66	85	107	103
Total	57	75	94	124	129
Cleared at initial sift first stage[a]	19	33	23	45	46
Cleared without in-depth investigation[b]	25	29	43	45	46
Settled	1	2	1	2	0
Full report issued	2	2	10	6	4
Ongoing at end of year	10	9	17	26	33

Source: Parliamentary Ombudsman for Northern Ireland and Northern Ireland Commissioner for Complaints, *Annual Report*, 1998–99 to 2001–02[39]
[a] These are described as 'cleared without enquiry' in the Commissioner's annual reports for 1998–99 and 1999–2000.
[b] Including those withdrawn or discontinued.

Table 3.6 Advanced outcome of all written complaints dealt with by the Northern Ireland Ombudsman, 1998–99 to 2002–03

	1998–99	1999–2000	2000–01	2001–02	2002–03
Brought forward	0	9	9	17	26
Received	57	66	85	107	103
Not investigated	42	61	62	79	78
Settled	1	2	1	2	0
Discontinued	1	0	3	10	12
Withdrawn	1	1	1	1	2
Upheld[a]	2	1	3	2	2
Not upheld	0	1	7	4	2
Ongoing at end of year	10	9	17	26	33

Source: Assembly Ombudsman and Commissioner for Complaints, *Annual Report*, 1999–2000 and 2000–01[40]
[a] Complaints that could be either wholly or partially upheld following full formal investigation.

Key aspects of complaints handling, outcomes and statistics

Perhaps the most notable characteristic of the United Kingdom's three health service Ombudsmen, from the perspective of dealing with complaints, is their comparative lack of authority. None of the ombudsmen has the legal right to insist – even in apparently serious cases – that an NHS body or practitioner must act on their recommendations (far from stern though these generally may be) when a complaint is upheld. Nor can they take disciplinary action against a health care professional or suggest that any such sanction should be applied. Nevertheless, there is a distinct bite in one aspect of the powers invested in these arbiters of complaints: complainants cannot appeal against the Ombudsmen's judgements – except in the most exceptional cases. And complainants have not been successful in appealing to the highest civil authority to intervene when they disagree with such a decision.

Are there any similarly noteworthy conclusions to be drawn from the mainland Ombudsmen's handling of complaints as expressed, for example, in the annual statistics for the period 1998–00 to 2002–03? Even accepting that significant proportions of complaints are found to be either premature or out of jurisdiction, the statistics appear to go nowhere near fully explaining the particularly wide chasm between the total number of complaints referred to the Ombudsman's office in the first place and the proportion that are investigated and out of that total upheld.

To illustrate, during these four years the majority of investigable complaints (an average of 68 per cent of the total over the period) were rejected for formal investigation in the three mainland countries as a whole. This left an average of 11 per cent of cases about which other action was taken and only around 21 per cent that were investigated. The number that were wholly or partially upheld after investigation was still smaller. (A similar pattern of a high proportion of complaints being rejected and low ratios accepted for investigation occurred in Northern Ireland during the same period. Like her mainland counterparts, the Northern Ireland Ombudsman receives a consistently large percentage of complaints that are either out of jurisdiction or have been referred prematurely.) The position for the United Kingdom in 2002–03 was broadly similar.

The share of complaints about the NHS that filters through to the Ombudsman
There is a huge disparity between the volume of complaints lodged annually with the NHS and the number that secures the Ombudsman's attention in the same period. During 2000–01, for example, the public health service in mainland Britain received nearly 157,000 written complaints (see Chapter 1). In the same year only 2,981 cases were referred to the Ombudsman concerned (Table 3.3). As already shown, a large proportion of this comparatively small number of complaints were found to be ineligible for jurisdictional or other reasons after screening, including those rejected on the grounds that they had been properly investigated and decided upon at NHS complaints procedure level. The picture is similar for preceding and subsequent years. But it does not answer the question about what yardstick the Ombudsman uses in order to reject 'investigable' complaints and decide the outcome of cases that then progress to a full investigation.

In his annual report for 1998–99 the ombudsman for mainland Britain confirmed that certain consumer organizations had expressed concern about the apparently low proportion of complaints that are accepted for investigation.[41] Earlier, it appears from one press report in particular that these groups included the National Consumer Council, the Consumers Association and the Association for Improvement in Maternity Service . Apparently they had suggested that the interests of patients were being neglected in the pursuit of administrative efficiency. The contention was that in a climate where complaints were rising to record levels the proportions being investigated had fallen. There had been 229 and 238 investigations completed during 1995–96 and 1996–97, respectively, but only 120 in 1997–98. The news report further pointed out that this drop had arisen 'just as the Ombudsman's remit has been extended into two new areas – clinical complaints and GPs'.[42]

The Ombudsman had further stated in his 1998–99 annual report that the issue of the low take-up rate complaints had been raised by the House of Commons Select Committee on Public Administration while considering his report for the previous year. He went on to say that the low numbers involved (4 per cent in 1997–98 and 5 per cent in 1998–99) were, in fact, misleading: 'Because it is based on the total number of complaints, including many on which I have no power in law to take action, it seriously understates the proportion of complaints on which I can and do take action. This is not helpful to complainants or those who advise them.'[43]

The explanation makes sense for cases referred to the Ombudsman that are found to be premature because of lack of local action through the NHS complaints procedure, and it also applies to complaints that were found to be out of jurisdiction. However, his comments do not seem to answer the questions raised in previous paragraphs in connection with the progress of cases about which he *is* in a position to make a judgement.

In his annual report for 2000–01 the Ombudsman wrote:

I continue to survey a proportion of all those who write to me, and the complainants and respondents involved in all investigations, and ask about the experience of contact with my office. More than 45 per cent of those surveyed responded to questions about the timeliness and clarity of communications, about the work of my staff and about their satisfaction with the service provided by my office. Comments were generally favourable this year, although the people whose complaints we upheld expressed satisfaction with our work more often than others. That said, there were justifiable concerns about the length of time taken to complete an investigation.[44]

The Ombudsman added that he had made some changes to the survey referred to in this extract in order that the information it provided should be more helpful. Moreover, he emphasized the importance of assessments of this kind being complemented from time to time by a more broadly based evaluation of opinion carried out by an independent organization about the work of his office. With this in mind, his plan was to commission such a survey during 2001–02. There is no further reference to this matter in the Ombudsman's annual report for 2001–02. Depending on how broadly based any independent appraisals have turned out to be (if they have taken place), the outcome could be more convincing than any resulting from one of the Ombudsman's own surveys.

Because the Ombudsman gave little information about his organization's survey in 2000–01, it is difficult for an outsider to draw conclusions. For instance it is not clear what level of satisfaction was shown by the complainants whose cases were not accepted for full investigation. The Ombudsman could also have provided figures on the views of those complainants whose cases had been investigated, irrespective of their outcome. Because of these omissions the statement about the Ombudsman's periodic internally managed research is not helpful.

Two years earlier, in his 1998–99 annual report the Northern Ireland Ombudsman noted that he was 'pleased to record that the office has received many letters of thanks, encouragement and support expressing the gratitude of complainants which, in my view, is an indication of the appreciation of thoroughness in an investigation, especially where the investigations have been complex and difficult'.[45]

Clearly the approbation thus described by him is not to be ridiculed. But was he talking about complainants whose grievances were upheld or those he had rejected – or both – following initial screening or subsequent investigation? And should not statements such as he made be qualified in these circumstances? One also wonders how many more satisfied respondents there might be – and how much more valuable their remarks – if complaints reaching the Ombudsman's organization were processed and investigated by more appropriately recruited personnel – from the top down? What is the objection, for instance, to staff being recruited from outside the health and civil services? (Are the public in Northern Ireland aware of the previous occupations of key personnel at the Ombudsman's office?)

In his annual report for 2001–02 for England, the UK mainland's Ombudsman suggested that two main factors could have contributed to the fall in the number of cases accepted for investigation.[46] First, the proportion of complaints reaching his office that were investigable continued to be 'disquietingly low' at 30 per cent. Secondly, many of the investigable complaints would previously have been considered by an independent review panel as part of the health service complaints procedure. (Presumably the Ombudsman was implying that the complaints he was referring to in the latter example had already received a thorough investigation and were rejected or decided upon in a way that was unacceptable to the complainants involved.)

The Ombudsman added that it was necessary to consider whether a statutory investigation by his organization was likely to be gainful. His contention was that an investigation when there was no evidence of unsound judgement by a health service review panel would raise false hopes on the complainant's part and he suggested that a high proportion of reports from such panels fell into this category. The Ombudsman also maintained that another investigation would impose an unfair burden on the health service and its staff, and waste public funds. (If the case history covered in Chapter 11 is anything to go by, the judgement of independent review panels and the Ombudsman's investigators could sometimes rightly be called into question. Indeed, it is on record that many complainants and patient support groups at the receiving end of decisions by these two parties have experience of this phenomenon.)

Yet, later in the same annual report the Ombudsman remarked that there was 'widespread dissatisfaction with, in particular... independent review panels'.[47] He added that their members are invariably regarded as not being independent and, in the experience of his office, 'their work varies in quality'. The Ombudsman further declared that the complaints system should include a component that is acknowledged by patients and their representatives, and health service staff, to be 'independent, impartial and authoritative'. He believed that the complaints body he fronted meets these obligations. (Chapter 4 looks at these and other aspects of the composition and role of the health service ombudsmen's organizations in the United Kingdom.)

This Ombudsman's justification for there being a consistently low proportion of cases that he was prepared to investigate does not explain the enormous disparity between the number of complaints entering the health service complaints system and those that he finally dealt with. While there is nothing wrong with grievances being resolved locally, it is questionable whether it should be mandatory for complaints to have to be considered locally before they can progress to the next stage of the NHS process – let alone being eligible for referral to an ombudsman. This position remains virtually the same in the reformed procedures for England, Wales and Northern Ireland although, in the case of Scotland, it is possible that a decision will have been made to allow complainants direct access to the ombudsman if there is dissatisfaction at local resolution (see Chapter 2).

It is not just the abysmally low proportion of cases fully investigated by the Health Service Ombudsman for England and Wales that might be considered cause for concern. Equally worrying is the length of time it could take a lucky few complainants to be in a position to refer their grievances to this final arbiter in the chain. Many months – sometimes years – could elapse before cases were eligible for referral following their passage through the earlier health service complaints procedure. The mainland's Ombudsman in office between 1996 and 2002 has confirmed that by the time his organization had completed reports of some complaints investigations, 'all too often' four or five years had gone by. (Only time will tell if the reformed NHS complaints procedure will improve the situation.) It is also disturbing that it was taking as long as this before a comparatively small number of complainants finally received an independent appraisal of their grievances. The low proportions of cases that any Ombudsman will investigate and the timescales involved in the complaints process as a whole contrast unfavourably with figures relating to certain comparable complaints bodies elsewhere in Europe (see Chapter 13).

It is accepted that the Ombudsman just referred to may have a point in stating that many cases found to be 'investigable' by his team will already have been closely examined by a review panel. Therefore, leaving aside concerns about the lack of independence in the earlier NHS complaints mechanism, he could argue that there was a greater likelihood of such cases being rejected by his examiners than otherwise would have happened. But that may be only part of the cause. The reason could also be connected with the basis upon which any Ombudsman decides or is obliged to exercise the powers that have been invested in them. There may be other underlying issues that are indirectly responsible for this apparently depressing state of affairs. These matters are raised in Chapter 4.

Final comments

It is difficult to draw a true comparison between the independent complaints bodies fronted by the health service ombudsmen in the United Kingdom and some of their counterparts on the continent. This is because the statutory powers of, for example, the Nordic models are appreciably greater than those of the standard British version. The jurisdiction of each of these northern European complaints authorities either extends to professional disciplinary issues or they are associated with another body that holds these powers. In addition, even in instances where local resolution is part of the system in this part of Europe, it is not compulsory for complaints to go through this process. Complaints about health care can progress straight to an independent investigation so the autonomous complaints bodies will normally accept cases directly and after they have passed through an inquiry by the health service (see Chapter 13).

Because of these important differences in the complaints procedures operated in other European countries when compared with that in the United Kingdom an exact statistical analysis of the treatment of complaints is also not possible. Nevertheless, it is interesting to make a general comparison of the figures showing the proportion of complaints accepted for investigation. They demonstrate that in contrast with the UK's ombudsmen the comparable Nordic complaints authorities, for example, not only directly accept and independently scrutinize complaints from the outset, but also pass a large proportion of these cases for full investigation. Many of these complaints are then upheld. Not only that, in instances where clinical error or negligence has been proven, disciplinary action of some kind is likely to follow and the case is then concluded. It is at least conceivable that complainants in the United Kingdom would welcome such facets in a system that concerns them.

CHAPTER 4

Is the Health Service Ombudsman really neutral and fair?

The jury isn't out, but it may need to be quite soon

Now, not a lot of people know this…but until recently many of the most important people at the Office of the Health Service Ombudsman for mainland Britain – right up to the chief himself – had previous occupational links with the NHS. Not only that, in their previous roles some will have been involved or associated with the internally regulated earlier NHS stages of the health service complaints system. By an apparently simple change of sides, these individuals were swiftly entrusted to investigate complaints that had come unstuck at the hands of investigators engaged or appointed by their erstwhile employer. They effectively investigated decisions by examiners from the same part of the NHS complaints mechanism in which some complaints investigators working for the Ombudsman could previously have been carrying out a similar function. In their new role under the Ombudsman, these recruits will also have become authorized to judge the conduct of other health service investigators in their examination of complaints that had progressed to the second NHS phase of the process. The above position is probably similar in 2005 and the reforms since April 2003 to the health service end of the complaints system will not significantly have altered things.

These former NHS personnel are invariably crucial components of the Ombudsman's independent statutory complaints investigating body. Their decisions mark the end of the line for the relatively small proportion of complaints that reach the Ombudsman for final judgement. This low number of cases involves complainants who have already survived the often long and arduous earlier stages of the NHS complaints procedure to get their grievances addressed and remedied. Can this cross-fertilization of complaints examiners be such a good idea when it comes to the crunch? Does a kind of conflict of interest arise? Or is there really no devil in the detail?

Recruitment to the Office of the Health Service Ombudsman

Up to around October 1999 the Office of the Health Service Ombudsman in mainland Britain had a policy of recruiting, screening and investigating staff on three-year rolling contracts from the health service. At the end of this secondment period, enlisted personnel would normally return to the health service and, presumably, to their previous complaints handling posts. It seems that moves were afoot at the time to offer permanency to recruits appointed in this way by the Ombudsman.[1]

By the beginning of 2000 secondment had apparently ended. The change in the Ombudsman's policy seemed to have been sparked off by situations where staff taken on by this means could be risking the loss of their previous jobs at the end of their secondment period.[2] Nonetheless, recruitment policy continued to include the enlisting of personnel from the health service – and seemingly still did two years later. So what proportion of key appointees at the Office of the Health Service Ombudsman came from this source?

Up to the spring of 2001, two out of the four directors of investigation and four of the nine investigations managers (the next tier down of management) came from the NHS. By contrast, all of the 54 (less senior) investigating officers were appointed – perhaps as a matter of policy – from outside the NHS.[3] Where they were recruited from is not known, though advertisements in the media normally used for recruitment by the Ombudsman suggest that a proportion could have come from the civil service. What are the roles and responsibilities of these main functionaries in the Ombudsman's team of complaints investigators?[4]

Investigating officers decide whether or not a case should be investigated, referring complaints that they are uncertain about to their managers. They undertake investigations, with help and guidance from these managers, and produce the first draft of the investigation results report.

Investigations managers have responsibility for managing their staff and the investigation process. They agree and sign some investigation results reports under delegated authority from the Ombudsman. Their duties include managing the workload within their own units, coaching investigating officers, collating statistics and giving talks to outside bodies.

Directors of investigation have wider spans of command than investigations managers and are responsible for several units. They are involved in the more difficult cases and agree and sign some of those investigation reports under delegated authority from the Ombudsman. (Other reports might go to the Ombudsman or the Ombudsman's deputy.) They manage their directorates, help to decide policy issues and represent the Office of the Health Service Ombudsman in dealings with outside bodies. Each director has responsibility over cases in a particular part of Britain and liaises with the NHS regional offices in that area.

In mid-2001 these officers were spread across the country as follows. In London the health service side of the Office had four directors of investigation, eight investigations managers and 44 investigating officers. A fifth director was in charge of the 'clinical advice directorate', a section made up of 11 internal professional advisers. The Edinburgh office had one investigations manager and three investigating officers who dealt purely with health service work. In the Cardiff office there was one investigations manager and five investigating officers who dealt with Welsh Administration Ombudsman and Health Service Ombudsman complaints.[5]

But strong previous links with the health service are not the preserve of senior and middle management at the Office of the Health Service Ombudsman (now responsible only for England and Wales because, since October 2002, Scotland has had its own Ombudsman). The Deputy Health Service Ombudsman in post until 2003 was recruited in early 1999 from the NHS where she had spent around 20 years, some eight to nine years as chief executive, including four heading a trust.[6] In this latter capacity she would have been a key player within the internally regulated NHS complaints procedure. (Her predecessor left to join the General Medical Council, the medical profession's self-regulating body, but it is not clear if she had similar previous links with the NHS.) However, from what can be ascertained, her successor has no past occupational connection with the NHS.

It seems that before his appointment in 1997 the Ombudsman in post until autumn 2002, a qualified statistician, had held a top position in the NHS for a short spell. In 1995–96 he had been chairman of a health service trust.[7] However, this officer clearly had an impressive career, mostly involving high-ranking posts in the civil service and government.[8] His successor, in post since October 2003, was previously the Legal Services Ombudsman for England and Wales, a position she had held from September 1997. She had also been a member of the Committee on Standards in Public Life since January 2000. Before this her career included posts in local government and the civil service.[9]

The role of the media

The issue of the occupational backgrounds of principal staff members in the Ombudsman's organization seems never to have been properly taken up by the media, nor even by patient and consumer groups. It is true that the information may not have been readily available, but it is hard to believe that a little enterprising foraging would not have uncovered the facts years ago, considering that this complaints body has been in existence since 1973. On the other hand, some of these media and public watchdogs may already have been aware of the situation and did not see that the recruitment of personnel from the health service by the Ombudsman to fill key roles in the Office of the Health Service Ombudsman can present a significant problem. Perhaps they still hold this view.

There is some oblique evidence that the latter might be the case. In early 2000 a number of representatives in the media and other contacts were presented with the facts of the matter by the author as the basis for a possible story. After initially expressing keen interest in the prospect of running a piece on the issue, each of them had a change of heart and finally pulled out. Either they ultimately considered the 'revelations' about the Ombudsman's organization to be not sufficiently newsworthy, or they had other undisclosed reasons for not going ahead.

However, one of the journalists on a nationally broadcasted consumer programme did write to say that the issue was too complex and wide-ranging to get a news angle on it – which was a fair comment. The reporter also felt that the greater proportion of the programme's followers would not consider as surprising or unreasonable that 'the Ombudsman's staff tended to be made up of health professionals'. (This view might appear to be valid on the surface. But a poll of the broadcast's followers, conducted on an informed footing, could paint a different picture.)

The journalist went on to say that it would be immensely difficult – if not impossible – to substantiate the belief that staff who have worked for the health service are automatically predisposed to be biased against complainants. 'One could just as easily say their experience of working in the NHS is a useful prerequisite to do their job,' the reporter added. All of these observations amounted to a misreading and an oversimplification of the issue as put to the programme-makers and, indeed, as presented in this chapter. Nor did the remarks face up to the converse reasoning that, by placing itself in an exposed position on the lines described, the Ombudsman's complaints body would inevitably attract widespread disapproval once the facts of its recruitment connections with the health service were revealed. Even so, the reporter's comments indicate that there are informed people in influential places, other than those with a vested interest, who have a different outlook on this issue concerning the Health Service Ombudsman's organization.

Doubtless, there will be others – especially those with an axe to grind – who see nothing improper about the health service origins of key functionaries in the Ombudsman's organization. Indeed, these believers in the practice may similarly have convinced themselves that there is great value to be had in hiring staff from what seems to be a natural pool of expertise. They might argue that these recruits will have had the experience and know-how about the system and the way it works, and that becoming part of the Ombudsman's team must, therefore, be regarded as a strength rather than a weakness. Accordingly, they could say, it must follow that the NHS is not only the most obvious source from which to recruit, but personnel taken on having this origin must have merit over those enlisted from elsewhere.

Potential problems in recruiting staff from the NHS for the Office of the Health Service Ombudsman

On the face of it, the reasoning may appear sound. But is it? Should it not be equally considered that some of the individuals who, presumably, continue to be drafted in by the Ombudsman for England and Wales from the health service come from a part of it that manages the internally regulated first stage of the NHS complaints system itself? What positions might these recruits have held in their previous employment or attachment with the health service? They could formerly have been complaints managers, conveners of 'independent review panels' or (in rarer instances) chief executives of trusts or health authorities and others associated with complaints handling in the NHS. (Is it possible that staff recruited by the Ombudsman from the health service have occasionally found themselves in a situation where they had to cast judgement upon the decisions of complaints handlers they may previously have known or worked with?) Assuming these are essentially accurate observations, the question arises of how the ongoing links with the health service can be properly justified, especially since the Ombudsman represents the only heavyweight independent component (for some) in the process of pursuing a complaint about the NHS. (Before the review phase changes already in place – and those still to take effect – in the UK's health service complaints system, described in Chapter 2, the Ombudsman was the sole independent examiner of complaints about the NHS.) Indeed, how can any such Ombudsman claim that their organization is entirely detached from the NHS?

There are additional issues to consider, such as the fact that the former fully self-regulated NHS complaints mechanism had racked up an inauspicious track record in dealing with complainants grievances. The previous Ombudsman based in England is well aware of the historical details of this undistinguished performance (as doubtless is the incumbent Ombudsman). Add to this the entrenched attitudes and culture that may have been picked up by hired staff in their previous roles, and questions about a kind of conflict of interest arise. Worthy of note is the much-vaunted declaration that the Office of the Health Service Ombudsman is a completely independent complaints investigating body[10] – a quality that, presumably, should be demonstrated both in its autonomous status as well as in its personnel.

To what extent can retraining and other similar measures taken by the Ombudsman eradicate mindsets already formed in personnel drawn from the health service? Is such remedial action effective, or is the nature of the investigations made by the Office of the Health Service Ombudsman merely a more sophisticated rerun of the still predominantly self-regulated system these recruits have left, and one in which they are able to settle comfortably? There are likely to be many on the outside who will take the latter view and consider that it is a simple case of poachers turning gamekeepers, so to speak, and a cause for concern. They may also find it hard to believe that these 'leopards' can entirely change their spots.

Other crucial questions arise. How can any Ombudsman justify recruiting from the same service – in particular from its complaints handling arm – that they have been entrusted to investigate when things go wrong? Indeed, how are the Ombudsman's investigators thus hired supposed to make a completely detached judgement about the decisions taken by complaints handlers working for their previous employer not to examine complaints? Not only that; in cases alleging maladministration, the responsibilities of the Ombudsman's investigators also involved judging the conduct of NHS arranged 'independent review panels' in arriving at their verdicts. (Chapter 2 shows that in April 2003 the review phase of the complaints procedure ceased to be set up and managed by the health service in Wales, while in England the practice stopped in August 2004. The situation for Scotland and Northern Ireland had not been officially settled late in 2004 although, in the case of the former, this was to become clear in spring 2005 when the reformed NHS complaints procedure was scheduled to be in place.)

Information appearing on its website in January 2002 shows that the Parliamentary and Health Service Ombudsman's organization had around 250 employees, of which approximately half were investigation officers. These officers examine complaints about maladministration in government departments and failures in the NHS. They were being recruited about twice a year for each facet of the Ombudsman's jurisdiction. It appears that these posts were advertised in the *Guardian* and the *Health Service Journal* (to attract staff from the NHS), and most of these positions were also advertised within the civil service. Moreover, periodically, clinical advisers were being engaged for guidance on specific complaints about the health service – such posts were advertised in the *British Medical Journal*. It is possible – or probable – that this approach to recruitment is similar today.

The benefits of Health Ombudsman staff being recruited from outside the NHS
Aside from all these factors, there are certain to be better sources from which the Ombudsman can hire staff. There must be many talented, capable, rational and more obviously neutral candidates in the world outside or unconnected with the health service who can fill any position in the organization. It is clear that a proportion of the workforce in the Office of the Health Service Ombudsman are recruited from outside the health care sector: why aren't all the staff enlisted from these sources? If they were there could be a double benefit: the quality of screening and investigations by the Ombudsman's team may improve and any charge of bias from complainants would be more difficult to justify. The problem is that a change of policy on this scale would involve a major clear-out of staff, especially of senior investigators recruited from the health service. It would be a high price to pay by

those concerned, but could well turn out to be a vital step towards gaining maximum public confidence.

Certainly, it is not inspiring for complainants and the public to discover that the same individuals who may have managed or adjudicated on complaints in the earlier health service complaints process had been taken on by the Ombudsman. These recruits will have been hired to examine and make vital decisions on cases that had already passed (unsuccessfully or unsatisfactorily) through the previous NHS procedure. This is likely to be especially disillusioning for complainants as such a small proportion of complaints ever reach the Ombudsman (see Chapter 3). Nor will it be gratifying for them to find out that, once there, an even smaller number is accepted for investigation by the Ombudsman's team – and still fewer are finally upheld.

However, the public is in no position to make any kind of informed judgement at present. The printed information and that provided on the Ombudsman's website is centred around the complaints process. These details explain who can complain and how, what complaints the Ombudsman can and cannot consider, and what will follow when a complaint is assessed or investigated.[11] There are no easily available facts about the structure of the organization; the pedigrees of screeners, investigators and their leaders; or the basis upon which complainants' grievances are assessed and examined. Nor have any validated assurances been provided of why 'complaints made by or on behalf of people who have suffered because of unsatisfactory treatment or service by the NHS'[12] will be looked at thoroughly, efficiently and equitably by those entrusted to do so by the Ombudsman.

The Health Service Ombudsman's clinical assessors

And what of the standing of the Ombudsman's internal and external clinical assessors? There are complainants who believe – and there is anecdotal evidence to show – that in some apparently questionable cases before the Ombudsman, medical advisers endorsed the opinions of their counterparts who guided 'independent review panels', as an example. (Chapter 11 may shed some light on the issue.) It is unfortunate that questions of confidentiality, a lack of transparency in the Ombudsman's operation and other contributing factors make it difficult to find substantial evidence of whether or not this is an endemic problem. (Can one be assured that the Ombudsman's clinical assessors will not behave in a similar way about judgements by their counterparts who advise the new review bodies?)

Some of the Ombudsman's internal clinical assessors could well have advised 'independent review panels' and other investigating components of the self-regulated NHS end of the complaints procedure. (Are they permitted to continue doing so while in his employ?) It would be interesting to know what proportion of the Ombudsman's external clinical assessors give advice, concurrently, to complaints handlers in the NHS, review bodies and those working for the Ombudsman. This suggestion may appear alarmist but, in the light of the discussion above it could be worth pursuing.

Of course, clinical advisers, unlike rabbits, cannot be drawn out of a hat. But if some of them turn out to be the same professionals who have participated in the culture of the earlier internally managed health service phase of the complaints system (or may take part in the reformed arrangements) questions of suitability or overlap could arise. After all, in this latter capacity they will have advised 'independent review panels' in adjudicating on (rejected) complaints – presumably not the same ones – which, subsequently, are referred to the Ombudsman. Just because someone happens to be a medical practitioner cannot automatically mean that tribal loyalties will always go out of the window when assessing the actions of another medical professional. The 'closing ranks' syndrome may no longer be considered as being endemic, but it seems that the label continues to be attached to the medical profession by much of the public.

The issue of engaging the services of internal and outside professional assessors by the Ombudsman (for England, Scotland and Wales) is explained in an item of internal guidance literature (not readily available for public consumption), which was circulated by the NHS Executive to health service trusts and similar bodies in 1996.[13] This occurred at the time the complaints procedure introduced in April 1996 was replacing the previous system and casts some daylight on the health service's involvement in the provision of clinical assessors for the Ombudsman's purposes.

The Ombudsman is recruiting medical and nursing advisers to his Office and intends also to engage external professional advisers to help him on a case-by-case basis. While independent of the NHS complaints procedure, the Ombudsman is a key component of the new complaints system. The prompt release by Trusts and other employers of professional staff invited by the Ombudsman to advise on particular cases will be essential in ensuring that he is able to discharge his new responsibilities effectively. Such release must be regarded as of equal priority to the release of staff to advise independent review panels.[14]

Depending on the extent to which any of this cross-flow of professional opinion occurs, one might sometimes be looking at a repeat performance – whether it is a correct assessment or not – by some of these clinical assessors in their extended role of advising the Ombudsman's investigators. The question then arises whether it might be more appropriate for the Ombudsman to call upon the services of professional assessors from a 'pool' that is not also open to use by 'independent review panels' or bodies? A separation on these lines could, arguably, reduce the incidence of possibly suspect clinical assessments of cases being examined by the Ombudsman, even accepting that health care practitioners can often find it difficult seriously to censure the actions of members of their fraternity. In this respect, any such division is likely to be a good move from a complainant's perspective.

The low number of complaints investigated by the Health Service Ombudsman

What effect could the in-built anomalies and other issues thus far outlined concerning the Ombudsman's operation have on the outcome of complaints that have been referred to him for judgement? Is there a correlation between these factors and the consistently low proportion of cases accepted for investigation and the still lower number of complaints that are then upheld by the Ombudsman's team?

Are there any other seemingly inequitable factors built in to the way complaints are evaluated by the Ombudsman's team that throw out the huge majority of cases referred from the earlier NHS complaints procedure? On what basis are his discretionary powers exercised in deciding whether or not complaints will be accepted for investigation? While accepting that a proportion of cases directed to the Ombudsman found to be ineligible for jurisdiction or other reasons will inevitably be rejected and referred elsewhere, it is only part of the picture.

As things stand, the comparatively small number of complainants (see Chapter 3) who are able to take their complaint to the Health Service Ombudsman are not doing too well. The last opening this complaints adjudicator provides for them turns out to be yet another kind of coarse sieve, which retains only a very small proportion of complaints for investigation and upholds even less, while denying access to countless other possibly justified ones.

This effect on complaints seems to be not entirely dissimilar to that relating to 'independent review' in the earlier internally regulated phase of the previous NHS complaints procedure. Here the vast majority of complaints failed to gain entry following unsuccessful 'local resolution' and most of those that did were dismissed at this stage (see Chapter 1). It is worth considering that the annual total of complaints received by the United Kingdom's public health service goes into six digits. By the time NHS complaints handlers have dealt with them, only a few thousand are referred to the Ombudsman.

Options for further action if complainants are dissatisfied with their treatment by the Health Service Ombudsman

Assuming that they have the resilience to go on after rejection at the hands of the Ombudsman or dissatisfaction with his judgement, what are disgruntled complainants supposed to do next? What they cannot do is contest the Ombudsman's verdict. There is no right of appeal against the Ombudsman's decision: it is the end of the line for a complaint investigated by the Ombudsman's Office.[15]

The Ombudsman cannot change the findings of a report on a complaint and will not generally enter into correspondence about it. Fresh evidence may influence the Ombudsman to start a new investigation, but it is extremely rare for that to happen.[16] Three choices – or a combination of any of them – remain open for discontented complainants: to apply for a judicial review, to take their case to the appropriate self-regulating professional body or to go to litigation. None of these routes guarantees that the complaint will receive resolution satisfactory to the complainant.

Unfortunately, judicial review will almost certainly turn out to be a blind alley: it appears that judicial proceedings have never been granted against the Health Service Ombudsman.[17] Taking a complaint to the General Medical Council or the Nursing and Midwifery Council (which, like its predecessor, the United Kingdom Central Council for Nursing, Midwifery and Health Visiting, continues to be funded by nurses' subscriptions) has usually been a daunting and protracted process. Historically, neither of these self-regulated bodies is considered by the public to have an auspicious record in dealing with complainants' grievances, although the reformed models are better constructed and seem likely to gain more trust from complainants. Court action is similarly lengthy and can involve high financial risk, with the only guaranteed and all-out winners being the legal profession.

The result of a complaint being upheld by the Health Service Ombudsman

There are other drawbacks for the lucky few fortunate enough to gain entry to the Ombudsman's exclusive club. Even when a serious complaint is upheld (see Chapter 11), about the best that a complainant can expect is an apology and an assurance by the health care parties concerned to mend their ways and do better for others. A statement of regret – unduly and misleadingly hyped by complaints bodies as being just what complainants say they are seeking – is not much of a gesture in the circumstances. And there are no guarantees that any assurances given about improving procedures will be honoured.

Invariably, practitioners seem to get off extremely lightly – even scot-free – because the health service is either reluctant or powerless to take firm action. Moreover, what meaningful value can one place on the Ombudsman's jurisdiction over complaints about clinical issues when he or she cannot reprimand, restrict the right to practise or remove a practitioner from the medical register? Those powers are in the hands of the self-regulating professional bodies, one of the next possible ports of call for complainants who are not satisfied with the results or remedies of the Ombudsman's investigation. This may suit erring clinicians and the health service, but it is probably of little worth to seriously damaged patients, or to complainants whose close relatives may have lost their lives following medical treatment. It is hard to see how they can come to terms with such outcomes when there is no form of automatic and consequential redress in cases where complaints are found to be justified.

The Ombudsman and his or her officers cannot be asked to give evidence in court, except in certain prescribed circumstances.[18] Section 15 (2) of the Health Service Commissioners Act 1993 (as amended) states: 'Neither the Commissioner nor his officers nor his advisers shall be called upon to give evidence in any proceedings, other than proceedings mentioned in subsection (1), of matters coming to his or their knowledge in the course of an investigation under this Act.'

The proceedings in subsection (1) refer to offences under the Official Secrets Acts 1911 to 1989, or offences of perjury, obstruction or contempt.

On the question of legal liability for defamation, section 14 (5) of the Act states: 'For the purpose of the law of defamation, the publication of any matter by a Commissioner in sending or making a report or statement in pursuance of this section shall be absolutely privileged.'

Lack of openness in the Office of the Health Service Ombudsman

It can be deduced from the observations made thus far that full openness and transparency are not qualities that can be readily ascribed to the Ombudsman's organization. Until such time as these attributes can be rightly claimed, complainants are in no position to make a valued judgement and affirm that the Health Service Ombudsman is the 'only hope' that their grievances will be independently investigated, as appears to have been expressed by some in their evidence to the House of Commons Health Committee in 1999.[19] One can only speculate on what the aspirations of those giving evidence would have been were they fully aware of the Ombudsman's way of doing things.

As the greater proportion of complaints received or those then deemed to be 'investigable' by the Ombudsman are rejected, there are probably large numbers of dissatisfied complainants with distressing tales to tell. It doesn't help that an adverse judgement cast at this hard-to-come-by last stage extension of the NHS complaints process is also the final straw for those who had expected much better from this much-vaunted independent complaints arbiter. Their dissatisfaction is likely to be even greater once they became aware of who does what and how in the Ombudsman's organization.

The apparent question marks over the orderliness of his Office had never seemed to stop the previous (mainland) Ombudsman handing out advice to others about complaints handling – including those operating internally regulated procedures. Comments in some of this Ombudsman's annual reports – and elsewhere – bear witness to that. In the first of a series of radio programmes on medical negligence broadcast in March and April 1999 he was not restrained in his excoriation of some clearly dubious aspects of the hard-to-come-by 'independent review' phase of the NHS complaints procedure and their undoubted adverse impact on those at the receiving end of poor decisions:

> Put yourself in the shoes of the complainant who says: 'Why should I accept this as a fair and independent tribunal? The convenor is almost invariably a non-executive of the body against which you are complaining. The third member is very often directly connected with the health service. It looks as though it's rigged.'[20]

The convenor is, indeed, normally a non-executive of the trust or health authority being complained about, who will decide whether or not a review panel will be set up to examine a complaint. This internal appointee is also one of two key players directing the process of investigation that may follow. And the third panel member is invariably a non-executive of another public health care body or someone else engaged in the health service. (As previously stated, this position for the review process has changed in England and Wales, and it may also alter in Scotland and Northern Ireland.)

In effect the same sentiments were repeated by the Ombudsman in an oral submission to the House of Commons Health Committee later that year.[21] Correct though he was to point out flaws elsewhere in the complaints system, it seems curious of him to have criticized aspects of the NHS complaints procedure when, as already suggested, his own organization has similarly significant faults. It should have occurred to him that probably many complainants whom he had dealt with believed that the system was rigged against them.

Northern Ireland's Commissioner for Complaints

Like Britain's Health Service Commissioner, Northern Ireland's Ombudsman in 2003 also affirmed that he is 'completely independent of the Assembly and of the government departments and public bodies'[22] that he has powers to investigate. That may be so, but he, too, was previously connected with the NHS, and more power-fully than his mainland counterpart. Before his appointment as Ombudsman – his blanket title covering the dual role of Commissioner for Complaints and Assembly Ombudsman – he was chief executive of one of the country's health and social services boards.[23] In this capacity, he was a key player in the complaints procedure during its health service regulated first phase.

However, unlike their previous leader (his successor was appointed in June 2003), whose post is a public appointment, all the staff in the Northern Ireland Ombudsman Office are seconded from the civil service. In theory, this is for a three-year term, but the duration can be extended. For example, if seconded personnel are happy to stay on, and the civil service departments from which they came are content for them to do so, then the transfer is lengthened accordingly. This arrangement between the Ombudsman's office and the civil service is informal and agreed in a way that suits both parties. Secondments occur from the civil service across the board.[24]

In 2003 the Northern Ireland Ombudsman had a total of 19 staff in his organization. These included his deputy, three directors of investigation, nine investigating officers and six support staff. The latter assist investigating officers in screening complaints that are referred to the Ombudsman for examination and judgement following dissatisfaction at the NHS phase of the complaints procedure.[25]

The Commissioner for Complaints (Amendment – Northern Ireland) Order 1997 became effective from 1 December 1997. This extended the Ombudsman's powers principally by bringing general health service providers (family health services) and independent health care establishments into her jurisdiction. In the process, the previous statutory bar on the Ombudsman's scope to investigate complaints about action taken in diagnosis, treatment or care of patients was removed.

The Ombudsman looks at complaints from people who claim to have suffered injustice through maladministration by government departments and public bodies. 'Maladministration' is taken to mean poor administration or the wrong application of rules. Examples include failure to follow correct procedures, avoidable delay, refusal to answer reasonable questions, failure to apologize for errors, and so on.[26]

In her role as Commissioner for Complaints, the Ombudsman has further powers to investigate the health service and personal social services. She also examines complaints relating to the private health sector where treatment is being paid for by the aforesaid public services. Her jurisdiction allows her to investigate complaints arising from the administrative actions of health service organizations such as trust boards and the exercise of clinical judgement by health care practitioners. Nonetheless, like the British mainland's health service ombudsmen, she will do so only when the NHS complaints procedure has been exhausted.[27]

Like her London-based counterpart, Northern Ireland's Ombudsman can recommend that the body being complained about should provide a remedy where she has found a complaint to be justified. But, again, she has no powers to enforce such a proposal, although the organization concerned will usually accept her recommendation. Under the Commissioner for Complaints legislation, complainants can go to court if a public body fails to put the proposed remedy in place. The Ombudsman will not normally investigate a complaint if the event to which it refers took place more than 12 months previously. This is a deadline similar to that applied by counterparts serving the rest of the United Kingdom.[28]

Action concerning medical negligence is the responsibility of the appropriate regulatory body and thus outside the Northern Ireland Ombudsman's remit so she has no powers to deal with compensation claims. What she can do is recommend a consolatory payment where a person has suffered because an organization has done wrong. Even so, the Ombudsman may consider an apology to be sufficient, having told the latter to mend its ways so that nobody else should have to tolerate the same experience.[29]

There appears to be no marked distinction between the powers and jurisdictions of the United Kingdom's three health service ombudsmen. Nevertheless, some may consider that the particularly restricted background of staff enlisted by Northern Ireland's Ombudsman is just as much of a disadvantage from a complainant's perspective as the background , for example, of some members of staff in the Office of the Ombudsman for England and Wales. It may seem extraordinary to complainants that civil servants, alone, are permitted to sit in judgement of their cases when there are surely more fitting candidates for the job from the much wider world beyond.

Conclusion

Apologies and promises by health service establishments and their practitioners to put their houses in order are all very well and relatively easy for the UK's three ombudsmen to extract. But, as already emphasized in this chapter, the real value of such expressions of regret and assurances in serious clinical cases is at best questionable, as it is unlikely to compensate for the damage that has been caused. And what is the point if the ombudsmen have no authority to compel the health care body involved to put words into action? It is difficult, therefore, to see how complainants can gain much satisfaction from the intervention of an Ombudsman and understandable why, despite the risks, an increasing number go to litigation (see chapters 8 and 9). Public confidence in the self-regulating professional bodies as a means of getting an equitable resolution is still not what it should be. However, as implied earlier in this chapter, it is possible that the not altogether ideal reforms to these institutions will make a difference, the question is, how much difference will they make?

Perhaps the most crucial defect in the character of British ombudsman organizations is the fact that they are defined as independent by those leading them in their position of final judges on complaints about health care. Their understanding of what constitutes an independent complaints body appears to be significantly different from that of their counterparts in the Nordic states (see Chapter 13). Senior figures representing parallel complaints authorities in some of these countries suggested that, given the previous occupational connections with the health service of key functionaries serving the previous Ombudsman (who was responsible for England, Scotland and Wales), as an example and in the way these have been described, the institution this officer headed could not be regarded as independent. (It is likely that they would hold a similar view in 2005.) They stated that a situation in which investigators and others are recruited from the same establishments whose conduct their body was set up to examine simply could not arise in their countries.

In the United Kingdom, by contrast, such an arrangement is considered to be an asset rather than impediment by those who are part of it, or else it may not have developed or been allowed to continue. On the other hand, there might be other more convenient reasons for the practice. Whatever the explanation, it is likely that the British people would find the Nordic system more acceptable. They may also consider that the powerful legal leadership factor generally built into the Nordic complaints systems would sit just as well in the Office of the Health Service Ombudsman, although probably only if the Ombudsman was given much greater powers. Perhaps they should be asked.

CHAPTER 5

Reformed medical self-regulation to rule, but will it be OK?

And will it gain trust and confidence by the public?

A new millennium it certainly is, but it seems that it is still not the time for British medical regulatory bodies to advance to truly independent control. There is no going the way of certain perhaps more enlightened European societies where medical practitioners of all categories are regulated by neutral bodies and managed free of their professions – and of government. After nearly 150 years since being established and for the foreseeable future, at least, the General Medical Council (GMC) will remain in the hands of its members.

Nonetheless, the latest reforms to this regulatory body for doctors that are in place or well advanced would seem to be dramatic by normal standards in Britain. Key structures and procedures have been adjusted in measures of which some implicitly – if not explicitly – address the question of redressing the balance between the public perception of bias on the part of the GMC and obvious impartiality in its handling of allegations against its members. These changes are part of wider action taken to overhaul and modernize the way this regulatory organization operates in the future.

There may be some who will say that the spate of especially alarming health care scandals that grabbed the headlines in the 1990s – particularly those that surfaced in the latter half of the decade – had spurred on the case for urgents reforms to medical regulation and to associated procedures in the NHS. Whatever the judgement here, it is at least possible that this long series of tragic events had influenced much of the initiatives by the government, seeing that many of the episodes pre-dated the latter's own efforts – in some cases by a number of years. Certainly the record will show that individual parliamentarians and the House of Commons Health Committee itself were sufficiently concerned by these episodes to make their own recommendations for remedial change as a consequence (see also Chapter 1).

Officially, though, the reforms can be traced back to a number of initiatives by the government in co-operation with the GMC and others as part of or linked with its national health service reforms. Among them were the Health Act 1999 and *The NHS Plan*, a document presented by the government in July 2000. There were other associated moves at around the same time – and later – in the drive to make changes to the existing system of medical regulation, but like the rest short of introducing an independently controlled and managed arrangement for the United Kingdom.

For example *Supporting Doctors, Protecting Patients*, a consultation paper issued by the Department of Health in 1999 and aimed primarily at doctors in England, discussed among other issues 'professional self-regulation in a modern context'. It drew attention to the government's commitment to 'permitting the health professions to continue to play a major part in defining and improving the quality of their own clinical practice, if such arrangements can be modernised to offer patients appropriate protection'. The statement was linked with the quotation 'professional self-regulation must remain an essential element in the delivery of quality patient services', taken from *The New NHS – Modern, Dependable*, also published by the Department of Health, except two years earlier.

Supporting Doctors, Protecting Patients stated that the 'primary purpose of professional self-regulation is to protect the public'. It listed the five principles – transparency, accountability, targeting, consistency and proportionality – set out by the 'Better Regulation Task Force' as the basis for good professional regulation in health care. The document then expanded on the point in providing a list of 17 axioms under the heading: 'Modern Principles of Professional Self-regulation in the Health Field'. It concluded that 'professional self-regulation itself must operate to a high standard and maintain public trust and confidence'. The paper added that 'with the advent of new structures and procedures to assure and improve quality in the NHS it is essential that the system of professional self-regulation adapts to support NHS organisations in fulfilling their duty of quality'. It further detailed how this support of the new NHS quality framework could be achieved. (The document added that its proposals for good regulation 'are generic and apply to all health professions'.)

The future make-up of and the path to be followed by the medical regulatory bodies was outlined in the *The NHS Plan*. Among its numerous initiatives, *The NHS Plan* called for the regulation of individual clinicians and of their professions to be strengthened. The view it expressed was that the self-regulated medical bodies had to change so that their respective councils would become smaller and have 'much greater patient and public representation in their membership'. Moreover, the view was that they should have faster and more transparent procedures and 'develop meaningful accountability to the public and the health service'. *The NHS Plan* added that these amounted to the 'minimum tests' that a reformed General Medical Council was required to meet.

It further stated that the regulatory body should look at introducing a 'civil burden of proof' in its disciplinary proceedings and put in place other reforms if it was genuinely to protect patients. The *NHS Plan* also indicated that formal co-ordination was necessary between the health care regulatory authorities. With this in mind, a UK 'council of health regulators' would be established to comprise all such bodies, including the GMC. In addition to helping these regulatory organizations to function efficiently together, the new group would act as a forum to establish and develop common ground across the professions, thus represented, to deal with relevant issues, including complaints against health care practitioners. The modernized and more accountable professional regulatory bodies emerging as a consequence from the planned overall reforms would work in close harmony with the NHS' own quality assurance agencies.

In May 2002 the government issued its consultation paper, *Reform of the General Medical Council*, detailing the propoals for change that had been developed in co-operation with the GMC and in consultation with the medical profession and representatives of the public.[1] Later that year the Medical Act 1983 (Amendment) Order 2002 came into force to allow the reforms to proceed. The account that follows provides a résumé of the GMC's roots and describes the body's composition and procedures under the erstwhile and reformed arrangements that are relevant to the focus of this book.

History of the General Medical Council in outline

The General Medical Council is the regulatory authority of the medical profession in the United Kingdom. It was established under section 3 of the Medical Act 1858 as the General Council of Medical Education and Registration and started operating the same year. The GMC was then incorporated under the same title through section 1 of the Medical Act 1862, and finally changed to its present name under provisions in the Medical Act 1950. It derived new powers from the Medical Act 1983 authorizing its role in medical education, registration and disciplinary proceedings.[2] Part 111 of the Health Act 1999 described the reforms that were necessary for the regulation of the medical profession, and the resulting changes that have been implemented since 2002 followed the introduction of the Medical Act 1983 (Amendment) Order 2002. In 2005 there are nearly 230,000 doctors on the GMC's medical register.[3]

Status of the GMC and introduction to the reforms

Doctors must be registered with the General Medical Council to practise medicine in the United Kingdom. In order to be registered with the body, these practitioners are required to have a recognized medical qualification. The GMC is responsible for setting the standards for good medical practice it expects of doctors throughout their working lives and dealing fairly and firmly with them when their fitness to practise is in question. It is also responsible for assuring the quality of undergraduate medical education and co-ordinating all stages of medical teaching in the United Kingdom.[4]

The latest reforms to the GMC have established revised rules, fitness to practise and other procedures and introduced (or are in the course of introducing) new requirements that members of the profession must meet. Among these obligations is 'revalidation', a process through which all doctors will be required to demonstrate at set intervals their continuing fitness to practise. When the details are finally decided the resulting arrangement will replace the requirement for a once-only check on a doctor's abilities. Another obligation is that every practitioner will need to hold a 'licence to practise'. At the time of writing these two elements of the reforms to the GMC were being reappraised following the Shipman Inquiry report in December 2004, with the timetable for their introduction unclear.

Before the reforms, the General Council consisted of 104 members, including 54 elected and 25 appointed medical practitioners and 25 lay members. On 1 July 2003 the new arrangements under the current reforms came into force. Now the Council has a total of 35 members, including 19 doctors elected by practitioners on the GMC's register and two other such professionals appointed by the Academy of Medical Royal Colleges and Council of Heads of Medical Schools.[5]

The balance consists of 14 lay members who are selected by the government (the Privy Council) on advice from the Department of Health through a more transparent process than hitherto. Their appointment to the Council, in this first instance, was the result of applications received from advertising in national, regional and ethnic press media. Applicants were provided with a clear description, previously agreed with the GMC, of the type of people being sought and their future role as Council members. They were chosen by the Privy Council from more than 350 applications that were received following interviews in which independent assessors also took part.[6]

The reduction in the number of Council members meant that it was necessary to recruit more unrelated personnel to assist in the GMC's functions. In 2004 there were 247 'associates' comprising 154 medical doctors and 93 lay people appointed through open selection to sit on conduct and other hearings with Council members. They were recruited in stages through press advertising and the GMC's website. Shortlisted applicants are interviewed by a panel consisting of Council members and independent assessors and the Office of the Commissioner for Public Appointments is also connected with the process. A three-day training course forms part of the selection procedure and the successful applicants receive a five-year service contract.[7]

Summary of the powers of the GMC and its complaints process in 2005

The GMC has legal powers to take action against erring doctors in the United Kingdom. Its authority covers registered practitioners in all fields of medicine or academic research, including hospital doctors and those engaged in general practice within the NHS and in private health care. Nevertheless, the GMC is not a general complaints body and can act only where there is evidence that a practitioner is unfit to practise.[8]

Anyone can lodge a complaint about a doctor with the GMC. The person may be a patient or some other member of the public, a doctor or health care professional, a NHS body or the police. In most cases, patients are recommended to pursue their grievances through the relevant health service complaints procedure before approaching the GMC. Similarly, if a medical professional has concerns about another practitioner, the GMC would normally expect the matter to be raised first locally.[9]

The GMC can take action if a doctor is unfit to practise because:

- of a criminal conviction
- there is evidence of professional misconduct that appears to be sufficiently serious to probably call into question the practitioner's right to continue in medical practice
- there is evidence of deficient performance that is a departure from good professional practice – whether or not it is covered by specific GMC guidance – and significant enough to call into question the professional's registration
- of evident health reasons.[10]

While the GMC is investigating a doctor's fitness to practise, and in exceptional circumstances, it can suspend the practitioner's name from the register (during which time the doctor cannot practise), or apply conditions to continued registration. For example, either action may occur when there is evidence that practitioners are a risk to patients, or to themselves; or where it is in the public interest.[11]

If a case goes to a fitness to practise hearing, there are a variety of sanctions that the panel can impose. As an instance, the panel can issue a warning to a doctor where the latter's fitness to practise is found not to be impaired but where there has been a significant departure from the principles set out in *Good Medical Practice*, the GMC's guidance for doctors. It will take the same action when there is serious cause for concern following a doctor's assessment, nevertheless restriction on the practitioner's registration is regarded as being unnecessary. Warnings are disclosed to doctors' employers and any other parties who have enquired (for a period of five years since they were given). A warning is not given where the concerns relate to a doctor's physical or mental health.[12]

Another sanction available to a fitness to practise panel is to place restrictions on a practitioner's registration such as a requirement to work under supervision or certain conditions. These panels also have the option to suspend a doctor's name from the register so that the person concerned is unable to practise for the period of suspension. If a panel decides to suspend a practitioner's registration or erase the doctor's name from the register, an order for immediate suspension may be applied to prevent the clinician from practising while the appeal period is in operation. In the most serious cases fitness to practise panels can strike a doctor off the register. Erasure from the register is for a minimum period of five years following which a doctor can apply for restoration.[13]

Some of the complaints about doctors where the GMC may take action can involve:

- serious or repeated errors in carrying out medical procedures, or in diagnosis when, for instance, incorrect dosages have been noted on prescriptions or inappropriate drugs prescribed
- a failure to examine patients properly or respond reasonably to their needs
- treating patients without obtaining their informed consent
- serious breaches of a patient's confidentiality
- sexual advances towards patients
- the misuse of alcohol or drugs
- fraud or dishonesty.[14]

The GMC will not normally consider allegations against doctors that are made more than five years after the event that are the subject of complaint, unless it judges it to be in the public interest to do so.[15] Also, cases that are outside its jurisdiction for taking action against doctors cannot be investigated.[16] The body's authority does not extend to other health care practitioners such as pharmacists, dentists, nurses and opticians. These and other medical professionals have their own regulatory mechanisms.[17] There are other instances when the GMC is unable to act. For example, it cannot provide advice or support to doctors whose employers are considering legal action against them. In these cases practitioners consult the medical defence organizations acting for them or the British Medical Association.[18] Nor can the GMC compel a doctor to apologize to a patient or professional colleague, or provide patients with the treatment they wish to receive.[19] Moreover, it cannot pay compensation to a patient or fine a doctor, nor order a practitioner to allow patients to examine their medical records.[20]

What follows when a complaint is lodged with the GMC
Before the GMC can investigate a case complainants have to provide relevant details about the subject of their grievances. This will include the names of the practitioner(s) involved and where they work, correspondence, medical records and also, where applicable, the names and addresses of anyone who can support the complaint. In order for matters to progress complainants must give the GMC their consent to disclose details of the case to the doctor(s) and health care

organization(s) concerned. Any subsequent comments by the practitioner(s) are normally shared with the complainants.[21] There is no specified time limit on investigations. Their length depends on the complexity and seriousness of cases being examined and the complainant and the doctor concerned are kept informed about progress.[22]

With the initial investigation completed, the case is considered by two GMC case examiners – one a medical professional, the other a lay person. Following this process the case examiners jointly decide on whether the complaint raises questions about the doctor's fitness to practise that need to be examined more closely before a fitness to practise panel hearing.[23] No case can be concluded or referred to a fitness to practise panel without their joint agreement. Where they fail to agree, the matter is considered by the newly formed Investigation Committee.[24] The latter also considers cases where the case examiners decide to issue a warning, but where the doctor concerned disputes the facts or requests that the matter is placed before a hearing of the Investigation Committee.[25]

The GMC provides the complainant and the doctor involved with a written explanation of whether or not it has been decided to take any action against the practitioner. Where it has been determined that further investigation of the case is necessary the complainant is provided with written guidance on the procedures that will follow. These next steps may ultimately involve the complainant giving evidence at a hearing held in public. In this event, the GMC pays the complainant's costs and expenses for the hearing, and support is available to alleviate what may be an intimidating experience for this person.[26] (A detailed account of the reformed fitness to practise procedures is given later in this chapter.)

Fitness to practise panels form the final phase of the GMC's complaints procedure. Panels comprise doctors and lay members of the public who hear the evidence and then decide if they need to take action against the practitioner concerned. Fitness to practise panels act in line with the standards and guidance published by the GMC. They may decide that a doctor's fitness to practise is not impaired and will either take no action or issue a warning. Where they find that the practitioner's fitness to practise is impaired they may take action in one of a number of the ways described earlier.[27] A doctor can be referred to an interim orders panel (IOP) at any stage of a case under investigation. An IOP can suspend or restrict a practitioner from practising while an investigation is in progress.[28]

On an associated though separate issue, decisions by fitness to practise panels can be referred by the Council for Healthcare Regulatory Excellence (CHRE) to the High Court in England and Wales or its parallels elsewhere in the United Kingdom. This will occur when the CHRE considers that such a decision is unduly lenient, or it is in the public interest. The CHRE has 28 days in which to make a referral following a doctor's 28-day appeal period. This body reviews all decisions by the GMC's fitness to practise panels where the erasure of a practitioner's name from the register has not occurred as a result.[29]

Undertakings by doctors, appeals and criminal convictions

Doctors can give an enforceable undertaking to the GMC about their future practise. Such an agreement allows the body to deal appropriately with cases where the questions are about their health or performance without having to refer to a fitness to practise panel. Undertakings might include restrictions on a practitioner's behaviour or right to practise, or they may involve a commitment to have medical supervision or re-training.[30]

Practitioners have 28 days in which to appeal to the High Court in England and Wales (or its equivalents elsewhere in the UK) about decisions made by fitness to practise panels. Decisions by these panels do not take effect until either the appeal period expires or judgement has been made on appeals. Nonetheless, fitness to practise panels can impose an immediate order of suspension if they consider that it is necessary to protect the public or it is in the best interests of the practitioner concerned.[31]

The GMC's rules allow it to deal promptly with doctors who have received a criminal conviction or have been subject to a judgement by a regulatory body in the United Kingdom or elsewhere. Such convictions or judgements are regarded as proof of an offence. In numerous cases – especially those involving a custodial offence – the matter will be referred directly to a fitness to practise panel for a hearing.[32]

Fitness to practise procedures prior to November 2004

Under the GMC's previous system incoming complaints were initially considered by one or more Council members appointed as 'screeners'. Cases were always examined first by a medical member, although a second, lay member was also involved in any decisions that were made. Once screened the relevant complaints were guided into one of three formal procedures dealing with issues of conduct, performance or health.[33]

This screening could show, for example, that instant action was necessary by the Interim Orders Committee (IOC) because the doctor concerned could pose an immediate risk to the public. In this event, the IOC could restrict the practitioner's right to practise, or issue a suspension order to take effect straight away.[34] (Doctors could be referred to an interim orders panel at any stage during an investigation.[35]) A complaint might be channelled to the Preliminary Proceedings Committee (PPC), Committee on Professional Performance or Health Committee, all three of which conducted their affairs in private.[36] The screening process was normally completed within six months of a complaint being received.[37]

If either screener considering a case decided that serious professional misconduct may have occurred, the GMC would write to the practitioner concerned setting out the allegations that were made. The doctor would be given another opportunity to comment before the case was considered by the PPC and asked if these remarks could be disclosed to the complainant.[38] The GMC's conduct procedures' panels considered allegations of serious professional misconduct (SPM), and dealt with doctors who had been convicted of a criminal offence.[39]

The Preliminary Proceedings Committee[40]

The PPC met in private session, with each panel comprising a quorum of three, of which one was a lay member, but panels usually contained between five and seven people. Before July 2003, all the PPC's medical and lay components were members of the (previous) Council. From then on, all those who were appointed to sit on panels of the committee were associate members of the new council. Each member of a PPC panel participated equally in the decison-making process, although lay members may have needed to be advised in cases involving clinical issues.

Where a case was referred to the PPC, a decision was made on whether it should be passed on to the Professional Conduct Committee (PCC) for a full formal inquiry in public. Additionally, the PPC could refer complaints to the Health Committee – as could the PCC, with its panels similarly comprising medical and lay members, who met to consider cases about misconduct. Each of the three basic formal procedures could produce a different outcome, and not all led to a practitioner being struck off the GMC's register. While members of the Council could form a part of committee panels, in other instances panels were made up entirely of externally recruited medical and lay people. (Under the new arrangements that are in place – described later in this chapter – members of the Council are no longer permitted to sit on fitness to practise panels.)

The Professional Conduct Committee[41]

Each Professional Conduct Committee panel consisted of a quorum of three, including at least one medical and one lay member, but normally panels were made up of five to seven people. Panellists were drawn from a list approved by the new Council in July 2003. Before this, those appointed to sit on panels were members of the previous Council. From that time the appointees who sat on committee panels were associate members of the new Council. Each panellist had an equal vote and was expected to exercise this right. The criminal burden of proof was applied in proceedings, and any resulting decisions were passed on the basis of a simple majority.

The Professional Conduct Committee was the final phase of the GMC's conduct procedures. Prior to the PCC convening for a full, formal inquiry in public, the GMC's solicitors would have arranged for witness statements, expert reports and any other evidence necessary for its case against the doctor concerned. During the proceedings this practitioner had an opportunity to respond to the allegations that were made, and the complainant could also be asked to appear as a witness. Where this happened, the complainant was required to give evidence under oath and could be questioned by the panel and the lawyer defending the doctor. The GMC paid the complainant's costs and expenses and normally offered the services of a solicitor, and its staff were available to explain procedures and assist in other ways to alleviate the stress placed upon witnesses giving evidence in public.

When doctors were found guilty of serious professional misconduct the PCC could:

* erase their names from the register
* suspend their registration
* impose conditions on their registration
* give them a reprimand.

In cases where doctors were not found to be guilty of serious professional misconduct, the PCC may have decided not to take remedial action, or it might have provided advice about the doctor's future conduct.

Performance procedures[42]

The GMC's performance procedures appraised doctors whose functions appeared to be significantly deficient. If information received suggested that a doctor was performing badly, it would first be established whether the details were true. Were it considered that there was a case to answer, the practitioner was invited to undergo a skills and knowledge assessment. The GMC provided a team of trained assessors to study the doctor's performance and give an assessment.

These assessors normally included two doctors with the relevant speciality and a lay member of the public. Their combined role was to evaluate the practitioner's attitude, knowledge, clinical and communication skills and medical records. With their work completed, the assessors provided details of their audit to the case co-ordinator, who was a medical member of the Council. The co-ordinator was responsible for supervising cases involving performance issues and decided which of the following three measures should be applied:

- take no further action, if the assessment had not revealed any serious performance difficulties
- ask the doctor concerned to improve his or her performance, where problems had been identified but did not pose a risk to patients
- refer the practitioner to the Committee on Professional Performance (CPP) if serious problems had been shown to exist; this could have resulted in the CPP suspending or placing conditions on the doctor's registration (unless expressly wishing to do so, complainants were not normally required to attend in person at CPP hearings).

In cases where a doctor had refused to accept an assessment, the matter was referred to the Assessment Referral Committee (ARC). This committee had powers to require the practitioner to be assessed within a prescribed period. The person who had reported the doctor to the GMC, in the first place, was allowed to state their case at the ARC meeting.

The Health Committee[43]

The GMC's health procedures could be applied if a practitioner persisted in practising despite serious ill health. This course of action was taken to protect patients and to encourage unwell doctors to be treated with a view to returning to work where this was possible. Especially critical cases were reported to the Health Committee, which could suspend or set conditions on a doctor's registration.

Like the PPC and PCC, Health Committee panels comprised a quorum of three, and included at least one medical and one lay member. The usual panel size consisted of between five and six people. Again, panellists were drawn from a list approved by the new Council in July 2003, and from that month panels comprised associate members of this body. (Before this, those appointed to sit on panels were members of the previous Council.) All panellists had an equal vote and were expected to exercise this prerogative; decisions passed were based on a simple majority. It was not usual for complainants to be present at proceedings of Health Committee panels.

The Interim Orders Committee[44]

This was a separate committee whose duty it was to consider the use of interim measures on a practitioner's registration while fitness to practise procedures advanced. Nevertheless, these steps would be taken only if there was evidence of a clear need to act immediately by suspending or restricting a doctor's right to practise. Examples are when practitioners may have been a risk to patients or to themselves, and when it was in the public interest. Complainants were not involved in Interim Orders Committee (IOC) proceedings.

The IOC, including the chairman, had eight medical and seven lay members. While the quorum for each panel was three, in practice there were usually at least five members (up to the maximum eight) present at sittings. Each member, whether medical or lay, had the same 'weight' on the committee; and the chairman had no casting vote. Here, too, the panellists were appointed from a list approved by the new Council in July 2003, and were associate members of the Council. (Before this, IOC panellists were members of the previous Council.) The criminal standard of proof was exercised in cases heard by the IOC.

Complaints (including enquiries and referrals) lodged in 2002 and 2003

Up to the year ending 31 December 2003 the GMC received 3,926 complaints (involving 3,592 doctors) compared with 3,906 in 2002. Out of the total, 3,821 related to the conduct or performance of doctors, or to a potential criminal conviction. The balance of 105 complaints referred to the possible impairment to a doctor's health. By the end of 2003, 4,468 cases had been concluded, in comparison with 5,539 in 2002.[45] Details about the sources and initial outcome of these cases are shown in tables 5.1 to 5.4

Table 5.1a Sources of complaints in 2002 and 2003[a]

	2002	2003
Members of public	2,913	2,928
Individuals acting for members of public	519	522
Doctors	231	249
Others (including private organizations)	161	122
Total	3,824	3,821

GMC, *Annex A – Work of the Screening Section*[46]
[a] Excludes those concerning a doctor's health

Table 5.1b Percentage sources of complaints in 2002 and 2003[a]

	2002	2003
Members of public	76	77
Individuals acting for members of public	14	14
Doctors	6	6
Others (including private organizations)	4	3

GMC, *Annex A – Work of the Screening Section*[46]
[a] Excludes those concerning a doctor's health

Table 5.2a Decisions by screeners at initial stage of fitness to practise process in 2002 and 2003[a<]

	2002	2003
Not SPM/SPD[b] or no prospect of evidence emerging	1,316	798
Referred to PPC	478	434
Referred to performance procedures	77	65
Referred to health procedures	13	7
Total	1,884	1,304

GMC, *Annex A – Work of the Screening Section*[47]
[a] Excludes those concerning a doctor's health
[b]Serious professional misconduct or seriously deficient performance

Table 5.2b Percentage decisions by screeners at initial stage of fitness to practise process in 2002 and 2003[a]

	2002	2003
Not SPM/SPD[b] or no prospect of evidence emerging	70	61
Referred to PPC	25	33
Referred to performance procedures	4	5
Referred to health procedures	1	1

GMC, *Annex A – Work of the Screening Section*[47]
[a] Excludes those concerning a doctor's health
[b]Serious professional misconduct or seriously deficient performance

Table 5.3a Cases concluded by screeners in 2002 and 2003, by category

	2002	2003
Sub standard clinical treatment	963	598
Dishonesty	35	28
Dysfunctional	15	22
Sexual assault/indecency	25	17
Violence	3	8
Others	275	125
Total	1,316	798

GMC, *Annex A – Work of the Screening Section*[48]

Table 5.3b Percentage cases concluded by screeners in 2002 and 2003, by category

	2002	2003
Sub standard clinical treatment	73	75
Dishonesty	3	4
Dysfunctional	1	3
Sexual assault/indecency	2	2
Violence	–	1
Others	21	16

GMC, *Annex A – Work of the Screening Section*[48]

Table 5.4a Cases referred to the PPC in 2002 and 2003, by category

	2002	2003
Sub standard clinical treatment	213	211
Dishonesty	112	97
Dysfunctional	28	29
Sexual assault/indecency	40	23
Violence	4	7
Others	81	67
Total	478	434

GMC, *Annex A – Work of the Screening Section*[49]

Table 5.4b Percentage cases referred to the PPC in 2002 and 2003, by category

	2002	2003
Sub standard clinical treatment	45	49
Dishonesty	23	22
Dysfunctional	6	7
Sexual assault/indecency	8	5
Violence	1	2
Others	17	15

GMC, *Annex A – Work of the Screening Section*[49]

In 2003 the Preliminary Proceedings Committee sat for 36 days and heard 496 complaints about 418 doctors compared with 35 days and 651 complaints that involved 546 doctors in 2002.[50] The overall outcomes and category of those heard are shown in tables 5.5 to 5.7

Table 5.5a Outcome of cases heard by the PPC in 2002 and 2003

	2002	2003
Refer to PCC	190	127
Refer to Health Committee or voluntary health procedures	19	11
Advice/warning letter	234	185
No action taken	100	94
Voluntary erasure	3	1
Total	546	418

GMC, *Annex B – Work of the Preliminary Proceedings Committee*[51]

Table 5.5b Percentage outcome of cases heard by the PPC in 2002 and 2003

	2002	2003
Refer to PCC	35	30
Refer to Health Committee or voluntary health procedures	4	3
Advice/warning letter	43	44
No action taken	18	23
Voluntary erasure	–	–

GMC, *Annex B – Work of the Preliminary Proceedings Committee*[51]

Table 5.6a Outcome of cases heard by the PPC in 2003, by category

	Sub standard clinical treatment	Dysfunctional conduct	Sexual assault or indecency
Refer to PCC	59	15	7
Refer to Health Committee or voluntary health procedures	0	0	0
Advice/warning letter	95	3	9
No action taken	60	3	7
Voluntary erasure	1	0	0
Total	215	21	23

	Dishonesty	Violence	Conviction
Refer to PCC	31	0	12
Refer to Health Committee or voluntary health procedures	0	0	0
Advice/warning letter	51	4	24
No action taken	7	0	1
Voluntary erasure	0	0	0
Total	89	4	37

GMC, *Annex B – Work of the Preliminary Proceedings Committee* [52]

Table 5.6b Percentage outcome of cases heard by the PPC in 2003, by category

	Sub standard clinical treatment	Dysfunctional conduct	Sexual assault or indecency
Refer to PCC	27	71	30
Refer to Health Committee or voluntary health procedures	0	0	0
Advice/warning letter	44	14	39
No action taken	28	14	30
Voluntary erasure	1	0	0

	Dishonesty	Violence	Conviction
Refer to PCC	35	0	32
Refer to Health Committee or voluntary health procedures	0	0	0
Advice/warning letter	57	100	65
No action taken	8	0	3
Voluntary erasure	0	0	0

GMC, *Annex B – Work of the Preliminary Proceedings Committee* [52]

Table 5.7 Outcome in other categories of cases in 2003

	Number	(%)
Refer to PCC	15	23
Refer to Health Committee or voluntary health procedures	11	17
Advice or warning letter	23	35
No action taken	17	26
Voluntary erasure	0	
Total	66	

GMC, *Annex B – Work of the Preliminary Proceedings Committee* [53]

The Professional and Conduct Committee panels considered 175 cases in 2003, including 128 new ones, 41 where they had resumed consideration and six applications by doctors to be restored to the register.[54] A breakdown of the outcome of these cases (and those considered in 2002) is given in tables 5.8a and 5.8b, and the sources of new cases about conduct are provided in Table 5.9.

Table 5.8a Outcome of all cases considered by the PCC in 2002 and 2003

	2002	2003
Not guilty/not proved	63	43
Guilty but no action taken	7	1
Reprimand	29	18
Conditions applied	33	25
Suspension	24	21
Erasure from register	48	29
Adjourned to Health Committee	4	1
Adjourned	10	8
Conditions revoked	6	17
Suspension lifted	6	6
Applications for restoration	8	6
Total	238	175

GMC, *Annex C – Work of the Professional Conduct Committee in 2003*[55]

Table 5.8b Percentage outcome of all cases considered by the PCC in 2002 and 2003

	2002	2003
Not guilty/not proved	26	25
Guilty but no action taken	3	1
Reprimand	12	10
Conditions applied	14	14
Suspension	10	12
Erasure from register	20	17
Adjourned to Health Committee	2	–
Adjourned	4	5
Conditions revoked	3	10
Suspension lifted	3	3
Applications for restoration	3	3

GMC, *Annex C – Work of the Professional Conduct Committee in 2003*[55]

Table 5.9 Source of complaints (new cases of conduct only) considered by the PCC in 2003

	Number	(%)
Public	35	31
Individuals acting in a public capacity	57	51
Doctors	8	7
Others (including private organizations)	12	11
Total	112	

GMC, *Annex C – Work of the Professional Conduct Committee in 2003*[56]

During 2003 the GMC's health screeners and health section dealt with 143 cases (compared with 202 and 181 in 2002 and 2001) concerning fitness to practise. The outcome of these initial health screening enquiries and subsequent medical examinations (including PPC cases) are shown in tables 5.10 and 5.11. In 2003 there were 135 new enquiries against 124 doctors (the ratio was 105 to 104 in 2002) relating to the possible impairment of their health (Table 5.12a).[57]

Table 5.10 Outcome of initial health screening inquiries in 2001 to 2003

	2001	2002	2003
Doctor invited to be examined	115	149	120
No further action: local measures adequate	20	11	14
No further action: name removed from register	13	27	3
No further action: insufficient evidence	30	13	6
Deceased	3	2	0
Total	181	202	143

GMC, *Annex D – Work of the Health Screeners and the Health Section* [58]

Table 5.11 Outcome of medical examinations (includes PPC cases) in 2001 to 2003

	2001	2002	2003
Unfit to practise	24	23	29
Fit to practise subject to recommendations	30	33	38
Fully fit to practise: no supervision required	24	15	34
Total	78	71	101

GMC, *Annex D – Work of the Health Screeners and the Health Section* [59]

Table 5.12a Sources of complaints involving practitioners' health in 2002 and 2003

	2002	2003
Public	11	8
Individuals acting in a public capacity	44	71
Doctors	24	11
Others (including private organizations)	25	34
Total (doctors)	104	124

GMC, *Annex D – Work of the Health Screeners and the Health Section* [60]

Table 5.12b Percentage sources of complaints involving practitioners' health in 2002 and 2003

	2002	2003
Public	11	7
Individuals acting in a public capacity	42	57
Doctors	23	9
Others (including private organizations)	24	27

GMC, *Annex D – Work of the Health Screeners and the Health Section* [60]

The Health Committee considered 146 cases concerning 141 doctors in 2003 compared with 152 cases and 137 doctors in 2002.[61] A breakdown of the outcomes in both years is given in tables 5.13a and 5.13b.

Table 5.13a Outcome of cases determined by the Health Committee in 2002 and 2003

	2002	2003
Conditions applied	68	63
Suspended	44	48
Indefinite suspension	12	7
Not seriously impaired	10	17
Adjourned	10	4
Deceased	4	1
Voluntary erasure	4	1
Total (doctors)	152	141

GMC, *Annex E – The Work of the Health Committee in 2003*[62]

Table 5.13b Percentage outcome of cases determined by the Health Committee in 2002 and 2003

	2002	2003
Conditions applied	45	45
Suspended	29	34
Indefinite suspension	8	5
Not seriously impaired	7	12
Adjourned	7	3
Deceased	3	1
Voluntary erasure	3	1

GMC, *Annex E – The Work of the Health Committee in 2003*[62]

During 2003, 71 doctors were referred to the GMC's performance procedures compared with 80 in 2002.[63] Action was initiated in 42 cases (67 in 2002), the types of which are shown in Table 5.14a.

Table 5.14a Outcome of assessments referred to the performance procedures in 2002 and 2003

	2002	2003
Performance found acceptable	14	13
Doctor not fit (referred for CPP[a] hearing)	18	12
Doctor fit within limits[b]	8	17
Voluntary erasure	16	0
To be given a case co-ordinator's decision	11	0
Total of completed assessments	67	42

GMC, *Annex F – Work of the Performance Section in 2003*[64]
[a] Committee on Professional Performance
[b] Statement of requirements given

Table 5.14b Percentage outcome of assessments referred to the performance procedures in 2002 and 2003

	2002	2003
Performance found acceptable	21	31
Doctor not fit (referred for CPP[a] hearing)	27	29
Doctor fit within limits[b]	12	40
Voluntary erasure	24	0
To be given a case co-ordinator's decision	16	0

GMC, *Annex F – Work of the Performance Section in 2003*[64]
[a] Committee on Professional Performance
[b] Statement of requirements given

The GMC's replacement committees, panels, procedures and registration rules

Under Part 111 of the Medical Act 1983 (Amendment) Order 2002, the GMC's committees and procedures were replaced by a new set of committees and panels on 1 November 2004 and operate as:

- the Investigation Committee
- one or more fitness to practise panels
- one or more interim orders panels
- one or more registration decisions panels
- one or more registration appeals panels
- the Education Committee (not included for the purposes of this book's focus).

These replacement mechanisms were constituted according to provisions in the Act and have the functions assigned to them under the legislation.[65]

Summary of initial consideration, referral and investigation of allegations procedures
The General Medical Council (Fitness to Practise) Rules 2004 requires that all allegations received by the GMC about practitioners are considered first by the registrar. Cases that meet the requirements of certain fitness to practise rules and fall within the relevant part of the Act are referred to case examiners (one a medical practitioner, the other a lay person) for consideration. Where it is judged that allegations are not covered by the Act or are out of time (because more than five years have elapsed since the circumstances that last gave rise to the claims being made) and the registrar considers that it is not in the public interest for them to progress further, the person who made the allegation (if any) and the doctor are notified accordingly.[66] The rules provide that there is a presumption that cases involving a criminal caution or conviction, or a judgement by another regulatory body, will progress directly to a fitness to practise panel, and to an interim orders panel in other circumstances.[67]

Having looked into a case that has been referred to them, the case examiners decide
unanimously on one of the following:

- that it should not proceed further
- agree an undertaking with the doctor concerned where there has been a performance or health assessment
- to issues a warning to the doctor concerned in accordance with the relevant fitness to practise rule

- direct it to a fitness to practise panel for determination.[68]

Cases can also be referred to the Investigation Committee but only where the medical and lay case examiners disagree, or when they are minded to issue a warning and the doctor requests an oral hearing.

Following the referral of an allegation the registrar notifies the practitioner involved in writing about the allegation and the issues that appear to raise questions with regard to their fitness to practise. The doctor is also given copies of any information received by the GMC in support of the allegation and invited to provide a written response within 28 days from the date of the registrar's notification. At the same time the practitioner is advised that, where appropriate, the content of their response will be disclosed to the person who made the allegation – where one has been made.[69] The criminal standard of proof continues to apply in conduct cases. In cases that involve a doctor's performance or health the civil standard of proof is exercised.[70]

The Investigation Committee

With the majority of decision-making on allegations lodged with the GMC delegated by Council to case examiners, the casework role of the Investigation Committee is on a limited scale. As explained earlier, the IC can consider only those cases where the medical and lay case examiners are unable to agree on a resolution, and in instances where the doctor in question has requested a hearing following a decision by the case examiners to issue a warning.[71]

As shown earlier in this chapter, the previous fitness to practise procedures had three streams: conduct, health and performance. Under the Investigation Committee rules a single investigation process has replaced the two previous screening and Preliminary Proceedings Committee phases, but the new Committee is not the PPC and screeners by another name.[72]

The Investigation Committee considers allegations made to the General Medical Council about a practitioner's fitness to practise. This applies to a person who is fully or provisionally registered, or who has limited registration. Additionally it is relevant to allegations relating to matters said to have occurred outside the United Kingdom, or at a time when the practitioner concerned was not registered.[73]

A doctor's fitness to practise is regarded as being 'impaired' by reason of misconduct, deficient professional performance or adverse physical or mental health. There is a presumption that cases where a doctor has received a conviction or caution for a criminal offence in the United Kingdom and Ireland will proceed directly to a fitness to practise panel for determination. The same applies to a conviction or caution elsewhere for an offence, if committing it in England and Wales would constitute a crime, and to judgements made against a practitioner by a body responsible under legislation for regulating a health or social care profession in the United Kingdom, or by a regulatory organization operating elsewhere.[74]

After its examination, the Investigation Committee determines whether an allegation should be referred to a fitness to practise panel for further investigation; if it decides to take this action, the Committee directs the GMC's registrar to make the referral.[75] Alternatively, the Committee may decide to take no action at all and it advises the registrar accordingly.[76] In either event, the registrar subsequently notifies the practitioner concerned and the person (if any) in the case who has made the allegation of the Committee's decision.[77] If the Investigation Committee decides that the allegation should not be examined by a fitness to practise panel, it may give a warning to the practitioner concerning future conduct or performance.[78] However, referrals to an interim orders panel is normally not the province of the Investigation Committee. This function is carried out by case examiners or the registrar who then inform the relevant parties in such cases about panel decisions.[79]

Fitness to practise reforms: rules and procedures
In circumstances where the case examiners or the IC decides that a warning should be issued, the doctor involved has a right to an oral hearing before a panel of the Investigation Committee prior to confirmation. This panel can refer the practitioner to a fitness to practise panel if it considers that 'the threshold for referral has been crossed'. Fitness to practise panels may also issue a warning where the facts found proven amount to a doctor's fitness to practise being impaired and justify action on registration by the GMC. There is no formal appeal against a decision to issue a warning – except through judicial review. Determinations by case examiners and the Investigation Committee are based on a 'sliding civil standard of proof', and warnings are valid for five years for the purposes of revalidation (referred to later in this chapter).[80]

When a fitness to practise panel decides that a doctor's fitness to practise is impaired to an extent justifying action on registration, it may:
- order removal of the person's name from the register (cases concerning health care excepted)
- issue instructions to suspend the practitioner's registration for a period of not more than 12 months
- require that the doctor's registration is conditional on complying, for a period up to three years, with requirements imposed by it to safeguard the public, or in the professional's own interests.[81]

In cases where a panel considers that a doctor's fitness to practise is not impaired it may still give a warning about the doctor's conduct or performance.[82] A fitness to practise panel can take further action concerning practitioners whose registration has been suspended in all of the circumstances just described.[83] It can also do so in other cases involving suspension from the register. To illustrate, the panel could direct that:
- the current period of suspension should be extended for a further period
- the name of the practitioner is erased from the register (except in health care cases)
- the doctor's registration, following expiry of the current period of suspension, is conditional on compliance over the term specified (but no more than three years) with the conditions it has imposed.[84]

Nevertheless, except in instances involving health care, a fitness to practise panel is not authorized to extend any period of suspension for more than one year at a time.[85] In cases where a doctor's health is concerned, these panels have powers to direct that the practitioner's existing suspension is extended indefinitely where it has already lasted for at least two years, and that the direction is given not more than two months before the date on which the suspension will have expired.[86]

However, in health care cases where a fitness to practise panel orders that a doctor's suspension should be extended indefinitely, the panel will review its decision if:

- the person concerned requests it to do so
- at least two years have passed since the panel's direction will have taken effect
- a minimum of two years have gone by since any previous reappraisal of the panel's direction.[87]

In instances involving such a review, the panel could confirm that the original direction still stands, order that the suspension should be ended, or give instructions that the registration is conditional on the practitioner complying with the requirements it has imposed for a specified period not exceeding three years.[88]

Where practitioners fail to comply with the conditions imposed on their registration in any of these cases, and in certain other circumstances referred to in the Act, a fitness to practise panel has powers to order their names to be erased from the register, except in cases involving a doctor's health, or to issue instructions that their registration should be suspended for a specified period, but not exceeding one year.[89]

In certain of these cases where a doctor's registration is conditional, a fitness to practise panel also has powers to

- direct that the name of the practitioner is removed from the register
- order registration to be suspended for a specified period up to one year
- call for the current period of conditional registration to be extended
- revoke any of these directions or quash or change any of the conditions imposed for the rest of the current period of conditional registration.[90]

However, in the instances just mentioned, the panel cannot extend any period of conditional registration for more than three years at a time.[91]

The registrar must immediately notify practitioners of their right to appeal under the Act where a fitness to practise panel has given instructions to:

- remove their names from the register
- suspend their registration
- allow them conditional registration
- vary any of the requirements for conditional registration.[92]

This notification also applies to cases where a period of suspension or conditional suspension has been extended by a panel.[93] Appeals against any of the aforesaid decisions taken by a fitness to practise panel must be made to the relevant court: the High Court of Justice in England and Wales; the Court of Session in Scotland; or the High Court of Justice in Northern Ireland.[94] All hearings by fitness to practice panels are in public, except in cases that involve a doctor's health.[95]

Interim orders panels

Interim orders panels decide on matters that involve both making and reviewing an interim order on practitioners in allegations that are referred to them by the registrar. If it is decided that a hearing for either purpose should take place, the registrar will serve notice of it on the doctor concerned in a reasonable time beforehand. Simultaneously, any evidence obtained by the Council that is relevant to the question of whether or not an interim order should be made or reviewed is supplied to the practitioner. Where a review hearing is involved, copies of the order to be reviewed and the documents considered at any previous hearing before an interim orders panel are also provided. Nevertheless, where the practitioner in question consents, an interim order can be reviewed by the chairman of an interim orders panel without a hearing. Ordinarily, interim orders panel hearings are held in private. The previous Interim Orders Committee rules were incorporated into those in force under the new system.[96]

Registration decisions panels and registration appeals panels
Applications for registration and erasure of registration are initially dealt with by the registrar who may refer any issue concerning an application to an interim orders panel for advice before making a judgement on the matter. Following this the registrar gives the applicant written notice of the decision that has been reached. Where it has been decided not to grant an application, the written 'notice of decision' gives the reasons for this and informs the applicant of their right of appeal to a registration appeals panel. If the registrar has considered the advice of a panel in arriving at a decision, a copy of the panel's written confirmation of its advice is also included The registrar can also ask a registration decisions panel to consider the case at a hearing.[97]

In instances where applicants have exercised their right to appeal to a registration appeals panel, the registrar forwards a 'notice of hearing' to the appellant in not less than 28 days before the hearing is to take place. The notice advises the appellant of their right to attend and be represented at the hearing and to request that it is held in public; otherwise the hearing is held in private.[98]

Rules about membership of panels and the Investigation Committee
The Council is responsible for assembling and maintaining a list of medical practitioners and lay people eligible to act as panellists (including that of chairman) on fitness to practise panels and on interim orders panels, and a list of such individuals who will be appointed to the Investigation Committee. Under the Medical Act 1983 (Amendment) Order 2002, only individuals who are not members of the Council can be appointed to fitness to practise, interim orders or registration appeals panels. However, members of the Council can be on the Investigation Committee. Someone who sits on an interim orders or a fitness to practise panel that has made an interim order concerning a particular case cannot be a member of a fitness to practise panel in any subsequent proceedings arising about the same matter. Anyone who is a member of the Investigation Committee or a registration decisions panel will not be allowed, simultaneously, to be part of an interim orders, registration appeals or fitness to practise panel.[99]

Quorum and rules for panels and the Investigation Committee
The quorum for fitness to practise panels, interim orders panels and panels of the Investigation Committee is three, including the chairman, a medical practitioner and a lay person. Proceedings of any of these panels or the Investigation Committee are unaffected by any defect subsequently found in the appointment of a panellist.[100] Decisions taken by all panels and committees are on the basis of a simple majority of their members. In instances where the votes are equal, the issue under consider-

ation must be decided in favour of the practitioner involved. The chairman of a panel or committee is not allowed a casting vote; nor can any of its members abstain from voting.[101]

In cases excepting those where evidence about a practitioner's health is being examined, or where it is otherwise specified elsewhere in the General Medical Council (Fitness to Practise) Rules 2004, fitness to practise panel hearings and those before the Investigation Committee are held in public. Nevertheless, panels or the Committee can decide that the public is excluded from their proceedings, or any part of them, if they consider that the circumstances of a case outweigh the public interest in holding the hearing in public. They can hold a hearing in public when it is about a doctor's health or it is to review or issue an interim order where, subject to certain conditions, they judge it is appropriate to do so. Also, a fitness to practise panel considering whether to review or issue an interim order can sit in public where the practitioner concerned has asked it to do so. Nevertheless, in certain instances the Investigation Committee, fitness to practise panels and interim orders panels may conduct their proceedings to the exclusion of all the parties involved – representatives included – and of the public.[102]

Appointment and functions of medical assessors and medical examiners[103]
The registrar maintains a panel of medical assessors and medical examiners, but none of the former is also a member of the Council. In selecting medical assessors and medical examiners, the registrar, case examiner or Committee (whichever applies) considers the nature of the physical or medical condition that is alleged to have impaired a practitioner's fitness to practise. The functions of medical assessors are to:
- advise fitness to practise panels on the medical significance of the information before them
- notify these panels if it appears to them that, without such advice, they may arrive at a faulty conclusion, either from the information in their hands or because it is insufficient.

Appointment and functions of specialist health and performance advisers[104]
The registrar also maintains a panel of registered medical practitioners to act as specialist health advisers and performance advisers, the latter also including lay persons. This assembled group is added to where it is necessary to provide special expertise at any assessment or panel hearing. Members of the Council cannot be appointed to fulfil either of these functions.

In selecting a specialist health adviser the registrar must make certain that the doctor engaged has not previously been part of an assessment team that has carried out an appraisal of the professional performance of the practitioner concerned in the case. Also at least one of the specialist health advisers should be a professional who is practising or has practised in the speciality to which the allegation concerned refers.

Specialist health advisers:
- advise fitness to practise panels about the medical issues before them concerning professional performance
- inform these panels if it appears to them that, without such advice, they may reach a faulty judgement either from the information they possess or because it is insufficient.

Advice from a specialist health adviser to a fitness to practise panel must be given in the presence of the practitioner and that person's representative if they appear at the hearing. Should such guidance be provided after the panel has started to produce its findings, the practitioner must be told about the nature of the advice that has been conveyed.

Performance advisers are components of 'assessment teams'. Each such group comprises a team leader who is a registered medical practitioner, and at least one other medical practitioner and one lay person. No person who has functioned as a performance adviser at a previous hearing of a case can be appointed as a member of an assessment team covering the same case. In appointing registered medical practitioners to an assessment team, the registrar considers the speciality to which the allegation concerned refers. This officer can appoint one or more additional members to an assessment team to assist in carrying out structured tests of a practitioner's performance and contribute to the team's resulting report.

In producing an assessment, members act either singly or with one or more members of the team. The assessment team passes on to the practitioner any written information or opinion it has received that, in its view, could influence its assessment of the level of the professional performance of the doctor whose case is being examined. It also gives the practitioner reasonable time to respond. On this basis and subject to any guidance provided by the General Medical Council, the assessment team adopts the procedures it considers to be necessary to evalute professional performance.

Physical and mental health assessments[105]

The Investigation Committee or case examiners who are considering cases about fitness to practice ask the practitioner concerned to agree to appear before two medical examiners for an assessment and report on their physical or mental condition within 14 days of being asked. Any relevant information that the GMC has received, including assessment reports by other practitioners who have recently examined this doctor, can accompany the request that the committee or case examiner has made for the medical professional to attend an assessment. However, if the Investigation Committee or case examiners feel that any such reports contain information that is irrelevant to practitioners' fitness to practise, or not in their best interests to see, they can instruct the registrar to remove it from the document. Any details that are excluded in this way must not subsequently be submitted to a panel.

Where a practitioner agrees to be assessed, the registrar arranges for the examinations to take place. However, it is the responsibility of the president of the Council to appoint the medical examiners. In their subsequent report, the latter must give an opinion on whether the doctor is fit to practise, either fully or part-time, and make any recommendations concerning the management of the case. Practitioners cannot be chosen to act as medical assessors in a case where they have previously been appointed as a medical examiner.

The role of legal assessors[106]

The Health Care and Associated Professions, Doctors: the General Medical Council (Legal Assessors) Rules 2004 set out the role of legal assessors assigned to the proceedings before the Investigation Committee, interim orders panels and fitness to practise panels. The functions of legal assessors include:

- advising the Committee or a panel on questions of law that are raised
- intervening to advise the Committee or a panel on issues of law where it appears that not doing so may result in a mistake being made
- intervening to advise the Committee or a panel of any irregularity in the conduct of proceedings
- advising on the drafting of decisions by the Committee or a panel despite legal assessors not themselves being parties to those determinations.

In all proceedings to which legal assessors have been appointed under the Medical Act 1983 (Amendment) Order 2002, the Committee or panel involved cannot hold any meeting or hearing that concerns those proceedings without the appointed assessor being present. Legal assessors are required to submit their advice in the presence of all relevant parties – including their representatives – at hearings.

The exception is where the Committee or a panel is considering its decision and believes that it would prejudice the way it discharges its duties. Where this occurs, the legal assessor concerned informs each of the relevant parties (or their representatives) at the hearing of the advice that has been given and the questions which led to it, and subsequently provides a written record of the matter to them. Copies of the latter are also available to parties who have not attended the proceedings but where the advice relates to them.

In cases where the Committee or a panel does not accept the advice of a legal assessor, the latter records:

- the advice that was given and the questions from which it arose
- the decision not to accept it and the reasons for the decision.

Again, copies of the record are given to all parties (or their representatives) to the proceedings.

Change in the system of registration for doctors

Under provisions in the Medical Act 1983 (Amendment) Order 2002 and following the Shipman Inquiry report in December 2004, the GMC is also changing the system of registration for doctors. Although the principle of recording the names in its medical register of those who are qualified to practise medicine in the United Kingdom continues, the new arrangement will also be based on a licence to practise and periodic revalidation. The details of this strengthened approach to registration were under renewed consideration at the time of writing.[107]

Future public confidence in the decisions of a newly constructed GMC

It is fair to say that even the snapshot of procedural and other reforms to the GMC recounted in this chapter is likely to raise public confidence in the regulatory body. One can add justifiably that the reforms, taken in their entirety, should further enhance faith in the system. On the good side, too, these adjustments (and the remaining few improvements in the process of implementation) appear generally to meet the requirements set out in *The NHS Plan* calling for the regulation of clinicians and their profession to be strengthened. What key aspects of the resulting overhauled GMC are likely to be beneficial from the perspective of complainants?

To begin with the reduction in the membership of the General Council to a third of its former size is clearly helpful. Probably even more favourable is the increase in the proportion of the Council's lay members from 25 per cent to 40 per cent of its total number. Both of these changes are in keeping with what was called for in *The NHS Plan*. The fact that members of the Council are no longer permitted to sit on fitness to practise panels – this function now assumed by associate members – is a further step in the right direction. (Nevertheless, Council members are allowed on the newly established Investigation Committee.)

The new situation where the two case examiners involved (one a medical professional, the other a lay person) must decide unanimously on the action to be taken in cases they are considering is, on the surface at least, another positive advance. (Otherwise the cases proceed to the Investigation Committee for consideration.) Also, the introduction of a 'sliding standard of proof' in determinations by case examiners and the Investigation Committee is some reflection of the recommendations in *The NHS Plan*. Another equitable factor is that the chairman, who is included in the quorum of three on fitness to practise panels, interim orders panels and panels of the Investigation Committee is not allowed a casting vote in an arrangement that is on a simple majority basis, and in which no panel or Committee member can abstain from voting. (It was shown earlier in this chapter that the chairman of an interim orders panel under the previous system did not have a casting vote.) There is also clear merit in the legal requirement that the Investigation Committee or any panel to which legal assessors have been appointed cannot hold a meeting or hearing without the assessors concerned being present.

A potentially strengthened approach to registration based on a licence to practise and periodic revalidation instead of the existing once-only check on a doctor's abilities has obvious worth, too. So it would appear was the formation in 2003 of the Council for Healthcare Regulatory Excellence and the powers invested in it, including that as an intervening mechanism in certain decisions by the GMC and other health care regulators. Its authority to refer decisions by the GMC's fitness to practise panels to the High Court in England and Wales and its parallels elsewhere in the United Kingdom is obviously an asset for complainants when such action occurs.

Taken as a whole, therefore, the improvements to the GMC could provide the faster and more equitable and transparent procedures sought after in *The NHS Plan*. Indeed, many observers are likely to agree that these reforms do add up to a significant change for the better within the parameters of medical self-regulation. Whereas others with a different outlook on the position of a regulatory authority like the GMC may consider that the changes do not go far enough even in that context. Their judgement might be that the GMC's reformed – and more concise – complaints handling process is not a dramatic improvement on the one it has replaced. It is possible that these detractors may be critical in particular of the process from the time a complaint is lodged with the GMC up to the point that a decision is made about its referral to a fitness to practice panel. Some of them may feel that even the revised fitness to practise procedures are not developments that are likely to inspire great confidence in those whose cases may be referred for judgement through this process.

There may also be reservations by some about the Council for Healthcare Regulatory Excellence. This is a body that is financed through the government's Department of Health with powers covering the nation.[108] Its governing council comprises 19 members, including one representative – normally the president – from each of the nine regulatory organizations in health care (including the GMC) and ten lay members unconnected with any of the latter.[109] Some might feel that a body of this kind in which the regulators are so comprehensively represented, could defeat certain of its objects in practice.

They could say also that the CHRE's powers in respect of determinations made on allegations received by the GMC are limited. This is because the CHRE will act only on decisions in cases that have been referred to fitness to practise panels that it considers are unduly lenient and that it is necessary to protect the public.[110] Information issued by the CHRE states that it can 'look at the decisions of the relevant fitness to practise panels and committees'.[111] The CHRE is not authorized to take action on decisions made by the GMC on cases in the initial stages, including any determination not to refer a case to a fitness to practise panel[112] – which some fault-finders might feel would have far greater worth. (Indeed, such critics may argue that an intervening body like the CHRE would not be necessary if the General Medical Council was an independent regulator in the first place.)

There could be other critics who question the whole issue of the reforms to the GMC when they consider that their purpose seems to be to perpetuate by propping up the anachronistic and indefensible – the practice of self-regulation itself, albeit with some seeming checks and balances put in place. If medical regulation will really be that equitable following the reforms what, they might ask, is it doing in the hands of a body that continues to operate under the patronage of the medical profession? They might want persuasive answers to other questions.

Is it really possible for the GMC to conduct its affairs in a completely detached and impartial way, however comprehensive the improvements are to its self-regulated system? Will the sweeping reforms 'develop meaningful accountability to the public and the health service' as it was called for in *The NHS Plan*? When fully in place, will the changes be enough to gain public trust and confidence in the GMC? Only time will tell if these few fundamental questions will be answered to the broad satisfaction of all in practice. But the odds may be against such an outcome.

CHAPTER 6

A renamed and reformed regulatory body for nursing has emerged

But self-regulation remains with more lay involvement and powers

'As a minimum, the self-regulatory bodies must change so that they are smaller, with much greater patient and public representation in their membership,' said Chapter 10 of the British government's *The NHS Plan*, which was presented in July 2000. The message was more unequivocal later in the report: 'There will be major increases in the citizen and lay membership of all the professional regulatory bodies.' The document added that, at the very least, these institutions must alter their ways to provide 'faster [and] more transparent procedures and develop meaningful accountability to the public and the health service'. To what extent, therefore, were these called-for reforms reflected in the legislation that followed? And how are they affecting the future regulation of nurses, midwives and health visitors in practice, particularly in matters concerning professional conduct and competence?

On 1 April 2002 the Nursing and Midwifery Council took over from the United Kingdom Central Council for Nursing, Midwifery and Health Visiting (UKCC) as the regulatory body for nurses, midwives and health visitors in the United Kingdom. The change came about as a result of the Nursing and Midwifery Order 2001, which came into force in February 2002. While many of the requirements of the Order are already in place, certain of the key arrangements of the previous UKCC are being maintained until they, too, are replaced by the newly authorized measures. This is especially true of the professional conduct rules and procedures.

Under the Order the NMC is required to continue keeping a register of qualified nurses and midwives (which is open to public inspection) and has established four statutory committees to replace the previous models. Other provisions in the Order oblige the regulatory body to set standards of education, training, conduct and performance and to put in place measures to ensure that the objectives are met. Its role further involves providing advice on professional standards and considering allegations of misconduct or unfitness to practise as a result of ill health. The NMC continues to be funded by the registration fees of nurses and midwives; as in the previous arrangements registration with the NMC is mandatory for practitioners in this category who practise in the United Kingdom.[1]

The Nursing and Midwifery Council has a membership of 35, including 12 'registrant' and 12 matching 'alternate' members; both these categories are elected by the practitioners on its register. An alternate member has the same functions as a registrant member but can attend and vote in Council meetings only if the corresponding registrant member is unable to do so. The remaining 11 Council members are lay members (not nurses, midwives or health visitors) appointed by the Privy Council.[2] Each serving member's tenure is for a four-year period, but members can be discharged if 'there is a change in qualifications, interests or experience' that, in the view of the Privy Council, results in the person no longer being able to contribute to the Council's duties.[3] A member can resign at any time but cannot be appointed for more than three consecutive terms.[4]

Members of the Council elect a president from among themselves for a term of four years but, for similar reasons, this period may not be served in full.[5] Past presidency by a member is not a bar to re-election,[6] but the Council cannot employ any of its members or those on its committees and sub-committees.[7] Nor can any of these appointees take part in proceedings of the Council in any period during which they are the subject of investigation, proceedings or a decision against them about their fitness to practise.[8]

Out of the registered professionals and other appointees that form each of the practice committees, at least one must be a registered medical practitioner. The number of registered professionals on each practice committee can (but need not) exceed the total of its other members, although any excess must be no more than one. Moreover, under the Order, only a Council member can be the chairman of a practice committee or one of its panels, and no person can be a member of more than one such committee. The NMC must follow the guidance issued by the Commissioner for Public Appointments when selecting non Council members for a practice committee.[9]

Sources and geographical breakdown of complaints received by the NMC

The highest proportion of complaints continue to come from employers, with those made by the public currently the second largest category. Police authorities are obliged to report to the NMC any nurse, midwife or health visitor who is convicted of a criminal offence. In 2002–03 the police reported 247 convictions. These ranged from minor cases such as motoring offences, which may not have led to action by the NMC, to serious crimes including the assault of patients and those that took place outside the workplace, such as rape and murder.[10]

Tables 6.1a and 6.1b show a breakdown of the complaints received by the NMC from 1999–2000 to 2001–02 (statistics for 2002–03 were not available at the time of writing); Table 6.2 provides figures of complaints received by the NMC by country from 2000–01 to 2002–03.

Table 6.1a Complaints received by the Nursing and Midwifery Council by source, 1999–2000 to 2001–02

	1999–2000	2000–01	2001–02
Employers	539	592	591
Public	249	276	415
Police	250	230	217
Miscellaneous	104	142	81
Total	1,142	1,240	1,304

Source: UK Central Council for Nursing, Midwifery and Health Visiting, *Professional Conduct Annual Report*, 2000–01, and Nursing and Midwifery Council[11]

Table 6.1b *Percentage complaints received by the Nursing and Midwifery Council by source, 1999–2000 to 2001–02*

	1999–2000	2000–01	2001–02
Employers	47	48	45
Public	22	22	32
Police	22	18.5	17
Miscellaneous	9	11.5	6

Source: UK Central Council for Nursing, Midwifery and Health Visiting, *Professional Conduct Annual Report*, 2000–01, and Nursing and Midwifery Council[11]

Table 6.2 *Complaints received by the Nursing and Midwifery Council by country, 2000–01 and 2002–03*

	England	Scotland	Wales	NI	Non-UK	Total
2000–01						
Received	1,015	81	81	49	14	1,240
As proportion of all complaints (%)	82	6.5	6.5	4	1	
As proportion of practitioners resident in country (%)	76	5	10	3	4	
2001–02						
Received	1,154	69	53	20	8	1,304
As proportion of all complaints (%)	79	10	3	3	5	
As proportion of practitioners resident in country (%)	88	5	4	2	1	
2002–03						
Received	1,109	97	69	14	12	1,301
As proportion of all complaints (%)	88.5	5.3	4.1	1.5	0.6	
As proportion of practitioners resident in country (%)	79.1	10.1	2.9	2.6	5.3	

Source: UK Central Council for Nursing, Midwifery and Health Visiting, *Professional Conduct Annual Report*, 2000–01, and Nursing and Midwifery Council[12]

The NMC's statutory committees

There are three practice committees – the newly named Investigating Committee (IC) and Conduct and Competence Committee (CCC), which succeeded the previous Preliminary Proceedings Committee and Professional Conduct Committee, and a re-modelled Health Committee – all of which came into effect in August 2004. A re-styled Midwifery Committee became operational in April 2002.

The practice committees consider allegations that practitioners on the NMC's register are unfit to practise including those attributed to physical or mental impairment. They also look at allegations that a statutory body regulating some other health or social care profession in the United Kingdom or elsewhere has determined that a practitioner is not fit to practise. Similarly, the practice committees deal with allegations involving matters said to have occurred outside the United Kingdom at a time when the individuals concerned were not registered practitioners.[13]

Key rules for practice committee panels
Practice committee panels considering an allegation or taking any other measures about fitness to practise, ethics or similar matters under the Order must comprise at least three members. These are selected with due regard to the previous, existing or proposed professional field of expertise of the practitioner in question and to the nature of the issues involved in the case.[14]

There are a number of provisos to be observed in the selection of members for these panels:

• At least one member of each panel must be listed in that part of the register of practitioners where the professional whose case is under consideration is or was registered, or has applied for registration.
• Panels must contain at least one lay member and, in cases where the health of a professional is in question, have a minimum of one registered medical practitioner.
• The person presiding over a panel can, but need not, be a member of the Council, while others on the panel are registrant and lay members, none of whom must be a Council member. However, the registrant members can exceed their lay counterparts, but by no more than one.
• No person who has been involved with the subject of a case can sit on the panel that is hearing it.[15]

Decisions by practice committee panels must be carried through by a majority vote of the members present. In the event of a tie, the chairman will have an additional casting vote. Where these concern decisions about fitness to practise, ethics or other similar matters (described in part V of the Order) the casting vote is made in favour of the practitioner who has been scrutinized. In other cases practice committees can exercise their powers even when there is a vacancy among their members. With the same exceptions, proceedings of practice committees are not invalidated by any flaw concerning the appointment of a member. Also, individuals who are members of the Council or a practice committee by virtue of their membership of any profession cannot take part in the proceedings of that committee in any period during which they are the subject of an investigation, proceedings or a decision against them about their fitness to practise.[16]

The Investigating Committee
When the NMC receives a complaint against one of its registered practitioners it is considered by the Investigating Committee, which decides if there is a case to answer, and whether there is enough supporting evidence. Some complaints are closed and go no further, but if an allegation is serious the IC examines the strength of the evidence to support the case. The criminal standard of proof is applied in such an investigation and, therefore, it is higher than that needed in employers' disciplinary hearings.[17]

In addition to considering allegations about lack of competence and unfitness to practise by the NMC's registrants the IC also deals with cases involving a conviction or caution for a criminal offence committed in the United Kingdom. Convictions for offences committed elsewhere that would constitute a crime in England and Wales, together with those by courts martial, are similarly treated. In addition the IC considers cases referred to it about fraudulent or incorrect entries in the register.

It refers allegations about misconduct to the Conduct and Competence Committee, and those involving unfitness to practise on grounds of ill health to the Health Committee.[18]

The Investigating Committee has four Council members. When it meets as a panel it comprises one or two of these Council members and three or four other panellists who are normally a combination of registered practitioners and lay appointees. In these respects and in the aforesaid ways, the IC resembles the Preliminary Proceedings Committee which it succeeded.[19]

In 1999–2000, 2000–01, 2001–02 and 2002–03 the PPC looked at 1,213, 1,627, 1,614 and 1,585 cases, respectively, and Table 6.3 shows how these were concluded.

Table 6.3 Outcome of cases considered by the PPC, 1999–2000 to 2002–03

	1999–2000	2000–01	2001–02	2002–03
Closed[a]	642	869	805	819
Further investigation required	295	399	352	418
Referred to professional screeners	82	105	66	66
Cautioned	30	33	75	42
Referred to the Professional Conduct Committee	164	221	316	240
Total	1,213	1,627	1,614	1,585

Source: UK Central Council for Nursing, Midwifery and Health Visiting, *Professional Conduct Annual Report*, 2000–01, and Nursing and Midwifery Council[20]
[a] No further action taken by the PPC

Some of the figures in Table 6.3 refer to cases that were considered twice. The large rise in cases handled by the previous PCC during 2000–01 (34 per cent), 2001–02 (33 per cent) and 2002–03 (30.7 per cent) compared with those dealt with by them the previous year is considered by the NMC to be a reflection of its success in increasing the number of PPC meetings to deal with the greater influx of complaints received and referred.

The Conduct and Competence Committee

The Conduct and Competence Committee (CCC) is broadly similar to the Professional Conduct Committee that it replaced and has a range of responsibilities. After consultation with the other practice committees, its duty is to advise the Council about the standards of conduct, performance and ethics expected of registered practitioners. This includes making recommendations about what is required in terms of good character and health from registered professionals, and how to protect the public from those whose fitness to practise is impaired.[21]

The CCC also considers complaints referred by the Council, Investigating Committee or Health Committee. It examines allegations about misconduct and, in addition, considers all applications for the restoration of practitioners' names to the register under the chairmanship of the president of the Council. In the latter case two references must be supplied, one from a current employer who is aware of the reason for removal of the practitioner from the register. Other questions must be addressed and answered by applicants to the satisfaction of the CCC before restoration to the register is approved.[22]

The CCC comprises 13 Council members including seven practitioners and six lay persons (with the president being one of the practitioner members), compared with seven Council members and one registered practitioner drawn from outside in the previous PCC. CCC hearing panels, usually involving three people, consist of committee members and others drawn from a reservoir of registered practitioners and lay individuals, which the NMC has established for the purpose. At least one of them is a member of the Council, another is a lay appointeee (either drawn from the Council or from outside) and one a registered practitioner with the relevant specialization.[23]

Conduct and Competence Committee hearings are held in public with the press normally present, as was the case under the previous UKCC, and others acting as observers can also attend. Exceptionally the hearings may be wholly or partially conducted in private, for instance to protect the identity of the victim in a child abuse case. The CCC is obliged to sit in the country where a case has originated.[24]

The PCC sat on 370 days in 2002–03 (compared with 297 days in 2001–02) and considered 326 cases of alleged misconduct (291 cases in 2001–02) and 19 applications for restoration to the register (19 in 2001–02). The leading categories of offence in 2002–03 concerned clinical practice (almost 30 per cent of all charges) and the physical or verbal abuse of patients (26 per cent of all charges).[25]

Physical or verbal abuse of patients has consistently been at the forefront in cases considered by the NMC. In 1998–99 and 1999–2000 this offence accounted for 30 per cent and 31 per cent, respectively, of all allegations received. At 6 per cent, poor record-keeping had been the third largest category of offence in 1999–2000. Decisions by the Professional Conduct Committee for the four years up to 2002–03 are shown in Table 6.4.

Table 6.4 Decisions by the Professional Conduct Committee, 1999–2000 to 2002–03

	1999–2000	2000–01	2001–02	2002–03
Practioner removed from register	96	104	113	154
Practioner cautioned	27	39	61	66
Misconduct proven but no further action	2	1	10	6
Facts or misconduct not proven	8	9	8	15

Source: UK Central Council for Nursing, Midwifery and Health Visiting, *Professional Conduct Annual Report*, 2000–01, and Nursing and Midwifery Council[26]

During 2002–03 some 8 per cent of the charges arose from criminal convictions.[27] A registrant can be called to account by the NMC for convictions related to offences outside work where these could damage public confidence in the professions. Failing to declare a criminal conviction when applying for employment is regarded as a serious offence and can lead to removal from the register.[28]

In 2002–03 the PCC looked at 19 applications for restoration to the register and accepted one. By comparison, five were successful from a total of 19 received the year before.[29] Practitioners who have been taken off the register can apply to have their names restored, although not during the first five years after their removal under the new rules.[30] (In the previous system it was recommended that a practitioner should not be restored to the register within one year of being removed.) It continues to be

NMC policy that practitioners who have been removed from the register after a serious criminal conviction should not be re-admitted, if doing so is likely to harm public trust in the profession the NMC regulates.[31]

The Health Committee
The Health Committee (HC) considers allegations of unfitness to practise by nurses or midwives on grounds of ill health and, like the Conduct and Competence Committee, can suspend a practitioner's registration. It also has similar powers to the Conduct and Competence Committee over the reinstatement of entries to the register and in the examination of cases that have been referred to it by the Council, Investigating Committee or Conduct and Competence Committee. The HC meets in private owing to the confidential nature of the medical evidence involved. It comprises three Council members, and when convened as a panel consists of one Council member, one lay person and one registered practitioner. The panel is supported by a legal assessor, and an examining medical practitioner is also in attendance. In its role and composition the new version of the Health Committee and its panels resembles the previous model.[32]

Table 6.5 shows the chief causes of cases referred to the Health Committee about allegations of unfitness to practise by nurses, midwives and health visitors from 1999–2000 to 2001–02. The figures for 2002–03 were not available at the time of writing.

Table 6.5 Referrals to the Health Committee on grounds of ill health, 1999–2000 to 2001–02

	1999–2000	2000–01	2001–02
Alcohol dependence	56	58	35
Mental illness	56	75	59
Drug dependence	27	26	24
Physical illness	7	5	5
Total	146	164	123

Source: UK Central Council for Nursing, Midwifery and Health Visiting, *Professional Conduct Annual Report*, 2000–01, and Nursing and Midwifery Council[33]

A practitioner can be referred to the Health Committee in one of two ways: directly by an employer (there were 74 referrals in this category in 2001–02); or, for professional conduct cases, by the CCC or IC if the practitioner may be unfit to practise (there were 105 referrals in this category in 2001–02). (The position was the same before August 2004, except that the practice committees concerned were the PCC and PPC.) In 2002–03 the number of referrals in each case was 34 and 68 respectively.[34]

Practitioners who are suspected by screeners to have a health problem are invited to be examined by up to two of the NMC's medical examiners. The results of this examination determine whether a referral to the Health Committee will follow.[35] Table 6.6 shows the results of referral in this category from 1999–2000 to 2002–03. In 2002–03 the Health Committee considered 204 cases, and 160 in 2001–02. Table 6.7 shows the conclusions it arrived at when considering these cases from 1999–2000 to 2002–03.

Table 6.6 Results of referrals to the Nursing and Midwifery Council for examination on grounds of ill health, 1999–2000 to 2002–03

	1999–2000	2000–01	2001–02	2002–03
Referral to Health Committee	122	122	121	112
Case closed	11	11	16	8
Outstanding cases	242	242	101	85
Total	375	375	238	205

Source: UK Central Council for Nursing, Midwifery and Health Visiting, *Professional Conduct Annual Report*, 2000–01, and Nursing and Midwifery Council [36]

Table 6.7 Conclusions drawn by the Health Committee when considering allegations of ill health of practioners, 1999–2000 to 2002–03

	1999–2000	2000–01	2001–02	2002–03[a]
Fitness not impaired – case closed	31	47	49	77
Fitness impaired – suspended	51	55	46	37
Fitness impaired – removed	7	0	5	13
Judgement postponed	28	30	41	24
Adjourned for further medical reports	2	13	19	43

Source: UK Central Council for Nursing, Midwifery and Health Visiting, *Professional Conduct Annual Report*, 2000–01, and Nursing and Midwifery Council [37]
[a] The Health Committee also considered nine applications to terminate suspension and accepted eight in 2002–03

Through the Health Committee and Investigating Committee the NMC has powers to suspend registration while an investigation is in progress if there is deemed to be a serious risk to the public in allowing an individual to practise or if such a step is considered to be in a practitioner's own interests. This includes cases where the person concerned is accused of stealing drugs for personal use. Practitioners who are under consideration for interim suspension have a right to be present and represented at hearings. All suspensions are reviewed after the first six months and every three months thereafter up to a maximum of 18 months.[38]

The Midwifery Committee
The Midwifery Committee has 12 members (compared with 20 on the model it replaced), including seven Council and five lay members with one of the former being a lay person.[39] Thus the professional and lay proportions on the Committee are equal. The chairman of the Midwifery Committee is a member of the Council and the majority of its members are practising midwives.[40] Selection of non-Council members by the Council must be carried out in line with guidance issued by the Commissioner for Public Appointments.[41] No individuals who are (professional) members of the Council or Midwifery Committee can take part in any proceedings of the latter in any period during which they are the subject of investigation, proceedings or a resolution against them about their fitness to practise.[42] The powers of the Midwifery Committee can be exercised even when there is a vacancy among its members, and none of its proceedings are nullified by any shortcomings in the appointment of a member.[43]

The role of the Midwifery Committee is to advise the Council on all affairs relating to midwifery, including proposals to establish rules under provisions in the Nursing and Midwifery Order 2001. Some of these rules involve regulating the practice of midwifery to determine the circumstances in which midwives could be suspended from practice and the procedure to carry out this action.[44]

How the Council deals with allegations about the unfitness to practise of registered practitioners

When the NMC refers a complaint to the Investigating Committee this Committee must promptly notify the practitioner concerned about the allegations and ask for a written response within a prescribed time. Once this has been received, the individual making the allegation may be asked to deal with any points the Investigating Committee has raised about the practitioner's account. The Committee will also take other steps to obtain as much information as possible on the matter and then decide if there is a case to be answered. Where a complaint concerns an alleged fraudulent or incorrect entry in the NMC's register, the Investigating Committee determines whether this has occurred.[45]

The complainant and the practitioner concerned are notified in writing about the decision that has been reached and the reasons why it was made. If the Investigating Committtee has concluded that there is a case to answer then, depending on the circumstances, it passes the case on to the Health Committee or the Conduct and Competence Committee for determination. In other instances the Investigating Committee will adopt the role of mediator or refer the matter for mediation by screeners.[46]

Options once a case has been decided
When either the Health Committee or the Conduct and Competence Committtee has decided that a case is not properly justified it makes a statement to that effect and gives the reasons for the conclusions that have been reached where it is asked to do so by the person who made the allegation and, in other cases, with their consent. The latter is notified of the right to appeal.[47]

On the other hand, the committee concerned can take any one of a number of steps where it has determinded that a case is legitimate.[48] It may:
- decide to take no further action
- refer the case to mediation or mediate itself
- direct the registrar to strike the practitioner involved off the register (a striking-off order) or to suspend the practitioner's registration for a specified period of no more than one year (a suspension order)
- issue an order imposing conditions that must be complied with by the practitioner concerned for a stipulated period, but not exceeding three years (a conditions of practice order)
- issue a caution together with an order directing the registrar to annotate the register accordingly; in this event, the entry remains for a set period of between one and five years duration (a caution order).

Practitioners can appeal to the appropriate court against any of these forms of disciplinary action, but must do so within 28 days of the date on which notice of the instruction was served.[49]

Hearings and preliminary meetings of practice committees at which practitioners concerned are entitled to be present are held in the UK country where these persons are registered or, if not registered and residing in the UK, in the country in which they live. Otherwise, these sessions take place in England. While registration is suspended, practitioners are treated as no longer being registered, even if they are still included in the NMC's register.[50]

Practioners who are struck off the register

Practitioners who have been struck off the register by one of the practice committees can apply for reinstatement subject to certain conditions being met. Any application for restoration to the register is referred by the registrar to the practice committee that made the striking-off order. Alternatively, where any previous applications have been made about the same striking-off directive, a submission to be reinstated is forwarded to the committee that last gave a decision on the matter.[51]

Before reaching a decision on applications, the committee involved asks applicants to present themselves and argue their case in line with rules and conditions laid down by the Council. The committee does not allow applicants to be restored to the register unless they satisfy certain requirements and, where striking-off orders have been issued, are also deemed fit and proper people to practise their profession. In cases where it permits reinstatement, the committee instructs the registrar to restore the person concerned to the register subject to any conditions imposed by the Council being met, and on payment of the registration fee. The committee might also make a 'conditions of practice order' with which the applicant must comply.[52]

If a second or further submission for restoration to the register made by individuals who have been struck off is unsuccessful, the committee that rejected the application can issue instructions to suspend their right to reapply indefinitely. However, the person who has received such an instruction can apply to the registrar for the order to be reviewed after three years. If unsuccessful, he or she can make a further application for review once a further another three years has elapsed. All such applications are referred to the committee that suspended the right of the applicant to reapply in the first place. In instances where cases are refused or made subject to applicants meeting conditions imposed by the Council, applicants can appeal to the appropriate court within 28 days of either decision being taken.[53]

Allegations of lack of competence

For the first time the NMC has a specific responsibility to handle allegations of practitioners' 'lack of competence'. There are distinctive sanctions if lack of competence is proven. Hitherto, the regulatory body considered cases of persistent incompetence within its misconduct processes. Under the new rules and procedures, the Investigating Committee initially considers lack of competence allegations. It may need to obtain specialist advice from expert witnesses, or it might appoint registrant assessors to advise on the issues raised in particular cases. Cases can be sent for investigation and may be forwarded for a hearing of the Conduct and Competence Committee if there is sufficient evidence to determine proof.[54]

The Council has established a clear definition for lack of competence and set out distinct criteria that have to be met before a case can be considered, but even if these criteria are not met the Investigating Committee may look at elements of an allegation that suggest misconduct has occurred: for example, a practitioner's refusal to undergo a programme of training and supervision. Equally, there may be a health issue that merits consideration by the Health Committee.[55]

If a lack of competence is proven at a hearing of the Conduct and Competence Committee, the panel can impose either a suspension order or a conditions of practice order. Under Article 29(6) of the Nursing and Midwifery Order 2001, a striking-off order cannot be made for lack of competence unless the person concerned has been continuously suspended or subject to a conditions of practice order for not less than two years. In either case, the matter must be reviewed three months before the expiry date.[56]

Legal assessors, medical assessors and registrant assessors
The role of legal assessors is similar to that in the previous body. They give advice and assistance to the practice committees, the registrar and to the Council (who appoints them) on questions of law arising from matters under consideration by any of them. This guidance can concern the registration or renewal of registration of practitioners, their readmission to the register and any appeals about these issues. It can also refer to all questions involving fitness to practise, ethics and other affairs.[57]

To qualify as a legal assessor a person must have held a general legal qualification for 10 years (section 71 of the Courts and Legal Services Act 1990). Alternatively, this appointee is required to be an advocate or solicitor in Scotland or a member of the Bar of Northern Ireland – in either case a legal professional with at least 10 years' experience. But a legal assessor cannot be a member of the Council or of a practice committee, nor a visitor, medical or registrant assessor or an employee of the Council.[58]

The Council appoints registered practitioners to act as medical assessors for the purpose of advising them, screeners, the practice committees and the registrar on questions within their professional scope arising out of issues being considered by any of these groups. These assessors may also be asked to discharge other functions under rules drawn up by the Council. A medical assessor cannot also be a member of the Council or of a practice committee, nor a visitor, legal or registrant assessor or an employee of the Council.[59]

Similarly appointed as medical assessors, registrant assessors advise the Council, screeners, its committees and the registrar on questions of professional practice emerging from issues being examined by them. The Council may require them to carry out additional duties. A member of the Council or of a practice committee is barred from being a registrant assessor, as is a visitor, legal or medical assessor or anyone who is employed by the Council.[60]

Key changes brought about by the legislation
Under the new regime all registered practitioners who are the subject of a complaint have to be notified from the outset when this happens. For the first time, the NMC deals with questions about lack of competence, and sanctions include orders for suspension and conditions of practice. Practitioners who have been removed from the register cannot apply for restoration until five years have elapsed; the Nursing and Midwifery Order 2001 limits a person's right to apply for restoration and the NMC may impose conditions on practice for those who are restored to the register.

These are some of the principal changes highlighted by the NMC that the new system has brought about.[61]

Nevertheless, probably just as significant are the adjustments that have been made to the composition of the Nursing and Midwifery Council. In step with one of the key changes called for in *The NHS Plan*, which was carried through by the Order, the Council has far fewer members (35, compared with 60 previously). Also, from the perspective of voting in Council meetings, the lay proportion of members is significantly greater than it was previously. Only the 11 lay members (47.8 per cent) and 12 registrant members (52.2 per cent) of the Council are permitted to vote. (The remaining 12 alternate members are also registered practitioners but, as mentioned earlier, they can attend and vote only when corresponding registrant members are unable to do so. In all other respects they discharge the duties of the other members, including attendance at Council meetings.) These voting proportions compare with 40 registered practitioners (66.7 per cent) and 20 other members (33.3 per cent), which comprised lay appointees as well as medical and nursing practitioners, in the previous Council.

Closing remarks

With the implementation of reforms covered in this chapter and other changes under the legislation not mentioned here, and with the passage of time, the record of the regulatory body in its new form may well turn out to be more effective and better regarded by the public than its predecessor as a mechanism for responding to allegations against its members. Certainly the Council is a more equitable arrangement than hitherto and, judging by some of the statistics provided earlier, the NMC appears to have made improvements in the handling of complaints that it is receiving.

All matters considered, though, it has to be said that the reforms under the Order are probably not sufficiently fundamental in scope to secure unconditional approbation from the public at large. Such approval is much more likely to be found for a completely independent regulatory and disciplinary body for nursing professionals – the brand of concept consumer and similar organizations in the UK have supported in recent years. The legislation could, for example, have called for a detached system covering health care and the professions, on the lines of the 'one-door' concept operated by the Financial Services Authority pointed to by the National Consumer Council in 1999, and gained such acceptance. As will be seen in Chapter 13, this kind of approach and other independent models directed specifically at medical professionals have been functioning with good effect for years in the Nordic countries.

But to have hoped that such a model would follow the UK's previous self-regulated form for nurses will have been over optimistic. Indeed, as in the case of the General Medical Council, it is unlikely that independent regulation of the nursing profession was seriously on the agenda leading up to the government's initiatives that induced only adjustments to the regulatory body as it stood. Thus, like the GMC we continue to have a body for nurses and midwives that remains generally self-regulating, albeit invested with greater statutory powers and subject to stronger rules and procedures. The NMC also continues to be financed by the practitioners over whom it has jurisdiction to authorize, regulate and investigate.

Chapter 5 describes how the government had sown the seeds for continued medical self-regulation in – among other initiatives – a consultation paper aimed primarily at doctors called *Supporting Doctors, Protecting Patients* issued in 1999. The document set out a list of commendable requirements headed 'Modern principles of professional self-regulation in the health field'. It claimed that the 'primary purpose of professional self-regulation is to protect the public'.

These are powerful words, but many of the obligations that are listed are more likely to be met with an independent system than through self-regulation. And members of the public are more likely to feel protected by an independent system than one of self-regulation, about which they may be cynical. So what would have been wrong with introducing a neutral regulatory body for nurses and associated practitioners to replace the previous model? Nothing, except that it would have upset many people in the profession and disturbed the status quo. It would also have set a precedent that may have affected the other areas in health care where self-regulation abounds, and perhaps elsewhere too. The idea of independent regulation remains anathema in certain quarters – some will say because its introduction would mean the loss of long-held rights and the advantages they give.

Although the more equitable arrangement that the Nursing and Midwifery Council provides is clearly superior to that of its predecessor, those who are in control will have to work hard to gain the public's trust and belief in the integrity of the new body. The statement by the government already referred to in Chapter 5, that 'professional self-regulation itself must operate to a high standard and maintain public trust and confidence', does not explain how the public's faith in the system can be maintained when it could be argued that many members of the public have little faith in the system to maintain. Moreover, all the applied checks and balances – however commendable – will probably not be enough to significantly transform this implied poor perception by the public. The fact is that anything short of real independence in medical regulation is unlikely to find universal acceptability outside the profession. We should not have to ask some of our Continental partners for confirmation.

CHAPTER 7

No all-inclusive patients' rights legislation in the United Kingdom

Instead guidance partially based on law is on offer

The United Kingdom has no specific patients' rights enactment. No single set of sweeping statutory provisions is in force covering the relevant interconnection between the public and NHS practitioners. Instead, the interests of patients and the position of those who attend to their clinical needs are provided for, collectively, via legislation, case law, set ethical criteria and health service policy rules. The accumulated entitlements and responsibilities, thus assembled, are laid out in official guidance for reference by those to whom the information applies.

In England the public and the health service can consult a number of individual printed guides and electronically replicated data (on the internet) giving information and advice for patients and their representatives about what they 'have a right to expect' in matters involving consent (or otherwise) to medical intervention. There is also an explanation about where patients stand when it comes to gaining access to health records and the extent of patients' entitlements relating to the use of personal details and tissue samples that have been taken.

Similarly, the separate official guidance directed to NHS establishments and clinicians clarifies their respective roles and responsibilities in the same issues involving patients. It contains advice on the ethical and legal positions affecting questions about patient consent, confidentiality and associated matters. Additionally, health care practitioners are provided with codes of practice guidelines that have been laid down by their regulatory bodies.

Like established policy in some other European societies, patients in the UK have been given direct and indirect support of a different kind, via legislation, in recent years. This back-up is delivered by special advice, liaison, safety and associated agencies, which operate either independently or as part of the NHS. Although these bodies (certain of which relate primarily to patients' complaints, while others refer to the protection of their health and the provision of medical care) apply largely to England, their remit in some cases extends to the nation as a whole.

What does all this mean for patients' rights in the United Kingdom? Are the rules and regulations sufficiently well founded and robust to ensure that the entitlements set out can be respected and met in practice? Or is there a case for enshrining a full array of patients' rights in law to avoid any misapprehension by those it will concern? A closer look at the present British way of doing things may provide some answers.

The NHS code of practice about confidentiality

In autumn 2003 the Department of Health published *Confidentiality: NHS Code of Practice*, a guide to required practice on matters of confidentiality relating to patients and consent to use personal information, aimed at those who work in or are contracted to NHS organizations. This 'evolving document' is considered by its authors to be a vital component of 'emerging information governance' measures for the NHS. Although primarily aimed at NHS personnel, it is regarded by the Department as being relevant to anyone working in or associated with health care, including those in the private and voluntary sectors.[1]

There was public consultation on what the new code of practice should be between October 2002 and January 2003. Those involved in the consultation process included the British Medical Association (BMA), General Medical Council (GMC), Information Commissioner (IC) and a variety of professional and private representatives. The exercise formed part of a broader strategy on guidance about patient confidentiality issues jointly conducted by the Department of Health and the NHS Information Authority (NHSIA).[2]

The code of practice declares that information about patients is 'generally held under legal and ethical obligations of confidentiality'. It points out that, except for powerful legal or public interest considerations, personal details given in confidence should not be used or divulged in a way that might identify patients without their consent. Broadly, the document:

- describes the notion of confidentiality and what confidentiality should be in practice when it involves health care
- gives an account of the main legal requirements
- recommends a common approach for sharing or disclosing information within the NHS
- provides examples in which information given can be disclosed.[3]

What is confidential patient data?
Sensitive information about the health care and other matters that patients entrust to the NHS or allow it to assemble is confidential. Thus health service professionals must not use or disclose any data that can identify patients for purposes other than those involving their therapy without the express consent of the patients concerned. The only exception is when such disclosure can be justified on the grounds of significant public interest or legal grounds, but anonymous information is not confidential and can be used with relatively few restrictions.[4]

Disclosure or use of confidential information about patients
It is most important that patients are advised about the extent of information that it is necessary to disclose about them – and to whom – so that they are provided with a high level of health care. This is especially relevant when the recipients of the data are not NHS organizations. Similarly, it must not be assumed that patients are content to have personal details about them used in ways that do not affect their health care, however worthy they may be. Medical research, protection of public health and health service management are areas that fall into this category.[5]

Disclosure or use of confidential information that identifies patients
In general, patients have a right to object to the disclosure or use of confidential data that will identify them, and need to be made aware of this entitlement. Should they then prohibit information being divulged to other health care practitioners, the result may occasionally be that limited therapy is available or, in very rare instances, it might even not be possible to propose certain treatment options. Patients must be told if their decisions about the disclosure of identifiable information will have an effect on the provision of therapy for them.[6]

In cases where patients have been advised about the disclosure and use of confidential data that is linked with their health care, the choices that are on offer and the implications of their choosing to place restrictions on how the information is handled, explicit consent is not normally needed from them for the way in which their personal details are used in order to provide the appropriate therapy. Nevertheless, practitioners should still check with patients that they understand what might happen, and that they are satisfied. Particular attention should be paid to this where children are involved.[7]

However, where the purpose of disclosing confidential data is not directly connected with patients' therapy, it is wrong to assume that patients would have given consent to the details being used or passed on. Consent is still required from patients or else measures that are not reliant on identifiable information will need to be taken. Nevertheless, there are instances where consent cannot be obtained, but the public good resulting from using or disclosing information that identifies patients outweighs their privacy. In these cases section 60 of the Health and Social Care Act 2001 will take effect. This legislation provides interim powers for information that identifies patients to be used without their consent when it is to aid a variety of important work such as clinical research and audit.[8]

Obligations for NHS personnel
In addition to fulfilling the terms of their employment or other engagement arrangements, individuals working in the health service should comply with the standards set out in the document *Confidentiality: NHS Code of Practice.* Where appropriate organizational procedures are not already in place to meet these requirements, the establishments concerned should be making all reasonable endeavours to do so.[9]

Provision of a confidential service for patients by those attending to them
The document puts forward a 'confidentiality model' describing the requirements that must be satisfied so that patients will have a confidential service. Those who hold records about patients must advise them of any intended use of this data, allow them to decide whether or not to give consent and protect their (identifiable) details from unjustified disclosure. The code of practice guidance sets out four key obligations with these ends in mind:

• Protect information about patients.
• Make certain that patients are aware of how information about them is used.
• Let patients decide whether details about them can be disclosed or used in a particular way.
• Continually look to improve the way each of these duties is observed.[10]

Protecting information held on patients
To begin with, procedures should be in place so that all NHS employees, contractors and others associated with them are well informed about their responsibilities on issues about confidentiality that affect the health records and interests of patients. Details about patients should be recorded accurately and consistently, and kept private. The data must also be held in a secure place, and any disclosure or use of it must be carried out with proper care.[11]

Advising patients on what can happen to information they give
Patients should be aware that the personal details they give those involved with the NHS may be recorded, shared (to provide them with appropriate care) and used for clinical audit purposes or other work to monitor the standard of therapy being provided. Health care personnel must therefore check, where possible, that patients have read and understood printed information on these matters. They also have an obligation to check that patients realize the different ways in which information about them may be processed. They must answer patients' questions (or find others who can do so), respect their rights and help them to exercise their entitlement to examine their health records.[12]

Giving patients a voice in the use of information about them
When treating patients and handling information about them those involved in their health care should take into account patients' divergent needs and values. They must obtain the consent of patients before using their personal details in ways that are not directly related to their care and, except in special circumstances, respect their decision to restrict the transmission or other use of this personal data. Moreover, they must ensure that patients recognize the implications of either consenting to or restricting the disclosure of information about them.[13]

Taking steps to improve practice in dealing with patient confidentiality
With best practice as the goal, health care personnel must familiarize themselves with all the issues involving patient confidentiality. They should obtain training or other support where their awareness is deficient and report breaches of confidence, or any risk of such inappropriate conduct.[14]

The use and discosure of confidential information about patients
When discussing patient confidentiality, *Confidentiality: NHS Code of Practice* affirms that 'the law and ethics in this area are largely in step', but that 'the law provides a minimum standard that does not always reflect the appropriate ethical standards that the government and the professional regulatory bodies require'. The code points out that the government and GMC agree that, while there are 'no clear legal obligations of confidentiality' applying to the deceased, there is an 'ethical basis' for requiring that the duties about patient confidentiality they have outlined must continue to be observed.[15]

The code reports that there are a number of statutory provisions limiting or prohibiting the use and disclosure of information in certain instances, and others that require the opposite. Nevertheless, it draws particular attention to four principal forms of law that restrict the use or disclosure of confidential personal health care data:

- the Data Protection Act 1998
- the Human Rights Act 1998
- the common law of confidentiality – described as not being 'codified in an Act of Parliament but built up from case law where practice has been established by individual judgements'
- administrative law – briefly outlined as that governing the actions of a public authority and, according to well-established rules, giving it 'the power to carry out what it intends to do'.[16]

The code comments that 'current understanding is that compliance with the Data Protection Act and the common law of confidentiality should satisfy' requirements in the Human Rights Act.[17] Some of the provisions of the two pieces of legislation that affect patient confidentiality are discussed later in the chapter.

Crucial questions for health care personnel about decisions on patient confidentiality

The code of practice for the NHS sets out a list of key questions and answers with a view to ensuring that the requirements of law, ethics and policy are satisfactorily addressed when decisions are to be made on the use or disclosure of confidential information about patients.[18]

- *If the purpose of disclosing confidential data is not health care or some other medical objective, what is the basis in administrative law for doing so?* Public bodies should carry out only those functions for which they have been established. While disclosure of information for medical purposes is permitted, it may not be divulged to other parties for a different application.
- *Is disclosure a statutory obligation or required by order of a court?* Any disclosure provided for by a statutory obligation or a court order must be complied with. However, disclosure should be limited to the legal requirement and there may be scope to ask a court to modify an order.
- *Is the disclosure needed to aid the provision of health care or to assure its quality?* Patients recognize that some of their personal information must be shared so as to provide them with care and therapy. Clinical audit carried out locally within health care bodies is also fundamental if the standard of care is to be maintained and enhanced. (Other types of audit that will be carried out across organizations or nationally require explicit consent.) Effort must be made to provide patients with information about prospective disclosure, check that it is understood, resolve any concerns and respect their objections. Where these steps have been taken, it is not necessary to obtain explicit consent each time information is to be shared.
- *If not associated with a patient's health care, is the disclosure to assist a wider medical objective?* While the use of information for purposes such as preventive medicine, medical research, health service management and other applications may not be understood by most patients, these are important and legitimate interests for health service bodies and their staff. Nevertheless, explicit consent must be obtained from patients to disclose their personal information for these purposes if it is in a form that will identify them. The exception is when disclosure is singularly warranted in the public interest, or there is interim provision for it under the Health and Social Care Act 2001.

- *Is the use of identifiable confidential information justified for its purpose?* Where the purpose is not connected with health care provision or to meet a legal requirement, disclosure should be checked for correctness and necessity. The object in taking this action is to anonymize disclosed information where it is feasible and reduce the extent of identifiable details that are to be revealed.
- *Has proper action been taken to advise patients about proposed disclosures?* There is a clear obligation to tell patients, in general terms, about who it is proposed will see their personal information. Where this is also to obtain consent, more specifics may be necessary and patients need to be made aware of their rights and how to exercise these entitlements.
- *Is a patient's explicit consent required for a disclosure to be lawful?* Except in certain circumstances, explicit consent is needed before identifiable information about a patient can be disclosed. The exceptions are when disclosure is for the purposes of health care, can be sufficiently justified in the public interest to warrant breach of confidence or is provided for under the Health and Social Care Act 2001.

Additional UK government guidance and recommendations about the positions of patients and those involved in their health care[19]
Extra and replicated guidance and recommendations on how issues arising between patients and health care providers should be addressed are also available. One example is the government document *Protecting and Using Confidential Patient Information – a Strategy for the NHS*. The guidance sets out some of the finer points about consent and the processing of confidential data, emphasizes the changes that are required to improve procedures and explains how these adjustments should be implemented.

It discusses the legal, ethical and policy issues involved and refers in particular to the 1997 Caldicott Committee study and recommendations about consent from patients and the use of their confidential information. The document goes further to touch on the extent to which this committee's proposals have been put into practice and where its recommendations can be built upon.

The legal rights of patients about their health records
Patients in the UK have long had some right of access to their medical records – as, indeed, have certain individuals connected with them, and provisions in the Data Protection Act 1998 broaden and strengthen these previous entitlements. Under Part II, 'Rights of data subjects and others', the 'right of access to personal data' and supplementary provisions, 'right to prevent processing likely to cause damage or distress', 'compensation for failure to comply with certain requirements' and 'rectification, blocking, erasure and destruction' are among a range of provisions that affect the holding of patients' health records.[20]

The Department of Health's Appendix A: the Data Protection Act 1998 draws attention to other aspects of these rights under the legislation, examples of which follow:

- Every 'living person' has a right to apply for access to their health records.
- This right applies to health records held in the public and private health sectors, and to such data kept by health professionals in private practice.

- It also applies to information that organizations hold on the physical or mental condition of their employees.

- Individuals applying for access to their health records are not required to give a reason for doing so and also have a right to be given a copy of this data.[21] In a similar way the Human Rights Act 1998, effective since October 2000, has provisions concerned with information held about the health of patients. Article 8 confers the right to respect for private and family life and provides for the protection of an individual's privacy and the confidentiality of their medical records.

Application by patients to examine their health records and what follows[22]
This process is described in Appendix B: Health Record Access Route of the Department of Health information referred to above. Should they wish to examine their health records patients must lodge a written request, including subsequently asking for copies to be supplied. They must apply to the relevant 'data controller' – an individual who is not a health care professional, general practitioner, practice manager or hospital records manager – and meet the request within 40 days. Where it is not possible to meet this deadline the applicant must be advised accordingly.

Before allowing a patient access to their medical records a data controller is obliged to seek advice from the health care practitioner responsible for the patient's clinical care. Only then can an applicant's request be granted. Information can be witheld if releasing it may cause serious harm to the physical or mental health or condition of the patient or another individual.

Before releasing a patient's medical records to the person it concerns, the data controller will check to see whether these files contain information that is recorded, on the one hand, as being stated by the patient about a third person or by a third person about the patient. In either event, the controller will establish whether:

- disclosing the information would reveal the third party's identity
- editing would conceal the identity of the third party
- the third party will consent to the information being disclosed.

Depending on the answers to any of these questions, parts of the records may not be shown to the patient; it is possible that the patient will be refused any access to them whatsoever.

In cases where parents have applied to inspect one of their children's medical records, the data controller will determine whether the child is capable of making a judgement about their health care. If the child is regarded as being able to do so, the parents must obtain the child's consent before their request is accepted. If solicitors have applied for access to medical records, the data controller may verify that the patients concerned understand that they have consented to the release of their whole medical record.

Individuals are required to pay a fee in order to inspect and copy their health records. The lowest charge (rising to the same maximum figure) is for viewing records, in whatever form (unless additions have been made in the previous 40 days), and taking copies of information from computerized files. Charges for copies of manual or a combination of computer and manual records rise to a much higher maximum amount.

Guidance on consent issues for NHS establishments and practitioners in England
The UK's Department of Health has produced several instruction booklets on patient consent issues aimed at NHS organizations and practitioners in England. The information covers wide-ranging aspects of the question and indicates the areas where existing law has an application and further reminds health service professionals to take account of any guidance issued by their own regulatory bodies on matters that involve consent. This information is also available on the Department's website.

A guide on good practice in consent for NHS organizations
First issued in November 2001, *Good Practice in Consent Implementation Guide: consent to examination or treatment* is aimed at NHS establishments. It sets out a 'model consent policy' and is part of the Department of Health's 'good practice in consent' initiative called for in *The NHS Plan* the previous year.[23] The information includes four model consent forms, the design of which health service organizations were expected to follow in their own individual versions.[24] They are:

• a patient agreement to investigation or treatment
• an agreement by parents (or those with parental responsibility) to investigation or treatment for a child or young person
• a patient–parental agreement to investigation or treatment
• a (form for) adults who are unable to consent to investigation or treatment.

The guidance information explains why consent is crucial. It states that patients have a 'fundamental and legal right to determine what happens to their own bodies'. Consequently, obtaining valid consent is vital in all forms of health care – from personal care to carrying out major surgery. Securing consent is also 'a matter of common courtesy between health professionals and patients'. Moreover, the guide draws the attention of social care personnel to their obligation to get consent before discharging certain functions, such as those that involve touching patients and clients.[25]

Consent is described as 'a patient's agreement for a health professional to provide care'. It may be indicated non-verbally (for instance patients offering an arm for their pulse to be taken), orally or in writing. For consent to be valid, a patient must:

• be capable of making the decision
• have been given enough information to do so
• not be acting under duress.[26]

In further describing aspects of consent, the guide explains that often the process of obtaining consent is more usefully characterized as 'joint decision-making' – mutual agreement being sought on the most appropriate way forward, based on a patient's values and preferences, and the clinical knowledge of the practitioner concerned. It also points out that where an adult patient temporarily or permanently lacks the mental ability to give or withhold consent, 'no-one else can give consent on their behalf'. Nevertheless, treatment may be provided if it is in a patient's best interests, but on condition that it has not been refused in advance through valid instructions.[27]

The booklet goes on to explore and give advice on other wide-ranging issues involving consent. For example, it states that it is necessary for practitioners to record clearly in writing a patient's agreement to a particular clinical intervention, where it is of a serious kind, and the discussions that led to that arrangement. This can be done via a consent form or an entry in the patient's notes (or both) that the latter has given consent.[28]

The guide also explains that it is rarely a legal requirement to obtain written consent, but that it is good practice to do so in certain specified instances. It provides additional advice on associated issues[29] and it sets out the procedures to be followed in cases where patients are not capable of giving or withholding consent.[30] The guide goes on to give detailed advice on how health service professionals should conduct themselves where other matters involving consent arise and deals with the following questions.

- When should patients be asked for their consent?
- When and what information should be given to patients about their condition and the treatment or investigation that is proposed?
- Who is responsible for trying to obtain consent?
- What is the procedure when a patient refuses treatment or consents to only part of a proposed therapy?
- What is the position – legal and otherwise – over the use of human tissue (including testing blood samples and other bodily fluids)?
- What is the procedure for clinical photography and conventional or digital recordings?[31]

The law in England on some key issues about consent

A separate Department of Health document, *12 Key Points on Consent: the law in England*, was circulated to health care professionals in England, which summarizes elements of the law on consent that arise daily.[32] This information is also available on the Department's website and is incorporated in the *Good Practice in Consent Implementation Guide: consent to examination or treatment* discussed above. A summary is given below.[33]

When do health professionals need consent from patients?

1. Before practitioners can examine, treat or care for competent adult patients they must obtain their consent.
2. Adults are always assumed to be competent unless otherwise demonstrated. Where there is doubt about their ability, the question to consider is whether or not the patient concerned has grasped and weighed up the information provided to make a decision. An unexpected decision does not prove that the patient is incompetent; it may signify a need for further information or explanation.
3. Patients may be competent to make decisions on health care in some instances, but not in others.
4. Seeking and receiving consent is normally a process rather than a single episode. Patients can change their minds and withdraw consent at any time. With this in mind, practitioners should always check that they still consent to the care or treatment to be (or being) provided.

Can children give consent for themselves?

5. Clinicians must ask for consent before examining or providing treatment or care for children. Patients who are 16 to 17 years of age are presumed to be capable of giving consent for themselves. Equally, younger children who fully understand

what is involved in a proposed course of action can give such consent although, ideally, their parents will also be involved. In other instances someone with parental responsibility must give consent on behalf of a child unless they cannot be contacted in an emergency. If a competent child has consented to therapy, a parent cannot countermand that decision. Nonetheless, parents can legally give consent where their children have refused to do so, except it is likely that taking such action will be rare.

Who is the right person to seek consent?

6. It is always best for the clinician who is to provide a therapy to ask for the patient's consent. Nevertheless, other practitioners can seek consent on that professional's behalf if they are capable of carrying out the procedure themselves, or where they are specially trained to do so for the therapy in question.

What information should be provided to patients?

7. Patients need to be given enough information, and in a form they understand, before they can make an informed decision on, for example, the benefits or risks of the proposed and alternative therapy. Otherwise, their consent may not be valid.
8. Consent must be given voluntarily – that is to say, not under duress nor undue influence of practitioners, family or friends.

Does it matter how patients give consent?

9. It does not. Consent can be written, oral or non-verbal. A signature on a consent form is not proof that consent is valid. The purpose of a signed form is to record a patient's decision and, increasingly, the discussions that have occurred. Individual NHS organizations may have a policy stating when their practitioners need to get written consent.

The position when treatment is refused

10. Competent adults have a right to refuse therapy – even when it will clearly benefit their health. (The exception is where the treatment is for a mental disorder and the patient has been detained under the Mental Health Act 1983.) Similarly, a competent pregnant woman can refuse any therapy, even if doing so will be harmful to the foetus.

Adults who are not capable of giving consent

11. No person can give consent on behalf of an incompetent adult. Nevertheless, such patients can still be treated if it is in their best interests. The meaning of 'best interests' is wider than that of best medical interests. Factors including the wishes and beliefs of patients when they were competent, their present wishes, general well-being and spiritual and religious welfare are other considerations. People who are close to the patient concerned may be able to provide information on some of these points. In cases where a patient has never been competent, relatives, carers and friends may be in the best position to advise on that person's needs and preferences.
12. Where incapable patients have clearly indicated in the past, while competent, that they would refuse treatment (an 'advance refusal') in certain circumstances, and one such situation arises, practitioners must abide by these patients' wishes.

Further guidance to health service practitioners on consent to clinical procedures
In its *Reference Guide to Consent and Examination or Treatment* the UK's Department of Health in 2001 states that there is a 'general legal and ethical principle' that valid consent must be obtained before commencing treatment or physical investigation of patients, or providing personal care for them. It adds that this axiom 'reflects the right of patients to determine what happens to their own bodies', and is a 'fundamental part of good practice'. Failure by health care professionals to respect this principle may make them liable to legal action by patients and disciplinary measures by their regulatory body. Their employers may also be held responsible in law.[34]

The booklet gives advice on English law affecting consent to physical interventions on patients – from assistance with dressing to the administration of drugs and major surgery and covers all health care practitioners (including students) who carry out such functions. There is also advice on the legal requirements in securing valid consent and about the circumstances in which there are exceptions to the common law obligation to get consent. It is pointed out that as the guidance provided applies specifically to consent for 'physical intervention on living patients', certain areas of consent are excepted. These include questions about patients' participation in observational studies, and the use of personal data about them and of their organs or tissue after death.[35]

The guide points out that, although there is no English statute setting out the principles of consent, case law (common law) has demonstrated that touching a patient without valid consent may amount to the civil or criminal offence of battery. If health service professionals fail to get proper approval for treatment they have given, any subsequent impairment to patients as a consequence may be a factor in a claim of negligence against them. It adds that mishandling of the consent process may also result in patients taking action against health care practitioners via the NHS complaints procedure, or through their disciplinary bodies.[36]

Attention is also drawn to the fact that case law had evolved considerably during the previous decade and that further legal developments might follow since publication of the guidance booklet. Accordingly, health care practitioners had a duty to keep themselves abreast of such advances (wherever they applied) and to take legal advice if in doubt about the validity, in law, of a proposed medical intervention. The booklet states that although much of case law refers particularly to doctors, it will also apply to other practitioners who are involved in examining or treating patients.[37]

The advice provided in this guide covers wide-ranging issues involving consent and concerns all patient categories: adults, young people (aged 16–17 years) and children who are either with or without capacity. Included are general principles, under English law, about the various aspects of consent in their application to each patient age group and capability. The principles affecting the withdrawal or withholding of life-prolonging treatment are also outlined, as are those that apply to the court when a patient's capacity is in doubt. The reference guide briefly itemizes the statutes that provide exceptions to the principles thus described.[38]

Guidance on consent for adults: what they have a right to expect
Before health service practitioners can examine or provide therapy for adult patients they must receive the latter's consent to do so. (This right of consent applies mainly to a physical condition and does not normally refer to patients who are in need of

treatment for a mental disorder.) Accordingly, patients who are asked to agree to any form of therapy can refuse the course of action being put forward, or ask for more information before reaching a decision. This may take the simple form of a patient complying with a doctor's request, for instance by opening their mouth if the doctor asks to look at their throat. In other cases, depending on the seriousness of what is being proposed, or whether the proposal entails risks and benefits, patients may be asked to sign a consent form.[39]

It is not how a person gives consent; more important is that the permission given is genuine or valid. This means that patients must be:

- able to give consent
- given sufficient information to enable them to reach a decision
- acting freely, rather than under the influence of others.[40]

Consent – What You Have a Right to Expect: a guide for adults points out that English law assumes that adults are capable of making their own decisions, unless it can be proved otherwise. Thus, providing that such individuals can understand and are able to assess the information needed to make up their mind, they should be capable of arriving at a decision.[41] The subject of consent to health care by adults is addressed in this Department of Health publication, the contents of which are also reproduced on the Department's website. (Similarly presented guidance has been produced by the Department aimed at children and young people, parents and relatives and carers. This is covered next in the chapter.)

Patients whose condition prevents them from making a decision
In cases where patients are unconscious following a road accident, for example, or when they cannot communicate because of a stroke, health care practitioners can generally provide the therapy that they consider to be in the best interests of those who are affected in this way. The exception is when patients have positively stated in advance, via a written record of their wishes (a 'living will'), that they do not want a certain treatment in the future and have advised those close to them of the fact. Such individuals must be precise about the therapy they are refusing, otherwise they could exclude health carethat might be acceptable. Also, they should inform close family members or friends of any change of mind so that this information can be passed on should this be necessary.[42]

Wives, husbands, partners or close friends cannot give consent to treatment on behalf of another adult, but they may be in a position to offer useful advice. They could, for instance, tell health care professionals about the beliefs and values of the person concerned, and whether or not the latter has previously accepted certain types of therapy. Additionally, they might have information indicating that this patient has strong views on certain health issues. The person concerned should already have discussed all such matters with relatives and friends in the event that anything of the kind might happen.[43]

Examination or therapy in the presence of students
There are instances when patients may be asked if they are willing to have students present while receiving health care. If unsure, they should ask what part the students will be playing (for example observing, examining or taking notes) and then decide

one way or the other. Patients can state their preference for either sex, but refusing to have students present should not affect the standard of attention they will receive.[44]

Information needed by patients to enable them to decide on consent
Patients require information about the therapy or medical investigation that health service clinicians are proposing in order to decide whether or not to give their consent. They should always ask more questions if uncertain about any aspects of the proposal, or if greater explanation is needed. There are a number of questions about which patients may want answers.[45]

- What will the proposed therapy involve?
- What benefits do the health care practitioners hope will follow such treatment?
- How good are the possibilities of these benefits being realized?
- Are there any alternative courses of action?
- What are the risks involved?
- If there are risks, do these refer to minor or serious effects?
- What might be the consequences of not receiving treatment?

There may be cases where those seeking consent to provide therapy are unable to answer questions put to them by patients. In this event, patients should ask them to find out or call someone else who can address the concerns they have raised. If preferable for them, patients can have a friend present when when they are seeking answers to their questions. They can also ask for someone of the same sex to be present while being examined or treated.[46]

How much do patients need to know?
Some people need to know all they can about their condition and the possible treatments that are available. to them. Others may prefer to leave the matter in the hands of the clinicians involved. Nobody who is to provide health care for patients will, for example, force unwanted information upon them about the risks of this treatment. Those in the best position to know what matters most to them are the patients themselves. Certain people are prepared to take some risks if there is also a chance of a very favourable outcome. Others may prefer to endure a degree of discomfort rather than have treatment which involves a slight risk of worsening the condition – even though there is a strong probability that therapy will improve it. Only the individual concerned can know what is personally of the greatest importance.[47]

How long can patients take to decide?
While health care professionals will probably encourage patients to accept a certain therapy if they believe that it would be beneficial, it is for the latter to decide whether or not to do so.

Patients who need more time to consider before reaching a decision should say so. It is often possible for patients to take as much time as they need to decide; nevertheless, in an emergency, a decision may need to be made without delay.[48]

Can patients state in advance what therapy they prefer?
Patients may wish to write down the types of treatment they prefer and their concerns about other kinds of procedures, but the wishes they have recorded are not

binding in the same way as the advance refusal mentioned earlier. For instance, they cannot insist on a particular type of treatment if the health care practitioner concerned does not consider it to be appropriate for them. Nonetheless, should a situation arise in the future when patients needing treatment are incapable of making a decision or conveying it to others, it would be helpful as a guide for the clinicians involved to know of the patient's previously expressed wishes in deciding what would be the best course of action. Nobody can ask for action to be taken that is against the law – euthanasia for example.[49]

What is the position of patients who are asked to take part in research?[50]
Patients may be asked to participate in research as part of their treatment, for instance to compare two different treatments. On the other hand, the request to take part may be separate, for example to provide extra blood samples for research purposes. In such an event, the research project will always have been first approved by a research ethics committee.

It is for patients to decide whether or not to participate in the research proposal being put forward. They would normally be given written information about the plan and are at liberty to raise additional questions before reaching a decision. Choosing not to take part should not affect a patient's care and, if they agree to co-operate in research, patients are still free to withdraw at any time.

Is there any advantage or disadvantage in participating in research?
Occasionally patients may be able to get a particular therapy only as part of a research trial because of its newness and the fact that it has been insufficiently tested. The practitioners concerned might suggest that patients could benefit from taking part in such a trial. In this event, the patients are free to ask as many questions as they want about the new treatment, the risks involved and the alternatives to participating in the test.[51]

In certain types of research neither the patient nor the patient's doctor will know whether the new or standard treatment – or possibly any therapy at all – is being given. Nevertheless, patients will be informed about the treatment options they have taken up in these cases, even though they will not know which one they will be given. They are also at liberty not to take part in this or any other kind of trial and instead to opt for the standard form of treatment that is available. In making their choice, patients will be aware that all types of therapy – including established ones – carry risks.[52]

The status of patients who have a mental illness
Under the Mental Health Act 1983 it may be necessary for patients with a serious mental illness to be kept in hospital involuntarily. They may also be given treatment for their mental disorder without their consent, although there are safeguards for patients in these circumstances. Nevertheless, the provisions in the Act apply only to mental illness. Patients may also have a physical disorder that is unconnected with their mental condition. In this event, they are entitled to decide whether or not to accept the therapy that has been suggested provided they are able to understand the available options in order to reach a decison sufficiently.[53]

Patients who are critical about the way they have been approached about consent
Where patients are dissatisfied with the manner in which they have been approached for consent they can raise their concerns with the health care practitioners involved. If still not satisfied, they are entitled to lodge a complaint. The procedure to follow is covered in the government's *Your Guide to the NHS* booklet, or it can be obtained from a designated NHS telephone helpline. Alternatively, patients can seek advice from the Patients' Advice and Liaison Services (PALS), units of which are located nationally within health service trust establishments. They can also approach charitable patient and other organizations for assistance on matters of consent.[54]

Guidance for children and young people on consent: what they have a right to expect
Although clear distinctions exist between the guidance for individuals aged under 18 and that referring specifically to adults, there are a number of common aspects. The official guidance in *Consent – What You Have a Right to Expect: a guide for children and young people*[55] covers:
• how consent is requested and given
• what a patient needs to know before giving consent
• how old a patient must be to give consent
• when parents can be involved in matters of consent
• when other individuals can give consent for a patient
• how a patient should respond to being asked to help in research.

How consent is asked for and what a patient needs to know before giving such approval
The meaning of consent, and how it is asked for and given in the case of patients aged under 18, is like that relating to adults. Therefore before consenting to therapy patients and their parents need the clinician involved to provide information on the treatment being offered and they should question matters that are unclear to them and ask for further details if they need them. The questions they should raise before giving consent are identical to those that apply to adult patients and, similarly, decisions on consent can be delayed except in certain circumstances, for instance in life-saving emergencies.[56]

When can patients give consent for themselves?
If between 16 and 18 years of age, a patient can give consent to examination or therapy on the same basis as an adult, without the practitioner concerned having also to get approval from the parents. Nevertheless, where a patient in this age group refuses a particular treatment, the parents may ocasionally become involved in the matter. In certain cases patients aged under 16 may also give consent about themselves on condition that they are able to understand what is involved in a therapy being proposed. Thus 13 to 14 year olds may be capable of agreeing to certain forms of therapy, investigation or immunization being performed, but not to other treatments. For instance the information that is needed in order to give consent to a heart operation may be too complex for patients to understand.[57]

When should parents become involved?

Even when children are capable of giving consent, health care professionals will encourage them to involve their parents in decision-making. Other closely connected adults such as grandparents or aunts can also be included in the process. In cases where these young people may not wish their parents to know that they are seeking certain kinds of advice or treatment (for instance relating to contraception), the practitioner involved will not tell the parents without their permission. The exception is when it is to protect the patients concerned or others from serious harm.[58]

When can other people give consent for patients who are under 18 years old?

This situation can arise when a patient has difficulty in deciding or understanding sufficiently in order to give consent to a proposed procedure. Here, the parents or guardian can give consent if the young person concerned is living with them or being cared for by the local authority with the parents' agreement. Where such a patient is under a care order, the parents or the social worker involved can give consent.[59]

In cases where a patient persists in refusing consent the rules are that, if the parents decide it is in the patient's best interest to have a particular treatment, they can give the go-ahead on behalf of the patient. But it is exceptional for this to happen. In especially serious or complex circumstances a court can be asked to decide whether it is appropriate for the practitioner to proceed with a particular therapy. This situation could arise when the patient and parents disagreed on whether an extremely serious operation should be performed.[60]

The position of those who are asked to participate in research

Those aged under 18 can respond in the same way as adults to being approached about taking part in research. They should ask as many questions as they wish about what will be involved in any such proposed study. Where all types of research are concerned they could enquire, for example, about the purpose of the investigation, the possible risks involved, the level of these risks and any conceivable benefits. In the case of research that involves a new or different therapy, patients can ask what the standard treatment would entail and what possible alternatives are available. For their part, the health care professionals concerned could suggest that a new trial treatment might have benefits, but also unknown risks. After due reflection of all these issues patients are still free to refuse participation in the research being proposed. Alternatively, they may wish to discuss the matter with their parents before reaching a decision.[61]

What patients can do if dissatisfied about the way they have been addressed about consent

In the same way as adults, those aged under 18 can raise their concerns with the practitioners involved, obtain advice from other agencies if still dissatisfied and progress further with their complaint through the standard channels set up for the purpose. Similarly, they can ask for additional help from charitable patient and other organizations.[62]

Guidance for parents on consent: what they have a right to expect

Parents are entitled to give consent to health care for children who are aged under 18 over whom they have parental responsibility. Mothers have automatic parental responsibility for their children. The same applies to fathers if they were married to the mother when the child was conceived or born, or if the couple were later married. Unmarried fathers do not have this automatic role – although a court order or a 'parental responsibility agreement' can give it to them. Grandparents or child-minders do not have parental responsibility but the parents concerned can authorize these people to take medical decisions for the children in their care. Nevertheless, depending on their age and level of understanding, there are times when children can give consent for themselves. Indeed, they gain increasing rights on matters of consent as they get older.[63] The subject of parental consent is dealt with in *Consent – What You Have a Right to Expect: a guide for parents.*

How do parents decide what is best for their children?
Parents are expected to make decisions on health care for their children based on what they believe will serve their welfare or is in the child's best interests. They should involve their children as much as possible in the process – even if they are not old enough to decide for themselves. As a consequence, children are more likely to feel confident about the therapy that is to be provided.[64]

When parents and the health care practitioners concerned disagree on therapy
Normally health care professionals cannot proceed with treatment for children if the parents disagree that it is in the latter's best interests. In these instances, it could help parents to obtain a second medical opinion, or discuss the issue with others concerned in the care of their children. When the health care practitioners involved believe that a certain therapy is vital or life-saving for a child, they can ask a court to decide on the matter if the parents will not give their consent. Similarly, parents can go to court to request or prevent treatment when they consider it is in the best interests of their child.[65]

When can children give consent on their own?
Once children are 16 years old they can give their consent to examination or therapy on the same terms as adults, and without the consent of their parents. Nevertheless, the rules also allow those aged under 16 to give consent independently on condition that they are sufficiently mature to fully understand what is involved. There is no hard and fast rule about who gives consent – the child or the parents – with much depending on the gravity or complexity of a proposed therapy. For example, a child may be capable of consenting to a commonplace vaccination but not to a heart operation. Even when children are mature enough to give consent exclusively, those providing the health care will advise them to involve their parents in reaching a decision. But if they refuse to do so the practitioners concerned must normally respect their wishes.[66]

What parents and their children need to know before consenting to treatment
Parents and their children need to be jointly given information about the therapy being proposed in order to arrive at a decision on the matter. Where parents and their children have not understood, or need additional details, they should ask for further information or explanation. The questions they should raise are like those suggested in the guidance for adults who decide for themselves whether they consent to

receiving treatment. The range of other factors about decisions on consent to therapy referred to in the guidance for adults equally apply to parents and children.[67]

The position when a child refuses treatment

There are occasions when children who are capable of making a decision refuse therapy that their parents want them to receive. In such cases, and with the parents' consent, the medical practitioners concerned can legally overrule the child and proceed with the recommended treatment, but stringent measures of this kind should be a last resort. Steps should first be taken to address the child's concerns and if the condition is not life-threatening it may be feasible to postpone treatment until the child agrees to its going ahead.[68]

Conversely, parents may not wish their child to be given a particular therapy or intervention – for instance being given contraceptives. In this event, provided the child is mature enough to understand what is involved and asks for certain treatment or intervention, the law allows health care professionals to provide the therapy or care they consider to be proper. Although they will always attempt to persuade children to keep their parents informed, practiioners must respect the child's wishes if they refuse to do so.[69]

Consent issues involving parents that are common in guidance about other individuals
The guidance on parental consent when the children concerned are asked to participate in research is like the advice (previously described) relating directly to adult and child patients. Parents can raise any concerns they may have with the practitioners involved, obtain advice from the same agencies and complain through the set health service procedure if they are not content with the way consent has been sought from their children. Again, they can ask charitable patient and other appropriate organizations for assistance.[70]

Guidance on consent for relatives and carers: what they have a right to expect

Consent – What You Have a Right to Expect: a guide for relatives and carers states that before health care practitioners can examine or treat patients they normally need the latter's consent. Provided the adult being looked after by relatives or a carer is able to understand what is involved in a proposed procedure or therapy, like anyone else over 18, that person is the only one who can give consent to proceed with the action.[71] (The issue has already been explained in the guidance about consent for adults.)

Nonetheless, there are exceptions to this rule. These can arise in extreme cases where someone is unconscious after an accident, is totally unable to communicate following a stroke or is too confused to make a decision on medical intervention because of advanced dementia. The exceptions can also include people who are capable of making simple health care decisions but because of a learning disability cannot understand the issues involved before giving consent to a major operation being performed upon them. In such cases, relatives or carers can become involved.[72]

How far are individuals in the care of others able to decide for themselves and give consent?
Neither carers nor health care practitioners should assume that patients seemingly unable to understand or communicate their wishes because of a learning disability

or dementia are incapable of reaching a decision about consenting to therapy. Once it has been established that such patients have, indeed, some ability to follow and consider what has been proposed for their health care, they should be encouraged to decide for themselves – even if the relatives or carers then disagree with the decision.[73]

What is the position of those who are completely unable to make a decison on their own?
Under English law, no person (including husbands, wives, partners, close relatives or carers) can give consent to health care on behalf of another adult. Therefore difficulties can emerge when patients are not in a condition to decide for themselves. In these instances, medical professionals are ordinarily permitted to provide the health care they consider to be in their patients' best interests. This means taking into account not only what might be most appropriate for their patients' physical health but also their general well-being and beliefs.[74]

Although relatives and other close associates cannot decide for patients who are unable to determine for themselves about consenting to therapy, they can inform health care practitioners about the latter's opinions and beliefs. This may include, for example, details about patients' previous refusal or consent to a certain treatment; or the fact that they have strongly held views about a particular health condition or therapy. Being provided with such information will assist medical professionals in deciding what is in a patient's best interests, unless it was given by someone the patient had previously made clear should not be involved.[75]

Whose opinion counts when deciding whether patients being cared for are sufficiently capable of giving consent?
Health care practitioners who consider that urgent medical action is necessary should not allow their view to lead to an assumption that the patient concerned is incapable of making a decision on the matter. Similarly, while relatives or carers may be in the best position to support those in their care, they will need to consider the medical opinion that is being offered. What usually emerges in these situations is general agreement about the best course of action. Should the parties concerned disagree on what is appropriate, either of them can get a court to decide what is in a patient's best interests. In no circumstances must relatives or carers be asked to sign a consent form on behalf of those they are looking after. But they can be requested to sign a document to show that they have been consulted.[76]

The position of relatives and carers where those in their care have refused therapy in advance through a living will
People can state in advance that they do not want a certain form of therapy should they become ill and no longer be capable of refusing consent. Any views expressed in a 'living will' are binding factors in decisions taken about the health care of the person concerned. Accordingly, relatives or carers should inform the clinicians involved if they know that those in their care have made a living will, or, if possible, hand over a document to that effect signed by the patient where such action has been taken.[77]

What relatives or carers can do if they are dissatisfied about how consent has been sought

The same courses of action can be taken by relatives or carers as that previously shown in the sets of guidance about other individuals to get their concerns addressed about the way they have been approached about consent. Similarly, they can seek additional advice on the matter from charitable patient and other organizations.[78]

The role, commitments and objectives of the NHS with patients in mind

In January 2001, the Department of Health issued the booklet *Your Guide to the NHS* and replicated the information on its website. One of the purposes of the guide is to help explain how the changes announced in *The NHS Plan* of July the previous year would affect the public at large. It also sets out what patients in England can expect from the health service and what they can expect in the future 'as improvements to health services are made'.[79] The guide superseded *The Patient's Charter & You* of 1996, which was similar in content.

Your Guide to the NHS attempts to answer the main questions individuals might raise and shows how they can obtain more information on public health care issues.[80] It underlines the commitment of the NHS to providing a high-quality health service and describes what the health service will do to serve this end. It will:

- provide a universal service based on clinical need, not ability to pay
- offer a comprehensive range of services, which it will mould around the individual needs and preferences of patients, families and carers
- respond to the varying requirements of different populations and work constantly to improve services and reduce mistakes
- use public funds earmarked for health care only on its patients and co-operate with others to provide a seamless service for them
- respect the confidentiality of patients and provide readily available information about services, treatment and performance
- support and value its staff.[81]

The guide summarizes members of the public's own responsibilities and provides a list of tips on how the population can stay healthy and safe. It then describes the course of action that anyone who is unwell should take, and what can follow in treating or caring for them at primary and secondary health service levels, and after they have been discharged from hospital. *Your Guide to the NHS* also sets out what patients can do if they have concerns about their care, including lodging a complaint, and what action the NHS will take as a result.[82]

Patient advice, liaison, advocacy and safety agencies, and other associated organizations

Since the turn of the 21st century the UK government has introduced a plethora of organizations to support the interests of patients across a spectrum of issues. There is an agency that offers advice and advocacy to patients and families who have raised concerns about standards in the NHS. A body has also been established to encourage the reporting by clinicians of adverse incidents involving patients as part of a wider and associated set of functions. More of the kind is being planned or has started, for instance patients' forums, which operate nationally within the NHS.

Other operating bodies that are either independent of the health service or connected with it, have also been set up with the interests of patients in mind. The purpose of these organizations includes setting standards for performance in the NHS and carrying out inspections to see that these and additional requirements are being met.

Patient Advice and Liaison Services
The role of the newly established Patients' Advice and Liaison Services (PALS) for advising complainants and assisting them with their grievances about the NHS in England has been described in Chapter 1. (It was also noted that this particular support network had replaced the previous system of community health councils to carry out these functions and that, by contrast, Scotland, Wales and Northern Ireland had retained their branches of this then UK-wide organization.)

Nevertheless, the scope of PALS activities extends to other areas. It provides information on the health service to patients, their families or carers, and the public; PALS staff listen to their questions and suggestions, and communicate with NHS personnel and organizations with service improvements in mind. The plan is for this patient support service to be a catalyst for change and improvement and to act as an early warning system in health care provision by trusts. PALS units are expected to submit regular anonymous reports to their respective trust boards.[83] Chapter 1 has described how the service can also function as an opening to other patient support agencies, including the Independent Complaints Advocacy Services (ICAS), which was set up in September 2003.

Independent Complaints and Advocacy Services
The Independent Complaints and Advocacy Service is an additional source of active help for complainants, the extent of which has also been covered in Chapter 1. While PALS units will make complainants aware of and refer them to ICAS, where it is necessary, health service trust complaints managers and agencies such as NHS Direct (a telephone information service) are also in a position to do so. ICAS receives guidance and other support in its work from the Commission for Patient and Public Involvement in Health.[84]

Commission for Patient and Public Involvement in Health, patient and public involvement forums and forum support organizations
The Commission for Patient and Public Involvement in Health (CPPIH) is an independent, non-departmental public body, which was established in January 2003. It is sponsored by the UK's Department of Health with a remit to involve the public in decision-making about health care and service provision in the NHS. The Commission operates at national, regional and local levels in England and, in December 2003, set up patient and public involvement (PPI) forums for all health service trusts (PCTs included) in England.[85]

The responsibilities of CPPIH include funding and monitoring this new network and overseeing and advancing the enlargement of the Independent Complaints Advocacy Services from its original interim countrywide form. The Commission appoints all the approximately seven members comprising each PPI forum. Recruited locally, members are given training and the Commission provides ongoing assistance to their forums both directly and through forum support organizations (FSOs).[86]

Health service staff, including board members of NHS and primary care trusts (PCTs), are eligible for membership of PPI forums, but not of those relating to the health service establishments with which they are connected in these ways. Similarly, such personnel belonging to strategic health authorities (SHAs) cannot be members of PPI forums put in place for trusts that are responsible to their organizations. Nor are any individuals associated with establishments who have been commisioned to provide services to PCTs allowed to join the forums to which the latter refer. Similar restrictions apply to local authority councillors: they are eligible for membership of PPI forums only on condition that they are not on their authority's executive, or are members of the relevant health service overview and scrutiny committee (OSC).[87]

PPI forums are not part of the NHS, but they have a statutory right to enter the premises of NHS trusts to carry out their duties. Similarly, they can go into buildings where primary care trusts are providing services or have commissioned other bodies to do so. PPI forums set up for PCTs are also permitted to enter and inspect the premises of primary care practitioners – GPs, dentists, pharmacists and opticians. For their part, NHS trusts and PCTs are required to provide information that is requested by PPI forums and respond to their reports. Strategic health authorities, also, must supply information that these forums have asked for.[88]

Forum support organizations are not-for-profit groups, with some of them consortia of not-for-profit organizations in their own right. They are managed geographically by way of nine regional centres. Independent of the NHS, their duties include helping to organize PPI forum meetings, providing all such assemblies with administrative support and encouraging them to work together.[89]

Part of the CPPIH's role is to submit reports to and advise the government on the way PPI forums are performing. It also connects with other national organizations – the Commission for Health Audit and Inspection (CHAI) for example – on matters involving patients and the public, and makes recommendations to them and the Department of Health. Additionally it is responsible for assembling data and opinion, gained through a shared information process, to ensure that the bodies it reports to are acting on the views of patients and the public.[90]

National Patient Safety Agency
The National Patient Safety Agency (NPSA) is a 'special health authority', which came into existence in July 2001. It was established with the aim of co-ordinating the endeavours of all NHS-funded health care organizations in the United Kingdom to report and learn from adverse clinical incidents and other service failures. Another key goal was to foster an open and fair culture in health service establishments where the fear of reprimand is removed when staff report such errors. The NPSA will then take action on these statements of intent to initiate appropriate preventive measures for application in the NHS across the country.[91]

National Institute for Clinical Excellence[92]
Part of the NHS, the National Institute for Clinical Excellence (NICE) is a special health authority that was set up for England and Wales in April 1999. Its role includes providing patients, health professionals and the public with authoritative guidance on what is current best practice in care and treatment. Some of its other responsibilities involve:

- promoting quicker access to the best and new treatments for patients
- helping to end the 'post-code prescribing' lottery
- assisting the NHS to provide the best possible health care from its available resources.

NICE has a patient involvement unit (PIU), which supplies it with independent advice on patient and care issues. The PIU seeks out patient and carer organizations that are interested in contributing to the Institute's work and provides them with the necessary wide-ranging (and ongoing) training and support. NICE has set up a 'citizens council' to find out what the public's view is of the main issues that form the basis for the guidance it releases on the application of treatments, and the care that patients can expect to receive in the NHS. NICE board meetings are held in public, and those of the citizens council's are open to the public.

(In April 2005 NICE absorbed the functions of the Health Development Agency to become the National Institute for Health and Clinical Excellence. Still referred to as NICE, the body's responsibilities are enlarged to provide national guidance on the promotion of good health and the prevention and treatment of ill health. Under these changes the 'patient involvement unit' has become the 'patient and public involvement programme' (PPIP). As its new name indicates, the PPIP's role extends also to involving members of the public in NICE activities.)

Commission for Health Improvement[93]

Until April 2004 the Commission for Health Improvement (CHI) was the independent inspectorate for the NHS in England and Wales. (The NHS Quality Improvement Scotland is the corresponding body in Scotland.) Its role included monitoring patient care and carrying out clinical governance reviews relating to organizations in the public health service. CHI was also in charge of the clinical audit programme for the two countries over which it had jurisdiction.

Additionally, the body assessed the extent to which the NHS met the guidelines for providing health care that are set out in the national service frameworks (NSFs). It investigated the serious service failures in the health service that central and devolved government – and the public – had brought to their attention. CHI published the results of these and other reviews, investigations and surveys, and produced an annual report on the position of patient care in the NHS.

Commission for Healthcare Audit and Inspection and the Commission for Social Care Inspection[94]

Set up under the Health and Social Care (Community Health and Standards) Act 2003, the Commission for Healthcare Audit and Inspection (CHAI) or Healthcare Commission began to operate in April 2004 (see Chapter 2). The same legislation also provided for the establishment of the Commission for Social Care Inspection (CSCI). These two new independent inspectorates were formed with the aim of strengthening the system for scrutinizing health and social care, streamlining regulation in these areas and providing clearer public accountability in the process. The bodies are being developed in parallel and have a legal obligation to work together.

Broadly, the purpose of the Healthcare Commission is to improve the quality of health care and services provided for recipients in the NHS and private sector. A single inspectorate, it has assumed the functions of the:

- Commission for Health Improvement (whose role was partially similar to that of the Healthcare Commission)
- National Care Standards Commission (dealing with private and voluntary health care provision)
- Audit Commission (with respect to national research involving health care efficiency, effectiveness and economics.

Also, the Healthcare Commission works in alliance with the Mental Health Act Commission (MHAC), whose function is to see that patients detained under the Mental Health Act 1983 are protected satisfactorily. It is expected to take on most of the duties of the MHAC, which is to be abolished at some point after April 2007. In addition, under the Human Rights Act 1998 the Healthcare Commission is obliged actively to promote respect for human rights. Moreover, as Chapter 2 shows, the Commission (whose activities mostly concern England) plays a key role in the reformed NHS complaints system – in particular dealing with complaints that have been referred to it for consideration.

A parallel body to the Healthcare Commission, the Commission for Social Care Inspection (CSCI) is an inclusive inspectorate covering social care. Its position is to integrate the work of the Social Services Inspectorate (SSI), the joint review group of the SSI and Audit Commission and the duties of the National Care Standards Commission (NCSC). The functions of CSCI include:

- promoting improvement in social care
- inspection of all public, private and voluntary social care establishments
- inspection of local social service authorities
- registering services that meet set national standards
- scrutinizing incoming complaints
- holding statistics on performance in social care
- publishing an annual report to Parliament and government on national progress in social care and associated issues.

In addition to working closely with the Healthcare Commission the Inspectorate operates similarly with the Audit Commission and Ofsted, the regulatory body for public education authorities. It would appear that the CSCI is staffed mainly by personnel previously employed by the bodies it has replaced.

Guidance to patients, health care professionals and the NHS in Wales, Scotland and Northern Ireland on questions surrounding consent , confidentiality and access to medical records

As in England, none of the three other UK countries has single, all-encompassing legislation devoted to patients' rights and the position of health care professionals. In much the same way their (devolved) administrations have issued guidance for patients and NHS personnel on questions about consent, the processing of confidential information and other associated issues. The form and content of these items of documentary advice are substantially akin to the English versions and have been drawn up to also take account of a combination of similar (or the same) legal, ethical and policy considerations.

What conclusions can be drawn from the present patients' rights arrangements?
There is, perhaps, one especially striking characteristic of the present British approach to delivering patients' rights – the apparent lack of an all-encompassing legal base for the entitlements and other considerations the system provides for. This is not to say that the arrangement, as it stands, is not adequately fulfilling its purpose. Nor can one declare that a complete array of rules set in stone will necessarily guarantee that those who are obliged to abide by them will assiduously do so at all times. Still, it is reasonable to suggest that statutory rights on this scale are less likely to be flouted than would otherwise be the case. Crucially, specific legislation for the purpose should provide greater clarity and certainty to the positions of the parties to whom it refers.

By contrast, with having to assemble and convey the messages received from various pieces of legislation, case law and other forms of guidance, the present arrangement of seting out patients' rights may be complicated for some people to absorb. It may also be confusing for patients and those who represent them to be told about what they 'have a right to expect', rather than what their rights are in their relationship with the health service.

It looks as if the decisions of law-makers in a clutch of European cultures (see chapters 13 to 15) to legislate for sweeping patients' rights were borne out of altruistic motives. Indeed, a desire to give citizens a powerful voice in matters about their health, well-being and privacy was probably the principal influence. Nevertheless, it is also likely that the legislators recognized the potential practicalities of the move in the run-up to making it legal. In conferring a set of meaningful entitlements the legislation enshrined in law the role and responsibilities of patients and their representatives, and the corresponding position of the health service and professionals who are involved.

There is no good reason why citizens of the United Kingdom should not also have a similar kind of compact assortment of all-inclusive legal rights and responsibilities of their own. It seems to make practical sense, and there is moral justification for it too. Certainly, it is hard to defend leaving things the way they are, even accepting that British law-makers have established institutions (not uniquely) to support the interests of patients in additional ways – directly and otherwise. The difficulty is that these legislators do not appear to have any plans to introduce specific patients' rights legislation in the forseeable future. By contrast, a (rising) number of other European governments have taken this issue seriously and the necessary legislation has been put in place. It would not be before time should the UK's administrations decide to do the same.

CHAPTER 8

Litigation is still the only game in town for patient compensation in the UK

But it may soon lose its monopoly

There is no mechanism in the United Kingdom that will automatically compensate victims of medical accident or malpractice, no universal system of compulsorily and independently assessing claims for compensation for any patient injury that occurred following health care in the public or private health service. The only recourse for a patient in these circumstances is civil litigation, an avenue long superseded by financially risk-free schemes, first introduced in Europe by Nordic countries and, apparently, catching on elsewhere on the continent. These open-to-all substitute schemes deliver unfettered access to compensation following clinical failure – even without fault having to be proved.

Yet a similar open door to compensation (of £100,000 in the form of a single sum payment) exists in the UK for severe disability caused by vaccination against any of a specified list of diseases. Financial redress is also available for personal injury that occurs outside the country's health service. For instance, in criminal incidents tariff-based compensation in levels between £1,000 and £250,000 is payable to those who have suffered physical or psychological injury. In certain cases involving lost earnings and special expenses such awards can exceed this range, rising to a maximum of £500,000. Moreover, specific social security benefits can be claimed in cases involving industrial injury – for an accident, injury or a disease that resulted from a person's work. (Chapter 9 expands on each of these three schemes.)

More than one mechanism, aside from the civil courts, invariably come into play when a claim is made for damages over clinical negligence in the NHS. These can include one or more organizations that will defend or settle claims for compensation made against NHS bodies, private health care groups or medical practitioners. The process of claiming recompense may also involve public legal aid groups set up to provide means-tested financial support in litigation referring to personal injury. As a result, anyone seeking restitution for alleged damaging medical error is likely to have their work cut out, especially if they may already have tried to obtain a satisfactory explanation via the statutory health service complaints procedure or some other process.

The key bodies dealing with claims about clinical negligence involving NHS trusts and community health services
Three out of the four United Kingdom countries have their own specially devised mechanisms for handling clinical negligence and other claims for damages against NHS trusts and community health services. These bodies are broadly similar in structure.

125

They are not independent by nature and the claims they are responsible for defending or settling are funded by the contributions received from their members or clients. The exception is Northern Ireland, where there is no such specific mechanism for dealing with compensation claims.

England

In England the body created for the purpose is the National Health Service Litigation Authority (NHSLA), a 'special health authority', which is part of the NHS. It was set up under provisions in the NHS Act 1977 and came into existence in November 1995. The NHSLA's principal duty is to administer schemes established under the National Health Service and Community Care Act 1990. This act allows the Secretary of State to introduce one or more schemes to help NHS bodies pool the cost of any 'loss of or damage to property and liabilities to third parties for loss, damage or injury arising out of the carrying out of [their] functions'.[1]

In 2003 there were five such schemes, which covered:

- liabilities for alleged clinical negligence where the original incident occurred on or after 1 April 1995 (the Clinical Negligence Scheme for Trusts or CNST)
- liabilities for clinical negligence incidents that took place before that date (the Existing Liabilities Scheme or ELS)
- the outstanding liabilities for clinical negligence relating to the former regional health authorities (RHAs)
- any liability to any third party where the original incident arose on or after 1 April 1999 (the Liability to Third Party Scheme or LTPS)
- any expenses incurred from any loss or damage to property where the original loss occurred on or after 1 April 1999 (the Property Expenses Scheme or PES) but excluding motor vehicle claims.[2]

The NHSLA is responsible for expenditure on the five schemes whether it is centrally funded by the Department of Health or by contributions from its members. Similarly, it has responsibility for the costs of administering the schemes and any additional duties agreed between the NHSLA and the Secretary of State.[3] Since 1 January 2003 these have included a Human Rights Act Information Service (HRAIS), the purpose of which is to reduce the cost to the NHS of obtaining legal advice concerning the application of the Human Rights Act 1998.[4]

Membership of the CNST, LTPS and PES is voluntary and open to relevant NHS bodies. Nevertheless, all NHS trusts and primary care trusts are members of the CNST and most of them belong to the LTPS and PES. Strategic health authorities are not members of CNST (since they do not directly provide patient care) but are eligible to join the LTPS and PES for non-clinical risks. Some have already done so as have certain special health authorities such as the Health Protection Agency. However, any NHS establishment – whether a member of the schemes or not – can apply for financial assistance under the ELS.[5]

The Secretary of State's stated overall objectives for the NHSLA in operating the schemes is 'to promote the highest possible standards of patient care and to minimize the suffering resulting from any adverse incidents'. In essence, the NHSLA will help to realize these aims through 'efficient, effective and impartial administration' of the schemes and also by means of their development in changing situations.[6]

With these considerations in mind, specific goals have been set for the schemes. These include keeping to a minimum the overall costs of clinical negligence, third party liabilities and property expenses to the NHS and in this way to maximize the funds set aside for patient care. The NHSLA sees a robust defence of unjustified actions, efficient settlement of legitimate claims and contributing, through incentives, to the reduction in the number of negligent or preventable incidents – clinical and non-clinical – as ways of achieving these objectives. Nevertheless, it will ensure that remedies, including financial compensation, will be made available to patients where liability is established.[7]

In managing the schemes the NHSLA's stated duty is to have 'due regard' for the interests of all the parties involved in its activities. At the same time it continues to be sensitive to the views of the schemes' members and other NHS bodies. Another of its considerations is that the confidence of NHS professionals is maintained and their legitimate interests kept in mind. Accordingly a 14-member policy advisory group (PAG) is in place to represent the interests of the schemes' members on 'all significant issues of operational policy'. In cases where the professional aspects of claims are unusual or contentious, the NHSLA is guided by a professional advisory panel (PAP) comprising a minimum of seven individuals present at all meetings. The obligation to consult these two groups does not prevent the organization from obtaining advice from elsewhere, however.[8]

Since 1 April 2001 the NHSLA has dealt with all ELS claims in-house and since 1 April 2002 it has handled all CNST claims in the same way. But the system of excesses still applies to the non-clinical schemes, although members can pay the body a nominal fee to handle such claims on their behalf. Where it is appropriate to admit liability at an early stage, the NHSLA may not involve lawyers at all. The same can apply where liability is not accepted: many relatively low value cases are dealt with solely by the organization's claims handlers.[9]

At the time of writing, in 2004, the NHSLA board comprised a non-executive chairman, four other non-executive members, the chief executive and a director of finance. As a group these presiding managers are professionals with experience of the NHS, litigation, clinical practice and insurance. The non-executive members are appointed by the Secretary of State in line with the Nolan Committee principles, details of which are set out in guidance by the Department of Health.[10]

The NHSLA is accountable through its chairman to the Secretary of State for Health. It is the latter who decides the broad policy objectives and the financial framework in which this body operates. The minister is also responsible for approving the corporate and annual business plans, but this does not extend to the day-to-day running of the NHSLA, or in the resolution of cases that pass through its hands. Every five years the Department of Health consults the organization to review its role and operation, as set out in the draft document. Nevertheless, either the Secretary of State or the chairman of the board can propose changes before the end of any such period if it is deemed to be necessary. The organization has a panel of 14 specialist firms of solicitors who are instructed on clinical negligence claims and also a 'non-clinical' panel of nine firms of solicitors.[11]

In 2001–02 the NHSLA received 4,675 (CNST) claims and substantially more were expected for the following year. This is attributed to the 'call-in' of such claims previously handled by NHS trusts and the continuing notification of new claims. During this period 1,287 CNST claims were closed, with damages agreed on an additional 1,154 cases – excluding outstanding legal costs. In the same year the body received 3,364 claims related to the LTPS and PES schemes. By the end of the period the NHSLA had assumed responsibility for an aggregate total of 13,146 claims for all its schemes compared with 11,339 at the end of 2000–01.[12]

The accumulated value of all these claims was estimated to be about £5.3 billion, including those 'incurred but not reported' (IBNR). This is not to say that the claims would be paid in the following year – in practice circumstances are such that they will be settled or resolved over a period of many years. Also, although the value of claims in hand had risen (and would further increase in 2002–03), the figure for 2001–02 refers to the increased number of claims of all types for which the NHSLA had become responsible. Potential liabilities for non-clinical risks were £69 million in 2001–02.[13] (Owing to developments, some already described, affecting the NHSLA's jurisdiction over claims and other factors, a detailed comparison with the statistics for any previous years is not provided.)

As predicted for reasons already given, in 2002–03 there was an increase in the number and value of claims handled by the NHSLA over the previous year. At the end of the year there were 19,580 claims involving all its schemes, with clinical negligence (CNST) claims also seeing a substantial rise – they had more than doubled from 4,675 in 2001–02 to 9,602. Inevitably also the estimated value of all claims received about trusts (which now include PCTs) has risen from around £5.3 billion in 2001–02 to £5.96 billion in 2002–03. Included in these figures are provisions for IBNR claims.[14]

Again it is emphasized in the NHSLA's 2003 report and accounts that the end of year total value of claims is not an annual payout for compensation and costs: 'it is a realistic estimate (provision)' of all the current known claims (19,580 at 2002–03) and IBNR provision to be dealt with over the coming years. The provision includes an increase partly to allow for continuing higher awards for injuries and the cost of care for patients who have suffered injury. The NHSLA chairman stated that the amounts involved in these cases may need to be revised in the light of the Courts Bill before parliament at the time – legislation that will enable the courts to order periodic payments instead of a single sum.[15]

In his statement the chairman added that there had been a 74% increase in the number of cases dealt with by formal mediation – a measure that the NHSLA continues to support. Also, in addition to reducing the number of 'older' (including the ELS) claims, the 'shelf-life' of claims had been reduced. For all CNST claims it was now 1.98 years from the notification of a claim to trusts until compensation is agreed, and 1.26 years from the time of notifying the NHSLA until compensation is agreed. This, the chairman stated, compared with five and a half years from claim to payment of damages, the duration reported by the National Audit Office (NAO) in its 2001 report. He further affirmed that there were only 218 outstanding claims five years after the NHSLA had been notified.[16]

Wales

The corresponding body handling clinical negligence claims in Wales is the Welsh Risks Pool (WRP), a mutual organization funded by all NHS trusts and local health boards (LHBs) in the Principality. Operating as the All Wales Risks Pool up to April

1996, it was set up in response to a rising tide of clinical negligence claims to help spread the cost of settlements. Commercial insurance for clinical negligence not being permitted, the alternative was to self-insure using the funds of individual NHS establishments.[17]

Three options were available at the time: fund risks from current revenue, generate reserves against future losses, or borrow funds to finance major losses when they occurred and repay them over an extended period. The 'mutual' concept was chosen because it allowed the risk to be spread across a number of health care organizations, thereby helping to even out peaks and troughs in claims being made. It also provided a pool of funds raised annually and, unlike conventional insurance practice or other mutual pooling schemes, no reserves are accumulated against future risks.[18]

The WRP is managed by Conwy and Denbighshire NHS Trust. It reimburses trusts and local health boards for the costs of meeting claims made against them, or when loss is caused through other means. Cover is provided for all risks, excluding motor vehicle claims and those about income-producing activities. Its responsibilities include setting policy, assessing and collecting premiums and reimbursing claims and ensuring that there are adequate resources to meet these demands. The WRP actively supports the development of risk management structures and introduced 11 'risk management standards' and six 'specialist services standards' in 1997. A further 21 similar measures were added to judge the performance of its members.[19]

Each year the WRP will assess the extent to which NHS trusts comply with 23 out of the 38 criteria that were in force by 2003. During the same year 'risk' standards specific to local health boards were also being developed. It appears that, at the time of its inception, the WRP's arrangements were not dissimilar to the Clinical Negligence Scheme for Trusts (CNST) operated by the NHSLA in England. However, in their greatly developed form since then, the measures in place for Wales are seen by the WRP to be more demanding and the cover greater than those apparent in the English model.[20]

Premiums set to finance the WRP are substantially dependent on the size of member organizations and to a small degree on their claims history. In the past the level of members' success in meeting the fixed standards also affected the value of excess payable by them on each claim. For instance, a 75 per cent compliance with these standards produced a reduction in excess from £30,000 to £25,000. There is an added incentive for NHS trusts, which if met will reduce this excess to £22,500. Nonetheless, the requirements did not apply to health authorities, with their excess being fixed at £35,000 per claim.[21]

The system of variable excesses in its application to local health boards ended with effect from 2003–04 when a nominal premium of £5,000 was charged to each of them at the start of the year. The premium will be reviewed as the level of exposure to risk posed by LHBs becomes apparent. On 1 April 2003 the variable excess was replaced by a standard excess of £25,000 per claim and applies to all NHS organizations. By contrast, the premiums paid by trusts and health authorities are arrived at by dividing the value of the total contribution figure determined for them by the number of members involved, and on the basis of their size and claims history. In 2002–03 the proportion of premium based on the claims record of these NHS establishments was increased from 15 to 20 per cent. (At the time of writing in 2004, the means of calculating the premium payable was under review and likely to be replaced by a risk-based model. Its effect will be to calculate premium based on the type and level of activity and risk management performance, rather than on size.)[22]

During the same year, clinical negligence cases accounted for over 90 per cent of all claims received by the Welsh Risks Pool and litigated by Welsh Health Legal Services, the group of solicitors acting on its behalf. The cost of claims rose from under £10 million in 1998–99 to just below £50 million during 2001–02, although the increase seems to have occurred almost entirely in the latter year. Between April and September 2002, the value of claims was roughly the same as that for the whole of the previous year. In 2002–03 the figure was slightly lower at £45.4 million.[23]

Scotland

The agency dealing with claims for damages against the National Health Service in Scotland has been around much longer than its corresponding bodies in England and Wales. Established by statute, the Central Legal Office (CLO) came into existence more than 45 years ago and is part of the Common Services Agency based in Edinburgh. The most recent primary legislation to have affected the way it operates is the National Health Service (Scotland) Act 1978, as amended by the National Health Service and Care in the Community Act 1990.[24]

Becoming a fee-charging organization in 1995, the CLO is managed as a business for its health service clients. In 2003 it employed around 40 solicitors and support staff – around 90 personnel in all. Its solicitors are divided into three groups covering litigation, property and contracts, with legal services provided to all NHS health boards and trusts in Scotland. While these health service bodies are obliged to use the CLO where it concerns clinical negligence claims, they are free to obtain legal services from elsewhere to deal with other claims that arise.[25]

In 2002–03 the value of compensation claims referring to health care received in these establishments had risen to £9.1 million from £6.5 million the year before and £3.2 million in 2000–01, but the rise from £1.5 million in 1990–91 has not been steady. Indeed, if a graph was drawn across the following 12-year period it would show an almost uninterrupted up-and-down pattern, although by far the greatest value of annual claims were those recorded for each of the last two years.[26]

Northern Ireland

Unlike the other three UK countries, there is no specially set up body to deal with clinical negligence compensation claims in Northern Ireland. From what can be ascertained, until 1993 such claims involving NHS hospital and community health services were handled by the country's four health boards. NHS trusts concerned then began dealing with these cases. However, the system was in the process of possible change, although details of its proposed new form appeared not to have been fully determined in early 2004.

Public legal aid in clinical negligence claims

Claimants seeking damages for injury allegedly caused by clinical negligence can apply for financial assistance in the form of legal aid from one of the three bodies operating in the UK. The cost of legal help or representation is covered to the extent of applicants' personal economic resources, or not at all if their finances are outside the set means-tested limits. In this latter event, claimants must pursue their cases independently through the litigation process. The account that follows gives the position in 2003.

In England and Wales the Legal Services Commission (LSC), through its 'community legal service', provides advice and legal representation for people pursuing a clinical negligence claim. Subject to certain conditions being met by applicants, the services are funded by the LSC and provided exclusively by legal firms – specialist ones in medical negligence cases – with which it has a contract. The provisions of the civil scheme are contained in the Access to Justice Act 1999, and in the 'funding code', guidance, regulations, directions and orders made under the legislation.[27]

Under the description of 'legal help' the LSC provides initial advice and assistance on any legal problem. 'Help at court' allows for a solicitor or adviser to speak on a person's behalf at certain court hearings, without formally acting for the individual in the whole proceedings. 'Legal representation' (formerly known as civil legal aid) allows a person to be represented in court and is available in two forms: 'investigative help', with funding limited to investigating the strength of a claim, and 'full representation', the cost of which is covered in legal proceedings. (If warranted, both these categories of funding can be granted in emergencies and if certain criteria are met.) In practice, funding for clinical negligence claims usually takes the form of investigative help and is extended to cover legal proceedings only if a case is found to have good prospects following investigation.[28]

To qualify for legal help and help at court or legal representation, applicants must show that their income and capital are within the current set limits. The income of a spouse or partner will also be taken into account, unless the couple are living apart because the relationship is over, or if there is a material conflict of interest between them in the matter being pursued.[29]

Some cases that were previously paid for by 'legal aid' are now carried out under a 'conditional fee agreement' (CFA) – a private arrangement between client and solicitor. This usually means that clients are not required to pay their solicitors' costs when an action is unsuccessful, but precise details may vary. However, as clinical negligence claims can be very complex, solicitors normally will not enter into a conditional fee agreement unless there is strong evidence that a case will be won.[30]

Although reform of clinical negligence procedures and funding is under consideration (referred to again later in this chapter), clinical negligence remains within the scope of 'community legal service' funding. In these instances applicants will need to show not only that their case has a reasonable chance of success but also that the possible value of the claim is sufficient to justify the costs involved. If the compensation is likely to be less than £5,000, funding will usually be refused. Where a claim is for less than £10,000, the LSC may require the client to pursue a complaint against the NHS before considering litigation.[31]

Qualification for 'legal help' and 'help at court'

Where disposable capital exceeds £3,000, or if gross income in the previous month was more than £2,288, the person concerned will not qualify. (A progressively higher income limit applies where a couple have more than four children.) Nonetheless, in cases where gross earnings are £2,288 or less but the disposable income is assessed as being more than £621 per month, the person concerned will still not be eligible for legal help or help at court. Applicants who are receiving income support or income-based jobseeker's allowance will qualify so far as their income is concerned, but their capital situation would still need to be assessed.[32]

No person who has qualified for legal help or help at court by reason of income or capital is required to contribute towards arising costs – the regional office of the LSC will cover these expenses. If money is recovered in the process, the solicitors concerned must use the funds to pay their bills. This is known as the 'statutory charge'. To illustrate, if £750 has been recovered and the bill is £100, the client will receive £650. Nevertheless, there are certain exceptions to this rule.[33]

Qualification for 'legal representation'

The Legal Services Commission decides whether a case satisfies the merits criteria and financial qualifications for legal representation funding. It then either issues a certificate, if the applicant does not have to pay a contribution, or makes an offer of one where payment is required. Once an offer is accepted, the person concerned must pay a contribution from capital immediately and make any such payment from income by monthly instalments starting straight away. A certificate is then issued, at which point the solicitor involved can start dealing with the case using LSC funding. The LSC must be notified where a person's income or capital has increased or reduced while a certificate is in force. This could lead to a reassessment of the person's means and affect the amount of contribution to be paid.[34]

In 2003 the disposable income limit was set at £707 for a person to qualify, but the applicant's case must also satisfy the merits criteria written into the LSC's funding code. Once these two sets of conditions are met, the applicant's monthly disposable income will decide whether or not a contribution towards the cost of legal representation will be needed. If these disposable earnings are no more than £267 per month payment is not required; if they are between £268 and £707 the person concerned must pay a monthly contribution to costs based on one of three income bands (see Table 8.1). The first monthly payment becomes due when an offer of funding by the LSC has been accepted. Anyone on income support or income-based jobseeker's allowance will automatically qualify for funding and also be exempt from paying a contribution.[35]

Table 8.1 Contribution towards the cost of legal representation, 2003

Band	Monthly disposable income	Monthly contribution
A	£268–393	1/4 of income over £263
B	£394–522	£32.50 +1/3 of income over £393
C	£523–707	£75.50 +1/2 of income over £522

Source: Legal Services Commission, *A Practical Guide to Community Legal Service Funding*, 2003[36]

Disposable capital will also decide whether a person qualifies for legal representation and will (or will not) contribute towards its cost. If this is no more than £8,000, funding will be provided, although in this case any disposable capital assessed as being over £3,000 will have to be contributed towards costs. The disposable capital of pensioners is calculated differently, with those who are 60 or over benefitting from an extra allowance. If the disposable income in such instances is less than £267 per month (excluding net income earned from capital) then a proportion of savings is disregarded (see Table 8.2). This means that applicants can still qualify for funding despite their total savings being above the set capital limit.[37]

Table 8.2 Disposable income and capital requirements for pensioners

Monthly disposable income	Capital disregarded
Up to £25	£100,000
£26–50	£90,000
£51–75	£80,000
£76–100	£70,000
£101–125	£60,000
£126–150	£50,000
£151–175	£40,000
£176–200	£30,000
£201–225	£20,000
£226–250	£10,000

Source: Legal Services Commission, *A Practical Guide to Community Legal Service Funding*, 2003[38]
[a] Excluding net income derived from capital

What follows the outcome of court action

Where a case is won, the amount a person will have to pay for legal representation depends on whether the other side is ordered to pay the plaintiff's costs, and does so, or the plaintiff is awarded any money that was at issue in the case. If the other party pays the claimant's costs in full, the latter may expect to be refunded the whole contribution that had been paid to the LSC. Where these cost are not paid in full, the LSC will deduct from any money ordered by the court or agreed to be paid by the other side (and paid) as much as is required to cover the costs. This is another example of the statutory charge, although in particular circumstances it can be postponed. In these cases, the money that is owed will be registered as a charge (like a mortgage) on the home of the person concerned and will be repayable at a simple (rather than compound) rate of interest. However, in most clinical negligence cases that are successful, costs are recovered in full so there is no statutory charge. Thus claimants receive their full damages.[39]

On the other hand, those who have received legal representation and lose their case normally pay no more towards solicitor's or barrister's fees than any contribution under the certificate previously issued by the LSC. The court will not usually order the plaintiff to pay the other party's costs, although it may do so in certain exceptional circumstances. In this event, the amount to be paid will depend on a person's means and their conduct in the dispute.[40]

(Separate though similar public legal aid mechanisms operate in Scotland and Northern Ireland. Akin to the model for England and Wales, the Scottish Legal Aid Board and the Law Society of Northern Ireland Legal Aid Department may provide funding for legal help and representation in clinical negligence claims. Again, any financial assistance is subject to means-testing and other criteria being met.)

The position for those seeking compensation

From what has been shown, the position of those who seek compensation as a result of clinical negligence in the UK is not encouraging – whether or not a claim reaches court. For instance legal aid in clinical negligence cases is not easily available, even when an applicant has passed a means test. The problem is that public funding for legal proceedings is provided only if a case is considered to have a good chance of success. Moreover, even when legal aid for this purpose is granted, the claimant may still have to contribute towards the cost of litigation, unless the case is successful. Another difficulty that can arise is that public funding is usually refused in instances where the compensation is likely to be less than £5,000 because of the high initial handling costs.

So where does this leave applicants in cases that either do not qualify for legal aid or where it is not on offer because the chances of success are not highly rated? Simple. Those who wish to pursue a claim for compensation in such circumstances must do so independently and foot the legal bill themselves – unless no-win-no-fee legal representation can be found. In either event, the cost of insuring against losing their case and having to pay the opponent's legal costs will need to be considered.

Alternatively, many who believe they have a case may simply decide against continuing their claim rather than take a chance in a challenging and invariably protracted process that offers no guarantees. Who knows how many more may simply not have the inclination to go through the motions of claiming at all. Indeed, it has been shown that a huge proportion of claimants give up before formally pursuing their cases. Even when claims have progressed further, it seems that a large percentage are then abandoned (see Chapter 9).

It seems that measures such as the Clinical Disputes Forum, set up in 1996; Lord Woolf's reforms to the civil justice system in 1999; the Access to Justice Act 1999; and steps taken by the Lord Chancellor's Department over use of 'alternative dispute resolution' procedures to settle legal cases and its other initiatives are having some effect in alleviating problems. But these recently introduced innovations, reforms, legislation and subsequent schemes can go only so far – probably not far enough to transform the situation about clinical negligence compensation as much as is needed.

The problem is that these indisputably commendable new adjustments, even with added no-win-no-fee incentives (when they arise), serve merely to improve a system that will probably remain inequitable. No amount of reform on these lines is likely to address what should be the basic issue concerning clinical negligence claims: providing ready and full access to compensation. Only total change to the system as it stands will do this, and deliver for damaged patients the sort of comparatively stress-free, redress-for-all arrangement that is available for other types of personal injury referred to at the beginning of this chapter.

Until this happens the position for claimants seeking damages for clinical negligence will remain bleak. The system will continue to be selective, unduly taxing and risky to take on. Plainly, there are not the same disadvantages for the health service or, indeed, medical practitioners who are on a similarly firm financial footing in compensation cases. The monetary contributions that they make to their respective legal defence organizations (the Medical Defence Union and Medical Protection Society, for example) secure for them the kind of guaranteed and powerful support that is not the privilege of damaged patients or their families who are looking for appropriate redress. Again, the system is skewed against these claimants.

Fortunately the issue of redress for personal injury caused by clinical error has finally been placed under detailed scrutiny. As a result radical change to adjust the imbalance between compensation for impairment occurring from care provided by the NHS and other kinds of personal injury may soon be on its way. The question is: to what extent will it correct matters when it arrives? Chapter 9 describes and assesses the proposals for sweeping reform that will affect negligence and compensation issues involving the NHS in England. Who knows, these recommendations may also turn out to be a template for the rest of the nation.

A patient redress scheme for England has been drawn up

It could even be a blueprint for the whole nation

There are indeed plans in England to change radically the way that clinical negligence and redressing its outcome are attended to in much of the public health service. In June 2003 England's chief medical officer (CMO), Professor Sir Liam Donaldson, announced his proposals to make this a reality where it involves NHS hospitals and community health services, and in certain situations outside the public health sector. Thus the recommendations for dealing with patient injury will not initially be all-inclusive, nor will the proposals necessarily affect the rest of the nation. Their additional application to NHS primary care in England and to the rest of the United Kingdom are matters yet to be determined.

Nevertheless, there are sure to be many who will be pleasantly startled at the apparent boldness of the proposals – especially after years of prevarication by legislators and no change to the poor position of those at the receiving end of medical error. These are certainly progressive recommendations and go a long way towards providing for a system with an open door for redressing claims. The question is: how wide open is the door?

Origins of the proposals for change

Professor Donaldson's report and recommendations for change were set out in the consultation document *Making Amends*, which followed a public consultation exercise he had carried out through the earlier paper, a 'call for ideas', *Clinical Negligence: what are the issues and options for reform?* The latter was issued in August 2001 and circulated to some 180 specific individuals (including the CMO's 18-member advisory committee) from a variety of organizations and institutions and to other relevant destinations in the United Kingdom.[1]

The CMO had also held meetings with his advisory committee of representatives from the legal and medical professions, the NHS, patient groups and medical defence bodies, and consulted the other interested parties on the 180-strong list of the paper's recipients. He had further commissioned research into various aspects of compensation relating to health care and reviewed reports on the way that litigation involving clinical negligence was working in the UK. Moreover, Professor Donaldson had considered how recent reforms to the civil justice system had affected the handling of clinical negligence claims. In the process of all this work he had received written statements from different parties responding to the document.[2]

In putting together *Making Amends* the CMO had further taken into account a number of reports and initiatives involving related matters that had been completed or were in progress at the time. These included the nationwide appraisal of the NHS complaints procedure (covered in Chapter 2 of this book) and an evaluation by the Lord Chancellor's Department of the reforms following Lord Woolf's report *Access to Justice* on civil litigation procedures in 1996. Among other items the CMO considered was a consultation paper *Damages for Future Loss*, also produced by the Lord Chancellor's Department and issued in March 2002. This applied to England, Wales and Northern Ireland and set out the position on whether the courts should be given powers to order periodical payments for future loss and care costs in personal injury cases.[3]

Introduction to the proposals for reforming the approach to clinical negligence and its outcome

'Legal proceedings for medical injury progress in an atmosphere of confrontation, acrimony, misunderstanding and bitterness. The process is anathema to the spirit of openness, trust and partnership which should characterize the modern relationship between patient and doctor.' So said England's Chief Medical Officer in his preamble to the long list of recommendations in *Making Amends*.[4]

He added that the whole nature of a legal dispute between two parties works against the wider interests of patients: the emphasis is on revealing as little as possible about what went wrong, clinical decisions taken are defended and information is released reluctantly. The CMO further pointed out that the 'tort' system in use for clinical negligence cases applies blame and retribution as its weapons of deterrence. This potential deterrent effect is greatly weakened in an age when the majority of cases are settled out of court, whereby lessons learned are restricted to those involved or associated with the case, rather than aimed at a wider audience.[5]

Professor Donaldson considered that a modern health service that seeks to improve safety should use the poor experience of one patient as a cause for 'rapid and systematic learning so that perhaps thousands of future patients do not suffer in the same way'. He felt that the ideal must be that anyone who has received a poor standard of health care or suffered harm as a result is given an apology, an explanation, remedial therapy and, where appropriate, monetary recompense, while 'the NHS as a whole learns the lessons'.[6]

The CMO cited a number of other apparently unacceptable contributing flaws in the present system of addressing clinical negligence issues:

- Complainants faced with complex and unfamiliar legal procedures feel disadvantaged and rarely believe that their concerns have been satisfactorily addressed – even after receiving compensation. Cases have taken too long to settle and, especially in low value claims, the legal costs have been disproportionate to the damages awarded. Larger claims for compensation can also be unduly lengthy and expensive because of the inevitable disputes that arise. Under current arrangements some people who have suffered severe injury caused by failures in health care will receive sizeable damages while others similarly harmed are paid nothing.
- Rehabilitation and facilities for the special care and education of children with severe mental or physical disability are not routinely available in the public health care sector.
- Despite the case put forward by many legal commentators, there is no escaping the fact that the tort system of addressing medical injury does not sit well in a National Health Service with an ethos of fairness and a desire to bring the greatest good

to the greatest number of people. Even a reformed tort system would be inequitable in that it will still compensate only a select few. Moreover, the mechanism presents no 'dynamic' for better and safer care for the large number of patients treated daily by the NHS. It also offers few incentives for health care providers to reduce risk to patients.[7]

Professor Donaldson stated that the proposals for change he had put forward were aimed at 'fundamental reform'. However, he added that these recommendations do not propose removing a patient's right to sue a NHS doctor or establishment. Instead, the role of tort would be moved from its existing central position to the 'outer perimeter' of the NHS.[8]

A new redress scheme for the NHS

Making Amends proposes that a NHS redress scheme should be established to investigate clinical incidents and the harm that is alleged to have resulted from them. Under this scheme the patient concerned would be given an explanation of what occurred and why, an apology and a description of what action is planned to avoid a repetition of the incident. The proposed mechanism would be a means of providing a prearranged set of measures involving remedial treatment, care and rehabilitation where it is needed.[9]

It would also determine whether payment should be made for pain and suffering, out-of-pocket expenses and care or therapy that the NHS is unable to provide. Initially, the proposed new redress scheme will be centred on patients receiving NHS hospital and community health services. Nevertheless, consideration would also be given to those who have received treatment in the independent or voluntary sectors in the United Kingdom or abroad under NHS funding arrangements.[10]

The mechanism would be implemented after an adverse incident or complaint has been inquired into locally by the relevant NHS establishment, or when the case has passed through independent review (in the new form described in Chapter 2). It could also be invoked after an investigation and recommendations by the Health Service Ombudsman. Additionally, claimants whose cases have been investigated by the National Health Service Litigation Authority (NHSLA) would be eligible for the proposed redress scheme. The conditions for receiving compensation would be that there were serious defects in the level of care provided, the impairment could have been avoided, or the adverse outcome was not caused by the natural progression of the illness.[11]

In the early stages of the scheme the NHS may have limited ability to provide a programme of care where it is required. Where this occurs, monetary recompense may be offered as a substitute. Meanwhile, the health service should start expanding its capacity to offer the necessary remedial treatment and care under the scheme. It is expected that the body replacing the NHSLA would give its support in the devising and implementation of care plans.[12]

Monetary redress would be limited to the notional cost of the period of care, or an alternative amount, 'at the discretion of the local NHS trust'. This payment could rise to a maximum of £30,000 where it has been authorized by the national body in charge of the proposed scheme.[13] The new mechanism will have a number of advantages over the existing arrangements. It will provide:

- a full investigation of a complaint or claim

- a programme of remedial care and rehabilitation where it is needed
- quicker resolution of cases and an offer of compensation where it is due
- reduced legal costs because lawyers would not routinely need to be involved.[14]

The suggestion is that the scheme should be piloted under existing laws to assist in fashioning the detail of new primary legislation. Until then, the pilot will be based on the 'Bolam' test of clinical negligence, in force in 2004; the batch of cases that are to be included in the pilot operation will be judged against alternative tests by a medico-legal panel. It is expected that the initial exercise as a whole will help give a clearer picture of the potential effect on the likely cost and number of successful claims in applying a lower qualifying threshold describing 'sub-standard care'.[15]

Care and compensation for babies who have suffered severe neurological impairment[16]
The redress scheme should allow for care and compensation in instances where babies have suffered severe neurological impairment, including celebral palsy. At present cases involving this kind of injury account for some of the biggest compensation payments by the NHSLA. The difficulty in proving causation and negligence means that one small group is compensated while another more sizeable one is not. Therefore, the new redress mechanism should be put on a footing that will more usefully meet the needs of a greater number of this category of seriously damaged children and their families.

A number of conditions would need to be met in order to qualify for the scheme. First, a child's birth must occur while in NHS care and any severe neurological injury (including cerebral palsy) be related to or result from the birth. Also, any claim for redress to the mechanism must be made within eight years of a child's birth. The programme of care and compensation would be based on a severity index assessed on a person's ability to carry out the activities of daily living. Genetic or chromosomal abnormality would be excluded from the scheme.

Redress would be given in cash and in kind according to the severity of impairment caused and the needs of the child concerned as a consequence. It would consist of a managed programme of care; a monthly payment (up to £100,00 in the most serious cases) for the costs of care that cannot be provided in this way; lump sum payments (up to £50,000 in very severe cases) for home adaptation and equipment at intervals throughout a child's life; and an opening payment, capped at £50,000, to compensate for pain, suffering and loss of amenity.

On application from the parents concerned, the programme determined would be managed by a national body following on the work of the NHSLA. A panel of experts would review the severity of the impairment that had arisen and decide whether it was connected with or a result of the birth. It is considered that the benefits of such a scheme would be to offer support and compensation to a wider cross-section of seriously disabled babies and children without negligence or fault having to be verified. The arrangement is also expected to control costs to the NHS by meeting care needs as they arise. Before establishing the form that the redress will take, the Department of Health would consult families whose children have been damaged in this way, their representatives and expert clinicians and care workers to settle the basis for the severity index that will apply to the programme of care.

A new national body to administer the compensation element of the redress scheme[17]
It is proposed that the national body to replace the NHSLA will have a new name, a wider remit and will administer the monetary redress aspect of the scheme nationally. The new body would be responsible for assessing all claims (other than those concerning neurologically damaged babies) from patients or families and recommendations for compensation payments by health service providers, complaints bodies and associated organizations. It would also monitor the care and rehabilitation programmes under the scheme that will be provided at local NHS level.

Other duties would include the levying of 'insurance' contributions to be paid by NHS providers that will finance the new arrangements. The new body would keep a check on local and national compensation awards and publish annual listings by these health service establishments to act as an encouragement to reduce risk to patients and improve their safety. It would also assess and manage claims for care (other than those for neurologically impaired babies) where damages of more than £30,000 are being sought under the tort system. Meanwhile, the body would take over the management of older clinical negligence claims for care provided before the start of the new scheme. After a reasonable period of evaluation it would consider raising the monetary threshold of the scheme and extending the system to cover primary care as well.

Retaining the right of individuals to pursue litigation
Under the proposed new measures patients or their families would retain the right to take civil action for clinical negligence instead of applying to the NHS redress scheme. This would be the case in addition to claims beyond the limit of the scheme. Nonetheless, once a patient has entered the scheme and accepted its proposals, the same case cannot subsequently be taken to litigation. It is expected that before an offer under the redress scheme is accepted, patients would be given a small payment to obtain independent advice on the fairness of the proposal.[18]

What should follow an adverse clinical incident or complaint
Each adverse incident or complaint should receive an appropriately comprehensive investigation. This should be followed by a simply written explanation to patients or their families of what happened, an apology where something has gone wrong and a report of the (local and national) action being taken to reduce the risk of it happening to others. There should also be an offer for a follow-up discussion with those affected, and an invitation for them to return to the hospital and observe the improvements that have been carried out as a result of the complaint. Moreover, under the redress scheme, NHS trusts should take prompt action to propose the treatment or rehabilitation considered necessary to remedy harm that has been caused. A senior member of staff should be responsible for organizing the initial response to the complaint, and become involved with the parties concerned in all aspects of the process of putting matters right.[19]

A designated NHS trust board member should have overall responsibility in the investigation of and learning from adverse incidents, complaints and claims
A NHS trust board member would be in charge of finding out the reasons, along a causal line, why an adverse incident occurred, instead of seeking to ascribe blame to

particular individuals. Such an investigation would allow for a full explanation to the patient or complainant involved and enable the measures necessary to avoid a repetition of the event to be identified. Patients should be told what these steps are and, where possible or relevant, be given evidence of the resulting changes.[20]

The NHS complaints procedure should proceed irrespective of a claim being made
In the existing NHS complaints procedure a complaint is halted pending resolution of the claim to which it refers. It is proposed that this requirement is removed in the reformed complaints mechanism so that an initial investigation at local level will automatically take place in response to a complaint. This would apply to claims being made through the NHS redress scheme and to cases involving larger sums that are pursued via litigation. It is predicted that a change on these lines may reduce rather than increase the number of people who decide to take civil action and that complainants and claimants may feel less dissatisfied than they are with the present state of affairs.[21]

Training in communication relating to complaints for NHS staff at all levels
Training should be given to staff at all levels in NHS trusts in communication relating to complaints – from the initial response through to conciliation and providing explanations to patients and their families. This will help overcome the defensive reaction that most complainants and claimants consider is the instinctive response to their concerns as matters stand in 2004. It would also complement the work that the Patients' Advice and Liaison Services (PALS) has already started.[22]

Effective rehabilitation in personal injury cases, including adverse clinical incidents
Effective rehabilitation services should be developed for those who have been injured as a result of therapy or other means. Research shows that following this course can lead to less time being spent in hospital, speed recovery and help prevent long-term disability. The ongoing pilot NHSLA scheme to offer early rehabilitation in appropriate clinical negligence cases should continue in the short term while being independently assessed. In the longer term, rehabilitation programmes should be developed under the NHS redress scheme, with attention also given to expanding the services to put these measures into effect.[23]

Improving facilities for children with severe neurological and physical impairment
There are a limited number of units providing special care and education amenities for severely brain-damaged and physically disabled children and their poor geographical spread invariably causes families to set up their own facilities at home. For this reason the Department of Health and patient and carer groups should study the prospect of providing a network of high grade units to provide this care, but at a lower cost than those operating in the private sector.[24]

Health care staff to report incidents without fear of disciplinary action
Conditions should be in place that allow a 'duty of candour' by health care professionals, yet exempt them from disciplinary action when they report incidents with a patient's safety in mind. Such a duty and exemption should be introduced in legislation requiring all health service practitioners and managers to notify patients

where they become aware that a negligent act or omission may have occurred. The exceptions would be if a practitioner has committed a criminal offence or when it would not be safe for the clinician to continue treating patients.[25]

*No disclosure in court of information compiled about adverse clinical incidents*Statutory provisions should be introduced to prevent the disclosure in a court of reports on adverse health care incidents provided locally or submitted to the National Patient Safety Agency (NPSA). This would reduce the disincentive for health service personnel to report errors. However, the proscription would apply only to reports of adverse incidents where a full account is also provided in the medical record. Information for use in court proceedings would have to be collected anew from the medical record and other sources.[26]

The Legal Service Commission's connection with the redress scheme
In instances where a claimant is seeking legal aid to pursue an action for clinical negligence, the Legal Services Commission (LSC) should establish whether the case has already passed through the NHS redress scheme. If so, what was the outcome? Information about the case could have an influence on decisions about applications for legal aid under the LSC's existing rules. These regulations should be updated to deal with cases in the longer term.[27]

Mediation before litigation for most claims outside the redress scheme
The organization that succeeds the NHSLA should require its panel of solicitor firms to assess each case for mediation and offer the service where it is appropriate. In addition to any non-material gains that mediation may provide, an out-of-court settlement of a substantial claim can follow. The Department of Health and the body that replaces the NHSLA should take steps to provide better information on the role of mediation to NHS staff and the specially set up patient advice and complaints agencies. These and other applicable bodies and groups should also work towards establishing an advanced mediation training programme about clinical negligence and look at alternative forms of dispute resolution for certain cases.[28]

Staged payment of damages in clinical negligence cases outside the redress scheme[29]
Provisions in the Courts Bill that allow the courts to order periodic payments without the consent of the parties involved can provide claimants with certainty for their future care needs. Distressing arguments about the life expectancy of claimants may also be avoided in the process, and allow the NHS to spread its costs in high value cases. The government indicated during the course of this draft legislation that circumstances in which periodic payments can be varied are to be tightly drawn so that frequent return to the court for reassessment will be avoided. Nevertheless, this legislation will apply only to clinical negligence cases decided in court, which accounts for less than one per cent of all such claims.

While the NHSLA has no power to enforce compliance with periodic payments in cases dealt with outside the NHS redress scheme, the legislation should encourage an increasing use of such staged settlements by the courts. On this basis the practice could gain ground and eventually become the norm in cases that are negotiated and decided.

Awards in NHS clinical negligence cases should not reflect the cost of private therapy
Section 2 (4) of the Law Reform (Personal Injury) Act 1948 allows for the care cost element of damages awarded to be based on that for private treatment in personal injury cases. The law should be changed to exempt clinical negligence cases where they refer to therapy that was provided by the NHS. Instead, the health service establishment concerned should agree to finance a stipulated programme of care or treatment over a specified period. It is expected that case managers working for the national authority that is to manage the redress scheme will produce such a programme and check its progress, so that patients do not have to deal with the NHS trust where the adverse incident arose. On an associated issue, special training should be provided for judges who hear clinical negligence cases because of the invariable complexity of such lawsuits and their comparatively infrequent entry into court.[30]

Controlling claimants' costs in clinical negligence cases
Finally, the Department for Constitutional Affairs (DCA) and the Legal Services Commission (LSC) should examine further ways of controlling claimants' costs in clinical negligence cases that are financed out of public funds. Also, the DCA and the Civil Justice Council should determine what additional measures could be taken to contain legal costs as a whole. At present, in cases that are successful and where costs are met by the NHS, claimants' costs are consistently considerably greater than those of the defence's, even if it is accepted that for unavoidable reasons there will always be some degree of imbalance in this respect. This situation of high legal costs could be improved by paying lawyers more in successful cases than in unsuccessful ones; such a measure may discourage some legal professionals from pursuing poor lawsuits. It is also suggested that the NHSLA's successor and the LSC should use common specialists in clinical negligence affairs as part of the drive to reduce expenditure.[31]

The Chief Medical Officer seeks the opinion of others
With the report completed and proposals set out for reforming the existing system of handling affairs about clinical negligence, Professor Donaldson circulated and publicized the resulting consultation paper with the aim of obtaining a wider sample of opinion on the subject. The views of respondents were especially called for over a series of questions that had arisen in the course of the study and preparation of his document.

Questions about the NHS redress scheme in its primary application were:
- What should the qualifying benchmark be: the 'Bolam' test, used in 2004 to assess clinical negligence or a wider definition of sub-standard care?
- If the latter criterion, what should its form be?
- Should there be a minimum qualifying standard relating to the extent of a disability expressed, for example, in days off work or in hospital, or by the degree of the impairment?
- Should there be an upper monetary limit for cases to be dealt with by the scheme? If so, is £30,000 the right starting amount?
- Should the monetary limit under the scheme apply to the programme of care and cash as a whole or just to the capital element?

- Should consideration be given to including primary care cases from the outset?
- Should patients or claimants be entitled to funding for legal advice to establish the fairness of an arrangement submitted by the redress scheme? If so, what limit should be set on the amount available?
- Will making it easier to get a programme of care and support as well as modest monetary compensation reduce or increase the number of claimants applying to the scheme? Why? Could this be mitigated?[32]

Questions about the NHS redress scheme as it applies to babies with severe neurological impairment were:

- What should the qualifying standard be: is 'birth-related severe neurological impairment' a reasonable test?
- Should a qualifying birth be restricted to one that took place in an NHS trust?
- Should patients or claimants be entitled to funding for legal advice to establish the fairness of an arrangement submitted by the redress scheme? If so, what limit should be applied to the amount available?
- Should patients be able to go directly to court, rather than use the scheme, if they believe negligence can be proven?
- Should the courts be permitted to examine the deliberations of an expert panel under the scheme when their arrangements for redress and compensation have been rejected and the case subsequently goes to law? What could the effect be on the numbers claiming compensation?
- Should the right to go to court be removed in favour of a new, faster and more responsive 'tribunal' system for all cases involving severe neurological impairment?[33]

Other questions raised for comment about the new scheme were:

- What kind of mechanism modelled on or developed from the NHSLA would not have a conflict of interest in managing the proposed NHS redress scheme and assessing claims or recommendations for health service compensation payments? Should the new body be a 'special health authority' or a non-departmental public body?
- If the cost of provision by the NHS is used to calculate future care costs, should the NHS be required to give guarantees for the treatment? (A change to this basis would mean repealing section 2 (4) of the Law Reform (Personal Injury) Act 1948.) If so, how could this be done? Would an arrangement involving independent case managers be needed?
- Are there more ways to encourage greater use of mediation and alternative dispute resolution procedures?
- What further steps could be taken to control legal costs in clinical negligence cases?[34]

How far do the chief medical officer's proposals stand up to close scrutiny?
In Britain when it comes to handing out rights or justice that happen to conflict with influential vested interests or entrenched attitudes at the seat of power invariably not much seems to materialize. Frequently unaffordable expense (where it can be applied) is given as a reason not to change a state of affairs even when it is indefensible. The best the public can expect (unless the shutters come down and nothing changes at all) is drip-feed reform, cosmetic change or

a sticking-plaster antidote to an unsatisfactory prevailing situation. Until now the prospect of an equitable approach to clinical negligence compensation for the nation has not been on the agenda at all; nor has the long-standing unsatisfactory litigation system altered in any fundamental way.

There is still no way that someone whose health has been damaged as a result of therapy will receive automatic monetary recompense. The person's claim normally must take the often protracted legal route and sometimes end up in court before it is finally resolved, and there are no guarantees of success even in apparently legitimate cases. Alternatively, owing to the injured party's lack of will, limited finances, fear of the consequences of failing or any other reason the matter will invariably stop short of civil action. Easily the greater proportion of claims (between 60 per cent and 70 per cent in the experience of the NHSLA) do not progress beyond initial contact with a solicitor or disclosure of medical records and nearly one-third of all claims are abandoned by claimants.[35]

There are many who will say that the recommendations for change are long overdue, but there is no denying that the CMO has taken a positive step in his proposals to start reforming the approach and response to clinical failure in the country's public health service. Certainly his argument against sole reliance on the tort system – even a reformed one – as a means of seeking compensation involving the NHS should be beyond dispute. Presumably only those with a vested interest in the litigation process would disagree with the CMO's reasoning. Even more importantly, what he has proposed amounts to an agenda for radical and equitable change from the current unsatisfactory state of affairs.

Nevertheless, the model scheme the CMO has recommended for redressing injury resulting from error or negligence in health care could have been more far-reaching in its scope. For instance it could have included a no-fault compensation element founded on a combination of the principles that support the schemes that are successfully in place elsewhere. In order to find out whether there was ever a serious intention to consider this one may need to look more closely at aspects of the CMO's report and recommendations in *Making Amends*. Some of the observations made and topics raised about no-fault compensation do not seem to be entirely convincing, nor stand up to close analysis.

In his report the CMO summarized the main arguments for no-fault-based schemes and the case put forward by critics against such a system.

The case for no-fault-based schemes is that they bring:
- fairness
- faster resolution of cases (usually taking months rather than years to settle) by removing the need to contest accusations of negligence in court
- lower running and legal costs in individual cases
- more certainty for claimants on the circumstances in which compensation is payable, and added consistency between claimants
- less tension between clinicians and claimants
- more willingness by clinicians to report errors and adverse incidents because 'blame' is eradicated.[36]

These are considerable advantages, which have been shown to work in practice (chapters 17, 18 and 19 describe the no-fault approach to compensation as it operates in Denmark, Finland and the other three Nordic countries, respectively). Not least is the point that a no-fault system of compensation need not be unduly expensive (for example the system costs 0.3 per cent of total hospital expenditure in Denmark's liberal scheme and 3.4 per cent for every person in Finland).

The case against no-fault-based schemes is that:

- Total costs will be greater than under a tort system because of the likely increase in the number of claims
- They will 'open the floodgates' to payments in damages and 'fuel a compensation culture'.
- Questions about causation remain, even if 'fault' is removed
- Questions about the amount of damages that will be paid remain, unless there is a tariff-based approach to any such scheme
- A tariff-based compensation scheme may not be sufficiently responsive to individuals' needs.
- It is difficult to separate injury from the natural progression of a disease in some cases
- explanations and apologies are not necessarily given in a system that focuses on monetary recompense alone
- A no-fault scheme does not of itself improve accountability nor ensure that lessons are learned from adverse incidents
- A no-fault system does not of itself guarantee that claimants will receive an explanation or apology.[37]

Professor Donaldson reaffirmed some of these perceived disadvantages and gave additional reasons in his report for rejecting the option of a (comprehensive) no-fault system. He included the following points:

- Total costs would be much higher than under the present tort arrangements because there is no need to prove negligence in a no-fault scheme and the number of claims would increase. Also, estimates from a survey published in November 2002 for the Department of Health suggest that depending on the use of a 'preventability' or 'causation' standard, even if the level of compensation was 25 per cent less than that being paid at the time, the annual cost of such a system would still range between £1.6 billion and nearly £4 billion if 19 per cent and 28 per cent of claimants, respectively, lodged a claim. This compares with £400 million under the present arrangements in 2000–01.
- It would be difficult to distinguish between harm done to a patient and the natural progression of a disease.
- No-fault mechanisms, by themselves, do not improve ways of learning from mistakes nor reduce the incidence of harm to patients.
- A no-fault system would be unaffordable. In order to be otherwise, compensation would have to be set at considerably lower levels than awards under the present tort system. Also, it would not necessarily meet the needs of patients who have suffered injury.[38]

An item-by-item examination of this case against a no-fault-based patient compensation system for the NHS shows that it may not be an accurate description of such a scheme, nor a good enough argument for not adopting it.

- A predicted increase, within limits, in the overall costs of a no-fault arrangement compared with those under a tort system is not a reason in itself for not opening up access to legitimate compensation claims. Consider for example Professor Donaldson's comments (reported earlier in this chapter) about one particular drawback in Britain's existing tort system. He drew attention to the fact that some people who have been severely damaged by failures in health care can receive substantial compensation while others who are equally deserving are paid nothing. Would it not be similarly inequitable to deprive a proportion of claimants of damages while others will be compensated under his scheme?

- Although the number of claims progressively increased after no-fault based schemes were established in the Nordic countries, the change meant that a greater proportion of legitimate claims are being processed and compensated than under the previous arrangements. This is very different from the forecasts by some that a no-fault system of compensation would 'open the floodgates' to payments in damages and 'fuel a compensation culture'. A compensation culture already exists in the UK and the introduction of a no-fault system of compensation might counteract it.

- It has already been established that, in practice, a no-fault scheme elsewhere in Europe can be affordable without compensation awards necessarily having to be set at lower levels than under the existing tort arrangements. While it may not be comparing like with like, the same could apply to such a system in the UK. In any event, who is to say that the British public en masse would turn their backs on a scheme that may result in lower compensation payments – which, nevertheless, are fair and cost nothing to claim – as opposed to larger sums that might be available via the perilous and protracted litigation route?

- In general, the no-fault schemes in Nordic countries seem to be handling satisfactorily the questions of causation and the perceived difficulty in separating injury from the natural progression of a disease.

- A 'tariff-based' approach to compensation is not common to all the no-fault schemes in operation, so that questions about the level of damages that will be paid may not arise. In cases where the arrangement is used, additional supporting redress is on offer to respond to individual patient's needs.

- A no-fault scheme by itself will not improve accountability and learning from mistakes, nor presumably is it intended to do so. It is surely the domain of the NHS and other appointed agencies to ensure that there is accountability for adverse incidents and that lessons are learned from them in order to reduce the incidence of harm to patients. This is the case in the UK and in Nordic countries where independent medical regulatory bodies can also play a dominant role in these respects (see Chapter 13).

- It seems curious to state that a no-fault system does not 'of itself' guarantee that claimants will receive an explanation or apology. Unless Professor Donaldson received confirmation of this point from those operating such schemes it is presumptuous of him to imply that clarification and a statement of regret are not given to claimants when dealing with their cases in a no-fault system. It is hard to believe that claimants will not already have received an explanation and apology following the separate and independent complaints or professional disciplinary processes that are common to all Nordic countries.

Earlier in his report, the CMO referred to the Royal Commission Review under Lord Pearson in 1978 about the prospect of introducing a no-fault scheme for personal injury and clinical negligence cases. Apart from being largely theoretical, since there was no practical gauge available at the time, the reasons (or some of them) given in the Pearson review for rejecting the use of no-fault compensation in medical negligence cases might now be regarded as being out-of-date and plainly wrong.[39] Since 1978 six countries have set up and continue to operate successful (if not perfect) no-fault based schemes. They may have adjusted or streamlined their mechanisms since first being introduced, but there is no question of them going back to their previous systems. Nor have these countries any plans for an alternative arrangement to deal with compensation claims involving health care.

Professor Donaldson further observed in his report that the Pearson Commission considered that the case for such a system covering health care was strong enough for it to be reviewed again over time.[40] Therefore it is a pity that when the matter is reviewed a second time similar theoretical arguments are still being put forward to reject a no-fault system again, when there is probably enough evidence to show that such a system would serve the interests of patients and health care providers. Evidence from other countries shows that clinical negligence compensation schemes of this kind can provide the greatest measure of all-round equity and be a viable proposition. Also, as suggested earlier, it would not be illogical to expect that a no-fault scheme for England – and indeed elsewhere in the UK – would actually reduce the number of cases taken to litigation.

The CMO added that the 'more comprehensive system of social welfare and social insurance support available in New Zealand and Scandinavia may affect the acceptability of the schemes in those countries'. He went on to say that, especially in Scandinavia, compensation payments are low compared with UK tort awards 'because they are topping up already generous social insurance payments for income replacement'.[41]

This position may be the case in the countries referred to, but it is still hard to believe that a suitable, no-fault-based compensation scheme cannot also be devised for England – and throughout the UK – if there is a will to do so. For a start, there would seem to be a solid base for the purpose: Britain's universal system of health and social care is similarly advanced and strongly resembles the Nordic model. Furthermore, the self-insuring mechanisms (the NHSLA in England, the WRP in Wales and the CLO in Scotland) already operating for health service establishments in the UK have basic similarities to an insurance-funded, no-fault system and its involvement with public health care. These facts suggest that it should not be difficult to make the necessary adjustments and establish an equivalent scheme for the NHS. Also, while it is true that compensation awards are lower in the Nordic countries compared with the UK tort settlements, they are not the result of a risky and drawn out process. Claimants are much more likely to be compensated than would be the case through litigation.

In presenting his report the CMO outlined the no-fault-based compensation schemes operating in New Zealand, Sweden and Finland. He also made a passing reference to those in Denmark and Norway, and described the similar systems that are in place for birth-related neurological injuries in the states of Virginia and Florida in the USA.[42] Nevertheless, the extent of these accounts does not appear to be sufficiently adequate for its purpose, nor a full representation of the no-fault schemes in existence and what these models have to offer injured patients. This is not to say that the CMO had overlooked the parallel systems in other countries. It is possible that he had obtained detailed, first-hand information about all the schemes in existence and for practical purposes decided not to include every example of the system in his report, nor to describe in greater detail those that he did mention. Whatever the reason, it would still have been useful had he given a fuller account of the no-fault schemes that operate elsewhere.

Certain observations the CMO made in his report about the no-fault approach to compensation involving health care, and to schemes in operation, seem to be generalized, inaccurate or misleading. Aspects of the report appear to be predisposed to favour the reasons for not adopting the no-fault approach for compensating claimants.

The CMO also drew attention to a number of common factors in the no-fault schemes reviewed in his report:
- All have tests of causation or avoidability; New Zealand and Sweden include a test of negligence similar to the Bolam category used in the UK's tort system.
- The severity of an injury must be in line with a set minimum level (often referring to days of disability or days in hospital) before a patient can qualify for compensation.
- There are limits to the kinds of damages that can be awarded; for instance compensation may not be available for 'pain and suffering' and there may be a cap on the amounts that are paid.
- The principal source of compensation is 'insurance payments, benefits or state-funded care', the no-fault scheme acting as a 'top-up'.
- In Scandinavia and New Zealand the volume of claims is higher than in the UK.
- Compensation payments in countries including New Zealand, Denmark, Finland, Norway, Sweden and it seems the states of Florida and Virginia (USA) are less than those typically awarded by courts in the UK.
- The scheme in New Zealand and to some extent those in Florida and Virginia restrict the use of court action.[43]

While these last-mentioned observations may broadly describe common features among some no-fault-based compensation schemes, the comments convey an imprecise overall picture. Some remarks appear to be unduly negative or misleading in their presentation and when applied to all such schemes are somewhat inaccurate. It seems that issues have been raised for the purpose of suggesting that aspects of the no-fault schemes operating in 2004 are a drawback, when this is not necessarily the case.

A point-by-point analysis may shed more light on a number of these additional concerns and considerations. It may even show that the CMO's observations do not altogether tally with the real picture (see chapters 17 to 19):
- A test of causation or avoidability, where it is used, in existing no-fault compensation schemes is not a reason to reject such a system.
- 'The severity of an injury must be in line with a set minimum level' is a somewhat simplistic and imprecise description of the conditions under which compensation is paid for patient injury, especially when applied to all the no-fault schemes in operation.

- In which schemes is compensation for pain and suffering not available? Certainly in the no-fault systems operating in Finland and Sweden, damages are payable in such cases. Having a cap on the sums that are paid is apparently not a serious obstacle in schemes that apply this policy.

- The principal source of monetary compensation in England (and most of the UK) is not very different from those that apply to countries operating no-fault schemes. Compensation payments made by the NHSLA, for example, come from 'insurance' premiums paid to it by NHS bodies (see Chapter 8). Moreover, what the CMO has proposed in his concept of a future scheme for England also includes state-funded care as part of any compensation package.

- The number of claims may be proportionately greater in Scandinavia and New Zealand, but if this also means that more legitimate claimants are being compensated – which they are – then it cannot be a bad thing. Open-access, no-cost and risk-free schemes must be expected to attract more claims. However, as Professor Donaldson later pointed out, compensation awards are generally less than those in the UK. (As referred to earlier, the CMO stated elsewhere in his report that in the NHSLA's experience 60 to 70 per cent of claims in England 'do not proceed beyond initial contact with a solicitor or disclosure of medical records'. Moreover, there was evidence that 30 per cent of claims formally pursued through the NHSLA are abandoned by claimants. Are these early withdrawals from litigation included in the aforementioned comparison between claims pursued in the UK and those received in countries with a no-fault compensation mechanism in operation?)

- Lower compensation awards need not be an insurmountable problem in devising a no-fault scheme for the UK – especially if non-monetary redress also forms part of the package.

- In none of the five Nordic countries is there a restriction on court action following a claim for compensation through the no-fault scheme in place. Moreover, claimants can first refer their cases to a powerful independent appeals authority before taking the litigation route.

Professor Donaldson backed up the case against a no-fault based compensation scheme with references to and brief tabulated data extracted from the survey (issued in November 2002) commissioned by the Department of Health.[44] But the information provided in *Making Amends* is not detailed or clear enough to make a hard and fast judgement on the likely veracity of the survey's results in practice. In order to do so one would need to be satisfied that the basis for these findings is sound.

The survey showed that the cost of a no-fault scheme for the NHS would range between £1.6 billion and nearly £4 billion (in certain set circumstances) for injury suffered by patients following treatment. By comparison, Professor Donaldson stated that £400 million had been spent on clinical negligence claims in 2000–01. But the CMO had also considered the implications of the Human Rights Act 1998 'if the quid pro quo for introducing a no-fault compensation scheme was the removal of the right to go to court' as had apparently happened in New Zealand. The CMO then went on to describe the potential or likely implications of implementing Article 6 of the European Convention on Human Rights, including those involving the NHS.[45]

The problem with the system that costs £400 million is that it is unfair and excludes a large proportion of would-be claimants, some of them likely to be legitimate, whereas a no-fault-based alternative within reason is unarguably more equitable and inclusive. Should cost be a (or the) key deciding factor in whether or not to change from a litigation-based system in these circumstances? Professor Donaldson appears to have answered this question as he concluded that, among the other considerations put forward by him together with the survey's results, 'a comprehensive no-fault scheme was unaffordable for the NHS' and therefore he had rejected it for all types of injury.[46]

However, each of the European countries running no-fault-based compensation mechanisms for their national health services (and in one or two cases including also the private sector) has found the system to be affordable. Some of them have shown that the cost involved is low, unlike the projected figures that emerged from the survey for the UK's Department of Health. Moreover, these no-fault systems (where applicable) are likely to be operating in accordance with the European human rights legislation (to which they are also signed up).

A close appraisal of the national no-fault schemes in operation globally (see chapters 17 to 19) will provide an opportunity to arrive at a system of compensation for the NHS that has merit, is legal and is affordable even in a not entirely similar social climate. It is fortunate that what Professor Donaldson has advanced has not yet been finalized and, as his proposals had not been implemented at March 2005, there may still be time to get things right from the outset. But that might be assuming minds have not already been made up.

Who were the contributors to Professor Donaldson's consultation paper?
Another issue connected with Professor Donaldson's report that is worth exploring is the pedigree of the individuals who formally advised him or contributed to this work in a less official capacity and the background from which they were drawn. Professor Donaldson's advisory committee was dominated by individuals from the public health service and medical profession. Out of its 18 members, five represented medical bodies, three were directly involved with the NHS and one was from a medical defence organization. Another three were senior legal figures and one was from a group of personal injury lawyers.[47] One might therefore argue that vested interests were disproportionately represented in a panel of people chosen to advise on a major issue affecting their future professional activities.

The rest of the committee included three representatives from patient and consumer bodies; the previous Health Service Ombudsman for England, Scotland and Wales; and the head of the Legal Services Commission in England.[48] (As a medical person by profession, and one also strongly associated with the NHS, Professor Donaldson's position as chairman further adds to the dominance of the medical and health service elements of his advisory panel.)

While it was clearly necessary for the advisory committee to contain some medical and legal people, should the ratio have been so high? It seems curious that greater input was not obtained from quarters outside these confines, sources that would still have had something worthwhile to contribute. Should not a specialist in citizens' and human rights have been on the committee? Perhaps most significantly there appears to have been no representation from the sources probably best equipped to offer advice – the individuals who have been running successful no-fault-based compensation schemes for years. Input from one or two such experts could markedly have altered the conclusions of the CMO's report and the proposals it made.

The group of 180 individuals (including members of the CMO's advisory committee) who were asked to contribute to the 'call for ideas' in the run-up to the publication of *Making Amends* was dominated by the legal and medical professions, in that order. From what can be seen there were only 12 representatives (two of whom were connected with the NHS) from patient and consumer groups; the rest were individuals involved in 'alternative dispute resolution' provision, academics, members of the Clinical Disputes Forum and people from organizations who had other interests.[49] Again, there was no input from citizens' or human rights groups, nor from anyone involved with the practicalities of operating no-fault-based compensation mechanisms.

Conclusion, and how does the proposed scheme compare with those for other types of personal injury

From the discussion above one might conclude that the proposals in *Making Amends*, while apparently generous, should have stretched to supporting an all-embracing, no-fault-based clinical negligence compensation system. Although it is likely that most of the public would accept the scheme put forward by England's chief medical officer over anything civil litigation has to offer, they would probably give it their greater blessing were it to offer them the kind of equity that some other civilized societies enjoy. Even something resembling the kind of enlightened measures that apply to other forms of personal injury in the United Kingdom might be welcome.

Already introduced briefly in Chapter 8, these include individual schemes where compensation is payable for vaccine damage and criminal injury. Moreover, benefit can be claimed from the state for industrial injury that has caused disablement – separate from any action for damages being pursued through litigation or other means by a claimant.

Vaccine Damage Payment Scheme

The scheme is operated by the vaccine damage payment unit of the nation's Department for Work and Pensions (DWP). It came into existence in 1979 following the Vaccine Damage Payments Act of the same year. Under the act– and subsequent amendments to it – compensation is available for severe disability caused by vaccination against a list of 11 specified diseases.[50]

Vaccine damage payment is in the form of a single, tax-free sum of £100,000 where a minimum of 60 per cent mental or physical disability has occurred as a result of vaccination. This level of disablement had reduced from the original 80 per cent, and the period during which claims can be made has also increased. In certain cases claimants under the previous rules can lodge a second claim, as long as it is before 16 June 2005.[51]

The scheme is open to anyone two years of age or over. Nevertheless, vaccination should have taken place before a person's 18th birthday – unless it was against poliomyelitis, rubella (German measles) or meningococcal Group C, or during an outbreak of the disease in the UK or the Isle of Man. Also, the vaccination must have been given in either of these two places, although compensation may still be paid if it occurred abroad under medical treatment provided by the British armed forces.[52]

Claims must be made on or before a person's 21st birthday (or if they had died, the date on which they would have reached this age – whichever is the later) and within six years of the vaccination concerned having been carried out. Compensation may also be available in cases of severe disablement where a person's mother was vaccinated against one of the listed diseases while being pregnant. It can also be paid where an individual's disability was the consequence of close physical contact with someone who had been vaccinated against poliomyelitis with vaccine that was administered orally.[53]

Compensation for vaccine damage is paid into trust, usually involving the parents or other family members. Otherwise it is made to another appropriate person (for example, a solicitor or legal guardian), or to the public trustee.[54] Table 9.1 shows the number of claims lodged and awards made between 1 April 2003 and 31 March 2004, and the total number in each case since the scheme started in 1979 until 30 November 2004.

Table 9.1 Claims and awards for 2003–04 and the total numbers involved since 1979

	2003–04	Apr–Nov 2004	1979–Nov 2004
Total claims received[a]	165	71	5,215
Total awards	5	4	916

Source: Department for Work and Pensions[55]

[a] The number of awards may have no connection with the claims shown to have been received in the same period as they invariably refer to claims lodged previously. Therefore the figures should not be regarded as proportions of awards against claims.

Vaccine damage payments can affect means-tested state benefits and entitlements that claimants may be receiving – although not necessarily. However, certain such benefits, including Disability Living Allowance or Incapacity Benefit, are unaffected by compensation that has been awarded through the scheme.[56]

Industrial Injuries Disablement Benefit
Also administered by the Department for Work and Pensions, in broad terms this benefit is payable to employees who are disabled because of an accident at work or those who have a listed disease or deafness that has resulted from their job. It is not available to a person who was self-employed at the time of the event. Industrial Injuries Disablement Benefit rates are the same for each of the three categories of disablement.[57]

For guidance purposes, at the time of writing in November 2004 the tariff ranged from £24.02 per week for 20 per cent disablement to £120.10 for 100 per cent disablement in adults. The corresponding rates for those under 18 years of age with no dependants are £14.71 and £73.55. Claims for Industrial Injuries Disablement Benefit because of an accident must be made after the person concerned has been disabled for two months. Claims relating to a disease or deafness are required to be lodged immediately, or else there may be a loss of benefit.[58]

There are other allowances managed by the DWP that may be awarded to those who have suffered industrial injury. For example, Reduced Earnings Allowance (at

£48.04) can be paid for an accident, a disease or deafness in this category that occurred before 1 October 1990 and where the persons concerned are unable to return to their normal job because of the effects of their accident or disease, or cannot do alternative work with similar pay.[59]

Constant Attendance Allowance (CAA) may be available for those who are receiving Industrial Injuries Disablement Benefit, need daily care and attention and if their disablement is assessed at 100 per cent. Where an 'exceptional' or 'inter-mediate' CAA rate is being received and the person concerned may also need permanent constant care and attention, Exceptionally Severe Disablement Allowance (SDA) can also be paid. CAA rates are the same for those who are disabled because of an accident at work or are ill or disabled as a result of a disease or deafness caused by their job. As a guide, the allowance is paid at one of four different levels ranging from a 'part-time rate' of £24.05 to an 'exceptional rate' of £96.20 per week. There are a number of other possible social security benefits for disablement that has arisen from a person's work. Also, Industrial Death Benefit can be paid to the wife or husband of someone who died before 11 April 1998 because of an industrial accident or disease.[60]

Criminal Injuries Compensation Scheme

Established in its original form in 1964, the Criminal Injuries Compensation Authority (CICA) represents one of the world's oldest criminal injuries compen-sation systems. It operates a scheme that grants financial awards for injuries suffered through violent crime in Great Britain, Northern Ireland having its own scheme.[61] Essentially, provided the crime took place within the previous two years claimants can apply for compensation if:

- they have been physically or psychologically damaged or
- they have a close relationship with someone who was the victim and they were present when the crime occurred, or involved immediately afterwards and their involvement in the incident caused them psychological injury.[62]

Claims for compensation can also be made in cases where a person's parent, child, husband, wife or partner died as a result of a violent crime and, normally, the death occurred within the last two years.[63]

Compensation under the scheme is not paid in cases where a single minor injury (a black eye for example) has been suffered. Nor is it available for those who are victims of sexual abuse or other sexual assault that ended before October 1979, and they and the persons who assaulted them were living together as members of the same family. Victims of road traffic incidents are also not eligible for compen-sation, unless a vehicle was used deliberately to injure them.[64]

Applicants for compensation should have fully informed the police and must fill in an application form giving as much detail as possible, including police and hospital reference numbers, to enable the CICA to establish the circumstances of the crime and the extent of the injuries sustained. In assessing a claim the CICA normally asks the police for a report of the incident and the doctor or hospital who provided treatment for an account of the injury that the person concerned has suffered.[65]

A conviction of the offender is not necessary for compensation to be paid but claims may be affected where applicants have not:

- reported the crime to the police or other authority as soon as possible after the episode
- co-operated with the police – for example they have refused to make a statement or attend an identity parade
- told the police that they agree to go to court and give evidence if the offender were to stand trial.[66]

Compensation is refused or reduced where, for instance, a claimant had started a fight or agreed to take part in it and was injured as a result. The same would apply if that person had provoked the assailant by behaving in an aggressive or threatening manner. In certain cases the CICA may also refuse or reduce a claim for compensation if the applicant (and in the event of an injury that causes death, the victim) has unspent criminal convictions.[67]

Two types of compensation are paid in criminal injury cases. One is a 'personal injury award' for pain and suffering – whether physical or psychological – and a possible additional payment against a claim for loss of earnings and special expenses. Those who were present when someone very close to them was injured as the result of a violent crime and suffered mental damage may also claim a personal injury award.[68]

Briefly, the CICA's scheme provides for a tariff of injuries and awards setting out what compensation can be paid (less any deductions) to someone who has suffered a criminal injury. There are 25 levels of compensation ranging from £1,000 (level 1) to £250,000 (level 25). However, compensation for lost earnings and special expenses (for specialist medical treatment or equipment as examples) can increase the total amount to a maximum of £500,000. The scheme lists more than 400 injury descriptions, against each of which is the level of compensation it represents and the amount that can be paid. Injuries not listed in the tariff but serious, nonetheless, can also be considered for an award, although in a different way.[69]

A 'fatal injury award' may be paid to a person whose parent, child, husband wife or partner has died as the result of a violent crime. (In 2005 this stood at £11,000 where there was only one claimant, or £5,500 each in the case of more than one.) A further claim can be made if the person depended financially on the deceased. The CICA may also refund reasonable funeral expenses.[70]

Recovery of compensation by the state
When someone who has had an accident, injury or a disease for which another party is to blame is claiming compensation, the 'compensator' (the person or organization who may pay the claim) must inform the 'compensation recovery unit' of the Department for Work and Pensions. The compensator is obliged to reimburse the DWP for the amount a claimant has received in social security benefit because of the impairment that has occurred.[71]

In the case of those who have had an accident or injury, the repayment will equal the benefit paid to the person concerned from the day after the incident to the date of the final compensation payment or for up to five years – whichever is sooner. Whereas, in instances when claimants of compensation have received social security benefit for a disease they have suffered, the amount the compensator must pay the DWP is calculated from the day the relevant person first claimed a benefit. As a result, in either situation the compensator may reduce a claimant's compensation.[72]

Endpiece
But the future for a health service compensation system in England, at least, may be more rosy than it looks. What Professor Donaldson has presented is a 'consultation paper', so some of the key issues raised here questioning aspects of his report may well be ironed out and acted upon, before final plans are put into place. Indeed, the outcome might pleasantly surprise us all. But it may not, unless respondents to his report and the final plan determined involved people who have operated successful patient redress and compensation schemes and therefore should know what they are talking about.

CHAPTER 10

The human cost of damaging health care can be hard to bear

With accountability and redress invariably a distant dream

Taking on the British health service complaints system is a daunting commitment at the best of times, but when the complaint is a particularly serious one, the going can – and does – get very rough indeed. And the chances of its being upheld, even in apparently legitimate cases, are frequently zero. What is more, in the comparatively exceptional instances when such complaints are sustained following investigation, the remedial action taken by the health care body concerned is certain not to reflect the gravity of the wrongdoing involved.

The best that complainants can expect in clinical cases is an apology and a promise that steps will be taken to prevent a recurrence of the same kind of mistake or malpractice. Any harsher action (other than criminal) is generally left in the hands of the similarly self-managed medical regulatory bodies to determine, once complaints have been referred to them.

Although some complainants may be satisfied with the outcome of their cases at the 'local resolution' first phase of the health service complaints procedure, there could be as many (or more) who are not. But, for private or other reasons, they decide not to proceed further through the system or to take other measures to get their concerns addressed and remedied. Nevertheless, even at this early stage of the procedure, it is probable that a proportion of disillusioned complainants pull out to pursue their cases via one of the professional regulatory bodies. Alternatively – or additionally – they may opt for litigation.

It is just as likely that some of those complainants who have decided to continue through the health service complaints mechanism take similar alternative action following dissatisfaction before or after the next phase of the process, or even once the Health Service Ombudsman has intervened and passed judgement. As the final arbiter in the complaints system – in an extended capacity – the Ombudsman is also its only independent component. (Chapter 1 and Chapter 2, in particular, show that the review phase of the NHS complaints procedure passed into the hands of independent bodies in Wales and England in 2003 and 2004, respectively.) Unfortunately, however, the Ombudsman's intervention is reserved only for a small and select group of cases. Even then there are no guarantees, with decisions made in the Ombudsman's name not always above suspicion.

The road to compensation, following failure through the complaints and regulatory mechanisms, is uncertain, too, and has its own pitfalls. Unless settled beforehand by mutual agreement, claims for damages can be pursued only through the courts and, inevitably, are a risky business. This is a course of action that also

157

invariably results in considerable monetary loss; the lives of claimants are blighted and they have nothing to show for their efforts except added disillusionment.

Large numbers of complainants will endorse many of the shortcomings described thus far about the process of pursuing complaints about health care. Many of them maintain that there is a lack of impartiality and accountability by the health service and medical profession in dealing with their concerns. Allegations abound, also, about attempts by health care providers to conceal or obstruct the truth in their investigations. Moreover, there have been accusations that information vital or relevant to complainants is withheld, preventing them from putting together their cases efficiently. Inadequate investigation by health service complaints handlers into grievances at the 'local resolution' first phase is a frequent criticism levelled at the complaints system. Another persistent accusation is that cases are unreasonably refused consideration by an 'independent review panel'. There is also a widely held view that complaints are all too often incorrectly rejected by independent review panels and referrals to the Ombudsman can similarly be turned down. Some of these points are demonstrated in the cases described below.

Case 1

For several years Mrs A suffered a severe chest pain intermittently during the night, which would then extend to her jaw and throat. The acute discomfort did not arise out of exercise and was attributed to a (non-existent) hiatus hernia. In 1993, after being given a stress exercise test and other cardiac checks, she was officially diagnosed as having a coronary artery spasm or 'prinzmetal angina' and immediately placed on appropriate drug therapy. Mrs A discovered later that the tests had revealed 'classic symptoms' of this apparently dangerous form of angina, which, over time, will damage the heart.

Early retirement from her senior teaching post followed on health grounds. But Mrs A was told that no clinical evidence of damage to her heart could be seen. So, it was a matter of some concern to her when some time later she became aware that the summaries of her consultations were misleading. Moreover, she discovered that certain of her medical records indicated serious damage to her heart had occurred.

After moving to another area, Mrs A tried to discuss her worries with the local cardiologists but claims that she was met with evasion and rudeness. Also, according to her, the information about the tests showing that her heart had been significantly damaged had not been obtained by these clinicians. Mrs A's subsequent attempts to get her concerns addressed and resolved through the NHS complaints procedure proved unsuccessful. Indeed, all three applications by her for 'independent review' of these and other grievances through the system were prevented – improperly from her account of the issues – from proceeding further.

She believes that, effectively, specialist cardiac care has been denied her by local cardiologists for a number of years. This is despite her having a well-established heart condition, significant associated medical problems and the clinical test data indicating other complications. Although the prospect of a major heart operation had been suggested, Mrs A feels that these clinicians are either unable or unwilling to treat her cardiac condition. Moreover, she says that a doctor has written that the prognosis for her is 'uncertain'.

Mrs A has a range of other criticisms about what she maintains has been an unsatisfactory level of health care provided to her. She considers that obstacles have been set up to frustrate her efforts to get matters corrected. For example, in 1996, requests to meet the regional medical officer and, later, the regional health authority's chief executive to discuss her concerns were refused.

At the start of the following year, while inspecting her medical records at a local hospital, she was taken ill with a bout of angina. Although someone noted in her medical records that she may have had a heart attack, it took two hours for a doctor to see her. This clinician was not a cardiologist, and she was refused admission to the cardiac unit. Following the episode, Mrs A made a verbal complaint. She subsequently received a discourteous letter from the hospital, after which she lodged a formal complaint.

A local resolution meeting – part of the first phase of the NHS complaints procedure – followed in 1997, and she recorded the event. At this session the medical director of the trust involved confirmed that her 'rest' electrocardiogram (ECG) had shown a heart attack, ischaemia and problems with her left ventricle. But the trust's chief executive did not send the obligatory summarized statement about what was discussed at the local resolution meeting, action that should have been taken within 20 working days following the event. Accordingly, Mrs A could not proceed to the next stage of the complaints procedure. She states that it was also impossible to obtain copies of certain information about her complaint to the trust. In these circumstances she felt there was no alternative except to complain to the Health Service Ombudsman – which she proceeded to do. But the Ombudsman did not support her.

Mrs A maintains that once a misdiagnosis and subsequent injury to a patient occurs, it becomes impossible to obtain a truthful, unbiased second opinion. Moreover, she claims that some of her records have been changed and critical test results have gone missing. Locally, she has been prevented from seeing her medical records for the purpose of correcting data that she knows, from evidence, is erroneous. Mrs A says she is now unwilling to seek medical treatment where she is unwelcome, because the stress is too much for her.

She believes it is the failure of the system to put patients first and its lack of impartiality in dealing with complaints that is at the root of the problem. In addition, there seems also to be an unfortunate perception that patients who have been damaged while being treated in the health service are merely potential litigants, not vulnerable human beings who are in need of medical attention.

Case 2

In August 1968, Mrs B, a young woman in her late 20s, suffered what is called a spontaneous subarachnoid haemorrhage, but was neither unconscious nor physically damaged. Five days later she was given an angiogram (an investigation with dye into the blood vessels of the brain) under general anaesthetic at a prominent neurological centre. No abnormality or aneurysm was found by this test.

Two days later, a second angiogram, again applied under general anaesthetic, also showed no aneurysm. However, on regaining consciousness after this angiogram it became clear that Mrs B had hemianopia – the loss of half the vision in both eyes. She also had an intense pain in her head, felt very ill and began vomiting profusely. Mrs B became extremely alarmed about her condition. The doctors told her that there was nothing abnormal in the blood vessels of her brain, and her partial loss of vision would probably go away.

Mrs B was then transferred to another hospital for recovery and was found to be pregnant. Continuation of the pregnancy was considered to be unwise, so a termination was carried out. A few weeks later, Mrs B was sent to a psychiatric unit where she was diagnosed as having hysterical vomiting. She was later found to be still pregnant, so a second termination (at 26 weeks) was performed. It is likely that she had been carrying twins.

In 1969, a local consultant told Mrs B that her partial loss of vision was caused by arterial spasm during angiogram because she suffered from migraine – an explanation she accepted and believed for nearly 30 years afterwards. The doctor added that she would remain half blind for the rest of her life. She was deeply upset by the news. It meant the end of her career as a nurse, loss of earnings and independence and no prospect of a pension. Mrs B felt that her life had been ruined forever, yet her difficulties were being ignored.

There were additional adverse consequences of her ordeals. Her reading ability was forever to be slow and troublesome. Indeed, even much routine visual activity had become a strain and often brought on headaches. Her balance, too, was slightly affected and she had falls, bad knocks and bruises over the years. Mrs B has been to casualty four times for X-rays and as an out-patient, and had seen her GP a number of times as well. She is unable to go out on her own to unfamiliar places since the damaging medical incident. Mrs B says that her limitations affected the lives of her two children and placed added responsibilities on her husband. Nonetheless, she and her family tried to make the best of an unenviable state of affairs and got on with their lives. But the story doesn't quite end there.

In 1994, when Mrs B went to an optician to have her eyes tested for reading glasses, she started to learn more about her disability. The optician felt she should have been registered as partially sighted in 1969. Mrs B maintains that many of the clinicians involved in the events of 1968 and 1969 were aware of her distress at the loss of half her sight. Yet they failed – neglectfully, she believes – to refer her to an opthamologist to be registered officially for the sight disability. In 1995, Mrs B was examined by such a practitioner and was finally registered as having partial vision.

In 1995 it came to Mrs B's notice that her medical records had been falsified. According to her, an official letter indicated that her partial loss of vision was clearing a few days after it had occurred. Moreover, some of the records she obtained seemed to be illogical. The solicitor Mrs B consulted in 1997 secured copies of her original angiogram X-rays, a process that cost her £300. Together with her legal fees and the cost of referral to neurological specialists for their opinion, the total bill rose to nearly £5,000.

One of these practitioners, a private neuroradiologist who examined the copies of the X-rays, told Mrs B that the first angiogram was normal. But the second such procedure revealed emboli that had resulted in infarction, thus causing hemianopia. The neuroradiologist's colleague, a neurologist, said it was normal in 1968 for a patient to be given two angiograms and that hemianopia was regarded as an acceptable, although unlikely, risk at the time. Four years later, in 2001, another neurologist and neuroradiologist who looked at this data made further observations. Mrs B was informed that, during the second angiogram, either thrombus formed and then embolized or, possibly, a verterbral artery had been dissected and a clot had arisen as a result.

The revelations from these clinicians came as a great shock to her, especially as she had accepted the word of the local neurologist in 1969 that her partial loss of vision had been caused by arterial spasm during the angiogram because she suffered from migraine. By contrast, neither of the two neuroradiologists she consulted in 1997 and 2001 detected any spasm in the angiograms. Mrs B believes that some of the details of the angiogram procedure are missing and that the hospital has refused to reveal the name or qualifications of the person who performed the angiograms.

Later Mrs B discovered that, according to the anatomy of the blood vessels to the brain, the way some of her records were presented would have meant that the hospital was going to tie off the wrong artery if they found an aneurysm. She drew attention to this point in writing to the hospital and asked if a clerical error had been made. (It so happened the hospital had sent Mrs B a second set of records, but had withdrawn certain data that previously was included.) The reply from the head of the litigation department was that Mrs B's correspondence had been passed on to the hospital's solicitors. Some months later she still had not received an answer to her question.

In May 2002 Mrs B sent copies of the relevant medical records to her Member of Parliament, who then took the case up with the appropriate head at the Department of Health. The response from the latter was that the trust concerned in Mrs B's case had done all it could to address the issues she had raised. Moreover, she was (correctly) told that government ministers and officials could not intervene in matters where the Health Service Ombudsman has made a decision and she should take legal advice.

Mrs B and her husband are not well off. In 2002 Mrs B received Disability Living Allowance and Severe Disablement Allowance amounting to a total of £77.40 a week. She was first awarded these benefits towards the end of 1995 and 1997, respectively, but neither was backdated for more than a few months. Mrs B does not receive a state or private pension.

Whichever way one looks at Mrs B's case, from the clinical incident itself to its consequences and her experiences since then, it is clear that she has suffered greatly. A clinical procedure that went badly wrong not only seriously damaged Mrs B's health: it ended a promising career and hugely reduced the quality of her life and her role in family affairs. It is not surprising that Mrs B feels badly let down by a system that has deprived her of appropriate reparation. Indeed, she continues to believe that there have been attempts to conceal or obstruct the truth about aspects of her case.

Mrs B maintains that the damage she has suffered at the hands of the NHS has not been properly addressed or investigated. Nor has there been any accountability on its part for her serious and longstanding problems. All her attempts to get an equitable resolution of her complaints have, so far, proved to be fruitless and a costly exercise. Unable to afford further solicitor's fees, Mrs B has been pursuing her case without legal assistance in recent years. She hopes that those concerned at the health service trust will eventually search their conscience, admit responsibility and finally compensate her for the damage to her health and the constraints she has been forced to endure for nearly 35 years. As of early 2003, she had not received a penny in redress, despite her efforts. (Sadly, Mrs B died later that year as a consequence of an unrelated condition.)

Case 3

Mr C, a 17-year-old teenager became unwell while at work in a retail store. He telephoned his stepmother to tell her that he had felt ill for several hours and had vomited. She collected the boy and took him to his doctor's surgery at 3 pm. A nurse took his temperature and 20 minutes later he was seen by his GP. After a thorough examination, the patient was told that he had a virus, advised to take paracetomol and to go home to bed.

Mr C followed the doctor's instructions, but at around 7 pm his stepmother contacted the surgery to say that, although feeling slightly better, her stepson was still poorly. She took him to the surgery again where he was examined by another doctor who told him that his temperature was lower and he had probably developed a virus.

Mr C went back to bed but his condition deteriorated. At 12.45 am the next day, Mr C's parents telephoned the doctors' night emergency service for advice. They were told to take their son to the surgery, but on the way there the boy collapsed; he died shortly afterwards, at the surgery, despite all efforts by the doctors present to revive him. The post mortem results showed the cause of death was '1(a) bilateral adrenal haemorrhage due to 1(b) septicaemia due to 1(c) N meningitis (meningococcus)'.

Mr C's father complained that the GP had failed to diagnose the illness, especially as his son had at least four symptoms of meningitis septicaemia when examined 11 hours before his death. Mr C's father lodged his grievance with the health authority as the circumstances of the case made it impossible for him to be directly involved with the local resolution phase of the NHS complaints procedure. He received a response from the doctor concerned but was extremely dissatisfied with it.

Following this, Mr C's father approached the local community health council for assistance and the community health council sent a letter to the health authority requesting that the complaint be considered for independent review. In due course, the case was accepted for investigation at this second phase of the complaints procedure and a date was set for a panel to convene. However, three days before the case was due to be heard, the panel meeting was called off because the medical defence body supporting the doctor concerned reported that the deceased's mother had begun civil proceedings. On legal advice, the health authority upheld the decision not to go ahead. Mr C's father wrote to the health authority asking for proof that civil action had been taken, but was told that written proof could not be produced. Accordingly, the community health council prepared a file on the case for Mr C's father to sign and the material was sent to the Health Service Ombudsman for examination.

The Ombudsman responded that his Office could take no immediate action and advised that a further request for independent review should be made to the health authority. Following this advice, Mr C sent another letter to the health authority requesting an independent review but the request was denied. As a result, the case file was once again sent to the Ombudsman for consideration. This second referral was also unsuccessful, with the Ombudsman stating that he could not take the matter further.

Consequently, the complaint was referred to the General Medical Council for examination, but with little success. The GMC wrote to say that no further action was found to be necessary, although the papers of Mr C's father would be held on the doctor's personal file for three years. This correspondence was passed on to Mr C's father with advice to consult a solicitor if he decided to continue with the case.

Case 4

Miss D was taken to her GP with rectal bleeding, but the symptoms were dismissed by the doctor as being 'normal'. Miss D made frequent further visits to the surgery but persistent symptoms were not recorded by the GP. A subsequent investigation showed that she had severe colitis, was seriously ill and required surgery.

When Miss D's mother tried to convey her concerns at the practice, another doctor saw her and threatened to remove her from the practice list if she made a formal complaint. Miss D's mother did make a formal complaint, however, but did not consider the response from the original GP satisfactory. Independent review of the case via the NHS complaints system followed with the panel accepting the GP's assertion that all important information had been recorded. Moreover, the doctors giving evidence refuted Miss D's mother's testimony and the panel found in favour of the practitioners, but the GPs accepted criticism by the panel of the practice complaints procedure. The case was then referred to the Health Service Ombudsman but was rejected on the grounds that there had been no maladminstration by the independent review panel.

Case 5

Ms E consulted her GP over several years about a persistent condition that failed to respond to treatment. Eventually a locum practitioner became concerned about Ms E's problem and referred her to a consultant, who diagnosed a gynaecological cancer, which required major surgery. After this Mrs E decided to make a formal complaint. The community health council acting for her wrote a letter of complaint to the GP concerned and also requested to see Ms E's medical records. Unhappy with the response to the complaint from her doctor, Ms E asked for her case to be examined by an independent review panel, the next phase of the NHS complaints procedure.

The complaint was accepted for investigation. In its subsequent report the panel criticized the GP's judgement, but he was not found to have acted irresponsibly. The GP wrote to the complainant disputing the panel's findings, and did not indicate what action would be taken as a result of the hearing. Moreover, there was no indication that the health authority concerned would monitor compliance with the panel's recommendations.

Ms E then referred her case to the Health Service Ombudsman who accepted it for investigation. The report that followed found that the GP's 'response to the findings and recommendations of the IR panel was inappropriate and insensitive'. That was the final verdict, and as far as Ms E could go via the NHS complaints procedure. Consequently, she took legal advice to pursue her case along the only other route left open to her – litigation.

Case 6

Mr F contacted a community health council about the conduct of his parents' GP concerning the care of his elderly father. In his mid-80s, the latter was suffering from first stage dementia and was using a suprapubic catheter, which required changing every 10 to 12 weeks. Mr F told the community health council that the doctor had consistently refused to change the catheter himself and had arranged for it to be changed at the local hospital's accident and emergency department instead. He alleged that on one occasion when the catheter needed changing the GP refused to do so. Instead, the GP asked Mrs F to inform the hospital that he had visited and that her husband was ill. However, the GP had not visited and in her subsequent conversation with staff from the hospital, when Mrs F was asked whether the doctor had visited her husband at home she told them that he had not. A few days later Mr F's parents were informed that they had been struck off their doctor's list. They had been attending the practice for more than 50 years.

The CHC then sent a letter of complaint to the GP concerned on behalf of Mr F, but the doctor failed to reply within the specified time limit and did not give a reason for the long delay in responding. Later, the GP reported than he was consulting his medical defence advisers, which resulted in further delay. He finally responded to Mr F's complaint with a conflicting version of events, but offered to meet him to resolve the issue. Mr F agreed to the proposal, but his father then died. Mr F wanted to pursue the matter, but his mother was too distressed to continue with the complaint and so the case came to an end.

Conclusion

Serious medical error causing or leading to the injury or death of a patient must be hard enough to bear, but when attempts are apparently made to obscure mistakes, or there is a failure to address the concerns of complainants fairly and frankly, the effects can be much more far-reaching. The distress to complainants can become still more acute when the statutory complaints mechanism set up to carry out an impartial investigation appears to be incapable of taking responsibility for these errors.

At the heart of the matter is the perception or conviction by complainants that self-regulation and a lack of adequate redress have loaded the system in favour of the health service and medical profession. Indeed, there are those (conspiracy theorists some may call them) who believe that the NHS complaints procedure was probably devised with these and other questionable objectives in mind. Certainly, the mechanism has shown itself to be an effective means of taking the vast majority of complaints – presumably including some legitimate ones – out of the system. To make matters worse, complainants then discover that there is no other easily attainable way of gaining a modicum of satisfaction.

The few cases profiled in this chapter illustrate the extent to which the lives of complainants and their relatives can be affected – often permanently – because of these factors. Countless more tales of injustice have made media headlines in recent years, and will continue to do so. Still, most disaffected complainants will, sooner or later, suffer in silence or try to put their experiences behind them. A few will fight their causes singlehandedly but, often, ineffectually. Others may join patient pressure groups for (mostly) moral support. None of them deserves to be forced into a position where, rightly or wrongly, they feel themselves to be cast aside and in a situation from which there seems to be little hope and no decent exit. It is a sad fact that much of this often endless despair would not have arisen had complainants been offered an equitable means of getting their concerns addressed and remedied from the outset.

CHAPTER 11

So you succeed in getting your complaint finally upheld

But what is it really worth, apart from confirming some of your worst fears?

Not only was engaging with the NHS complaints procedure invariably an intimidating experience, it could take more than two years to go the full distance in serious cases. But what could complainants really come up against if they were allowed to pursue their grievances to their conclusion through the system? What were the odds of a favourable outcome, and would the redress on offer reflect the seriousness of the complaint, or be worth the time and energy taken to make the case?

To begin with, complainants came up against bias and inadequate examination – contrived or otherwise – of their grievances at 'local resolution' by the health service body concerned. Usually anything close to a satisfactory investigation occurred only if complainants were lucky enough to get their cases placed before an 'independent review panel'. Even then, the health service pedigree of certain key component parts of these panels could – and did – come in the way of a guarantee that complaints would be dispassionately judged.

It was only when the grievances about the most fortunate complainants of all were approved for investigation by the Health Service Ombudsman that a reasonably thorough examination would take place. However, there are complainants and patients' agencies who still believe that the judgements of even this independent arbiter frequently appear to be questionable. (Chapter 4 has suggested one possible explanation for this phenomenon.)

That was the invidious position for complainants under the system that took effect in April 1996 – an arrangement in the process of being replaced by a reformed model for each of the four UK countries. Nonetheless, it is not a foregone conclusion that the changes to the system that are already in place or in the process of implementation will eradicate many of the drawbacks thus far mentioned. What, then, is to stop this happening?

For one thing – and crucially – it continues to be mandatory for complaints to be lodged initially with the health service. And all these complaints continue to be examined by the NHS, with the vast majority dealt with exclusively by them and not proceeding further. Like the earlier procedure, it is only after this process that complainants can seek a review or approach the relevant health service ombudsman for an independent inquiry and judgement. Nor are the checks and balances – current and future – to local resolution, in particular, likely to offer a reasonably cast-iron guarantee that the lot of complainants will improve dramatically under the new regime. Moreover, the character, functions and ways of doing things of the Ombudsman's organization remain apparently unaffected. For these and other considerations, the account that follows is still likely to be of relevance.

The story told in this chapter describes a catalogue of abysmally poor professional practice concerning the care of a patient admitted to hospital on each of two unconnected occasions. She recovered from her first stroke at an acute hospital and then a rehabilitation unit, despite experiencing some measure of sub-standard care. Five years later she had a second stroke, after which there was a near wholesale breakdown in attending to her. The patient's condition rapidly deteriorated while she was in the care of the community hospital of her admission. She died 24 hours later, within a few hours of being transferred to the district general hospital.

Stunned by the seriously questionable chain of events leading up to her sudden death, the patient's husband raised his concerns with the two hospital authorities involved. The authorities both produced unsatisfactory reports of the internal investigation they had carried out. Consequently, the complainant asked for his wife's case to be examined by an 'independent review panel'. He then took steps to obtain independent medical advice and was soon talking to a senior clinician in the National Health Service. Unfortunately, this doctor was unable to help the complainant with his case but he did offer another kind of advice: 'Forget the NHS complaints procedure. It's a waste of time. You will get nowhere. What you need is a good lawyer who knows the ropes.'

Despite this advice, the complainant approached instead another high-ranking NHS specialist, explaining his wife's case and asking for assistance. This practioner made a damning set of observations on the standard of care and treatment that had been given to the patient. His remarks also confirmed the complainant's own worst fears about those in whose charge his wife had been placed, and further justified his decision to ask for the case to be investigated more thoroughly. As a result, two separate independent review panels were subsequently convened, but the complainant was not satisfied with the panels' judgements and referred his grievances to the Health Service Ombudsman. The case, summarized here, illustrates the extent to which poor professional practice in the care of a patient was systematically overlooked by complaints examiners operating within the NHS complaints system. Each set of complaints went the full distance and took nearly five years to complete in an overlapping investigation process.

Background
Early in 1992, Mrs G suffered what her GP described as a slight stroke after examining her in bed. Stating that the stroke could extend, the doctor arranged for Mrs G to be immediately admitted to one of the two closely associated and located acute hospitals serving the area. Soon after her arrival Mrs G received a second and more thorough examination in the ward, which resulted in a similar diagnosis.

A couple of days later the stroke began to extend, affecting Mrs G's left side and leaving her unable to use her left arm and leg. Fortunately, its impact on her speech was only slight – even unnoticeable. Nevertheless, by this time she had become seriously ill, was under close observation and care and unable to be moved from her bed. However, a week after being admitted her condition began to improve and, with nursing assistance, she was moved from her bed to the bedside chair each day.

During the next five weeks or so, with medical care and daily physiotherapy, Mrs G slowly progressed and movement gradually returned to her left leg. Nevertheless, her balance, though improving, was still significantly affected, but she had started to walk with physical and mechanical assistance during her regular sessions in the physiotherapy unit of the hospital. Unfortunately, despite therapy, Mrs G's left arm was to remain permanently useless. Midway through this period Mrs G had two serious and closely occurring accidents. These resulted from elementary mishandling by nursing and medical staff, respectively, and had potentially severe consequences. Indeed, after the first accident (resulting in a severely wrenched shoulder on her affected side), Mrs G had to be put on painkillers, which she was taking when she had the second accident (a bad fall) a couple of days later.

At the first opportunity, and within about three hours of the second accident, the ward's staff nurse asked Mr G to sign a disclaimer, a step that would have absolved the hospital of responsibility for this fall. Mr G declined the invitation and instead lodged a written complaint with the general manager of the hospital trust; he received no reply from the manager himself. Instead, someone else, presumably a member of the complaints staff, arranged to meet him. The meeting was entirely unsatisfactory for Mr G. No apology was given, nor any trace of compassion shown for the physical and possibly psychological injuries suffered by Mr G's still-recovering and seriously disabled wife.

Mr G intended to pursue the complaint further, but Mrs G was now being given the 'cool treatment' by a once very friendly nursing staff. She was extremely concerned that her steady progress – despite the two accidents – would be prejudiced unless the complaint was dropped. Mr G agreed and took no further action on the matter. He had also been at the receiving end of the ward nurses' standoffish manner.

After six weeks at this hospital, and following advice given to Mrs G and her husband by the senior physiotherapist and clinicians in charge of her health care, she was transferred to what was referred to as the 'stroke rehabilitation centre' for the region. But the place turned out to be a shadow of its impressive description. To begin with, the 'centre' amounted to a couple of prefabricated, shed-like Second World War structures, which were wholly inappropriate for the well-being and rehabilitation of still-recovering stroke patients. Its unsuitability became especially apparent during the long, hot summer that was to come. The sister in charge retired within a couple of weeks of Mrs G's admission, closely followed by the departure of the two senior physiotherapists, both of whom had gone on maternity leave. While the new sister, inexperienced in the care of stroke patients, was receiving training during the next two and a half months, the ward was mostly being run by a young staff nurse supported by auxiliary nursing helpers. During this period, the adjacent physiotherapy unit continued to be short of its two senior professionals.

According to Mrs G's husband, the running of the ward left a lot to be desired, with poor professional practice and other failures (some too shameful or incredible to describe) a common occurrence. The living conditions in the ward were similarly deplorable and not the kind that recovering yet still fragile stroke patients should have been expected to endure. Mr G thought that these patients persevered with their lot in the expectation that they would soon be well enough to return home. It didn't help that there appeared to be no suitable alternative establishment for those of them who would have wished to be transferred. After more than two months at this so-called stroke centre, none of the patients had regained sufficient mobility to be discharged, although in other respects their recovery was much more conspicuous.

Mrs G, other patients and their visiting family members had told Mr G that physiotherapy sessions were cancelled by the understaffed physiotherapy unit, which also took in out-patients. Mr G considers that these unfavourable circumstances were probably at least partly responsible for the apparently slow progress of his wife and some other patients since she was transferred from the acute hospital. However, three and a half months after her admission at the centre and two weeks before she was officially due to leave, Mrs G and her husband could see no more benefit in her staying on any longer. Fortunately, by then, Mrs G had gained sufficient mobility to be easily transferred to and from their car. Indeed, her husband had already taken her out on several trips during the previous few weeks. So, after a lengthy incarceration, and with huge relief, Mrs G returned home to be cared for by her husband and social services. Mrs G's diary entry for the day of her departure read: 'Left…Hospital. Thank God!'

For the next two years Mrs G received a measure of regular physiotherapy treatment until, in July 1994, the trust involved terminated it altogether. During this period Mrs G's husband had also provided (daily) physical therapy and exercises – which he continued to give in the following few years. By July 1994 Mrs G had progressed considerably, although she had not regained the use of her left arm and would never be able to walk without combined physical and mechanical aid. To all other intents and purposes she had fully recovered. Her speech was normal, she was mentally acute and was able to perform most tasks that did not involve walking about unassisted. In mid 1993, Mrs G had been put on permanent anticoagulant therapy; two years later she was diagnosed as being diabetic and prescribed drugs to control the condition.

Five years on
Five years after her first stroke, Mrs G had a second stroke, this time affecting her right side. Mr G told her that he would ring for an ambulance, but his wife implored him not to, asking him to contact her GP instead. Mr G was connected to the 'on call' GP answering service; he left details of the emergency and was told that a doctor would telephone shortly. Mr G then went to get a district nurse (who happened to live a few houses away) to take care of her in the meantime. When he returned, Mrs G reported that the telephone had rung so he dialled the doctor's number again. This time the GP 'on call' answered and confirmed that he had returned Mr G's original call.

Shortly after this conversation the doctor arrived and after a brief examination, while Mrs G remained seated in her wheelchair, diagnosed a 'mild' stroke. Then the doctor went to make a call on his carphone. When he returned, he told Mr G that his wife had suffered what appeared to be a mild stroke but there was a risk that it could extend. He had arranged for her to be admitted to the community hospital and for an ambulance to take her there. Mr G noted that the doctor's decision to opt for the local community hospital contrasted with that taken by Mrs G's own GP five years earlier. On that occasion, she had been admitted directly to one of the two acute hospitals serving the area.

What happened to Mrs G when she was taken to hospital after her second stroke
Mr G arrived at the hospital shortly after his wife and stayed with her until the end of visiting time a couple of hours later. During that time Mrs G was sitting upright

propped against pillows on the bed, in the position she had been left by the ward nurses. She was able to respond verbally to Mr G, although on a reduced scale, and could still use her newly affected right arm and leg, but again to a lesser degree than before this second stroke. Mrs G had not been changed from the clothes in which she had arrived during this period. (It later transpired that Mrs G had also not received a follow-up examination, as had been the case at the time of the first stroke, at the community hospital.)

Immediately before leaving the ward, at around 8.15 pm, Mr G made a point of asking the staff nurse in charge to be sure to telephone him if there was a downturn in his wife's condition during the night. He asked this primarily out of consideration of the GP's remark about the possibility of the stroke extending, and from his experience of Mrs G's deterioration after her first stroke five years earlier. At the same time he told the staff nurse that he had brought two nightdresses and other personal effects for his wife. She suggested that it would be advisable for him to bring some more of Mrs G's nightwear when he visited the following morning.

Two hours later Mr G telephoned the hospital and was told that there was no change in his wife's condition. He was further encouraged by the fact that, up to 2.30 the next morning, when he went to bed, there had been no more word from the hospital. So it was with some optimism that he telephoned the ward for news when he rose later that morning. But the news was dire. The ward sister who was leading the day shift told him that Mrs G had been very sick during the night, was now unconscious and not responding. Mr G asked why he had not been contacted about the downturn in his wife's condition, as expressly requested by him the previous night. The sister said that she could not answer his question. She was also unable to provide a proper explanation of the events that had led to Mrs G's unconscious state. It further came to light during the conversation that the duty doctor had not been called. The ward sister said that she would look into the matters Mr G had raised and hoped to be more helpful on his arrival at the hospital later that morning. (Months afterwards it came to light that Mrs G had suffered three progressively serious setbacks starting from either 3 am or 4 am until around 7.40 am, when she became unconscious and unresponsive. It was also to emerge that the doctor had been told about Mrs G's dire situation when he happened to telephone the ward at 8.30 am, following Mr G's conversation with the ward sister.)

However, there was still no further information of consequence for Mr G when he visited his wife. The duty doctor had still not seen her and the ward sister told Mr G that the doctor was busy in the adjacent out-patients minor injuries unit. Meanwhile, Mrs G lay in deep coma and was not seen by the doctor until 11.30 am – three hours after he had been told about her condition. When the doctor finally arrived and examined Mrs G, he agreed with her husband that she should be transferred to the district general hospital immediately. (Mr G was later to discover that one of the remarks in the doctor's admission note to this hospital read: 'No facility to monitor sugar/INR here. Transfer to [name of acute hospital].') However, despite all efforts taken at the acute hospital to save her, Mrs G's condition had deteriorated to a point beyond which medical intervention could have saved her life. She died a few hours later with her husband by her bedside.

Two weeks after Mrs G's death, Mr G had still not received an explanation of the events leading up to his late wife's comatose state, nor why he had not been contacted as he had requested on the night she was taken in to hospital. So he called without warning at the ward one evening to find out what was causing the hold-up. His unannounced visit appeared to alarm the staff nurse who greeted him (she was one of those who had been on duty during the night in question). She seemed also to be strangely defensive and had no answers to the concerns he had originally raised with the ward sister. Mr G had the impression that the clinicians involved had either not taken his concerns seriously or were burying their heads in the sand in the hope that he would abandon his complaint.

Within a few minutes of Mr G returning home, a doctor (not one of the two involved in his wife's care) at the hospital telephoned to enquire about the purpose of his visit there. When told, the doctor gave Mr G assurances about the painless and peaceful demise of his wife and recommended that Mr G should seek counselling. The doctor could not answer the questions Mr G had raised about his wife on the morning of the day she died. From this conversation, also, Mr G had the feeling that, until then, the practiioners concerned had not expected him to pursue the matter.

Mr G lodges a set of official complaints with the health service trust involved

As he had no further information from any of the practitioners concerned in his wife's care before and during her admission to the community hospital, Mr G was advised by a health authority official to complain directly to the trust concerned. A month after his initial verbal complaint Mr G wrote to the trust's complaints manager giving his written account of events from the time of Mrs G's second stroke episode up to immediately before she died at the acute hospital. Although not at all familiar with the health service complaints procedure, Mr G also asked for answers to a number of still outstanding questions concerning the care of his wife. He had seven questions.

1. As a clearly very sick patient, on what lines and how frequently was Mrs G's condition monitored during the night she spent at the community hospital?
2. Bearing in mind that Mrs G had just suffered a stroke, were any special instructions given to senior ward staff regarding her care at the time of admission?
3. At what time during the night did she get 'very sick'?
4. When did Mrs G become unconscious?
5. Was the duty doctor told immediately?
6. Why was Mrs G not admitted to the acute hospital without delay when she had got into difficulties?
7. Why was Mr G not notified when Mrs G's condition deteriorated, as he had requested?

Mr G points out that he had raised these issues when he first complained, at a time when he had been told very little about his wife's care and treatment at the community hospital. As a result these questions were not as well informed and probing as they could have been. In his letter of complaint Mr G added that, in his view, the on call local GP had made an error of judgement in admitting his wife to the community hospital. He stated that, as a precautionary measure, Mrs G should have been admitted directly to the acute hospital. The fact that this doctor had observed there was a risk of the stroke extending should have been sufficient reason for him to take that step.

On the point of lodging his complaint, Mr G received a letter signed by the ward sister giving the nurses' version of events at the community hospital from the time of his wife's admission until she was unconscious and eventually transferred to the acute hospital. Mr G considered that the story she had put her name to was distorted, superficial and left outstanding questions. Her account painted a picture of caring nursing staff who had done their best for Mrs G. However, Mr G suspected that cover-up and closing of ranks was more likely to be the case. Mr G then expressed all these sentiments in a second letter to the trust's complaints manager. A few days later he received an acknowledgement from the trust's chief executive stating that he had initiated a full examination of the case.

Seven weeks after his initial complaint, Mr G had written to the trust expressing concern at the length of time the investigation was taking and asking the reason for the delay. The trust apologized for the hold-up, stating that it had been necessary to speak to all the medical and nursing staff involved in Mrs G's care. It added that sometimes the process could take longer than planned. About three months after he had made the complaint, Mr G received the report of the trust's investigation.

Summary of the trust's report on its investigation into events at the community hospital
The GP who was called to Mrs G's home had been informed about her previous medical history of diabetes and the left-sided stroke that had left her handicapped. He was also told about her current symptoms – a sudden right-sided weakness and loss of speech – and he carried out a clinical examination, which confirmed Mrs G had suffered a further significant stroke. After assessing the situation, the practitioner decided to admit Mrs G to the community hospital for observation and nursing care. She arrived at the hospital by ambulance at about 6 pm.

Although the admitting GP did not see Mrs G again before going off duty at 6 pm, he recorded in her case notes that she had previously suffered a severe left-sided stroke. He wrote that there was evidence to suggest that Mrs G had experienced a further stroke affecting her right side and that, in particular, her right arm and leg movements had been weakened. The doctor added in the notes that Mrs G was unable to speak or walk and that her blood sugar level had been low. In view of the latter, he recommended that her Metformin dosage should be reduced to 500mg twice a day and the Warfarin anticoagulant therapy kept at the level advised in her INR records.

The period following Mrs G's admission to the community hospital was 'essentially one of watchful waiting'. The trust's clinical director of medicine had confirmed that this period of observation is the norm in cases of stroke, when the first 24 to 48 hours indicate the severity of such an event. Ward nursing staff were familiar with Mrs G's medical history and were trained in the care of stroke patients. Accordingly, they were capable of interpreting the doctor's findings and formulating an appropriate care plan until further review.

Two qualified nurses and an auxiliary were on night duty in the ward to which Mrs G had been admitted. They were fully briefed about Mrs G's condition during the changeover with the afternoon–evening shift. It was confirmed that she would be watched throughout the night but generally left to sleep although, if she awoke, her position would be changed to keep her comfortable. Observations were taken on her admission.

Mrs G's condition had deteriorated very gradually during the night so it is extremely dificult to state precisely when she became unconscious. Although very serious, her condition had been 'comparatively stable throughout the night'. 'No obvious signs of deterioration were recorded from her admission at approximately 6.30 pm'. (It was to emerge in later investigations that there were indeed obvious signs of deterioration.) When the night staff took over at 8.30 pm Mrs G was 'sitting upright'; she 'appeared extremely tired' and 'her only responses were by moving her head or facial expression'.

Although restless, Mrs G had slept throughout the night. No obvious change in her condition was noted until around 4 am when she vomited. After being attended to by nurses, she was laid on her side. Mrs G was still responding by facial expression. The next clear change came at 6.30 am when she was found to be feverish and a fan was switched on to make her comfortable. Her temperature and blood sugar were measured again. With hindsight, the trust believed that the nursing staff 'should have' taken four-hourly observations. Nonetheless, it does not consider that Mrs G's condition 'materially deteriorated' until early the next morning. The matter of these infrequent observations has been brought to the attention of the nurses. They have since been 'counselled about the importance' of ensuring that patients' observations were properly monitored and documented.

By 7.15 am, when the day nurses arrived on duty, Mrs G's condition and level of consciousness, although poor, were not judged to have 'significantly altered', but at 7.40 am she vomited again. The ward sister noticed that Mrs G's 'levels of consciousness were deteriorating' and there was 'no obvious response' from her to handling. It was at this point that the trust considered that a 'significant downturn in her condition had occurred'. At 8.30 am, after attending to Mrs G, the duty GP was informed about her condition.

The doctor has confirmed his opinion that despite the continuing deterioration in Mrs G's condition overnight, she was unlikely to have been given further treatment, other than to be made comfortable. He added that, in the light of the overnight downturn in Mrs G's condition and her previous medical history, an earlier transfer to the acute hospital would not have influenced the course of events. This view has been supported by the trust's clinical director of medicine, who stated that it was extremely unlikely that any more active treatment would have been given to Mrs G at the acute hospital. He has further commented that the eventual outcome of such an illness is often determined by a patient's response during the crucial first 24- to 48-hour period.

Mr G has described how, just before leaving the ward on the night in question, he requested that he should be contacted immediately if his wife's condition deteriorated in any way during the night. The staff nurse he spoke to recalls promising Mr G to do so if there were any significant change in her situation. This procedure is the policy in all the trust's hospitals and is vigorously applied. At 10.30 pm Mr G telephoned the ward. The nurse he spoke to remembers telling him that his wife was not very well and that he would be informed if there was any noticeable change in Mrs G's condition.

The nursing staff's perception of Mrs G's capabilities 'is at variance' with Mr G's account of her competency. In her earlier letter to Mr G, the ward sister had reported that his wife was 'unable to communicate' with the nurses and was immobile and nurses have since confirmed that Mrs G could not or 'was reluctant to respond verbally to them' other than by nodding her head or facial expression. (Mr G maintained in his earlier complaint that when he had sat with his wife after she had been admitted to hospital she had been able to communicate with him verbally and move her newly affected right arm and leg. Were this not the case, Mr G had stated later in his ongoing complaint, he would have insisted that a doctor be called. Moreover, Mr G asked how his wife could have remained sitting upright and steady for at least two hours if, in addition to the existing limitations of her left side, the right side of her body was now not functioning. If that were the case, would it not be unlikely that the nurses would have succeeded in placing Mrs G in a sitting position in the first place?)

Mr G asks, given that the GP who examined his wife at home told him that the next 36 to 48 hours would be crucial, should not the doctor have admitted Mrs G to the district general hospital immediately? The practioner who admitted Mrs G to the community hospital has stated that, in his clinical judgement, it would not have been appropriate to admit her to the acute hospital, nor would it have changed the eventual outcome if she had been sent there. Indeed, neither of the two doctors responsible for Mrs G's care during the period in question considers that an earlier transfer to the acute hospital would have influenced the course of events. The treatment would have been the same at the acute hospital, a point that has been confirmed by the trust's clinical director of medicine.

In his earlier written complaint Mr G asked what documentary evidence could be supplied to show that his wife had received regular nursing attention at the community hospital during the night in question. If she had been properly cared for, why was it that the nursing staff did not notice Mrs G's deterioration? The trust reiterates that Mrs G did receive appropriate nursing care throughout the night, but the general plan was to allow her as much rest as possible. Again, as previously stated, Mrs G's condition had deteriorated very gradually and was extremely difficult to pinpoint until she became ill at 7.40 am. Mr G had further questioned the delay in calling for the duty doctor to see his wife the following morning. The practioner was informed of her condition at about 8.30 am, soon after the ward sister had finished her telephone conversation with Mr G, but he had been unable to see Mrs G immediately. In answer to Mr G's question about the delay in calling for the duty doctor to see his wife, the trust emphasizes that this delay had little bearing on the ultimate outcome.

Mr G enquires why it had taken a month for the staff at the community hospital to respond formally to the points he had raised in conversation with the ward sister. Ward personnel had initially tried to deal with his concerns informally. Subsequently, the ward sister spoke to the nurses in charge of Mrs G's care on the night in question and she then wrote to Mr G. Staff have since been reminded that cases where serious concerns are expressed by complainants must be promptly referred to the trust's patient services department at the acute hospital for formal handling.

In reply to Mr G's question about whether the facilities and expertise at the community hospital were sufficient to deal with stroke patients, the trust states that as a community hospital it is not equipped to provide 'such high levels of monitoring or medical intervention' as the trust's large acute hospital was. Nonetheless, all the nursing staff are trained to 'exactly' the same standard as their counterparts at any of the other trust hospitals.

Mr G responds to the trust's report on its investigation

While the trust's 14-page investigation report was much more extensive than the statement received from the ward sister, Mr G considered that the questions he had raised about his wife's care had not been satisfactorily addressed. He also felt that the trust's account of events during the evening and night in question was inaccurate, defensive, and left a number of still unanswered and crucial issues. The report had revealed to him a picture of wide-ranging professional negligence and abysmally poor levels of care about which he had not been previously aware, despite attempts by the trust to minimize their significance and effect. Moreover, it became clear to him that the trust was doing all it could to protect the medical and nursing practitioners involved. Even its clinical director of medicine was brought in to give an opinion on dubious claims concerning Mrs G's care. As a result, Mr G detailed his objections in a widely critical page-by-page response – too lengthy to cover here – and asked for his case to be considered for independent review.

Mr G lodges a separate complaint with the health authority

In his written complaint to the trust, Mr G had questioned the on-call GP's brief examination of his wife at home and this doctor's subsequent decision to admit her to the community hospital. This was because it had become increasingly clear to him that the hospital was poorly equipped – professionally and technically – to manage her condition. He also suggested that this practitioner must have known that the hospital was not equipped to deal with his wife's stroke, monitor her pre-existing diabetes and manage her anticoagulant control. Once the initial confusion in the demarcation line between the jurisdictions of the health service trust and health authority, respectively, had been resolved, these aspects of his case became the subject of a separate complaint to the health authority.

The health authority's complaints manager subsequently approached the GP concerned for his comments on the events up to and including his decision to admit Mrs G to the community hospital. In his letter to the manager, the doctor stated that he had been informed about Mrs G's relevant medical history and current problem – a sudden right-sided weakness and loss of speech. He had carried out a clinical examination, which confirmed the position, and concluded that Mrs G had suffered a further stroke.

The GP went on to say that it was his 'carefully considered judgement' that Mrs G should be admitted to the community hospital. He did not believe that the specialist services of the acute hospital would be suitable. Although there was some possibility of the stroke extending, admission to this acute hospital could not prevent that happening. The doctor wrote that he did not see Mrs G again that evening as he had completed his period of duty at 6 pm, but he intended to review her position at 12 noon the next day. He maintained that admitting Mrs G to the acute hospital would have made no difference to the final outcome.

The health authority's complaints manager invited Mr G to respond to the practitioner's remarks. In his subsequent letter Mr G suggested that a 'clinical examination' should have involved more than a few minutes examining his wife while she remained in her wheelchair. In these circumstances, and in the interests of Mrs G's safety, the doctor should have taken no chances. He should unhesitatingly have admitted Mrs G to an acute hospital – as her own GP had done after her first stroke five years earlier. Mr G also pointed out that the doctor was well acquainted with what was available (or not) in terms of clinical support at the community hospital ward to which his wife had been admitted.

Mr G questioned the practitioner's opinion that the specialist services available at the acute hospital were inappropriate for Mrs G and his view that admission to this hospital could not have prevented the possibility of the stroke extending. Mr G's point was that there was no justification in taking unnecessary chances with a patient's life when the option of specialist care and equipment for stroke patients was available.

Mr G also wanted to know why the doctor had not carried out a follow-up examination of his wife at the community hospital when, it seemed, he had been present and still on duty at the time of her admission. Failing that, why had he not left instructions for the replacement duty doctor to do so? Mr G added that, either way, it could have altered the course of events. Finally, he stated that his wife had suffered only a partial loss of speech, a point that had already been covered by him in previous correspondence.

A 'conciliator'- a recently recruited retired person – was then brought in by the health authority to intercede between Mr G and the doctor who had admitted Mrs G to the community hospital. From what Mr G has to say, the conciliator was an inappropriate person for the job of mediation. His poor aptitude for the role was substantiated by his seemingly unquestioning acceptance of this practitioner's decision and the supporting views of other doctors connected with the trust concerned who had become involved in the case. Judging by the remarks in his letter to Mr G, it was clear the conciliator had merely replicated comments attributed to these clinicians in the earlier investigation report by this trust about events at the community hospital.

The conciliator observed that 'all fully appreciate Mr G's concern' as to why his wife was not admitted to the acute hospital. He further wrote that the doctors involved had 'reiterated their belief that transfer [to the acute hospital] at whatever time would not have saved Mrs G. This point has been confirmed by the clinical director of medicine.' The admitting GP 'did all that was possible' for Mrs G, but, 'sadly, her condition deteriorated and any transfer [to the acute hospital] would not have influenced the course of events'. He then quoted the words of a literary hero suggesting that Mr G should put the episode behind him and move on.

Mr G then wrote to the health authority expressing his dissatisfaction with this flawed attempt at conciliation and requesting that his complaint be considered for independent review. He concedes that intercession of even the highest calibre would have been absurd when it meant trying to persuade him that black was white. By then it had become crystal clear to him that a number of clinicians had a lot to answer for concerning the care of his wife.

Independent review approved and initiated by the trust

The results of the trust's and health authority's investigations were unacceptable to Mr G so he asked for each of his complaints to be considered for 'independent review'. Around six months after Mrs G's death, the convener appointed by the trust agreed that an independent review panel (IRP) should be set up to investigate Mr G's complaint. After a discussion with Mr G, the convener wrote to the chief executive of the trust involved setting out the principal terms of reference for the IRP to investigate the relevant aspects of the case. There were two questions to be considered.

1   With knowledge of her serious condition and previous medical history, was the care provided by the on-call medical service appropriate for Mrs G?
2   Was the nursing care provided for Mrs G during her period of time in the community hospital of the appropriate standard?

The convener sent Mr G a copy of his letter to the trust's chief executive. To his surprise the terms of reference suggested that a follow-up medical examination had been carried out at the community hospital, when it had not. He wrote to the convener to set the record straight. Despite Mr G pointing out this error, the terms of reference remained uncorrected in the independent review report of its completed investigation. Fortunately, though, the IRP seemed to pick up this point during its investigations.

The IRP comprised the convener, a lay chair, another lay member and two nursing and two medical assessors (GPs). Its subsequent report contained wide-ranging criticisms – some serious or crucial – by the advising medical assessors about the actions and statements of those who were involved in Mrs G's care at the community hospital.

What the trust's independent review uncovered, its observations and Mr G's comments
There had been a vague reference in the trust's earlier local resolution investigation that the GP who had admitted Mrs G to the community hospital 'did not see' her following admission, but the independent review investigation confirmed what Mr G had meanwhile discovered – that the GP had not carried out a further examination of Mrs G at the hospital. Nor had he left instructions for the night duty doctor to do so. Indeed, Mrs G was examined only at 11.30 the following morning, by which time she had been in deep coma for four hours. It was also 19 hours since her first and only previous examination at her home.

The trust's independent review investigation had uncovered a catalogue of other crucial errors by nurses during the evening and night in question. At 7.30 on the evening of her admission, Mrs G's blood pressure and temperature had risen dramatically, yet the duty doctor had not been called, nor had Mr G been informed, even though he was present in the ward at the time. Had he been told about this clearly serious development, Mr G says that he would have insisted that a doctor was called. He has no doubt that this would have led Mrs G being transferred to the district general hospital.

At around this time, Mr G had informed the staff nurse that his wife was having difficulty swallowing her tablets (Metformin and Warfarin). He now knows that this was a significant development and should have been a further signal for the staff nurse to contact the duty doctor after checking its severity for herself. But the nurse took no action. Instead, after Mr G had left the hospital, his wife had been given ice cream, a step that should not have been taken in the circumstances. Indeed, it was likely that the dramatic deterioration in Mrs G's condition and crises later that night and in the morning were directly connected with these critical errors, as well as with additional mistakes and the poor care provided by the nurses.

The next obvious crisis – following the earlier (ignored) vital signs concerning blood pressure, temperature and swallow reflex – occurred at either 3 am or 4 am (the precise time was never established) when Mrs G suffered her first bout of vomiting. Nurses attended to her but did not take the vomiting as a sign that this was a crucial downturn in Mrs G's condition. Indeed, one of the nurses who contacted the duty doctor at the time did so, it seems, only to discuss the question of catheterization. It had not occurred to the nurse to mention Mrs G's vomiting, although it was the first time she had vomited since her admission.

Mrs G suffered two further and more serious attacks of sickness and other conspicuous signs of critical deterioration that morning. It appears the first of these additional setbacks took place at 6.30 am and the second less than an hour later. A few minutes afterwards, Mrs G lapsed into deep coma, but even then no doctor was called to attend her. Nor had any attempt been made to advise Mr G of her deteriorating condition.

Only after Mr G had telephoned the ward sister some 40 minutes later and was told about his wife's perilous condition did the sister speak to the duty doctor and then, it seems, only after the latter had contacted her. This was nearly an hour since Mrs G had become unconscious and when the prospect of saving her life was probably already lost. As previously noted, the duty doctor finally arrived three hours later. Mr G considers that the ward sister was handed the job of picking up the pieces left behind by the stunningly negligent night staff. He feels that she may also have been occupied trying to find a way of saving their skins instead of calling him and the doctor.

The more qualified of the two nursing assessors advising the trust's independent review panel confirmed that the duty doctor should have been called when Mrs G's blood pressure and temperature were found to be high at 7.30 pm. She added: 'I would also question whether admission to…Community Hospital for a new stroke was appropriate, particularly as Mrs…needed careful monitoring for her diabetes and anticoagulant control.' This was a direct reference to the GP who had arranged Mrs G's admission to the community hospital. Between them the two nursing assessors went on to criticize the nurses' failure to carry out crucial clinical tests, the substandard level in the frequency of recording vital signs, the poor state of nursing records and the nurses' lack of communication with Mr G about his wife's condition.

Yet, this wide-ranging and apparently strong disapproval was not reflected in the assessors' conclusions. One assessor stated that 'the nursing care provided [for Mrs G] was of the appropriate standard'. The other affirmed that 'the nursing care provided [for Mrs G] was of an acceptable level'. The opinions of the two medical assessors generally seemed to defend the conduct of the doctors and nurses concerned in the case, despite evidence indicating poor practice by all the practitioners involved in Mrs G's care.

These (GP) assessors remarked that the short journey to the community hospital, where Mrs G was already known, seems to have been appropriate for her condition at the time. They added that following admission 'there would appear to be no real need for her to have been examined again since her serious condition, after suffering a second stroke affecting the opposite side, would have precluded specific treatment other than rest'.

Moreover the assessors did not believe that the 'coagulability' of the blood was crucial in the management of Mrs G's illness. They could not say with certainty whether she had 'suffered a bleed from a major artery or a blockage of an artery by a clot that later extended due to brain swelling'. The assessors further stated that the deterioration suggested a haemorrhage, but added that clinical impressions can be unreliable. They drew attention to the fact that neither a CT scan nor a post-mortem had been carried out to provide a true diagnosis.

The assessors went on to say that, 'although the INR was outside the therapeutic range, it was not grossly so and required only a minor adjustment as recommended by the laboratory'. They pointed to guidelines in the British National Formulary stating that, 'in the presence of severe bleeding, Warfarin should be stopped'. Nevertheless, the assessors did not consider that stopping Warfarin at the time of Mrs G's admission to the community hospital would have altered the eventual outcome. But they made no mention of the fact that the patient's INR was recorded the day before and, accordingly, could well have risen in the intervening period.

They stated that the decision to continue with a reduced Metformin dosage was the standard treatment and that 'although taken infrequently, the paucity of blood sugar measurements was not responsible' for Mrs G's demise. They also remarked that 'at no time were there clinical signs consistent with low or high blood sugars and the readings bear this out'.

The assessors then referred to the long delay before the duty doctor attended to Mrs G. They stated it was 'unfortunate' that the practitioner did not attend until 11.30 am, but felt unable to comment on the level of priority given to this patient in the absence of detailed information about the doctor's other commitments in the minor injuries unit. However, the assessors were certain that, given Mrs G's critical state at the time, earlier attention to her would not have made any difference to the final outcome.

They added that 'from the detailed nursing observations' given to them, their view was that 'the fatal stroke extended at approximately 7 am' on the day in question. The medical assessors considered that Mr G would have been contacted about his wife's condition at the first possible opportunity had he not telephoned first. By contrast, the review panel's two nursing advisers indicated that the 'observations' referred to by the GP assessors were inadequate. One of them further implied that the duty doctor should have been told earlier of the seriousness of the situation and added that Mr G should also have been called. (These and other comments made by the GP assessors in particular were to be seen as flawed in the independent and more thorough investigations that were to come.)

The rest of the review panel, including the convener (a non-executive board member of the trust against whom the complaint had been made), lay chairman and lay member (a non-executive of the regional health authority board) added their signatures to the assessors' conclusions. Effectively, the overall verdict was that the clinicians involved in Mrs G's care had no case to answer.

Even before the independent review involving the trust, Mr G had become convinced that the grim state of affairs surrounding his wife's care at the community hospital was not an isolated episode. He continues to believe that the inferior professional practice exemplified in her case was probably endemic and part of a culture that may have existed for some time in the ward before his wife's admission.

The independent review panel's recommendations and the trust's response
Soon after receiving the report of the independent review panel, the trust's chief executive wrote to Mr G confirming acceptance of its recommendations and that action was being taken to implement them. The proposals indicated that GPs who admit patients to community hospitals should provide written and detailed instructions for their clinical care and treatment. The panel recommended that the trust needed to review its policy concerning the calling of on-call practitioners (duty doctors) to attend patients at community hospitals. Finally, the panel recommended that the trust should review its policy on the notification by hospital staff of relatives of seriously ill patients.

Following this, a new operational policy affecting the ward at the community hospital where his wife had been admitted was formulated and recorded in a substantial document produced by the trust. Mr G says that the changes in place following this could be regarded as an indication of the poor standards of care previously given to patients in the ward.

In particular, the document laid down new rules for the admission and care of patients, including those with acute illnesses. One of the rules states that patients who require nursing or medical care that cannot be provided at home will not be admitted to the community hospital ward if their condition 'would be expected to need the more specialized care available at a district general hospital'. Moreover, it is now necessary that all staff who are involved in a patient's care 'are in agreement about the admission', and that the resources and expertise available are considered to be 'sufficient to effectively meet the patient's needs'. Mr G is astonished that these elementary rules had not been in force through the ward's previous operational policy. Nonetheless, he considers that the very basic but crucial failures by medical and nursing staff in the care of his wife had little connection with past trust policy and everything to do with very poor practice and supervision.

The sweeping changes seemed to have addressed all the questions about poor professional practice and procedures that Mr G had focused on in his complaint. A representative of the trust wrote to Mr G saying he hoped that Mr G would 'regard this as a very positive outcome' from what had been 'clearly a very distressing experience' for him. Saddened though he still is, Mr G says that the most distressing experience of all was that experienced by his late wife, who did not survive her ordeal, but it would have been too much to expect the head of corporate affairs who signed the letter to have alluded to her suffering.

Nevertheless, Mr G believes that some good may already have come out of his wife's case, but it is of no great consolation to him that it has taken the death, in at least dubious circumstances, of his nearest and dearest relative to have brought about these remedial changes. He believes that the atrocious medical and nursing conduct surrounding the community hospital ward should have been noticed much sooner by the trust's management. Indeed, he says, who knows how many other patients before his wife may have suffered a similar fate?

An independent review is initiated by the health authority to consider Mr G's additional complaint
Meanwhile Mr G's request to the health authority for independent review of his additional complaint about the doctor's examination of his wife at her home, and

the practitioner's decision to admit her to the community hospital had been accepted by the appointed convener. However, Mr G became concerned when he discovered that this official (a non-executive board member of the same health authority) had also been on the panel of the earlier trust independent review. In view of his objection, a replacement was appointed. Under the terms of reference, the panel to be convened would examine the events before Mrs G's admission to hospital and in particular the decision taken by the GP to admit Mrs G to the community hospital instead of the district general hospital.

Observations by the health authority's independent review panel, its conclusions and Mr G's comments

The independent review panel set up by the health authority was in session nine months after that of the trust's and the report of its investigation completed three months later. In the view of the panel's medical assessors, the visiting doctor's examination of Mrs G 'was brief and not recorded on the...contact sheet'. They went on to say that 'it is uncertain whether pulse and blood pressure were measured'. (In evidence to the panel, the GP stated that he could not remember whether or not he had measured Mrs G's pulse and blood pressure.) In addition the assessors remarked that there 'appears to have been a failure' on the GP's part 'to record the precise details' of Mrs G's examination on the contact sheet used for the purpose. They affirmed that 'while the examination was adequate to make the diagnosis of a stroke, it should have been more thorough, especially as it was to suffice as the admitting examination' for the community hospital. Also, it seemed to the assessors that this doctor did not adequately discuss with Mr G the questions of his wife's condition and treatment.

The medical assessors drew attention to the GP's remark that he now felt more careful consideration should have been given to the possibility of a haemorrhagic stroke, which in retrospect may have led him to admit Mrs G to the acute hospital. But they felt that it was 'quite impossible to differentiate between the various types of stroke in the acute phase' and that treatment at this stage would not have affected the result. The assessors concluded that the kind of hospital to which Mrs G had been admitted was 'an appropriate place to manage a stroke as there is little that can be done during the acute phase in any hospital setting to influence the outcome'. In arriving at this conclusion they did not mention anywhere in their report that, in addition to suffering a new stroke, Mrs G's pre-existing diabetes and anticoagulant control needed careful monitoring. The assessors knew that the community hospital did not have the facilities to deal with these matters, which Mr G felt was possibly the reason they made no reference to them. In his view it was curious that, having formed part of his evidence in the review panel's report of its investigation, the issue was not raised or commented on in the panel's conclusions or elsewhere in the document.

The assessors made no comment about the point that, at the time of Mrs G's first stroke (diagnosed as being 'slight' after an examination at home) five years earlier, her own GP had unhesitatingly admitted her to one of the two acute hospitals serving the area. This was despite the fact that this matter had also been raised by Mr G in his evidence to the review panel. Unsurprisingly, therefore, Mr G is unimpressed by the assessors' conclusions and suggests that they are an example of the way in which medical practitioners will put up a defence of others in their profession even if there is evidence that they should not do so. He considers that there are clinicians who are so inured to tragedy involving others not connected with them that they will overlook dubious professional practice that may have led to the injury or death of a patient.

In agreeing with the individual criticisms by the medical assessors, the other panel members were concerned that the GP did not examine Mrs G again at the community hospital to which she had been admitted. They observed that the situation here was more favourable for the purpose than that he had encountered at Mrs G's home, where she had been sitting in a wheelchair at the time. It was 'regrettable', they added, that Mrs G was not seen by a doctor until 11 am (other evidence indicates it was 11.30 am) the following day. This was about 19 hours since she was first examined at home by the visiting GP, eight hours since she first got into difficulties and four hours from the time she had lost consciousness.

In his evidence to the panel, the doctor concerned stated that even if he had diagnosed a haemorrhagic stroke, he would still have admitted Mrs G to the community hospital. Yet, in an earlier statement to the panel, he had said that he had not previously admitted patients to this hospital as his own practice was in another nearby town. (Oddly, in his evidence to the earlier independent review panel set up for the health service trust, the doctor stated that he often admitted his own patients to the same community hospital. Mr G has still not been told which of these two versions is correct. Even the investigation that was to be made by the Health Service Ombudsman did not get to the bottom of the inconsistencies in the GP's statements.)

So, what was the final judgement by this second independent review panel of the conduct of the doctor involved? It concluded that his 'initial decision' to admit Mrs G to the community hospital 'was not unreasonable in the circumstances, and that this in itself does not appear to have determined the eventual outcome'. Apart from a few additional but repetitious remarks that, effectively, was the sum total of the panel's conclusions. Mr G regarded these findings to be as inaccurate a reflection of the facts as those exemplified in the outcome of the earlier trust IRP investigation.

Mr G seeks advice from an independent consultant neurophysician

After the two local resolution inquiries, but before the two independent review investigations, Mr G had consulted a NHS consultant neurophysician about his late wife's case. This doctor's subsequent observations more than substantiated all the concerns Mr G had already raised about his wife's care and treatment. The clinician criticized the GP's inadequate examination of Mrs G at her home and his decision to admit her to the community hospital instead of the acute hospital. He remarked that Mrs G's outcome could have been very different had she been admitted to the acute hospital directly, or transferred there from the community hospital later during the evening in question. Although the acute hospital did not have a dedicated stroke unit at the time, it had sophisticated facilities and designated clinical staff to deal with stroke patients. In its position as the predominant acute hospital in the region, it was well known for the care and treatment of strokes.

Mr G cited the cases of two acquaintances who had also suffered severe strokes in the 1990s and benefitted considerably from therapy at the acute hospital. Indeed, 13 years later in 2004 one of them, then over 90, continued to be mobile. The other, who had been admitted to hospital three times for especially severe stroke attacks, survived another two years, during which time he, too, was able to walk unaided. Mr G drew attention, once again, to the case of his late wife at the time of her first serious stroke. With no bed available at the district general hospital, her GP had admitted her to another acute hospital, where she made much progress despite sustaining two accidents during her stay (as reported earlier in this chapter). As a result, after having initially been unable to walk, among other restrictions, Mrs G eventually became partially mobile, and it was another five years before her second stroke.

The consultant neurophysician's further comments focused on a number of instances of crucial and culpable clinical neglect by the doctors and nurses at the community hospital. These included the lack of a follow-up medical examination of Mrs G, the nurses' failure to take any action when her blood pressure had risen significantly and neglect on their part in not monitoring her condition and carrying out other essential procedures. The neurophysician heavily criticized additional instances of poor practice by medical and nursing staff. These and other comments were made shortly before the trust's independent review panel had started its investigation into the course of events following Mrs G's admission to the community hospital.

The consultant neurophysician's key observations based on case information supplied to him (these exclude remarks in parentheses)
The outcome could have been very different if Mrs G had been admitted directly to the acute hospital. First, a CT brain scan would have shown whether she had suffered a cerebral haemorrhage, although it may not have been clearly apparent for 24 hours. This would have had an influence on whether to omit or reverse her Warfarin therapy. Secondly, there was a good chance that the probable aspiration pneumonia could have been prevented or at least actively treated with antibiotics and physiotherapy before Mrs G's condition became critical. Acute medical treatment for stroke includes the maintenance of vital functions with adjustment of blood pressure, if necessary, as well as preventing aspiration pneumonia from inappropriate feeding or vomiting. The best medical and nursing practice dictates that feeding by mouth should be avoided in the acute stages of stroke until it is established that swallowing is safe. This is to prevent inhalation of food and contents into the lungs causing chest complications and pneumonia. The question about the dangers of oral feeding or drinking involving stroke patients, particularly those with a recurrent stroke, was obviously not realized by the nursing staff at the community hospital.

Reference to Mrs G's medication was given in the doctor's brief admitting note advising a reduction of her Metformin therapy and continuation of her Warfarin dosage. The latter had been recommended by the acute hospital's haematology department following an INR reading taken the day before her stroke. (The procedure was part of Mrs G's routine and ongoing anticoagulant control and the INR level and Warfarin dosage were recorded in a booklet provided for the purpose.) Was the practitioner who wrote the note aware that the INR level was abnormally high at 4.3? (Yes, because he studied the booklet beforehand.) In any case, he should have considered the possibility that Mrs G had suffered a cerebral haemorrhage and reduced the Warfarin dosage as a precaution.

As a diabetic and on Warfarin, Mrs G had an unstable condition, a fresh stroke, that needed monitoring and investigations to determine the best course of treatment and management. Was the community hospital ward the most suitable place for this, and did it have appropriately trained personnel to provide these acute procedures and care? It may have been correct to admit Mrs G to the ward at this hospital if these conditions were met and if there were facilities for carrying out acute medical tests including blood sugars and INR to ascertain the suitability of her medication. The possibility of a cerebral haemorrhage was clearly apparent. Accordingly, Mrs G's Warfarin dosage should, at least, have been reduced. It may have been more sensible to stop this therapy for 24 to 48 hours to assess the clinical position.

If the community hospital was regarded as the right place for Mrs G, why was she not examined properly after admission and why were no blood tests taken? What instructions about observations were given to the nursing staff? Assuming that there was no change in Mrs G's overall condition until 4 am (it could have been 3 am) the following morning, was there any other cause for concern at this time other than that she had vomited? Was there any change in her level of consciousness or weakness when this happened?

It seems that Mrs G's condition at 7.40 am was very dire with deep coma, stertorous breathing and a rising temperature. There also appears to have been some delay in advising the duty doctor (at 8.30 am) about Mrs G's serious state, but his delay in assessing her until some three hours after being told seems inexcusable. The medical die and clinical course was fully established by then and the subsequent outcome (Mrs G's death) later that day at the acute hospital was inevitable and unpreventable.

It was probable that transferring Mrs G to the acute hospital earlier on the morning in question would not have had a significant effect on the outcome, but there was 'certainly the possibility' of this with full and appropriate medical and nursing care. However, if Mrs G had been admitted directly to the acute hospital the previous afternoon or evening, 'it could have been an entirely different matter and outcome'.

'Watchful waiting' (this was the description used by the trust in the report of its investigation and refered to by the consultant) needs skilled nursing and medical observations. There is plenty of evidence to show that this is best carried out in an acute stroke unit where a better result is secured for patients. The advisability of admitting patients to a skilled observation ward is partly dependent on their previous health and fitness. The fact that Mrs G made a good recovery from her first stroke should have been ample reason for all efforts being made on her account. Skilled nursing care is required to prevent inhalation pneumonia resulting from disturbed swallowing response and also to avoid other complications. Was it the trust's medical director's opinion that these careful observations and treatment of acute stroke are the norm in the community hospital? (Mr G subsequently invited this trust clinician to answer this question but he did not give evidence at the independent review that followed.)

The duty doctor at the community hospital should have been told about Mrs G's condition at 4 am (or 3 am) or 6.30 am. The practitioner who replaced him should have seen Mrs G shortly after he was notified about her condition at 8.30 am. It is a sad commentary that this duty doctor stated that, in his view, no further active treatment was likely to be planned, and that an earlier transfer to the acute hospital would not have influenced the course of events. The trust's investigation report stated that its clinical director for medicine had said it was extremely unlikely that any more active treatment would have been given to Mrs G at the acute hospital. This begs the question of when she would have been admitted there and to what stage in her illness he was referring.

No statements have been made about what medical instructions – written or otherwise – were given to nursing staff (on the evening of Mrs G's admission). It appears that Mr G was told (by the ward sister) the following morning that his wife had been very sick in the night. Presumably this referred to the occasion at 4 am (or 3 am) when Mrs G was attended to by nursing staff. It was reported (in the trust's report of its own inquiry) that she was responding by facial expressions to the nurses at the time. Her vomiting was probably a direct result of her stroke and an indication of a deterioration in her condition. Nonetheless, ward nurses recorded no such observations and no effort was made by them to alert the duty doctor or to seek medical advice or assessment.

It was also stated (in the trust's report) that Mrs G was feverish and found to be incontinent at 6.30 am. Yet, once again, staff made no detailed neurological obser-vations, nor did they obtain medical help at the time of this obvious deterioration in Mrs G's condition. As already noted, Mrs G was probably developing aspiration pneumonia following her vomiting. It is not known (from the trust's account of events) when it was considered that Mrs G's condition 'materially deteriorated early the following morning'. However, this was clearly at either 4 am (or 3 am) or 6.30 am, but on neither occasion was action taken to assist her, nor was antibiotic therapy to manage or arrest her likely pneumonia considered.

The consultant neurophysician's comments are included in Mr G's ongoing case

When giving evidence to each of the two independent review panels, Mr G incor-porated the neurophysician's medical advice. He considers that, but for this independent clinician's observations, the panels' investigations may have been less probing than they were, but what the neurophysician had to say was to make no difference to the panels' conclusions – judgements that absolved all the practitioners involved of any responsibility.

Mr G had the impression that the inclusion of this externally obtained clinical advice in his evidence to the independent review panels did not go down well with their members. He believes that this may have been one of the reasons why the meetings he attended with them turned out to be sometimes defensive and confronta-tional. Mr G added that his introduction of externally obtained medical opinion may also have provoked each of the two independent review panels to take an inappro-priately stubborn stance in their decisions on his grievances.

Mr G refers his case to the Health Service Ombudsman, but his complaint is rejected

Lack of success at the independent reviews led Mr G to refer the two sets of complaints to the Health Service Ombudsman early in 1999. He sent all the accumu-lated material on the case to this final destination in the health service complaints procedure and further complained to the Ombudsman that there had been malad-ministration by the two independent review panels in dealing with his grievances.

Around four months later, Mr G was informed that the Ombudsman had rejected his case for investigation. Effectively, all concerned in assessing his complaints had given their total support to the conclusions reached by the two earlier health service managed independent review panels. Mr G's additional complaint that there had been maladministration of his case by the two independent review panels was similarly turned down. The investigations manager who wrote to Mr G stated that his grievances had been taken seriously and dealt with correctly. Also, he hoped that Mr G would be able to 'take some comfort from the comments of the Ombudsman's medical and nursing advisers'. In the light of the (inappropriate) support that these clinical assessors had given their counterparts on the independent review panels and, effectively, to the practitioners being complained against, Mr G considered this statement to be absurd.

Mr G lodged a wide-ranging and critical response to the decision by the Ombudsman's team not to investigate his complaints. Additional items of correspondence were exchanged between himself and the Ombudsman's office during the four months after he was notified that his case had been rejected. The process ended with a second detailed letter from Mr G explaining why he did not consider that his complaints had been properly evaluated by the Ombudsman's screeners. In it he added that a number of crucial and serious aspects of the case had been overlooked by these assessors, but Mr G received no acknowledgement in the following weeks and he resigned himself to what seemed to be the end of the line for his grievances.

The Health Service Ombudsman decides to investigate Mr G's case after all

Six weeks after Mr G had last written to the Ombudsman's Office, a top-ranking official at the Ombudsman's office telephoned Mr G to say that she had 'raised eyebrows' about aspects of his case, and to state that the set of complaints was to be considered again for investigation. A further six weeks later Mr G was formally advised that his case was to be re-investigated. The grievances to be examined were as follows.

1 The GP's clinical assessment of Mrs G's condition was inadequate and his decision to admit her to the community hospital was inappropriate.
2 The independent review panel convened by the health authority failed to consider all the available information relating to the case.
3 The medical care given to Mrs G at the trust's community hospital was inadequate – in particular she was not examined on admission, no instructions were given to nursing staff about her care, and there was an undue delay before the duty doctor saw her on the morning in question.
4 The nursing care given to Mrs G in the community hospital was deficient – in particular she was inadequately observed, and nursing staff failed to inform medical staff, or contact Mr G, when her condition deteriorated.
5 The independent review panel convened by the trust failed to consider all the available information.

After this development Mr G expressed concern that the investigations manager and his boss, a regional head of investigations who had supported his subordinate's previous decision not to investigate the case, were now once again to oversee the examination of his set of complaints. But, apart from assurances given to him, there was to be no change to this situation. Mr G presumed that for regional job-function considerations it would have been awkward for the Ombudsman to remove these two individuals from the case and temporarily replace them with a pair of similarly senior, but more detached managers. There seemed to be no choice for him but to accept matters as they were, but the high-ranking official who had telephoned Mr G in the first place undertook to sign the resulting investigation report

It also became clear to Mr G that the investigating officer (see Chapter 4 for job-function) who had been involved in the initial stages of the earlier screening process that rejected his complaints in the first place would carry out the oncoming investigation. But Mr G received a clear assurance that this examiner's previous involvement in his case had not been significant. He was told that, by the time clinical advice had been obtained from internal professional advisers, this investigating officer had gone on extended leave and someone else took over the screening of his case on the previous occasion. In the circumstances – and to avoid any risky delays – he accepted the arrangement as it stood.

The same official at the Ombudsman Office rang Mr G again before the process of taking evidence began and told him that the Ombudsman was determined to have no 'loose threads' in the investigation that was to come. When he received the Ombudsman's draft report of the investigation a few months later, it was clear to Mr G that substantial aspects of his complaint were unaddressed. In his view, loose threads remained, with numerous matters of significance excluded from the draft document. So Mr G responded with a detailed account of the evidence and issues that seemed to have been disregarded in the Ombudsman's investigation. He also identified a number of errors and pointed to one or two items of new but minor evidence that had been picked up by the examiners.

In responding, Mr G drew special attention to the fact that only a very tenuous reference was made to the consultant neurophysician who had advised him. He further remarked that he would like to have seen at least the basic details of the neurophysician's wide-ranging comments on vital clinical questions concerning his wife's care included in the draft report. Mr G added that this omission was especially disappointing since the Ombudsman's investigators had received copies of all the neurophysician's documented observations.

He went on to point out that, by contrast, the trust's head of nursing quality – who was not in post at the time and had no connection with the case – was interviewed by the investigators and her comments given exposure in the Ombudsman's report. She criticized the standard of nursing and medical assessments, the inadequate monitoring of Mrs G's 'vital signs' after her admission to the community hospital and felt that 'more observations, especially blood pressure in the light of the initial high reading, should have been done'. Nonetheless, she concluded that Mrs G had been 'adequately observed, but that there was inadequate nursing documentation to provide evidence of the care given'. The report further remarked: 'However, while she thought there had been some shortcomings, she thought the key issue had been that [Mr G's] expectations were very different from those involved in [Mrs G's] care.' (The precise meaning of this observation is not clear.)

In his response to the draft report, Mr G had stated that his 'expectations were perfectly realistic and straightforward'. He had gone on to say that the catalogue of nursing and medical failures identified in the investigation of his complaints was surely the key issue in this case. Mr G regards the curious conclusions of this trust staff member to have been a predictable and silly last-ditch attempt to minimize the culpability of some of her associates.

The Health Service Ombudsman's findings and Mr G's observations

When the Ombudsman's final report was completed and sent to him, the signatory to the covering letter (the same top-ranking official with whom he had been in contact) stated that 'no matter of significance has been overlooked'. Mr G was, therefore, disappointed to find that this was not the case, especially as he had already drawn attention to numerous significant issues that had been overlooked when he had responded to the draft version of the report. Indeed, apart from the professional assessors' opinions and the Ombudsman's findings, the two documents were virtually identical.

Despite its being an academic exercise, Mr G responded in writing to the Ombudsman's final report. Once more, he pointed to the important matters that had been disregarded in the investigation and itemized wide-ranging aspects of the findings he found to be flawed, questionable or incomplete. He also criticized what he felt was the unreserved acceptance by the signatory to the findings of some of the illogical and openly biased comments made by certain of the Ombudsman's assessors. Mr G went on to list elements of the nursing and (GP) medical assessors' statements he regarded as being dubious or otherwise faulty.

Although not obliged to do so, the signatory to the report was good enough to respond in writing to the concerns that Mr G had raised, but this high-level respondent maintained that the complaints had been 'considered thoroughly' and 'stood by' the findings in the document. Moreover, Mr G's particular criticism of what he regarded as being a deeply flawed defence by the Ombudsman's two GP assessors (each having seemingly inappropriate specialties for his case) of the actions of the doctor concerned before and after Mrs G's admission to the community hospital was similarly rejected. So were his concerns about some of the observations made by the Ombudsman's nursing assessor.

But Mr G had some cause for satisfaction as the Ombudsman upheld three out of the five complaints in his case in one way or another. However, his first complaint, that the GP's assessment of Mrs G's condition was insufficient and his decision to admit her to the community hospital instead of the acute hospital – arguably the most crucial factor in her future care – was not one of them. Accordingly, his second complaint, alleging maladminstration by the independent review panel convened by the health authority in considering this doctor's conduct and judgement before Mrs G's admission, could not be upheld.

The signatory to the Ombudsman's report agreed with the (GP) assessors that 'while [the doctor's] examination was very brief, as an experienced GP, he established enough information to reach a conclusion both about [Mrs G's] condition, and about the need for hospital admission'. These assessors had disagreed that Mrs G's condition of a fresh stroke, combined with her diabetes and the need for anti-coagulant therapy, merited admission to the acute hospital. Their advice was that Mrs G's 'anti-coagulant status was within the normal range and did not require management in a general hospital setting'. The Ombudsman's assessors' view was that 'different management would have been extremely unlikely to lead to a different outcome'.

Once again, the signatory to the Ombudsman's report accepted the assessors' view of this issue and added that the reasons given by the GP for admitting Mrs G to the community hospital also 'withstand scrutiny'.

The doctor concerned had told the Ombudsman's investigators that admission to the community hospital was appropriate to the patient's condition, especially as there was no immediate active medical treatment that she could be given. He considered that Mrs G would have been in familiar and less stressful surroundings where staff knew her; she would have been seen by her own GP after the weekend; and it was easier for Mr G to visit her there than at the acute hospital.

Mr G feels that the Ombudsman may not have been prepared to uphold all his complaints, despite seemingly compelling evidence that this is what should have occurred. One reason he gives for this view is that the apparent wholesale breakdown in professional conduct in the care of his wife had involved an inordinately and, perhaps, embarrassingly large number of clinicians. As a consequence, it seemed to him that the signatory to the Ombudsman's report may have decided to accept some patently suspect clinical advice from the assessors together with the absurd comments of the GP concerned in defence of his actions. Mr G had already expressed these views to the Ombudsman.

He had also previously commented in detail during the earlier health service investigations about the examination given to Mrs G by the visiting GP and the latter's decision as a result. From all evidence arising and commented upon during the case it seems clear that the examination was brief and flawed, an observation that was in marked contrast with the view expressed by the Ombudsman's (GP) assessors. Indeed, one of the independent review panels was 'concerned that the doctor could not remember whether or not he had measured the patient's pulse and blood pressure' at the time. The panel added that there 'appears to have been a failure' on his part 'to record the precise details' of Mrs G's examination on the contact sheet provided for that purpose. Even this panel's medical assessors stated that the patient should have been more thoroughly examined, 'especially as it was to suffice as the admitting examination at the community hospital'. Mr G considers that the poor level of treatment the doctor gave his wife and his failure to carry out a follow-up examination after Mrs G's admission to the community hospital do not demonstrate the actions of an 'experienced GP'.

One of the assessors advising the trust's independent review panel had questioned the appropriateness of Mrs G's admission to this hospital following a new stroke, 'particularly as [Mrs G] needed careful monitoring for her diabetes and anti-coagulant control'. As has already been stated, the consultant neurophysician who advised Mr G held a similar opinion and had made other apparently significant observations in support of his view. Mr G suggested it was likely that this specialist stroke consultant, a practising doctor in the NHS, would be more familiar with the capabilities of acute stroke management at a major general hospital than the Ombudsman's (GP) assessors who seem to have had the opposite view.

Mr G also pointed out it was misleading of the Ombudsman's assessors to say that his wife's 'anti-coagulant status was within the normal range'. In the first place, at 4.3 Mrs G's INR was outside the 'desired therapeutic range' of 2.5 to 3.5 set by the acute hospital's haematology department. Probably even more significantly, the 4.3 reading had been taken the day before. In the light of subsequent events suggesting a possible – perhaps probable – haemorrhagic stroke, the actual INR may well have been higher. But there was no way of establishing this as, unlike the acute hospital, the community hospital was not equipped for the purpose. Nor did the latter have facilities to perform a CT brain scan. Mr G had previously drawn the attention of the Ombudsman's investigators to these considerations, as well as to the essentially similar observations made by the consulting neurophysician, but his explanations seem to have been overlooked or ignored.

After the independent review and during the Ombudsman's investigations Mr G had written to point out what he considered to be the unsound reasons given by the GP for admitting his wife to the community hospital. He cited Mrs G's own doctor's decision to admit her directly to an acute hospital at the time of her first stroke five years earlier. Here, too, his remarks appear to have fallen on deaf ears. The inconsistency of the general practitioner concerned in telling the first independent review panel that he had often admitted his own patients to the community hospital, and then informing the second one he had not previously done so seems not to have been checked or corrected by any of the investigators examining Mrs G's case.

Mr G's third complaint, that the medical care given in the Trust's community hospital was inadequate, was upheld to 'the extent' of the shortcomings in the communication by the relevant doctor with nursing staff, 'and his failure to examine [Mrs G] in the community hospital'. The signatory to the findings added that the practitioner would be expected to 'take note' of the comments in the Ombudsman's investigation report and 'take them into account in his future practice'.

Mr G's complaint about the undue delay by the duty doctor in attending to his wife on the morning in question was not upheld. The signatory to the Ombudsman's report stated that it was 'clearly of concern' that it had taken up to three hours for the duty doctor to see Mrs G. Nevertheless, it was accepted that this doctor had established an 'appropriate priority' for the patients he had to attend and that even if he had seen the patient earlier, it was very unlikely to have made any difference to her outcome. Mr G suggests that the doctor could not have accurately established her condition until he had seen and examined his wife. He considers that it was disgraceful of the practitioner to have mitigated his actions in this way. Mr G wonders whether this doctor would have taken the same stance had the patient been closely related to him.

Mr G pointed out that it was not until the Ombudsman became involved that the delay in examining his wife had been properly investigated – and then only after considerable pressure from him. The Ombudsman's report shows that the doctor concerned had come on duty at 8.30 on the morning in question. He telephoned a patient whom he then advised to attend the minor injuries unit at the community hospital. His next call was to the ward sister to say that he expected to arrive at the hospital at about 10 am. She explained the situation concerning Mrs G and it was agreed that he would see the patient on his arrival. During the next half-hour the doctor spoke to three more patients on the telephone and then visited one of them at home.

The doctor arrived at the community hospital soon after 10 am to find that 10 patients were waiting for him in the minor injuries unit, adjacent to the ward where Mrs G had been admitted. Mr G considers that this doctor's decision to deal with these patients ahead of one who was in a critical condition across the corridor was highly questionable. Only an hour and a half later and three hours after he first knew about her predicament did the clinician cross the corridor to examine Mrs G. In view of these circumstances, Mr G cannot understand how the signatory to the Ombudsman's report could not uphold his complaint about this doctor's actions. He accepts that this aspect of the case relating to his wife's care may not bear strong comparison with the other examples of poor clinical practice that had come to light.

Mr G's fourth complaint, that the nursing care given to Mrs G at the community hospital was inadequate, was upheld. However, the signatory to the findings referred to the significant clinical and other procedural changes that had taken effect since Mr G's complaint was made. These included 'nursing handover' now taking place 'on the ward so that any changes in a patient's condition would be immediately apparent'. 'Nursing documentation' had been improved, and there was evidence that nursing staff are 'more aware of the need to undertake observations'. The signatory to the findings also suggested that the trust concerned should consider a number of 'other issues raised by the Ombudsman's nursing assessor'.

Mr G's final complaint, that the 'independent review panel' convened by the trust failed to consider all the available information, was also upheld by the Ombudsman. Although critical of 'some of the panel's and lay chair's actions', the signatory to the findings did 'not think it would be helpful to recommend any remedial action specific to this trust' – whatever that was supposed to mean.

The Ombudsman's findings focused on the failure by the trust's independent review panel to reflect properly the observations of certain clinical assessors in its conclusions. In particular, the latter recounted the criticisms by one of the two nursing assessors on the independent review panel over a number of crucial issues.

1 In view of Mrs G's high blood pressure on admission to hospital, nurses should have checked her blood pressure again during the evening.
2 Mrs G's blood pressure was so high that nurses should have called a doctor.
3 Observations should have been carried out more frequently.
4 Nurses should have called a doctor earlier in the morning.
5 The ward sister should not have become involved in Mrs G's care – instead she should have called a doctor and Mr G.
6 Nursing documentation did not accurately reflect Mrs G's deterioration.

The findings of the Ombudsman's report pointed out that, having made these critical observations, the nursing assessor (in the trust's independent review panel) then concluded that 'the nursing care was of an appropriate standard'. The signatory to the findings agreed with Mr G's view that this conclusion seemed to be at odds with the criticisms the assessor had already made, but added that if her judgement was sustainable it was not supported 'well enough' in her report. It was further mentioned that the other nursing assessor's statement did not show that she agreed with these criticisms, that is to say, apart from a comment that observations of Mrs G should have been carried out more frequently.

For the signatory to the Ombudsman's report and findings to conclude that, 'while shortcomings in practice have been identified, they were not at a level that compromised her [Mrs G's] care' is a ridiculous and disgraceful observation from Mr G's perspective. He considers the remark to be a bogus reflection of even the

Ombudsman's own investigation and what it revealed about the abysmally poor level of care given to his wife – and said so in his follow-up comments.

Mr G is also critical of additional – and in his view – presumptious and erroneous remarks by the signatory to the Ombudsman's findings: 'I certainly understand [Mr G's]... concerns about his wife's care. Inadequate communication between clinical staff and [Mr G]... led to different expectations of [Mrs G's]... likely prognosis.' Considering this person's other dubious conclusions in the face of compelling evidence and argument to the contrary, Mr G fails to see how his anxieties can have been appreciated. He added that poor communication with him had nothing tangible to do with the near total breakdown in standards of clinical practice by the practitioners concerned in this case.

Mr G went on to say that, in the circumstances, it was depressing to find this high-level and, supposedly, independent complaints adjudicator apparently accepting the doubtful prognoses of the patently suspect clinicians involved. Moreover, flawed though they were, the conduct and attitude of these practitioners before his wife's admission to the community hospital and up to the time she was made comfortable for the night implied that their forecast for her – certainly during this period – was clearly nothing like the mostly grim one that emerged following his complaint. Mr G made the point that the casual manner in which his wife was attended to at this time did not indicate a critically or fatally ill patient.

In his evidence to the trust's independent review panel, the GP who had admitted Mrs G to the community hospital stated that as 'he had not been informed of any concerns by the staff nurses on the ward' he did not examine Mrs G again. The doctor had added that 'he expected to be able to see her [Mrs G] the next day' when he was on duty again. Mr G suggests that these statements do not suggest that the doctor thought his wife a perilously ill patient who was not expected to survive, which was the view expressed or intimated by certain nurses giving evidence to the Ombudsman's investigators.

However, it is plain to him that the now well-established and dangerously flawed medical and nursing care given to Mrs G were directly responsible for her subsequent rapid deterioration and death. In these circumstances, he suggests that the prognosis issue put forward in the Ombudsman's report is misleading, unnecessary and an attempt to evade the real question of the near total failure to attend to Mrs G's clinical needs from the outset.

The signatory to the Ombudsman's report of the investigation also commented that 'no matter of significance has been overlooked' and that 'all aspects of Mrs G's care have been scrutinized'. Mr G strongly disagrees with each of these remarks. He had previously drawn attention to a plethora of significant matters that had been disregarded in the draft report, but without effect. Virtually all these points continued to be ignored, with the final version of the Ombudsman's report – apart from the findings and clinical assessors' comments – an almost total replica of the draft.

Included in Mr G's written response to the Ombudsman's final report was a question addressed personally to its signatory. Would the Ombudsman's report and conclusions have been regarded as an example of equitable judgement, in the way it had been expressed, if the patient concerned had been a similarly close relative of the signatory? Mr G did not expect a reply to his question – and did not get one. Nor had he received a response to the same question put to other senior investigators about their decisions during the passage of his late wife's case through the earlier stages of the health service complaints procedure.

With tongue in cheek, Mr G also enquired if the three upheld complaints called into question the competence of the two senior managers at the Ombudsman's office who had comprehensively rejected all his complaints in the first instance. He suggested that their conduct also begged the question of how often they may have dealt similarly with the legitimate grievances of other complainants. Would they now be considering their positions, or did the Ombudsman still have confidence in these two senior staff members and given them another chance?

The signatory to the Ombudsman's report replied to Mr G that the two senior managers concerned 'had exercised their responsibilities in both initial consideration' of his complaint and, subsequently, to the Ombudsman's 'complete satisfaction'; moreover an altered decision of the kind shown in his case was seen by the Ombudsman as a strength of the latter's system, rather than an issue for concern. The fact that it had taken sustained pressure from Mr G over a four-month period contesting the earlier judgement by these managers did not seem to be a cause for any uneasiness or regret by the Ombudsman's respondent.

The consultant neurophysician's key observations on the Ombudsman's report

The consultant neurophysician made various comments on the Health Service Ombudsman's report: there was an element of 'whitewashing' in the report over the care and action taken by medical and nursing staff at all levels in dealing with Mrs G's illness. In the first place, she was briefly and inadequately examined by the visiting GP. It was also obviously wrong not to have examined her again and not carried out a more careful assessment of Mrs G's condition after her admission to the community hospital. A satisfactory written note containing the results of this action should have followed and the nursing staff more clearly advised about Mrs G's condition and the preparation of an agreed care plan. The arrangements should also have been discussed with Mr G, who was present in the ward shortly after his wife's admission.

Nursing staff initially had observed that Mrs G's blood pressure was high. Her blood pressure should therefore have been checked again soon after it was first taken that night, and medical advice obtained or therapy provided if it remained high. Also, Mrs G should have received four-hourly observations, at least, and no food or drink by mouth until it was demonstrated that her swallowing was normal – which, almost certainly, it was not. Furthermore, the nurses should have taken action to prevent and subsequently to treat the chest infection that, in hindsight, was virtually certain to have been an aspiration pneumonia associated with Mrs G's vomiting. The Ombudsman has acknowledged shortcomings in the standard of nursing care provided. Therefore, the attitude of the trust's head of nursing quality and her attempts to minimize these defects, and to state that Mrs G was given good overall care, are considerably dismaying. (This senior practitioner had given evidence to the Ombudsman's investigators, although she had not been in post at the time of Mrs G's admission to the community hospital.)

Finally, Mr G should have been contacted at 4 am (or 3 am) when his wife's condition had deteriorated and she had first vomited. It was even more necessary to do so between about 6 am and 7 am when her condition had obviously deteriorated further. The care and attention that followed was slow by all concerned – especially the duty doctor – and indicated a very poor standard of practice, but had the doctor attended Mrs G at 8.30 am, it would probably already have been too late to save her.

It was incorrect to suggest that no additional care could have been given to Mrs G, and that no alternative handling would have altered the outcome. Multiple studies have indicated that acute stroke units produce the best results for stroke patients – in survival and in residual mobility. (Although the acute hospital in question did not have a dedicated stroke unit at the time it had high-level acute stroke facilities and was widely and effectively used by stroke patients.) Management of stroke can be formulated 'only on the basis of a full assessment and correct diagnosis, which includes a brain scan'.

Mr G's view of the health service complaints system in action

Mr G is convinced that there is an endemic reluctance at all levels in the health service complaints procedure seriously to condemn inappropriate practice by health care practitioners. He maintains that there are large numbers of complainants, patients' agencies and others who agree with this view. Even in apparently open-and-shut cases (such as his own), the gravity of neglectful clinical practice is often mitigated, played down or ignored, with legitimate complaints being unjustifiably rejected in the process. Mr G believes this state of affairs to be a natural product of any self-regulated health care complaints system and, for that matter, of a modified arrangement that is all but internally managed – exemplifed by the new procedures either in place or in the process of taking effect.

He considers that similarly faulty decision-making is at work among those carrying out investigations in the Ombudsman's name. Mr G has evidence that his own poor experience of investigators operating under this final arbiter in the system is shared – perhaps even more acutely – by many other complainants. It seems to him, even when a major complaint is upheld by the Ombudsman, its seriousness can be unreasonably moderated in the investigation report, implying that the professional conduct being complained about was not really all that bad. He regards such failures by the Ombudsman's examiners to be especially troubling in the light of this officer's position as head of what was – and to some extent still is – the sole independent component of the complaints system.

Moreover, Mr G feels that there is nothing like enough satisfaction to be gained from favourable decisions by the Ombudsman. He asserts that the best a complainant can expect is an apology and an assurance that steps will be taken by the health service body concerned to mend its ways. This was the result received by him when the Ombudsman decided largely in favour of his case. Fortunate though Mr G judges himself to have been in receiving this verdict, he feels that it is of such nominal value as to be of little consolation to him – especially as his case had involved the death of a person in dubious circumstances. The signatory to the Ombudsman's report hoped that Mr G would 'find some support in this independent consideration' of his late wife's care and of the complaint he had lodged. Mr G has pondered on how he was supposed to do this when the Ombudsman's neutral position was not reflected in the way his case had been handled.

Finally, Mr G believes that, in practice, the 1996 version of the NHS complaints procedure was a highly defensive mechanism that operated excessively in favour of those being complained about. He considers that far too much onus was placed on complainants to prove their case. Not only that; he maintains the system was not transparent enough, with complainants often being given an incomplete picture about the subject of their complaints, especially in the early stages of the process. Its effect was that complainants were not sufficiently equipped to pursue their cases and consequently there must have been many who became dissillusioned and prematurely gave up. The problem arising for those who decided to proceed further, and were lucky enough to be allowed to do so, was finding the time to take on the system. Mr G says there could not have been many complainants who were able to give up the time involved over two or three years for the purpose. And for what achievement in the end? He cannot see that such an adverse portrayal of the system will improve dramatically (which he maintains it needs to) in his understanding of the reformed complaints regime.

Enough said.

CHAPTER 12

Ireland's complaints system is under reform

But the proposals don't go as far as independent regulation

Ireland is heading for a statutory health care complaints system that may look suspiciously like either the United Kingdom's basic NHS model, established in April 1996, or the reformed mechanisms that have replaced it, or are in the process of doing so. Under the Irish government's Health Strategy 2001 proposals, action would be taken to 'strengthen the customer focus of service providers'[1] across a range of health service areas, including the handling of patients' complaints through 'formalized' procedures at local level.[2]

In this latter respect, the health strategy paper declared that legislation would be introduced to provide for a statutory procedure that would give 'greater clarity and uniformity in dealing with complaints, structured local resolution processes as well as the opportunity for independent review'.[3] Details of the statutory framework for these arrangements were to appear in a new Health Bill, which was due to be published in autumn 2004. In its wider context the Bill will specify the form that a planned new Health Service Executive (HSE) is to assume[4] as a unified national administrative body for the delivery and promotion of health services,[5] in place of the existing less integrated system.

Legislation enacted following the Health (Amendment) Act, passed on 8 June 2004, and its 'statutory instruments', has provided for, among other requirements, the 'cessation of the office of the members' of existing health boards, area health boards and the Eastern Regional Health Authority, and the formation of an 'interim health service executive'. The latter was charged with planning for the setting up of the finished model,[6] an event that was scheduled for January 2005.[7]

Another issue that the Health Strategy 2001 objectives focus on is the perceived inability under present procedures to question the actions or decisions taken by medical practitioners on clinical matters. While the proposals acknowledged the need for freedom in exercising clinical judgement, they also recognized the necessity for a stronger framework for questioning and investigating clinical decisions in certain situations.[8]

Chapter 5 of the health strategy paper stated that forthcoming legislation on statutory registration of health care professionals will contain 'adequate machinery' to investigate complaints against individual practitioners.[9] The document further declared that the situation surrounding complaints lodged with and handled by the relevant professional bodies needed to be strengthened.[10] It added that the government was also committed to toughen existing legislation covering the registration of professionals such as doctors, nurses and pharmacists.[11] These issues are addressed in the Medical Practitioners' Bill, which was at an advanced draft stage in summer 2004 and due to be passed by the following autumn.[12]

The health strategy paper additionally noted that statutory registration, currently applying to doctors, nurses, pharmacists, dentists and opticians, would be introduced for other health profession groups under new legislation. These would include health and social care professionals such as physiotherapists, occupational therapists, social workers and child care specialists.[13] The legislation in particular is the Health and Social Care Professionals Bill, which was expected to be passed in late 2004.[14]

All legislation on statutory registration of health professionals will be formally reviewed within five years of its introduction. This re-appraisal will pay special attention to the accountability of regulatory bodies to the Oireachtas (Irish parliament) and to the significance of their having regard to the public interest in the conduct of their work.[15] The legislation for professionals with existing registration and those to be registered for the first time will also provide for consumer representation on their statutory registration bodies and authorize registration boards to establish a system requiring regular re-accreditation of practitioners. This procedure will be based on a structured form of continuing education and training.[16] In addition, the government has put into place machinery to explore how best a system of registration can be set up to cover practitioners in alternative and complementary therapies.[17]

The health strategy proposals also focus on the role of the Irish Ombudsman. This officer already investigates complaints about maladministration against the Department of Health and Children and the health boards. The paper declared that the government considers the existing Ombudsman to be 'the appropriate person to deal with complaints relating to the health system', and aims to enlarge this officer's jurisdiction to take in voluntary hospitals and other like health care establishments. Indeed, the legal implications of such an advance have been under scrutiny for some time[18] and it is suggested that such a development would be a logical extension of the Ombudsman's responsibilities. (It does not seem clear whether this means that the Ombudsman will be given powers to examine complaints involving clinical issues in the new legislation – an area that is within the remit of his three opposite numbers in the United Kingdom.)

The Ombudsman still in post in 2004 made clear his own views on aspects of the present health service complaints procedures in Ireland. He is a 'great supporter of bodies having their own internal complaints system' and in line with this it appears that his Office has supported a number of initiatives aimed at improving the quality of the existing procedures covering health care.[19]

The Ombudsman has stated that complaint handling in the health service is heavily dependent on the goodwill and co-operation of medical staff.[20] In several cases studied by him in recent years he found there was a marked reluctance by doctors, and consultants especially, to engage wholeheartedly in patients' complaints. Indeed, he was struck by the lack of a procedure to oblige consultants to co-operate fully in the process. He pointed to the contrasting situation in the British health service complaints system where there is a process of independent review in the handling of grievances. The Ombudsman observed that at this phase of the United Kingdom's procedure, in certain cases an independent panel is set up with the authority to obtain clinical advice during its investigations.[21] (The 'independent panel' he refers to is explained in the closing paragraphs of this chapter.)

The position of internal complaints systems operated by the health boards in 2004
Each of the 10 health boards (seven operating individually, three jointly within a health authority) in Ireland manages its own individual, although similar, internal complaints system. While basic similarities in style exist across these procedures, some appear to be more streamlined or sophisticated than others are. In one example a major health care provider has put its own complaints mechanism under wide-ranging scrutiny with the aim of providing a more equitable and efficient system for handling complainants' grievances.

The review of the Eastern Regional Health Authority
In March 2000 the country's Eastern Regional Health Authority (ERHA) was formed to take over responsibility for health, social and personal services in counties Dublin, Wicklow and Kildare.[22] Some 14 months later the ERHA set in motion a sweeping review of the way complaints were being handled in the region. By September 2001, the working group appointed for the job had produced an interim report pin-pointing the gaps in existing procedures and specifying the changes necessary to remedy these deficiencies.

Among the areas under focus in the review was the quality of training programmes for staff dealing with complaints in health boards and voluntary institutions. Issues of care standards and good practice in relation to complaints and appeals procedures and in other respects were also addressed.[23] In 2002, hospital and community services in the three counties were provided by as many area health boards and 36 voluntary providers. There were also 400 smaller voluntary agencies operating in the health care system.[24]

The report proposed that patients, clients and their families should be encouraged to complain if they were dissatisfied with any service, as complaints provided valuable information about how the quality of a service could be improved. Patients made complaints on various subjects, such as communication difficulties and the behaviour of health service staff; lack of facilities, equipment and therapy services; cancellation of and waiting times for appointments; and admission procedures.[25] The working group considered the existing training for staff dealing with complaints to be inadequate and commented on the absence of recognized qualifications for these staff. It recommended that these matters should be addressed, that there should be effective publicity about complaints procedures and an IT regional database to support complaints handling. It also proposed that an efficient first phase local resolution avenue for complaints and a procedure for the review of unresolved grievances following the initial complaints stage should be introduced. The working group underlined the value of promoting patient–client advocacy and developing customer services, and made other recommendations.[26]

So what is the position on complaints procedures in the region in 2004? Under the Health (ERHA) Act 1999, the Eastern Regional Health Authority is obliged to plan, arrange for and oversee the provision of services within its boundaries. It also has powers to set up a complaints and appeals system and introduce measures to assess the value of all these procedures. Being subject to the Ombudsman's juris-diction, the ERHA could also provide a means by which patients and clients of health care establishments not under health board control (but funded by the ERHA) have access to the Ombudsman.[27]

Local complaints managers are the first to investigate grievances. If dissatisfied after this initial phase, complainants can take their case to the director in charge of customer services, complaints and appeals. A detailed investigation then begins and can continue for any time from a few days to a couple of months. The director's decision is passed on to the parties concerned in the case, after which the complainant has a right of appeal to the Ombudsman.[28]

Acute, non-acute and voluntary hospitals, intellectual disability units and other establishments not under health board management also have procedures and designated staff to investigate complaints. Some have even set up their own internal appeals process. However, if a complainant is not satisfied with an investigation outcome, there is no right of appeal to the Ombudsman. In this event, the only recourse is to the courts or, in relevant cases, to the Medical Council, the doctors' regulatory body. Before 1 March 2000, some of these complaints were referred to the Department of Health and Children, but since then such cases have been handled by the ERHA.[29]

There is a difference between the complaints and appeals systems in the area health boards and those operating in the voluntary sector. In the latter, complainants are denied equal access to procedures set up to deal with appeals. As such, the disparity may be regarded as being out of step with the principles of equity and equality, and accountability outlined in *Shaping a Healthier Future – Health Strategy 1994*, the Irish government's previous paper about reforms for the National Health Service.[30]

The ERHA review showed that 80 per cent of health service providers have a complaints policy. Half of those who do not are intellectual disability establishments. The research also showed that 76 per cent of health care providers advise patients, clients and their families about any complaints procedures that have been set up and 17 per cent of service providers had an assortment of people to deal with complaints. Designated personnel vary according to the type of complaint received, so a director of nursing, one of the management team or a patient representative could also be responsible for dealing with grievances. Of the health care establishments that have a designated person to handle complaints, this role is usually carried out by complaints officers, chief executive officers (CEOs) or patient services managers. In 46 per cent of all cases, the person dealing with complaints holds a full-time position.[31]

The health care providers who responded (80 per cent of the total in the Eastern Region) gave estimates of the number of complaints they received each month. Figures ranged between one and 48, although most providers received from one to seven complaints. Unsurprisingly, the larger health care providers generally received more complaints than the smaller ones.[32]

Some of the respondents found it difficult to give an average length of time that it took them to deal with a complaint. They pointed out that the time taken depended on the nature and source of the grievance and on the mechanisms in place for attending to them. The majority of respondents reported that a complaint would be dealt with in between one and four weeks, but 10 per cent of them said that action was taken immediately a complaint was received. Around 28 per cent of health service providers took an average of four weeks to address complaints.[33]

Some 35 per cent of respondents, about two-thirds of whom are in the specialist hospital sector, had seen an increase in the number of complaints lodged during the previous year or two. In contrast, 14 per cent reported a reduction in the total number of complaints received during this period. In this case, there were no significant differences in replies according to sector: 19 (65 per cent) of the service providers surveyed have an internal complaints review procedure.[34]

In 38 per cent of cases, respondents stated that the chief executive officer puts his or her signature to decisions made on complaints. This is mostly prevalent in the intellectual disability and specialist hospital sectors. Where the CEO is not involved in this part of the process, responsibility for the job is assigned to someone else, who may be a complaints officer, director of nursing, patient services appointee, corporate services manager, risk manager or other person, according to the nature of the complaint under investigation.[35]

The ERHA's survey also showed that 82 per cent of complaints were made by patients and clients and that family members or relatives were the next largest source of grievances, especially those relating to intellectual disability establishments. Virtually all respondents who specified 'other' sources of complaints mentioned family members and relatives in that context.[36]

Subjects of complaints were: communication difficulties (about 50 per cent); staff behaviour (30 per cent); problems in accessing services such as therapies, or the absence of them (29 per cent); and difficulties with the appointments process, including delays and cancellations (21 per cent). Other grievances concerned lack of facilities and equipment, admission procedures and reaction to bereavement. There was no important difference in the nature of replies received by different health care sectors.[37]

In their report the ERHA working group then drew attention to what was called a National Patient Perception of Quality of Care Survey carried out in 2001 by the Irish Society for Quality in Healthcare. The appraisal centred on a number of hospitals – including some in the Eastern Region – and focused especially on the existing complaints procedures from a patient perspective. A number of telling facts were uncovered: 74 per cent of patients were unaware that complaints mechanisms existed; 66 per cent of complainants felt that a grievance they had was not acted upon or put right; and, where complaints were made, 79 per cent complained to a ward sister or nurse, 6 per cent took their protest to a matron, 5 per cent to a consultant, 3 per cent to a clinician below this level, 3 per cent to a manager and 4 per cent to other personnel.[38]

Until recently, no formal training courses were in place for personnel delegated to deal with complaints in the Eastern Region. The same applied to frontline staff such as doctors, nurses, paramedics, attendants, receptionists and porters, but since 2002 the ERHA has provided training programmes to remedy the situation. In addition, and on their own initiative, a small proportion of health service providers have set up internal courses for their employees. In 2002, no formal qualifications, experience or specific skills were required of staff engaged in complaints handling duties. As previously noted, those assigned for the job included patient services managers, directors of nursing, management personnel and CEOs.[39]

The ERHA's working group considered that 'staff training and personal development was the key to making a complaints procedure work effectively'. It believed personnel needed to be trained and given powers to deal with complaints, and that proper procedures should be set up so that information gained from complaints was used to improve service quality.[40] A number of principles were picked out as being necessary for a complaints mechanism to function efficiently.[41]

- The complaints mechanism should be simple to understand and use.
- Responses should be made quickly, with fixed time limits for action.
- Complainants should be kept informed about progress of their case.
- Confidentiality should be observed at all times.
- Investigations should be fair and detailed.
- Appropriate remedies should be put in place where necessary.
- The system should be monitored and audited regularly.

Additionally, the working group's advice was for health care providers to encourage a 'let us know' culture, improve staff skills and attitudes, avoid defensiveness and apologize when mistakes were made. Their interim report cited examples of good practice in dealing with grievances, such as providing support for staff to deal with complaints on the spot and removing the fear of discrimination from complainants.[42] Also, the working group believed that once the statutory framework for complaints handling in health care outlined in the Irish government's 2001 health strategy document and the recommendations of the ERHA's review were in place, an effective way of dealing with complaints should result.[43]

In September 2003 the ERHA announced its new framework for handling complaints in the region of its jurisdiction. The arrangement includes its review proposals to overhaul the way complaints are handled, and the necessary structures for this were scheduled to be in place by the end of 2004.[44]

The South Eastern Health Board
The complaints procedure operated by Ireland's South Eastern Health Board appears to be similar to that being run by the Eastern Regional Health Authority. At its Waterford Regional Hospital, for example, a 'patient services officer' is the designated person for handling complaints. Grievances can be lodged with this official in person, by letter or by telephone. Formal complaints are those for which complainants are seeking an investigation and explanation from the senior member of staff concerned or the patient services officer.[45]

The hospital's complaints procedure states that all complaints received from patients or service users should be acknowledged in writing even if there has been a prior verbal settlement.[46] It also specifies that complaints should be acknowledged in writing within two working days of being made, and that investigations by the patient services officer or person in charge should be completed in no more than two weeks.[47] The time limit for responding to complaints in writing is three weeks from the date of receipt. In cases where this is not possible, complainants should be informed about the delay. In any event, three weeks is the maximum extension time allowed for replying to complaints.[48]

Grievances involving clinical issues can be made directly to the relevant consultant, the health board or to a senior staff member. However, it is the consultant's responsibility to examine the clinical aspects of such complaints and try to resolve the matter quickly. This can be done in writing or discussion with complainants. Where a delay is expected, complainants should be informed and told the reason for the hold-up.[49]

Any non-clinical aspects of complaints received directly by a consultant are referred to the patient services officer for attention. Alternatively, where a complaint having a clinical content is received by the general manager or patient services officer, a copy is sent to the consultant involved to respond to its medical aspects. Then the general manager or patient services officer usually sends a written reply to the complainant once the clinical issues have been dealt with by the consultant.[50]

Verbal complaints received by members of staff are passed on to the ward sister or head of department, and also to the patient services officer. Where verbal grievances cannot be resolved at the initial discussion or it is considered that they should be in writing, complainants must be advised to complain in written form to the patient services officer. In cases where complainants are unwilling or unable to lodge a written complaint but want their grievance to be examined further, the senior member of staff dealing with the matter must arrange for a written record to be made on complainants' behalf. The complainants are then asked to sign this statement and given a copy of the document.[51] Written complaints must be forwarded to the patient services officer, who sets up an investigation with the involvement of the hospital's general manager or a senior officer designated by the latter. Complaints made in writing are also referred to the relevant consultant, director of nursing or head of department for scrutiny and a report.[52]

Waterford Regional Hospital has a complaints committee made up of the general manager, deputy manager, patient services officer, director of nursing and a member of the medical board. The role of the committee is to review the incidence and nature of complaints received and to deal with grievances in a manner that is in keeping with the rights expressed in the hospital's 'patient's charter'. But this does not include complaints relating to the exercise of clinical judgement.[53] Complainants of all kinds who are dissatisfied with the outcome of an investigation are advised of their right to appeal further up the scale and ultimately to the chief executive officer.[54]

The hospital's 'patient's charter' statement is straightforward. It confers on patients the right to complain about any of the hospital's services, to have grievances investigated and to be told about the outcome as soon as possible. It states that details about the complaints procedures in place and the name and telephone number of the designated complaints officer should be posted prominently throughout the hospital. It affirms the right of patients to have unresolved complaints referred to the hospital's complaints committee and confirms that using the complaints procedure does not affect patients' statutory rights to complain to the Ombudsman, the Medical Council or An Bord Altranais (the Nursing Board).[55]

The South Eastern Health Board has a separate but similar complaints procedure covering psychiatric care. As an example, the system is operated by Kilkenny Mental Health Services based at St Canice's Hospital, Kilkenny, one of five county psychiatric establishments within the health board's jurisdiction. Complainants who are dissatisfied with the outcome of a complaint following this process can exercise their statutory right to refer the matter to the Minister for Health, the President of the High Court, the Registrar of the Wards of Court or the Inspector of Mental Hospitals.[56]

The North Eastern Health Board

Although similarly internal in character to those already outlined, the complaints system established by Ireland's North Eastern Health Board has some differences in style. A complainant can be a patient or a patient's representative, a close relative of the patient or a local representative such as a health board staff member or a public figure. Concerns or complaints are raised initially with the relevant staff member or head of department. This could be a ward sister, senior social worker, community welfare officer or one of a number of other designated personnel.[57] In especially serious cases this referral process can be bypassed, with the management stepping in to take action immediately. The three broad categories of serious complaints are those alleging criminal conduct, those where there is *prima facie* evidence of negligence and those for which the health board has a statutory investigative responsibility.[58]

Where complaints include allegations of a 'medico-legal nature' the board's chief executive officer can nominate appropriate internal personnel to investigate the claims. External professionals having relevant experience may also be called in to advise.[59] Cases in which initial evidence indicates there are *prima facie* grounds for suspecting that criminal activity has occurred are referred to the Gardai (Irish Police). Pending a police investigation, the health board may suspend its own inquiry.[60]

Complaints do not have to be in writing unless they remain unresolved after discussion or are serious. In these cases, written complaints are addressed to the appropriate senior designated local officer. All formal complaints are acknowledged in writing – or exceptionally by telephone – within three working days of being received. Grievances are investigated and complainants notified of the outcome in no more than 21 days from the time they were received. If this is not possible, complainants are given reasons for the delay in advance and the likely date that they will receive a response.[61]

All written replies to complainants contain a summary of the complaint, details of the investigation that took place and an explanation of its results. An apology is included if appropriate, as are details of any remedial action taken and complainants' rights to a review.[62] Complainants who are dissatisfied with the board's response are told how they can obtain a review of their case. Usually this is carried out by a more senior officer than the person who made the initial decision, but the board's chief executive officer may decide to nominate an appropriate member of staff to undertake the review.[63]

The Mid Western Health Board

The internal complaints policy of Ireland's Mid Western Health Board is described as one where 'all staff are responsible for handling complaints so that the system is realistic, workable, and responsive to the needs of the individual'.[64] Accordingly, when verbal complaints are made to front line staff or line managers, they are investigated and responded to at that level.[65] Only when such complaints cannot be resolved at this initial approach are they referred to the next tier of management.[66] If grievances are still unresolved, complainants can make a written complaint or complete a 'feedback form', which is sent to the local 'feedback co-ordinator'.[67]

Among a range of responsibilities, the feedback co-ordinator has a duty to acknowledge all written complaints within 48 hours and advise complainants about what is to follow. The complaints are then referred back to the relevant manager for investigation and a response. Where cases cannot be resolved within 28 days, complainants are notified. They are also advised of their right to appeal to the

Ombudsman if they continue to be dissatisfied after all possible avenues have been explored.[68]

The role of Ireland's Ombudsman up to 2004

The Office of the Ombudsman came about as a result of the Ombudsman Act 1980, and was opened in January 1984. It is based on an international model and deals with allegations made by complainants who claim to have been adversely affected owing to maladministration by a public body. Where allegations of maladministration are found to be justified and the complainants adversely affected the Ombudsman will recommend that suitable redress is made by those guilty of such behaviour.[69]

Although obliged to report to the Oireachtas (Irish Parliament), the Ombudsman's Office is independent of government. In investigating a complaint about maladministration by a public body, the Ombudsman has powers to obtain information, documents or materials that are relevant to the cases being examined from any person or the organizations involved. Any individual – including officials of the organization concerned – who may have information can be called before the Ombudsman. However, the Ombudsman's Office has no authority to rescind any 'impugned' action or decision that resulted in the complaint, nor does it have powers to impose a legally binding solution. Nonetheless, no recommendation made by the Ombudsman has ever been rejected by the body that was the subject of a complaint.[70] Also, of the more than 50,000 complaints received since the Ombudsman's Office was established, 40 per cent involved some form of redress being gained.[71] The current arrangements, which allow a large proportion of case work to be handled informally by the Ombudsman's Office, are considered to be an advantage that is of benefit to both parties in a complaint.[72]

A number of public bodies are currently within the jurisdiction of the Ombudsman's investigations. These include health boards and An Post (postal service), government departments and offices, and local authorities of various forms. The Ombudsman (Amendment) Bill (being drafted at the time of writing early in 2003) is likely to add many more such organizations to the list once it is enacted and comes into force.[73]

Probable candidates are FAS (Training and Employment Authority), public voluntary hospitals, third-level education establishments and other publicly funded organizations. The Courts Service could also be included and subject to the Ombudsman's powers.[74] As indicated earlier in this chapter, the Eastern Regional Health Authority is looking at the prospect of all its service providers being brought within his jurisdiction.

In 2003, the Ombudsman's remit did not extend to 'actions taken solely in the exercise of clinical judgement in connection with the diagnosis of illness', nor did his powers cover matters about health care provided to patients. Moreover, since they are not health board units, the majority of hospitals in Dublin are outside his jurisdiction – although they are almost entirely funded by the Exchequer.[75] Primary care, too, is outside the Ombudsman's influence.[76]

In November 2001 the Ombudsman stated that his Office received around 4,000 complaints each year, of which about 3,000 were within jurisdiction. Roughly 50 per cent of the valid complaints referred to civil service bodies, around 25 per cent concerned local authorities and about 17 per cent involved health boards. Surprisingly, the greater proportion of complaints relating to health boards were about entitlement to Supplementary Welfare Allowance, a benefit that is not strictly a health service issue. Nonetheless, some of these grievances referred to patient care. There was a sharp increase in the volume of complaints received between 2000 and 2001 relating to the health services.[77]

The Office of the Ombudsman is an independent complaints body that operates in an inquisitorial rather than adversarial way. The service offered is relatively informal and is cost-free to complainants.[78] Complaints can be made in writing, by telephone or by calling at the Ombudsman's Office in Dublin. His staff are also available to the public each month at citizen information centres in four other locations in the country. In addition, a sequence of visits to other provincial centres is made annually.[79]

Details of a complaint are always put to the public body involved. Depending on the response, the Ombudsman's staff may examine the latter's files and will invariably also discuss the case with the officials involved. Once these stages are completed, and having considered the matter, the Ombudsman's officers generally discuss the position again with the complainant. To some extent, the procedure as a whole serves as a kind of mediation, and it can often result in a settlement that is acceptable all round. In only a small proportion of cases does it become necessary to resort to an investigation report containing formal findings and recommendations. This formal means of responding to a complaint occurs in cases where a complainant has suffered unduly and the public body concerned is unwilling to take proper remedial action. Formal written reports are also prepared if they concern issues of general importance and wider application.[80]

The Ombudsman publishes an annual report, which may contain recommendations about matters within his jurisdiction. The incumbent in 2003, who had been in post since 1994, saw his Office as an alternative to the litigation route, yet complementary to the role of the courts. His view was that where complainants consider their cases to have been properly determined – especially when redress has been provided – the effect must be to reduce the incidence of civil actions, but going to the Ombudsman is not a bar to taking a case to court subsequently.[81]

Conclusion

The proposed initiatives – and those already put into practice – by regional health care providers to upgrade their dealings with patients are obviously commendable. So are their moves to enhance care standards and professional practice, and to assess the value of their internal procedures and services to the public. Even more praiseworthy is the plethora of objectives in the Irish government's seemingly exhaustive national health strategy plan of November 2001.

However, the aims outlined in the proposals for a statutory health service complaints procedure and associated arrangements of 2001 could have been a little more courageous. Of course, it would be premature to visualize what will result from the proposed legislation in these respects. But if the shape of things to come for a complaints handling mechanism in Ireland is indeed a kind of mirror-image of the one that existed at the time and operated in most of the United Kingdom until 2004, then the issue deserves longer and closer inspection before legislation goes through. There is good reason for this.

First, we now know that the complaints procedure in question was self-regulated throughout its health service phases, with a major lack of independence in the way it was structured. Not only was the 'local resolution first phase' internally managed, but so was the following 'independent review' stage of the process – and it was nowhere near as neutral as it sounded (see Chapter 1). Indeed, its trust-building description was a misnomer and its true nature quite another story. The only seemingly redeeming quality of this second phase of the procedure was that its investigations were undoubtedly more extensive than those conducted at the first stage, with external clinical assessors brought in to advise the investigating panel. (Chapter 2, in particular, shows that the local resolution stage of the UK's reformed complaints procedures in 2005 continues to be in health service hands – except that its potentially upgraded character could improve performances.)

Secondly, the final judgements of these panels on complaints under their examination did not always reflect the clinical advice given to them by the assessors. Thirdly, there was no truly independent and suitably qualified person (preferably a legal professional) presiding over proceedings to reduce the risk of this happening or, for that matter, the possibility of biased advice from the clinical assessors themselves being accepted by the panel. Indeed, it was not uncommon for medical practitioners to go along with erroneous decisions made or action taken by (especially) their peers in the profession to get the latter out of hot water. There are members of the medical fraternity who have admitted, on record, that this could and did happen. A case of 'there but for the grace of...' is what they invariably offered in mitigation.

Chapter 1 shows that not much value could be ascribed to the independent review phase of this preceding British health service's complaints procedure. To recap, even the convener of an independent review panel was normally a non-executive board member of the health care body being complained against. This officer would also decide whether or not a complaint was accepted for independent review. The convener was also a key player in the setting up, management and conduct of an independent review panel. Even the lay chairman – the second member – appointed to the panel was recruited by the health service. Significantly, also, the third panel member was either a non-executive of a health authority or some other person drawn from the health service. So much for independence.

Could it be coincidence, therefore, that a very small proportion of complaints referred to convenors was approved for independent review? Was it also pure chance that of those grievances given the go-ahead for further investigation, a similarly low percentage succeeded in being upheld? It would be naive to imagine that there isn't some connection, at least, between these figures (explained in Chapter 1) and the pedigree of certain complaints handlers at the review phase of this earlier NHS complaints process in the United Kingdom. Chapter 2 demonstrates that both independent review and local resolution in their existing (1996) forms had considerable room for improvement.

The health service end (that is, the local resolution and independent review stages) of the mechanism had been the focus of widespread public excoriation during much of its existence since April 1996. It had failed to gain the confidence of complainants and probably of most patient agencies and similar support groups. In fact, it would not be wide off the mark to say that this British model was generally regarded as a thoroughly discredited mechanism for handling complaints in the health service.

Why else would Britain's Department of Health have commissioned a national evaluation of the system, put forward proposals for reform and introduced legislation to carry out its intentions? But, as already pointed out in Chapter 2, this overhaul of the NHS procedure will still mean that only a tiny proportion of complaints entering the system is likely to progress to review – independently conducted though it may be.

There were sages in Ireland who seemed to think that the way complaints about health care was being handled in a part of the United Kingdom was essentially a good idea. In a report made public in April 2002, the Joint Committee on the Strategic Management Initiative in Ireland cited the statutory complaints system in Northern Ireland as a possible model for the Republic. In principle, and 'without limiting the right of access to the Ombudsman', the group recommended the adoption of such a structure that 'builds on a three-tiered approach involving local resolution, independent review and referral to the Ombudsman'.[82]

Conditional though they were, the recommendations may not be a great idea for the reasons given earlier, because the complaints mechanism in Northern Ireland at the time was effectively a mirror-image of the one operating in the rest of the United Kingdom. Exponents of this prevailing British system in the Republic of Ireland would do well, therefore, to think longer and harder before embarking on a similar path – unless in the interim they have devised a more revolutionary plan.

Not that there is anything wrong with a local resolution process. All the health care complaints mechanisms in the Nordic countries – arguably the most enlightened to be found anywhere on the planet – offer this avenue for resolving patients' grievances as a first resort. But there is a key difference. Complainants do not have a statutory obligation to use the local resolution route as a first resort. (Nor is there a second health service phase to consider.) They can bypass this avenue altogether and take their cases directly to the independent investigating authority set up for the purpose (see Chapter 13).

In their detached position the Nordic complaints mechanisms are logically best placed to address the question of evenhandedness in the examination of health service complaints and those directly concerning medical practitioners. However, similar to their counterparts in the United Kingdom, it could be that Irish lawmakers may be reluctant to go so far as to introduce total independence into the way complaints about health care are investigated in the future.

Update

It appears that the existing health service complaints procedures (a representative sample has been given in this chapter) continue to be applied in Ireland. However, the position is likely to change when the Minister for Health and Children introduces new regulations under the Health (Amendment) Act 2004 – scheduled for the autumn of 2005.[83] The role of the Ombudsman also remains effectively unchanged for the present.[84]

Some of the changes referred to in the early paragraphs of this chapter have now come into force. For example, on 1 January 2005 the Health Service Executive (HSE) assumed full operational responsibility for administering Ireland's health and personal services. As a result, each of the former seven health boards and one authority (four of which figure in this chapter) is now known as a Health Service Executive Area.[85]

(Also, as expected, the Health and Social Care Professionals Bill was published at the end of October 2004.)[86]

Each of the eight HSE areas (the Eastern Regional Area for instance) has a Complaints and Appeals Office – inherited from the previous arrangement – that considers referred complaints where the complainants are dissatisfied with the handling of their grievances locally. Once a decision has been made here the Ombudsman can become involved to give a judgement.[87]

CHAPTER 13

Independence with legal leadership: the founding principles of Nordic complaints investigating mechanisms

And no lengthy assault course to get grievances addressed and resolved

Self-regulation has no real place in the examination of complaints about health care and the medical profession in any of the Nordic countries. All key investigating mechanisms operate autonomously and are independent of those whose actions they have been specifically appointed to scrutinize. Moreover, the strong legal leadership base assigned to these bodies is regarded as being a similarly crucial factor in the work of investigating aspects of the health service, including the conduct of the health care professionals who work there.

The nature of Nordic-style patient complaints procedures means that they are effectively one-stop mechanisms delivering independent decisions on complainants' grievances. This is not to say that inquiries into complaints at local level in the first place do not take place. Indeed, the framework for this exists for the purpose in each of the five countries concerned, but none of these local procedures is compulsory for complainants and decisions made have no legal authority. Nevertheless, complainants may initially decide to use this informal amenity before approaching the statutory independent complaints body (or bodies) that is in place to investigate their grievances formally. Alternatively, they can (and do) lodge their complaints directly as a first resort. The result of all this is that there is no enforced and drawn-out preliminary 'sifting' procedure for complaints to pass through before they can be independently examined and resolved.

Denmark

Take Denmark's Patients' Board of Complaints (Sundhedsvæsenets Patientklagenævn) as an example. Here we have an autonomous and independently operating public body that is completely detached from the authorities who run the health service and whose authority extends to the private health care sector.[1] Complainants normally lodge their grievances directly with the Board in Copenhagen. In certain special instances, grievances can be within the jurisdiction of the state regional authority (Statsamt) and sometimes complainants may contact the medical officer of health (MoH) located at one of the regional administrative centres.[2] However, the role of the MoH is to collect all case information and pass it on to the Patients' Board of Complaints for examination and judgement.[3] Complainants have a legal right to be given assistance in putting their complaint together, if that is what they want. This prerogative is written into Denmark's Patients' Legal Rights and Entitlements Act 1998.

Once all the evidence is obtained from the parties concerned in a complaint, a detailed investigation follows. The testimony provided for the case may also include information given by medical professionals not connected with the complaint in question. An evaluation is then prepared and sent to the complainant and the health care personnel involved for their comments. When they have responded, the case is passed on to the Board's investigating panel for examination and resolution, but the matter will be referred back for further inquiries if it is considered to have been insufficiently investigated.[4] The panel consists of two lay assessors representing the health service and two independent medical practitioners. It is chaired by a high-ranking legal practitioner. In 2001 the chairman would have been any one of the four city court judges and high court judge, who were assigned to the Board for the purpose.[5]

The Patient' Board of Complaints panel sessions are closed to complainants and those being complained about, and all judgements made are final. Rulings by the Board cannot be appealed against at another administrative authority. However, the Danish Ombudsman will look into cases where the parties concerned have complained to this official about the way their complaint has been handled.[6] Either party can also look for a solution in the civil courts if a decision is regarded as being unacceptable. On average, it takes around three months for the Patients' Board of Complaints to resolve simple cases brought before them. Decision-making in complex cases runs to a little over six months.[7] Complaints must normally be made no more than two years after the date when the adverse clinical event to which they apply occurred. In exceptional circumstances the Board may extend this time limit.[8]

The majority of complaints received by the Patients' Board of Complaints are accepted for full investigation (see Table 13.1) and a relatively high percentage of cases examined by this body are found to be justified in one way or another.

Table 13.1 Complaints received and processed by the Danish Patients' Board of Complaints, 1988 to 2000[a]

	1988	1989	1990	1991	1992	1993	1994	1995	1996	1997	1998	1999	2000
Rejections	366	278	268	244	285	354	427	450	472	576	482	536	433
Reopened	0	0	0	0	0	0	0	0	0	0	224	112	100
Accepted	941	822	885	923	1,164	1,363	1,484	1,581	1,577	1,992	2,003	1,926	2,141
Total	1,307	1,100	1,153	1,167	1,449	1,717	1,911	2,031	2,049	2,568	2,709	2,574	2,674

Source: Sundhedsvaesenets Patientklagenaevn (Patients' Board of Complaints), 2001[9]
[a]The population of Denmark in 2005 is about 5.3 million.

Using the year 2000 as an example, the table shows that a total of 2,674 written complaints were received by the Board, including 100 that were requests by complainants to re-evaluate already decided cases. Of the balance of 2,574 (new) complaints, 433 (16.8 per cent) were rejected on grounds of being mostly outside the Board's jurisdiction.[10] The remaining 2,141 (83.2 per cent) were accepted for investigation. It will be seen that a similarly high percentage of complaints was approved for investigation for each of the earlier years.

Over the four years up to and including 2001 (not covered in Table 13.1) an average of approximately one in five cases examined by the Board was upheld in favour of complainants. That is to say, the clinician(s) involved was judged to have made a mistake or been negligent. The annual proportions during this four-year period were 22 per cent in 2001, 20 per cent in 2000, 17.6 per cent in 1999 and 18.3 per cent in 1998. An average of around 20 per cent was also recorded for the preceding few years, albeit with the odd blip such as the 28 per cent registered for 1994.[11]

Akin to a couple of other Nordic countries, Denmark's Patients' Board of Complaints has jurisdiction over grievances about medical practitioners and other health care professionals throughout the public and private health service. The country's National Board of Health (Sundhedsstyrelsen) has a similarly powerful connection with the medical profession. This is reflected in its control and operation of the official authorization system for doctors, nurses, physiotherapists and other such qualified health care professionals. In this capacity, the Board has powers to withdraw the licences of these practitioners to practise in certain circumstances.[12]

Finland

Although similarly independent and having a strong legal component as in Denmark, four dominant bodies exist in Finland to deal with complaints about health care. These are the National Authority for Medicolegal Affairs, the provincial governments, the Parliamentary Ombudsman and the Chancellor of Justice. Complainants can lodge their grievances with any one or more of these bodies simultaneously. Nor is it a prerequisite that cases must first have been examined at local level, where an additional opening exists for complaints to be addressed.

Aggrieved patients or complainants can – as they invariably do – first approach the 'patient ombudsman' in the health care establishment involved. Employed by individual health service units, this officer's main function is to advise complainants of their entitlements under Finland's Status and Rights of Patients Act 1998. However, the ombudsman is there also to assist them with their concerns, the result of which could mean that a grievance is satisfactorily resolved. Where this happens, the alternative of complaining to the director of the establishment concerned is avoided. Nevertheless, grievances can be taken directly to this chief executive officer, in whose hands formal responsibility lies to respond to complaints and make decisions at local level.

Cases that are referred to the National Board of Medicolegal Affairs, the Parliamentary Ombudsman or the Chancellor of Justice are prepared and investigated by qualified and experienced legal professionals. These jurists are assisted in their work by independent medical practitioners who submit their opinions in writing about relevant aspects of the cases being examined. Where the National Board of Medicolegal Affairs is involved, clinical advice is provided by resident practitioners, each of whom will have specialized in a particular medical field.[13]

Once a case has been processed, it is referred for approval and a decision by the head of the complaints body concerned – either the National Board of Medicolegal Affairs, Parliamentary Ombudsman or Chancellor of Justice. In each of these institutions this principal official is a legal professional. Complaints that are directed to the provincial governments are handled by health care experts (inspectors) rather than investigators who are experts in law. Recruitment policy is such that only qualified personnel with experience in legal, health and medical affairs are eligible to fill positions within any of these complaints bodies.[14]

The National Board of Medicolegal Affairs and the provincial governments have powers to issue a serious reprimand to health care practitioners. The former can also restrict or withdraw a clinician's right to practise, in either case until further notice. Any of the four complaints cum regulatory bodies can refer especially serious cases to the courts for criminal proceedings.[15]

Whatever their destination, complaints relating to health care are usually in written form and there are no oral hearings, but complainants are given an opportunity to file a rejoinder before their cases are resolved. There is a statutory requirement that decisions on complaints are made within a reasonable period, although the law does not specify a time limit. No appeal is allowed against decisions arrived at by any of the four complaints bodies.[16] The total numbers of complaints received and/or investigated in recent years by each of these institutions are listed in tables 13.2 to 13.5. Their outcomes following examination are also briefly outlined.

Much of Finland's health care complaints and regulatory system encompasses the private health care sector as well as the public one. Grievances relating to this area can be referred to the National Authority for Medicolegal Affairs or one of the provincial governments, but not to the Parliamentary Ombudsman or Chancellor of Justice.[17] Besides these avenues, complaints can be made to the director in charge of health care at the private medical establishment involved.

Table 13.2 Complaints received and investigated by the National Board of Medicolegal Affairs, 1996 to 2000

	1996	1997	1998	1999	2000
Received	176	189	113	209	189
Investigated	67	74	56	168	159
Measures taken:[a]					
instructions	5	6	12	9	12
reprimand	1	4	6	3	11
serious reprimand	4	7	5	4	5

Source: Ministry of Social Affairs and Health, Helsinki[18]

[a] 'Instructions' – This is guidance given to the health care professional(s) in question about the proper procedures that should be followed in future. 'Reprimand' – This action is taken where it is evident that a practitioner has acted incorrectly or reprehensibly, although not in a very serious way. 'Serious reprimand' – This step is taken where professional conduct has been significantly poor. The National Board of Medicolegal Affairs can impose restrictions on or withdraw the right of a practitioner to practise as a registered health care professional until further notice; it may also refer especially serious cases of professional misconduct for prosecution.

Table 13.3 Complaints investigated by the Parliamentary Ombudsman,[a] 1996 to 2000

	1996	1997	1998	1999	2000
Received	145	196	166	214	213
Measures taken:[b]					
proposal	0	1	3	1	0
instructions	4	11	9	14	10
reprimand	0	0	1	7	1

Source: Ministry of Social Affairs and Health, Helsinki[19]

[a] The Parliamentary Ombudsman reports the number of complaints that have been investigated, not those received.

b 'Proposal' – For example, this might be a proposal to the Ministry of Social Affairs and Health to consider new legislation or directions for the health care professionals concerned. 'Instructions' – This is guidance given to the health care professional(s) in question about the proper procedures that should be followed in future. 'Reprimand' – this action is taken where it is evident that a practitioner has acted incorrectly or reprehensibly, although not in a very serious way. The Parliamentary Ombudsman can also refer particularly serious cases of professional misconduct for prosecution.

Table 13.4 Complaints received and decided by the Chancellor of Justice,[a] 1996 to 2000

	1996	1997	1998	1999	2000
Received	43	51	62	53	64
Measures taken:[b]					
proposal	1	0	1	1	0
instructions	1	2	2	1	1
reprimand	0	0	0	0	1

Source: Ministry of Social Affairs and Health, Helsinki[20]
[a] The Chancellor of Justice reports the number of health care related complaints received, not those that have been investigated.
[b] 'Proposal' – For example, this might be a proposal to the Ministry of Social Affairs and Health to consider new legislation or directions for the health care professionals concerned. 'Instructions' – guidance given to the health care professional(s) in question about the proper procedures that should be followed in future. 'Reprimand' – This action is taken where it is evident that a practitioner has acted incorrectly or reprehensibly, although not in a very serious way. The Chancellor of Justice can also refer particularly serious cases of professional misconduct for prosecution.

Table 13.5 Complaints received and investigated by the provincial governments, 1998 to 2000[a]

	1998	1999	2000
Southern Finland			
Received	250	214	284
Investigated	173	261	250
Measures taken:[b]			
instructions	48	54	51
reprimand	8	11	11
serious reprimand	3	1	1
Western Finland[c]			
Received	(102)	(150)	201
Investigated	(75)	(65)	145
Measures taken:[b]			
instructions	(27)	(13)	39
reprimand	(13)	(1)	4
serious reprimand	(3)	(1)	2
Eastern Finland			
Received	87	61	111
Investigated	66	60	82
Measures taken:[b]			
instructions	8	9	16
reprimand	2	3	2
serious reprimand	1	0	1

Oulu

Received	118	65	71
Investigated	[–][d]	91	49
Measures taken:[b]			
instructions	[–][d]	15	12
reprimand	[–][d]	2	1
serious reprimand	[–][d]	2	4

Lapland

Received	apprx 30	apprx 30	31
Investigated	27	37	11
Measures taken:[b]			
instructions	4	4	4
reprimand	4	3	0
serious reprimand	1	0	0

Total for all provincial governments[e]

Received	(587)	(520)	698
Investigated	(341)	(514)	537
Measures taken:[b]			
instructions	(87)	(95)	122
reprimand	(27)	(20)	18
serious reprimand	(8)	(4)	8

Source: Ministry of Social Affairs and Health, Helsinki[21]

[a] The population of Finland in 2005 is about 5.2 million.

[b] 'Instructions' – This is guidance given to the health care professional(s) in question about the proper procedures that should be followed in future. 'Reprimand' – This action is taken where it is evident that a practitioner has acted incorrectly or reprehensibly, although not in a very serious way. 'Serious reprimand' – This step is taken where professional conduct has been significantly poor. In addition to issuing a 'serious reprimand', the provincial governments have powers to refer especially serious cases of misconduct for prosecution.

[c] These figures refer to information received from only three out of the four offices representing Western Finland and, accordingly, are less than the actual totals.

[d] Information is not readily available concerning complaints investigated and decided upon in Oulu during 1998.

[e] The aggregate figures shown under 1998 and 1999 involving all the provincial governments are less than the actual totals for reasons given in note c, above.

(Statistics for the two previous years are not appropriate for comparison purposes because of reforms within the provincial governments that became effective in 1998. Therefore they have not been provided.)

The Parliamentary Ombudsman reports on the number of health care related complaints that are investigated, rather than those received. Conversely, the Chancellor of Justice gives an account of complaints received, but not the proportion that are investigated. As a result the statistics shown in tables 13.3 and 13.4 are generally less illuminating than those provided by the National Authority for Medicolegal Affairs and provincial governments in tables 13.2 and 13.5, which include both categories.

Moreover, the figures relating to these latter two complaints authorities show that a high proportion of grievances investigated were upheld, one way or another, during the same period. Perhaps significantly, each of these bodies appears to possess more sizeable powers, especially in the case of the National Authority for Medicolegal Affairs, whose jurisdiction extends to medical regulation.

Norway

Independence and a strong legal component where it counts are also founding principles in complaints handling and medical regulation in Norway. Here, the Norwegian Board of Health (Statens helsetylsin) has overall responsibility for national surveillance and control of the health services. Complaints handling and medical regulation form part of these duties. The Board is an autonomous authority, which operates in collaboration with 19 county medical officers who represent it at countrywide locations.[22]

Complaints are normally lodged with county medical officers, although serious cases can be referred directly or indirectly to the Board of Health. Here they are dealt with by the Department of Medical Law, one of six departments within the Board. All complaints are examined by qualified and experienced legal and medical professionals, including jurists, lawyers, doctors, nurses, psychologists and others. In cases where county medical offices are involved, the county medical officer is formally in charge of all complaints investigations. There are no hard-and-fast time limits to be followed in examining complaints and reaching a decision.[23]

The provisions of the Health Personnel Act 1999 come into play in dealing with complaints about health care staff. The Norwegian Board of Health has powers to give a warning to those who intentionally or negligently breach the Act's regulations, if doing so is liable to compromise safety in the health service or harm patients. Where applicable, authorization or a licence or certificate confirming completion of training can be revoked if a health care professional persists in failing to comply with statutory requirements.[24]

The same action can be taken by the Board against practitioners who are unfit to practise their profession in a responsible way. This may be because of severe mental illness, physical or mental impairment, or alcohol or substance abuse. A gross lack of professional acumen or conduct considered to be incompatible with good professional practice are examples of other cases that can be similarly treated by the Board. The right to prescribe drugs can also be revoked if a medical practitioner or dentist acts irresponsibly in the prescription of such medicinal remedies. This can involve a partial or total ban to be applied either temporarily or permanently.[25]

The number of complaints received annually by the Board of Health has been remarkably stable in recent years up to 2002, hovering at around 1,800 each year, most of which are handled and resolved at county medical officer level. About 15 per cent of this figure refers to serious and grave complaints received directly by or transferred to the Board of Health for further investigation and final decision.[26]

The Norwegian Board of Health investigated 241 complaints in 2001. In 60 per cent of cases no formal measures were taken and the complaints were rejected. Fifteen medical doctors had their authorizations or licences to practise rescinded during the same year. Six cases related to sexual exploitation of patients, four to substance abuse and five to infringements of the Health Personnel Act. In the same year, the licences to practise of 17 nurses were withdrawn on grounds relating to substance abuse and other forms of misconduct (see Table 13.6).[27]

Table 13.6 Types of formal action taken against health care personnel in 2001 by the Norwegian Board of Health[a]

Type of practitioner	Warning given	Licence rescinded
Doctor	22	15
Dentist	2	3
Psychologist	2	1
Nurse	7	12
Auxiliary nurse	1	5
Midwife	1	0
Physiotherapist	1	0
Chiropractor	2	0
Total	38	36

Source: Statens Helsetilsyn, 2002[28]
[a] Norway's population is about 4 million in 2005.

During 2001, seven health care professionals were reported to the police authorities. Also, there were three cases where medical practitioners had lost the right to prescribe drugs in groups A and B (high and medium dependency). In addition, formal action, chiefly criticism, was taken against 19 hospital and other health care establishments.[29] The jurisdiction of the Norwegian Board of Health extends over a wide spectrum of health care provision and its powers and procedures cover both the public and private sectors.

Sweden

No less than in other Nordic countries, autonomy and a powerful legal element where it is considered to count most is the philosophy behind complaints handling and medical regulation in Sweden. In this country there are a number of complaints procedures and associated mechanisms for addressing alleged medical errors, with the formal kind operating in parallel with informal ones. Indeed, the arrangement is common to a number of countries, except that its character can vary dramatically from place to place.

Complaints are initially dealt with informally in the hope that official action or litigation can be avoided. One argument put forward in Sweden for the merits of such a procedure is the apparently large number of complaints (between 85 per cent and 95 per cent of those received) that are related to poor communication between patients and health care practitioners.

The two key health care complaints mechanisms in Sweden are the National Board of Health and Welfare (Socialstyrelsen) and the Medical Responsibility Board (Hälso-och sjukvärdens ansvarsnämnd, or HSAN as it is also known). In addition, complainants can take their grievances to one of 30 county complaints boards (CCBs) or patients boards (Patientnamnder). However, unlike the two regulatory bodies, CCBs have no medical disciplinary powers, nor can they be involved in decisions on patient compensation. Every county or local authority is obliged to set up one of these units to serve its area.[30]

The role of county complaints boards is to provide patients with the information they need in order to 'gain from the health service'. This includes giving advice about making a complaint and to promote better communication between patients and health care personnel. Their responsibilities also extend to taking an active part in measures to improve the quality of service being offered by health care providers. CCBs are required to report annually to the regional units of the National Board of Health and Welfare.[31]

Regional offices of the National Board of Health and Welfare deal with complaints from patients and reports from health care providers about adverse medical incidents that have occurred. The Board also takes action on its own initiative in the form of visits to and inspections of health care establishments. Complaints received from patients can result in this body criticizing medical practitioners or reporting them to HSAN for action. Similarly, health service establishments can refer matters to HSAN where medical errors or negligence are attributable to members of staff. The Parliamentary Ombudsman and the Chancellor of Justice also can complain to this body.[32]

Under Sweden's Health and Medical Personnel (Duties) Act 1994 (which was replaced by new legislation in 1999), HSAN can impose disciplinary sanctions on health care practitioners who intentionally or through negligence do not appropriately discharge their duties. Disciplinary measures take the form of a reprimand or warning and can also be enforced on health care professionals who may have changed their job. Effectively, HSAN has regulatory powers over the performance and competence of health care practitioners right across the medical profession. Issues about medical examination, treatment and information, and matters involving consent to therapy and the preparation of medical certificates are some of the areas that can come under its scrutiny.[33]

The Medical Responsibility Board has authority to refer especially serious cases of professional misconduct to the public prosecutor. Once criminal proceedings have been filed against health care practitioners, disciplinary procedures cannot also be started or continued concerning an alleged offence, but notification of the complaint in question can be given in these situations. Disciplinary action that refers to cases being decided through criminal proceedings can commence only if the alleged offences have not been classified as a crime for a reason other than lack of evidence.[34]

Unlike one or two other Nordic countries, Sweden's Medical Responsibility Board is separate from its supervisory body, the National Board of Health and Welfare. It's adjudicators are made up of nine members, eight of whom represent patients and the medical profession between them, and an independent chairperson who is (or must have been) a practising judge. This panel is appointed by the government for a three-year period, during which time similarly qualified and experienced lawyers are on hand to take over proceedings in the chairperson's absence. In the same way, stand-ins are assigned to step in for the other HSAN panel members. The composition of this complaints and regulatory mechanism resembles that of a court.[35]

Complaints to HSAN must be made within two years of the date when the adverse medical incidents to which they refer occurred and failure to do so means that they cannot be accepted for investigation. In principle, complaints before this body are open to the public gaze, although they can be declared confidential in exceptional circumstances. After preparation, cases are reviewed by medical experts designated by HSAN. The panel will then study all the evidence and a judgement will follow, but in certain situations the chairperson alone will examine cases, once an assessment by the medical professionals is obtained.[36]

While case decisions are in the public domain, the normal rules of medical confidentiality still apply. Judgements by HSAN can be appealed against but must be lodged no more than three weeks later. Appeals are addressed to one or more of three bodies set up for the purpose: the County Administrative Court (Lansratten), Administrative Court of Appeal (Kammarratten) and Supreme Administrative Court (Regeringsratten), all of which are in Stockholm.[37] Sweden's health care complaints system is not confined to the public sector. As in Denmark and Norway, patients receiving private health care have the same rights as those using the public health service, with complaints proceeding through the same process of investigation and resolution by the relevant statutory examining bodies.[38]

The most important aspect of HSAN's role is considered to be its responsibilities in contributing to patient safety. It has powers to decide whether the standard of care provided by health care professionals who have been complained about is of an acceptable level. Moreover, this body has official authority to take disciplinary action (warning or admonition) against anyone who is licensed to work in the health service. However, the number or severity of sanctions received in this way does not affect a practitioner's right to practise. Nevertheless, HSAN has powers to withdraw the licences of health care professionals, and to limit their right to prescribe drugs. It appears that those who are removed from the health register each year are mostly nurses and doctors.[39]

Table 13.7 Complaints received and decided by the Medical Responsibility Board, 1994 to 2001[a]

	1994	1995	1996	1997	1998	1999	2000	2001
Received	2,417	2,521	2,659	2,860	3,119	3,064	3,070	3,250
Decided	2,053	2,337	3,032	2,896	2,986	3,377	3,188	3,132
Warning	150	180	226	212	208	183	151	120
Admonition	112	150	184	179	193	195	184	157
Total sanctions	262	330	410	391	401	378	335	277
Sanctions (%)	17	18	17	17	17	14	13	12
Given warning (%)	57	55	55	54	52	48	45	43
Given admonition (%)	43	45	45	46	48	52	55	57
Judgements made	1,591	1,844	2,427	2,310	2,366	2,733	2,578	2,459
Not accepted[b]	462	494	603	586	620	644	610	691
Cases about certification	48	50	59	61	80	81	81	60
Certification withdrawn:								
doctors	7	5	8	8	16	10	7	6
dentists	2	4	4	1	1	2	1	1
nurses	11	8	6	14	7	15	14	12
others	[–]	[–]	1	[–]	2	2	[–]	[–]
Total	20	17	19	23	26	29	22	19
Proportion of appeals (%)	[–]	29[c]	24	23	24	24	27	28

Source: Halso-och sjukvärdens ansvarnämnd (HSAN or Medical Responsibility Board), Stockholm, 2002[40]
[a] The population of Sweden in 2001 was approximately 8.8 million.

A new disciplinary measure came into force in 1999 whereby, in certain circumstances, HSAN can put health care personnel on probation (provotid) following medical error. Any subsequent breach within the next three years can result in the withdrawal of a practitioner's licence to practise without further notice.[41]

From a total of around 3,000 complaints received by HSAN each year between 1997 and 2001 (Table 13.7) concerning medical professionals, around 75 per cent were made about doctors, 10 per cent about nurses and 7 per cent about dentists. Patients or their relatives initiated most of these complaints, with the balance generally coming from the National Board of Health and Welfare. In more than 80 per cent of cases medical practitioners were found not to be at fault.[42]

Iceland

Like the other Nordic countries, Iceland's health care complaints and medical regulatory mechanisms are independent of the health service, but there seem to be key differences that exist in certain other areas. One of these concerns government involvement in the way the system as a whole is set up and functions; the other is ministerial powers in the medical disciplinary process itself. However, autonomy and impartiality appear to be the norm in the operations of the two bodies that have been established to deal with complaints.

Patients who have a grievance about medical treatment lodge their complaints either with the Directorate-General of Public Health or the Committee on Dispute Settlement. Complaints or comments about other issues connected with health care are directed to the central management of the establishment involved. Personnel in health service units are obliged to give guidance to patients or their relatives who wish to lodge a complaint or forward an opinion on how either action should be put into effect. Patients or complainants must be given a written response to their concerns or observations without undue delay. The principal management in health care institutions is under an obligation to look into the comments of staff when they indicate that the rights of patients are being infringed. All these rights and procedures are written into Iceland's Rights of Patients Act 1997 and Health Service Act 1990.

Three out of the five members of the central administration of local hospitals and primary care centres are elected by the municipalities' governing bodies, and Iceland's parliament nominates four of the seven members who serve in the management board of the National University Hospital. No special qualifications are required of any of these personnel as they mostly deal with non-medical complaints, such as patient waiting times, charges and the like.

The head of the Directorate-General of Public Health and this officer's deputy are appointed by the Minister of Health and Social Security. Both of these appointees must be qualified medical professionals and also have wide management experience. (Their precise credentials are described in Article 3 of the Health Service Act.) Other staff recruited by the Directorate-General are similarly qualified and include medical doctors and nurses with a record in management.[43]

Complaints received by this body are processed under the supervision of its deputy head. The Minister of Health and Social Security is responsible for issuing regulations about the role and professional observations of the Directorate. These rules are established in co-operation with bodies representing health care practitioners, the medical faculty of the University of Iceland and the Icelandic Medical Association.[44] The three members of the Committee on Dispute Settlement are also appointed by the Minister, with two of them nominated by the Supreme Court of Iceland. None of these officers must be employed by the public health service, and one is required to be a lawyer who presides as chairperson. The Committee is in place for four years at a time and, in collaboration with its members, the Minister issues the regulations governing their role and function for the duration. The key difference between the Directorate and the Committee is that the latter also decides whether or not a medical professional is at fault, and if the patient concerned is entitled to compensation. The Directorate determines only on the medical issues in patients' complaints.[45]

Article 18 of the Medical Doctors Act 1998 defines the procedure that is followed when the care or treatment of a patient goes unexpectedly wrong. It identifies those who are responsible for reporting the incident, and the other parties whose duty it is to investigate the complaint. These functions are always discharged by qualified and experienced health care managers.

When a doctor's actions break the rules laid down in the Medical Doctors Act 1988 – or any other relevant legislation about the health service – it is the responsibility of the Directorate-General to deal with the situation. Where this involves a reprimand, it is given in writing and a copy is sent to the Minister of Health and Social Security. If a practitioner continues to err, the Directorate-General is obliged to suggest measures that the Minister should take to remedy the problem. The latter has powers to revoke the doctor's licence to practise (in part or as a whole), although any such decision can be appealed against in the courts. As in other countries, serious violations concerning health care can result in a prison sentence.[46]

The majority of complaints refer to events involving emergency clinics, orthopaedic surgery, gynaecology and obstetrics. Over the past 10 years there has been a progressive rise in the number of complaints. A little more than a decade ago, about 170 were processed by the Directorate across a 12-month period. In 2001 these had increased to around 400, and another 30 were handled by the Committee on Dispute Settlement during that year.[47] The summary figures in tables 13.8 and 13.9 may be useful to get a picture about complaints received and, in the case of the Committee, their basic outcome during those years.

Table 13.8 Treatment of complaints received by the Committee on Dispute Settlement, 1997 to 2001

	1997	1998	1999	2000	2001
Opinions[a]	12	9	13	7	0
Dismissed	9	0	2	1	0
Under investigation[b]	0	1	0	0	7
Total	21	10	15	8	7

Source: Heilbrigdis-og tryggingamálaráduneytid, Reykjavik, 2002[48]

220 *Fair Play and Foul?*

a Decisions that appear to be wholly or partially in favour of complainants.
b Cases still under investigation at the end of the year.

Table 13.9 Complaints involving doctors received by the Directorate-General of Public Health, 1990, 1995, 2000 and 2001ᵃ

	1990	1995	2000	2001
Total	188	261	373	356

Source: Heilbrigdis-og tryggingamálaráduneytid, Reykjavik, 2002[49]
a The population of Iceland in 2001 was estimated to be around 280,000.

It appears that, on average, two-thirds of complaints to the Directorate-General of Public Health are regarded as being unreasonable and, therefore, are rejected. Around 10 per cent are said to be about difficulties in the relationship between doctors and their patients.[50] If this includes a problem with communication between the two parties, then it seems to be in strong contrast with the picture revealed earlier in this chapter about the situation in Sweden.

Iceland's patients' complaints and medical regulatory system is said to receive the broad approval of both the public and the medical profession. In practice, however, it is the Directorate that is 'in the frontline' when it comes to dealing with grievances about health care. As such, it is this body that is said to have especially gained the confidence of the Icelandic people.

Conclusion

The well-established and almost unique independent complaints and regulatory mechanisms operating in each of the five Nordic countries may not be the be-all and end-all of the way grievances about health care should be examined and judged. But it would not be difficult to argue that what is on offer for those at the receiving end of medical error or malpractice is a more equitable arrangement than the kind provided for by any self-regulated model. The work of the health service and that of medical practitioners in Denmark, Finland, Norway, Sweden and Iceland has not been undermined in getting the balance right for the examination of complaints about health care. A case of a dose of evenhandedness never doing anyone any harm, so to speak.

So what are the essential finer points of these complaints and regulatory systems? First, and to emphasize, they are autonomous and genuinely detached from the health service and medical professions they were set up to investigate. Moreover, the nature of these mechanisms is such that a situation is unlikely to arise – or will have occurred – in which their investigators or judges could previously have discharged similar duties in health care itself. For that reason the prospect of a kind of extended conflict of interest by examiners (which can and does happen in parallel complaints systems elsewhere) is also a non-starter. Further value is probably added to the cause of the independently operating model in the shape of a generally high order of legal leadership in the investigations into complaints. Nonetheless, a separate informal procedure for local resolution of grievances about health care also has a role in the Nordic countries. This is available but mostly not compulsory for complainants before their cases are independently investigated by the proper complaints bodies.

In what other – tangible – ways are these seemingly commendable features of the Nordic complaints bodies reflected in their handling of complainants' grievances? To begin with, it is clear that a generally large percentage of complaints received is accepted for investigation. More accurately, it could be said that all grievances lodged (except for those out of jurisdiction or ineligible for some other similar reason) are formally – and independently – examined from start to finish. Also, it can be seen that the proportions of complaints upheld as a result can be quite high.

Crucially, both public and private health care are within the jurisdiction of the complaints and regulatory authorities in Denmark, Norway and Sweden. Finland is nearly there, with much of the private sector also subject to the same regulations and procedures as the public health service. Presumably the view of these countries' lawmakers is that there is no good reason why equal rights should be the preserve of some but not all users of health care.

Perhaps this is another reason for the apparently broad approval these autonomous statutory authorities receive from the citizens they serve. With independent investigation and the delivery of seemingly high calibre case judgements being par for the course on this and other health care fronts, it would be hard to reject any claim that the Nordic countries have got more satisfactory arrangements than most others when it comes to redressing the balance. One might even say that the enlightened way they run these affairs sets them apart in this respect from certain developed nations who have still not caught up. Nor, it seems, intend to do so in the foreseeable future.

CHAPTER 14

A specific patients' rights act for Finland and Norway

But in Sweden these rights are provided for in various pieces of legislation

'Oh well, they would do that, wouldn't they?' The remark may once have been a recognizable description of the occasionally patronizing accommodation given to aspects of enlightened Nordic tradition by spokespersons elsewhere. In the process it may have served as an elementary device to blur faults in their own conventions. Who knows, the advances in public rights about health care in these northernmost of European states might also have come in for this kind of oblique disparagement, but these days it is more fashionable to hail much of their liberal conventions as a benchmark to aspire to, even if not always as a cue for other societies to follow suit. Indeed, the advances made in patients' rights by the Nordic countries are generally impressive.

The standards that have been set for the entitlements of patients in Finland and Norway, for example, are no exceptions to the rule. Nor does it seem to be a problem for the Finns and Norwegians to find out about their statutory entitlements and know where they stand. Printed material describing what these patients' rights are can be collected at health service and associated establishments where designated officers are on hand and under an obligation to give advice to those seeking guidance on these and other related matters.

Each of the two countries has specific legislation in place covering patients' rights across a wide range of questions. Written into their respective enactments is the basic right of individuals to receive health care, through to a plethora of more complex entitlements. These include personal and clinical issues, some of which could arise in the process of patients receiving health care. The question of patients giving consent to health care, the involvement of those who may represent them in such decisions and patient confidentiality and access to medical records are all important. In all these matters the role of clinicians is identified and included in the provisions of the legislation. The rights of patients in relation to the complaints procedure and to compensation when health care may have gone wrong are other matters that are covered by the enactments.

Although Sweden is alone among the five Nordic countries in having no specific, all-encompassing patients' rights legislation, this is not to say that an array of such entitlements does not exist. The difference is that patients' rights – or the less formal 'position of patients' concept as some in Sweden prefer to describe the term – form part of enactment. They are also integral to the periodic regulations that cover health care in a wider sense and in items of legislation involving other obvious components of the health service and areas that overlap

Finland

What entitlements does Finland offer its citizens in their dealings with the health service? To begin with, the extent of these prerogatives is incorporated into the Status and Rights of Patients Act 1992, legislation that took effect from March 1993. Under one of the Act's introductory provisions, the country's Council of State has powers to appoint, for four years at a time, a national advisory board on health care ethics and issues that concern the status of patients. Additional provisions on the composition and role of this board are issued by directive progressively. The advisory board is linked with the Ministry of Social Affairs and Health.[1]

Under the Act, every permanent resident of Finland has a right to health care according to their needs and within the limits of available resources at the time. The entitlements of those who are temporarily domiciled in the country are covered either by special existing arrangements or by reciprocal agreements with other states.[2] Provisions on the obligations of municipalities and the state to organize health care services are laid down in separate pieces of legislation. Among others, these include the Primary Health Care Act 1972, Specialized Health Care Act 1989 and Mental Health Act 1990.[3]

Finland's Status and Rights of Patients Act 1992 has established the right of patients to 'qualitatively good health care', provided in a way that is also described as preserving their dignity and respecting their privacy and convictions. Under the Act, and as far as possible, a patient's first language, individual needs and culture must be given due consideration in all dealings by the health service.[4]

Access to treatment

When treatment considered to be necessary by a health care practitioner is not readily available, patients must be asked either to wait until the therapy can be provided or be taken to where it is obtainable. The chosen course will depend on the patient's state of health and the urgency ascribed to it. If treatment is not immediately accessible, a reason must be given for the consequent hold-up as well as an estimate of its duration.[5] However, patients in need of urgent medical attention must be treated without delay or, alternatively, admitted for therapy in a way stipulated in other health care legislation. This includes the Primary Health Care Act 1972, the Specialized Health Care Act 1989 and the Health Care Professionals Act 1994.[6]

The right to be informed

The Status and Rights of Patients Act requires that information is provided about a patient's condition, the significance of the proposed treatment, any alternative forms of therapy and the expected outcome in either case. Details about other associated factors must also be given. Clinicians must advise patients about their state of health clearly, ensuring that the details are understood. If health care practitioners cannot speak a patient's language, or are unable to understand a patient because of a sensory or speech defect, interpretation assistance must be provided if possible.[7] Nonetheless, it is not permissible for clinicians to advise patients if such advice is against the patient's wishes, nor when it is clear that it will raise a serious threat to their life or health.[8]

The right of patients to be informed about matters concerning their health care takes other forms. Their entitlement to check data about themselves in medical records is covered by provisions in Finland's Personal Data File Act 1999. The right of patients to be allowed to examine this information in the first place is provided for in the Openness of Government Activities Act 1999.[9]

The right to self-determination

'Patients' right to self-determination' is the heading in the Status and Rights of Patients Act 1992, which covers the rights of patients and those acting for them about consent – or otherwise – to health care. Under the Act's provisions, if patients refuse a certain treatment or procedure, another agreed form of therapy must be provided, as far as this is possible.[10] On the other hand, where a patient is prevented from reaching a decision about a prescribed form of treatment because of a mental disorder or for some other reason, one of the patient's representatives must be consulted. This is normally a family member, another close associate or a legal representative whose consent must be obtained for the therapy to be provided.[11]

Any such approval must respect patients' previously expressed wishes, or their well being if no wishes had been conveyed.[12] If one or other of those acting for a patient forbids the prescribed care or treatment, another clinically appropriate course of action must be adopted, which has the representative's consent.[13] Where approval cannot be obtained because of differing opinions of representatives, care or treatment with the best interests of the patient involved must be provided.[14] Treatment given irrespective of the wishes of patients is covered by provisions in the country's Mental Health Act 1990 and in other items of relevant legislation.[15]

The position and powers of patients' representatives

A patient's representative (family member, close associate or legal agent) is entitled to receive any information that will help in reaching a decision about treatment and giving consent where the patient is unable to do so because of a mental illness or for some other reason.[16] In similar circumstances, the right to be informed about the condition of a minor and deciding on the treatment is passed on to the parent(s), guardian or legal representative.[17] However, this does not necessarily apply where the minor is of an appropriate age and maturity to decide on a prescribed therapy. In this event, the minor's opinions must be considered and the person(s) acting for the under-age patient is prevented from receiving these details if that is the latter's wish.[18] Moreover, the representative of a patient – whether a minor or an adult – cannot prohibit treatment that is necessary to avert any threat to the life or health of the person being represented.[19]

Emergency treatment

The Status and Rights of Patients Act 1992 takes into account matters concerning emergency treatment. Patients whose health or lives are threatened must be given the necessary therapy if, owing to unconsciousness or for some other reason, their wishes cannot be established. But no treatment procedure can take place that does not reflect their earlier and competently expressed request.[20]

Patients' medical records and asociated data

Health care professionals must ensure that patient documents contain the information necessary to arrange, plan, provide and monitor the care and treatment of those whom they are attending. Independent health care units and practitioners are required to retain such medical records and any samples containing biological material arising from examinations and therapy, and models of organs. The retention of this material must be for a suitable period during which treatment is being arranged and given to a patient and, similarly, for the purposes of investigating possible compensation claims and for scientific research. Once these considerations have been met, all the retained material must be disposed of without delay.[21]

Patient confidentiality[22]
The information contained in patient records is confidential and may not be disclosed to outsiders (those not involved in or related to a patient's care) without the written consent of a patient. If the latter is unable to do so intelligently, permission can be given by a legal representative. The confidentiality obligation required of health care practitioners remains in force after a change of post or termination of the relevant employment contract. Any breach of this constraint is punishable under the law.

Nonetheless, information in patient records can be passed on where express provisions exist, or when there is a right of access to it stated in law. Data that is essential for a patient's examination or treatment can be given to another hospital or practitioner. Similarly, a summary of the therapy can be conveyed to the party (or parties) who referred a patient, and to any doctor who may have been appointed to care for that person at a health centre, after oral or some other obvious form of consent (in the absence of written approval) has been received either directly or from the patient's legal representative. The granting of consent must be voluntary and with the full knowledge of its destination, use and significance. Data released in all these ways must be recorded in the patient's records.

The same kind of information can be provided, without consent, to another Finnish or foreign health care unit or professional if, owing to a mental health disorder, some other comparable condition or unconsciousness, patients are incapable or unable to indicate agreement themselves. This assumes that the patients concerned have no legal representative to give permission on their behalf. Again, the data released must be recorded in the patient's medical documents.

Information about the identity and medical condition of a patient can be supplied to a family member or other close person in cases where treatment is being given following unconsciousness. It can also be made available when therapy has been prescribed after some other similar adverse event has occurred, but these details cannot be released if there is cause to believe that the patient would have forbidden it.

Data about health care that was given when a deceased person was still living can be supplied to another individual if it is justified, and to the extent that it is vital to establish the latter's interests or rights. It is illegal to use or pass on such information for some other purpose. Data in patient records that is released for scientific research and statistics is subject to provisions in the Openness of Government Activities Act 1999, the National Personal Data Registers for Health Care Act 1989 and in the Personal Data File Act 1999.

Complaints about health care
Finland's health care complaints procedure is influenced by the provisions of the Status and Rights of Patients Act 1992. Patients who are not satisfied with the

therapy or related treatment that they have received have a right to complain to the relevant director of the health care unit concerned. The complaint must be responded to in a reasonable time. Lodging such a complaint does not affect a patient's right to take the grievance further to the health care complaints and regulatory bodies concerned.[23]

The provisions of the Act extend further into the complaints process. If it comes to light that patient care or other treatment (or lack of either) could result in liability for injury under the Patient Injury Act 1986 or indemnification according to the Torts Act 1974, patients are entitled to be given guidance on how they can seek redress, and from whom. They will be similarly assisted if they are considering taking legal action, and in cases that may result in the restriction or cancellation of the right of health care staff to practise or in disciplinary proceedings under another law.[24]

Provisions in the Act mean that every health care unit – or group of them – has a 'patient ombudsman' to give such information. This officer is responsible for advising patients about the application of the Status and Rights of Patients Act 1992, their rights, the complaints procedure and ensuring that due entitlements are being respected and implemented. Printed copies of a simplified version of the statutory rights of patients under the Act are available at hospitals and other health care units.[25]

Norway
Norway's latest patients' rights legislation is similarly wide-ranging in its jurisdiction. Adopted in July 1999, the country's Patients' Rights Act came into force in January 2001 and provides an array of rights and entitlements to all citizens. The primary objectives of the legislation include the provision of equal access to health care for all in a climate of trust and respect between patients and the health service.[26] So how far do these obligations go?

General right to health care
Patients are entitled to emergency medical services and to receive necessary health care from their municipal health service. This right extends to the publicly funded specialist (acute) sector, and the health service must give anyone who asks for or needs health care the necessary clinical information that they are entitled to receive. The right to health care applies only if patients are expected to benefit as a result and that the cost is reasonable compared with the anticipated outcome of the therapy that is to be provided. Patients' entitlement to health care also includes other establishments with which a county municipality has entered into an agreement to provide the required services within the limits that their capacity allows.[27]

Medical assessment and re-assessment, choice of psychiatric clinic and case plans
Patients who have been referred to a public hospital or out-patient clinic are entitled to receive an assessment of their medical condition within 30 working days. Simultaneously, they must be told about the expected date on which treatment will be given. Where there is a serious or life-threatening issue involved, the timescale must be correspondingly reduced. Upon referral from a GP, patients are also entitled to a re-assessment of their condition in a specialist health care establishment. However, this right applies only once for any one condition.[28]

In psychiatric cases patients can choose the health care establishment where treatment is to be carried out, but not the level of therapy, and this choice does not extend to instances involving child and adolescent psychiatry. Patients who need long-term, co-ordinated health services are entitled, under provisions in various relevant legislation, to have an individual plan set up for the purpose. (This item, although part of the Act, was not effective when the latter came into force on 1 January 2001.)[29]

Involvement of patients and next-of-kin in treatment decisions
Participation in the implementation of medical treatment is also an entitlement conferred on patients under the Act. This includes the right to choose between one available form of examination or treatment and another. Nonetheless, the degree of such involvement depends on the ability of patients to absorb information and to express an opinion. Where they are unable to give informed consent, their next-of-kin have a right to be included in the decision-making. As far as possible, patients' wishes for others to be present while they are receiving health care must be granted.[30]

The right to be informed
Patients are entitled to be informed about their medical condition, how it is to be treated and the possible risks and side-effects involved in doing so. This information cannot be disclosed against their expressed wishes, but it can be divulged if it is to avoid the adverse outcome that a planned therapy was likely to produce, or if it is laid down in law. Conversely, information can be withheld where a patient's life or health could be endangered, or for some other crucial reason. Patients are entitled to be told if serious complications or damage to their health has occurred. When this happens, they must be made aware of their right to apply for compensation through the Norwegian patient compensation scheme.[31]

Information to patients' next-of-kin
Where patients have given consent – or circumstances justify it – their next-of-kin will be told about the medical condition and the treatment being provided. If the situation concerns patients who are over 16 years of age but clearly incapable of managing their affairs because of a physical or mental handicap, both they and their next-of-kin are entitled to be given relevant clinical and other information as expressed in s.3 (2) of the Act.[32]

Information about minors
Patients under 16 years old must be told about their medical disorder and the therapy that is being involved in treating it. Their parents or those holding parental responsibility for them will be similarly informed. Nonetheless, such information is not passed on to these parties when a patient aged 12 to 16 years gives a good reason why it should be withheld, but clinical information about patients who are under 18 years of age is disclosed where it is crucial to a parent's (or legal representative's) responsibilities. Under provisions in the Children's Welfare Act 1992, the children's welfare service is subject to the same rules in all respects where it has taken over the custody of a child below 16 years of age.[33]

Presentation of information to patients
Information about a patient's clinical disorder must be presented to them in a way that is in keeping with their age, maturity, culture and language, and expressed in a sensitive way. Health care personnel must ensure – as far as possible – that patients have understood the meaning of what they have been told. An entry explaining what has occurred is then made on the patient's medical record.[34]

The right to protection against the release of information
Health-related and other personal data must be treated in the same way as current provisions relating to confidentiality, and with due care and respect for the individual to whom they refer. The principle of confidentiality ceases to apply to the extent of any consent otherwise given by the person concerned. Nevertheless, health care staff can reveal information where a statutory duty to do so applies. In such cases, and insofar as the situation allows, it is obligatory for patients to be promptly advised about the nature of the material that has been divulged.[35]

General rules about consent
Health care can be given only with patients' consent, except when there are legal grounds for doing so without their approval. In order for the consent to be valid, patients must have been fully informed about their medical condition and provided with details of the proposed treatment. Consent can be withdrawn, but in this event the patient concerned will be told about the consequences of the therapy not being provided. Consent can be either expressly or implicitly granted, although there may be instances when regulations stipulate that this must be in writing or given in some other formal way.[36]

Who has the right of consent? [37]
Adults (over 18 years) and minors of more than 16 years are entitled to give consent to health care, unless special provisions or the nature of a proposed clinical measure dictate otherwise. Also, the right to consent can be rescinded, in part or as a whole, because of a patient's physical or mental deficiencies. Nonetheless, after assessing these and other relevant issues, the practitioner(s) concerned must make an effort to ensure that the health care to be given has the approval of the patient involved.

If it is decided that, owing to a physical or mental disability, a patient is unable to give consent to health care, written reasons must be provided to support that decision. Where possible, both patient and next-of-kin will immediately be given this information, but if there is no next-of-kin, the issue is discussed with other clinicians and a decision made on the treatment to be given.

Consent on behalf of children
Parents or others holding parental responsibility are entitled to give consent to health care for patients below 16 years of age. Under the provisions of the Children's Welfare Act 1992, the children's welfare service also has this right where it concerns minors in the same age group who are in their care. Nonetheless, children who are less than 16 years old must be listened to before a decision on their health care is taken. Indeed, on reaching 12 years of age, children are allowed

to express an opinion about personal health questions, and the value of what they have said is gauged according to their age and maturity.[38]

The parents of or those holding parental responsibility for children between 16 and 18 years of age have a right to give consent to health care for the latter if they are not competent to do so themselves. In the same way, the children's welfare service is entitled to give its approval to health care where it concerns similarly aged young people in their charge. However, health care cannot be provided if patients in this age group object, unless special provisions exist to override their disapproval.[39]

Consent for adults not competent to give consent
In cases where an adult patient is not competent to grant consent, the health care provider involved can decide on a less invasive type of treatment, having regard for its extent and duration; alternatively, the patient's next-of-kin can give consent to another proposed form of therapy. Moreover, some other kind of medical intervention can be provided if it is considered to be in the patient's best interests and likely that the latter would have approved. The views of the patient's next-of-kin can be sought in determining this question, but in none of these instances can therapy be given if patients disapprove, unless special provisions dictate otherwise and take precedence.[40]

Consent for the legally incapable and others not competent and without next-of-kin
Patients who have been declared legally incapable can, to the fullest extent of their abilities, grant consent to receive medical treatment. Where they are unable to do so, those legally responsible for them can give approval on their behalf. The Patients' Rights Act 1999 allows for a similar arrangement for patients who are not competent to give consent and have no next-of-kin. In these cases, the health care practitioner concerned, in collaboration with other clinicians, is permitted to decide on the therapy to be provided.[41]

The right to refuse health care in certain circumstances
There are other examples under the Act where the right to refuse health care can apply. For instance, where religious or other strong convictions are a factor, patients are entitled to decline blood or blood products and refuse to call off an ongoing hunger strike. Patients who are dying have a right to reject life-prolonging treatment, but if they are incapable of communicating their wishes about any proposed therapy the clinicians involved can withdraw treatment if the next-of-kin gives their consent to do so. Such a course will be followed only if an independent opinion obtained by the clinicians shows that it is what the patients would also have wanted. In all the cases just mentioned, health care practitioners must ensure that patients are adults, have been informed and understand the consequences of refusing treatment.[42]

The right of access to medical records[43]
Unsurprisingly, under the Act patients are also entitled to look at their medical records and any additional notes, and to be given a copy of this data and a brief explanation of their content. But access can be denied if this is essential in order to avoid endangering patients' lives or seriously damaging their health. It can also be refused

where it is shown to be clearly unwise from the perspective of people who are close to a patient.

A legitimate representative is allowed to look at information denied to a patient – as is a medical practitioner or lawyer – unless there are clear grounds for refusing it. Where patients have given consent, others such as a parent, guardian or next-of-kin are permitted to see their medical records. The next-of-kin have a right of access to patients' clinical records following their death, except when there are special reasons for not allowing it.

Medical records – correction, deletion, transfer and release of data
Norway's Patients' Rights Act 1999 also confers rights about the correction, deletion, transfer and release of medical records. This means patients can insist that data in their clinical records is corrected or deleted in line with provisions in the present Health Personnel Act 1999. Furthermore, they have a right to stop the disclosure of any such material, in part or as a whole. Nor can the information be disclosed if there is cause to believe that a patient would have refused permission, if asked. Data can be divulged when there are exceptional grounds for doing so, but any transfer or disclosure of clinical records must be consistent with the provisions of the Health Personnel Act.[44]

Special rights of children
The rights of children are covered in other respects by the Patients' Right Act 1999. Children are entitled to necessary medical care – as well as that in the form of health control – in the municipality where they live or visit. They have a right to be accompanied by at least one parent or guardian during their entire stay in a medical establishment. The exception is when this is inadvisable in the interests of a child, or if any right of contact has ceased to apply under provisions in the current Children's Act 1981 or the Children's Welfare Act 1992. Children of compulsory school age are also entitled to receive stimulation and become involved in activities – to the extent that it is advisable – while staying in a health care unit. During their stay they have a right to be given tuition in keeping with the requirements of the Tuition Act, amended in December 2000 and in force on 1 January 2001.[45]

The right to complain
The Patients' Rights Act 1999 has a statutory link with the complaints procedure relating to the health service. Thus, patients (or their authorized representatives) who consider that their rights about aspects of health care provided for under the Act have been breached can ask the health service provider to explain its actions. This step must be taken within three weeks from the time a particular complainant had or should have received adequate information to lodge such a complaint.[46]

If the health care body refuses to respond, or believes that no infringement has occurred, the complainant can refer the case to the county medical officer. This must take no more than three weeks from the time the complainant was advised, or should have been told, about the outcome of the initial approach to the health care provider. The complaint must be in writing and signed by the patient or any representative involved. Errors or omissions can be corrected and additional information supplied within a time limit set by the county medical officer.[47]

The provisions of Norway's Public Administration Act 1970 can also be a factor in complaints under examination and being determined by the county medical officer, insofar as they have an application in cases being dealt with by this agency under the provisions in Chapter 7 of the Patients' Rights Act. On a separate point, complainants can ask a health service organization to take action against their staff where they consider that requirements in the Health Personnel Act 1999 have been infringed. The Act was amended in December 2000 and came into force on 1 Januray 2001.[48]

Patient ombud
Under the Patients' Rights Act, every county municipality is required to have a 'patient ombud' with jurisdiction over the specialist (acute) health care sector. These officers are required to carry out their duties independently and centre on protecting patients' rights, interests and legal entitlements about health care. Anyone can approach them to deal with a grievance, but they will also act independently of any such complaint where it is seen to be necessary to improve the service being provided.

Complaints lodged with the patient ombud can be either oral or in writing, and complainants have the right to remain anonymous. The patient ombud will decide whether a grievance has sufficient grounds for investigation. If it is determined not to proceed further with the case, the complainant is notified and told the reason for the decision. Public authorities and bodies providing services to them are required by law to supply information to the ombud when asked to do so. This officer is also allowed access to all premises where public health services are provided, and to comment on all jurisdictional matters. These can include recommendations to improve a service, although their implementation is not mandatory.

Under provisions in the Act, complainants must be advised about the outcome of their case once the handling process has been completed and given an explanation of how it came about. Where a follow-up by the management of the health care body concerned is required, the patient ombud will notify them about what is involved and ensure that the remedial steps to be taken are made known.[49]

Sweden
Patients' rights – or the 'position of patients' as it is sometimes referred to[50] – is included to a fair extent in Sweden's Health and Medical Services Act 1982, amended in March 2000. As its title implies, the Act sets out the role and responsibilities of the health service in the provision of medical care, treatment and services for the public. In the process the legislation outlines the requirements of the health service in some of its closer relationships with patients. The balance of patient entitlements appears to arise out of associated or overlapping legislation, among which are the Health and Medical Services (Professional Activity) Act 1998, the Patients' Record Act and the Secrecy Act 1980.

Requirements to be met in the care or treatment of patients
The health service must provide patients with a high standard of care that is readily available, on equal terms for all and about which they feel secure. Priority must be given to those with the greatest need. In providing this level of care or treatment it must respect the free will, dignity and privacy of patients and foster good relations

between them and their attending health care professionals. Except where manifestly unnecessary, a prompt assessment must be given of a person's state of health.

Patients are also entitled to specific details about their medical condition and the treatment procedures that are available. Where such information cannot be given to them, it must be passed on to a close relative, but neither party can be informed if doing so is in breach of the Secrecy Act or the Health and Medical Services (Professional Activity) Act.

The health service must work for the prevention of ill health and injury. Where appropriate, it must provide advice to patients on how such impairment can be avoided. Wherever health care is being provided, the necessary staff, facilities and equipment must be available to give an acceptable level of service. On an associated issue, where a person has died the necessary arrangements involved must be carried out respectfully and with consideration for surviving relatives.[51]

Responsibilities of the health service concerning the population and patient care
Every county council has an obligation to provide an acceptable level of health and medical services to those living within its boundaries and to others residually registered under section 16 of the Civil Registration Act 1991 and living permanently within the county council boundaries. This health care provision is also available to those who are not residents of Sweden but are entitled to illness and maternity benefits under the relevant EEC regulation involving the social security rights of migrant workers, self-employed individuals – and of their families. County councils are obliged to provide emergency health care where it is needed by non-residents who happen to be present within the area of their jurisdiction.[52]

In cases where several alternative therapies proven as being clinically sound exist, patients must be allowed to express their preference, but the chosen treatment will be given only if the illness or injury involved and the cost of the procedure are seen to be justifiable. Treatment outside the county council area of a patient's residency is not allowed for a condition if medically proven therapy is already on offer where that person lives.[53]

Patients with a life-threatening or especially serious illness or injury can obtain a medical reassessment within or outside the locality where they are resident. Such reassessment is made only if there are grounds for doubt about any already proposed medical intervention or fears that a patient could be placed at risk if the therapy was applied. Reassessment will also be approved if it is considered to be of significant importance to a patient's future quality of life. The recommended therapy decided upon as a result can then go ahead.[54]

Rights provided for by other legislation and regulations
Sweden's Patients' Record Act now states that a note must be made in patients' medical records of the information given to them by the clinicians who have attended them. Additionally, documentation about what was discussed between patients and practitioners about the available treatment options and the choices that were made – including those resulting from a second opinion – should form part of the record. Under regulations stemming from other legislation, patients have a right to participate in what is noted about them in their medical records, be given access to this data and have any disparaging descriptions of their medical condition removed and

destroyed. The right of individuals to abortion and sterilization is provided for in separate regulations.[55]

Conclusion

The introduction of detailed legislation specific to patients' rights in the Nordic countries probably arose out of mostly honourable motives. Adjusting the scales more equitably between patient and health care provider could have been at the heart of the matter, but the sound practicalities of levelling things in this way are likely also to have been part of the plan to produce the blueprint for a procedure that would allow all concerned to know exactly where they stood. Whatever the true reason, the results don't seem to be a bad deal for patients nor, indeed, for those who deliver their health care.

It should not be surprising that there is a powerful common theme running through the new-look patients' rights legislation passed in Finland and Norway during the 1990s. Essentially, this is to do with a set of precisely defined entitlements covering what, arguably, are most of the key issues about patients and their representatives in their links with the health service. In this respect they have strong affinities with legislation passed at more or less the same time in non-Nordic countries: The Netherlands in 1995, Lithuania and Israel in 1996 and Belgium in 2002. The next two chapters show that Denmark and Iceland closely followed Norway, with similar types of statutory patients' rights. It looks very much like a growing trend.

CHAPTER 15

Denmark, too, has an array of patients' rights set in stone

Succinct, valuable and clearly defined? They seem to be

The lawmakers in Denmark didn't waste much time in the general drive to update patients' rights legislation in the Nordic world during the 1990s. The result was the Patients' Legal Rights and Entitlements Act, which was passed in July 1998 and became effective on 1 October of the same year. Similar to the parallel models endorsed six years earlier in Finland and the following year in Norway, the Danish enactment confers a sizeable set of rights on patients in their links with the country's health service and medical practitioners. The entitlements of individuals speaking for patients and, indeed, those of the health care providers themselves seem just as explicitly supported.

Most of the rights incorporated in the Patients' Legal Rights and Entitlements Act 1998 are common to the latest pieces of legislation in other Nordic countries and a few countries elsewhere in Europe and beyond. Nevertheless, the few distinctions that there are in each case can be significant, as the model in Denmark will show.

The need for informed consent before treatment

Under the Act no clinical procedure can be started or continued without a patient's informed consent, unless it is otherwise provided for in law or stated elsewhere in the Act. Informed consent is described as approval given by patients after they have received adequate information from the clinician involved. Consent can be given orally or in writing – implied or otherwise – and can be withdrawn at any time. In cases where patients are not capable of protecting their interests, their legal rights can be adopted by individuals authorized to do so under the law where it is necessary to safeguard entitlements that are due.[1]

The Act requires that patients have a right to be told about their state of health, the treatment options available and the complications or side-effects that could arise. The guidance given must also include advice on the consequences of therapy not being provided, but patients are entitled to turn down such advice. Information about a patient's illness, examinations or any planned treatment must be provided regularly, in an easily understood and considerate way and allowing for factors such as the recipient's age and maturity. More detailed guidance must be given in cases where treatment involves a high risk of serious complications or side-effects. Where patients are seen to be unaware of factors that could affect their decisions about therapy, attending practitioners are obliged to advise them about these issues, unless this guidance has already been rejected.

Provision for minors
As in patients' rights legislation in most other Nordic countries, the Act contains specific provisions for minors. Minors of 15 years and older can give their informed consent to any treatment, a decision in which the custodial parents will also be involved. However, if a clinician believes a patient of this age to be incapable of understanding the consequences of their decisions, consent rests with the patient's custodial parents. Under provisions in the Act, 15-year-old patients are allowed access to their medical records and can give consent to the transfer of information from these files to other clinicians for an opinion on their proposed treatment.[2]

The position about treatment for patients who are permanently unable to give informed consent
In cases where patients are permanently incapable of giving informed consent to treatment, their next-of-kin have a right to do so on their behalf. Otherwise the patients' legal guardians will act for them and give consent in line with provisions in the Guardianship Act 1997. Where there is no next-of-kin or guardian, the attending practitioner is entitled to provide the planned therapy, subject to approval by another clinician who has not previously been involved in treating the patient concerned, and will not do so in the future. But attending doctors can treat patients without involving another practitioner if the therapy is of a less invasive kind in scope and duration. Where the next-of-kin or guardian has consented to treatment that will clearly damage a patient or produce an adverse outcome, the clinician involved can carry out other therapy with the approval of the relevant health care inspectorate.[3]

The status of temporarily or permanently incapable patients who need immediate and crucial therapy
Sometimes patients need immediate and crucial medical intervention but are temporarily or permanently incapable of giving informed consent for this to go ahead. In these cases attending clinicians are allowed to begin or continue a therapy that is necessary to achieve a significantly better result than would otherwise be the case, essential for the patients' survival or to improve their prospects in the long term. Nor is approval from the next-of-kin required before treatment is given. The same authority applies to similarly placed patients under 15 years of age and to their custodial parents or guardian, neither of whose prior assent is required.[4]

Involvement of patients who are unable to give their informed consent
Nonetheless, patients who are unable to give informed consent must be advised and involved in the discussions about available treatment. This applies insofar as what has been explained is understood, unless providing such information could adversely affect them, but comments from patients that are considered to be worthwhile or relevant must be taken seriously.[5]

Action to be taken by clinicians prior to providing therapy
Before providing treatment, medical professionals are obliged to:
• obtain the informed consent of patients
• get the approval of another clinician

- secure the agreement of the relevant health inspector
- keep patients informed and involved in discussions about their therapy,

in each case consistent with the requirements of the Act.[6]

Hunger strikes and treatment involving blood transfusion or blood products
If a patient is clearly on a hunger strike, and has been advised about its consequences without effect, the attending clinician must not intervene to stop it. Nor
can any therapy involving blood transfusion or blood products be started or
continued without the informed consent of patients. The latter can refuse any such
measures to treat a current illness following advice given by the practitioner
involved of the health-related consequences of not accepting the therapy. In
instances where clinicians consider it to be ethically wrong not to provide
treatment involving blood transfusion or blood products, their patients can be
referred to another practitioner. The exception is in cases of urgently needed
medical attention as those indicated in the relevant part of the Execution of the
Medical Profession Act 1992, now superseded by new legislation passed in 1998.[7]

Terminally ill patients and living wills
The right of terminally ill patients to refuse any treatment that will merely be life-
prolonging is included in the Patients' Legal Rights and Entitlements Act. Where
patients in this condition have become incapable of making a decision, the
attending doctor is entitled not to start or continue what is clearly life-prolonging
treatment. Terminally ill patients can be given painkillers, tranquillizers or similar
drugs that are necessary for palliative support even if doing so may result in accel-
erating death.

The legislation also covers the issue of 'living wills'. Individuals of 18 years of
age and over who have no guardian to take care of their personal or health care
arrangements, as defined in the Guardianship Act 1997, can make a living will.
By this means they can state their last wishes about treatment should they become
terminally ill and lose the capacity to express themselves.

A living will can state that the person concerned does not wish to be given life-
prolonging therapy if terminally ill. It can also make clear that life-extending
treatment is not to be provided if illness, advanced weakening through age,
accident, cardiac arrest or the like has produced such a high level of disability that
the individual involved will no longer be physically or mentally able to cope.

Life-prolonging treatment is defined in the Patients' Legal Rights and
Entitlements Act as therapy that provides no prospects of cure, recovery or
improvement other than extending the duration of a patient's life. Before an
attending clinician can start or continue life-prolonging treatment in cases where
a patient has become incapable of making a decision, the Danish Living Wills
Register must be scrutinized to verify whether a living will has been made. The
wish of a testator not to be given life-extending therapy in the event of terminal
illness is binding on the medical practitioner concerned, whereas any such
expression about a medical or physical condition that prevents a patient from
being able to cope must be looked upon as directional when considering
treatment.[8]

Medical records: handling and their inspection by patients

Provisions in the Act apply to case records and similar data that are prepared by medical personnel and stored in public and private hospitals, clinics, out-patient units and private practices. The rules also cover medical records about treatment in private homes, as well as in other public or private establishments in which patients receive therapy as part of the health services on offer. Registers kept by public authorities and registration records kept for scientific or statistical purposes are not included in the regulations.

On request, patients must be advised in a straightforward way whether any part of their medical record is being passed on by automatic or other means. If it is, patients must also be given a straightforward explanation of a number of points. These will include the type of data being conveyed, the purpose of doing so, the kind of individuals receiving the transmitted information and details about the origin of this action. These rights may be limited in cases where it is found that patients' motives in asking for these facts are inappropriate. The whole procedure must conform to regulations laid down in European Community Directive 95/46/EC of October 1995 on the protection of individuals concerning the processing of personal data and on the free movement of such information.

Decisions on the rights of patients to inspect their medical records are made by the authority, establishment or clinician in possession of this data. Where access is granted, one or other of these parties will also decide if inspection of the records is to take place on site or by means of a copy being sent to the patient concerned. If a request to inspect clinical records has not been granted or refused within 10 days of being received, the patient involved must be given reasons for the delay, with an indication of when a decision is expected to be made. While an attending clinician has authority over patients' medical records, overall responsibility for allowing the records to be inspected rests with the health care body involved.[9]

Consent to transfer of patient information

Provisions in the Patients' Legal Rights and Entitlements Act give patients the right to confidentiality about information that attending practitioners have gained about them in the course of their duties, including health and other personal details. Where the clinician involved has been authorized to pass on this data, the ultimate responsibility to ensure that it is carried out in keeping with the law rests with the health authority concerned.

Provided patients have given their consent, attending clinicians can transfer medical and additional personal information about them to other practitioners involved with the patients' treatment. Consent can be given orally or in writing to the clinician passing on the data, or to the practitioner receiving it, and this consent is entered in the patients' case records. In certain circumstances these details can be handed over without a patient's consent, for instance when this information is a necessary measure to support a patient's ongoing therapy. (In this situation, patients are still entitled at any time to stop their details being passed on.)

Patients' consent to the transfer of personal information about themselves is also not needed when it is necessary for obvious reasons, or to protect the interests of a patient, the attending practitioner or others who may be involved. (In this case, the patient concerned will be told about the transfer and the reasons for doing so.) Nor is approval required if the information is given to a patient's general practioner by a doctor who is standing in for the latter. But in all cases concerning the handing over of patient information where no consent to do so is needed, the clinician holding this data will decide whether its transfer is justified.

Having obtained consent from a patient, the attending clinicians can pass on details about the patient's state of health and other personal facts to authorities, organizations or private individuals for non-medical purposes. Consent to do so must be received in writing (although departure from this rule is allowed if it is justified by the circumstances of a case) and entered in the patient's case records. Any such permission received from patients becomes null and void one year after being given.

In some cases, information can be made available to one or other of these last-mentioned recipients without the prior consent of patients. This can happen if it is provided for in law that it is permissible to do so and is considered to be of significant value to a receiving authority in its case-handling duties. The same conditions apply when it is necessary to pass on this confidential data for obvious reasons or when it is to protect the interests of the patient concerned, the attending practitioner or any others who are involved. (In any of these circumstances, the patient concerned will be advised about the transfer and the reasons for doing so.) The consent of patients is also not required when the supplying of information about them to an authority is essential to carry out the latter's supervision and inspection procedures. However, in all cases of passing on patient information where no consent to do so is needed, the medical practitioner holding these details will decide whether its transfer is justified.[10]

Releasing details about patients' health care to the next-of-kin
Provisions in the Act allow a doctor to tell the next-of-kin of a patient who has died the cause of the patient's death and the way in which death occurred, if doing so is not regarded as being against the wishes of the deceased. Consideration for the latter or other relevant private issues must also be taken into account in giving these details. The next-of-kin can be given this information when it is obviously correct to do so or when it is to protect the specific interests of the deceased patient, the hospital clinician involved or other relevant individuals. The deceased person's GP or the clinician who treated the patient in hospital can also obtain the patient's medical details from another hospital or doctor, but only if asked to do so by the next-of-kin.[11]

Transfer of health care data for special purposes
The Patients' Legal Rights and Entitlements Act 1998 covers the transfer of health care data for research, statistics and other special purposes. Information about a person's state of health, personal details and other confidential material obtained from case records can be provided for scientific or specific biomedical research purposes without consent, subject to its use being approved by provisions in the Scientific Ethical Committee System Act. If information is needed for research purposes not affected by this additional legislation, it can be passed on for use in a specific scientific study project of significant public interest with the approval of the National Board of Health, which specifies the terms upon which data can be transferred. After such approval is given, any contact with individuals to get more information is allowed only if the clinicians who treated them give their permission. The assent of the

National Board of Health must also be obtained before confidential patient information can be handed over for statistical or planning purposes and the Board stipulates the terms for using the data. However, the Board's approval is not needed in these cases if there is provision in law that allows such information to be passed on. Any confidential information about patients that is obtained for research, statistical or planning purposes must not subsequently be used in any other way. Furthermore, publication of this data can be made only in a form that cannot be related to its source.[12]

Complaints and penalties

Complaints about issues covered in the Act may be lodged with the Patient's Board of Complaints under rules set out in Denmark's Health Care Sector Central Administration Act, unless a specific complaints procedure has been provided for in law. Judgements by the Board cannot be appealed against to another administrative authority. Those who unjustifiably convey or use confidential patient information as a whole and referred to in Part 5 of the Patients' Legal Rights and Entitlements Act will be penalized under the relevant sections of the Danish criminal code.[13]

Conclusion

The Patients' Legal Rights and Entitlements Act is strong on the rights of patients, their representatives and those who are responsible for the delivery of health care, and entitlements extend to a wide range of issues in the relationship between patients and the health service. Prerogatives that arise in situations that occur infrequently are also covered and one or two might be considered questionable by some outsiders. The final result may fall short of perfection, but what the Act has to offer Danish citizens in its package of sweeping and generally valuable rights appears to be not far off target; it offers the kind of privileges that are available in only a handful of developed nations.

CHAPTER 16

How far do patients' rights go in Iceland?

Quite a long way, by all accounts

Like specific legislation passed and effective in three out of the four other Nordic states, Iceland's Rights of Patients Act 1997 confers an array of entitlements across health care and associated areas. The Act has a powerful impact on patient consent about treatment and the provision of information about a patient's medical condition and any proposed therapy. Other issues affected are confidentiality on the part of health care professionals, their handling of patients' records and the entitlements of patients who wish to see their medical files and of those who retain them. The legislation also provides for special rules concerning the care of sick children and for the right of patients to complain. Perhaps uniquely, the question of scientific research related to the health service forms a sizeable part of the Rights of Patients Act.

A stated principal aim of the Act is to secure specific entitlements for patients in their connections with the health service at a level corresponding with the benchmark for human rights in general. The purpose is also to strengthen the legal status of patients and to support the necessary confidentiality between them and health care personnel. The legislation prohibits discrimination against patients on the grounds of gender, religion, beliefs, nationality, race, skin colour, financial position and family relation or status in other respects.[1]

Under the Act, patients have a right to the best available health care and professional expertise relative to their condition and prognosis at all times. Health workers must try to develop a secure relationship with those in their charge. In the process, patients are entitled to receive continuous care and the co-operation of practitioners and the institutions involved in their treatment.[2]

The Ministry of Health and Social Security is obliged to see that information is available about the rights of patients, and about patients' associations and social security schemes. This data must be accessible to patients on the premises of health care establishments, including those of self-employed practitioners. Efforts must be made by the Ministry to advise the public about the causes and consequences of illnesses concerning both children and adults.[3]

Essential provisions of the Rights of Patients Act 1997

After the accounts that have been given in the two previous chapters about patients' rights in other Nordic countries, to provide an analysis of the legal rights of patients and those involving associated factors in Iceland will be seen as another, mostly repetitive, exercise. Nonetheless, while there are admittedly major similarities in the content of the Rights of Patients Act and that of the parallel legislation in Denmark, Finland

240

and Norway, in particular, even the few – and not always – significant differences that exist do not cancel out the need to provide full details of what is provided for under the Icelandic enactment.

Rights affecting information, consent and action in health care
Patients are entitled to information regarding their state of health, medical condition and the prognosis, and details must be provided about any proposed therapy, its duration, risks, benefits, other possible remedies and the consequences of not being treated. The Act specifies that all these procedures must be recorded in a patient's medical records. Moreover, communication of this kind with patients must be carried out when there is a reason for doing so and in circumstances and a way that it can be understood. If a patient does not understand Icelandic or is dependent on sign language, the information provided is required to be interpreted in a way that can be followed.[4]

However, any of these details must be withheld where patients do not want to be told, or if they have designated someone else to receive the information. Either situation – including the name of the nominated individual – has to be entered in the records of the patient concerned, but if a patient is simply unable to understand what is being conveyed, the information has to be given to a close relative or the legal guardian, whoever is applicable. The identity of those representing patients who are either under age or intellectually incapable of making a decision must be similarly recorded in patients' files.[5]

The right of patients to decide whether or not to accept treatment must be respected. Provisions in the Legal Majority Act 1997 cover the question of consent to treatment of patients who, for intellectual or other reasons defined in that Act, are not capable of deciding about therapy for themselves. Nonetheless, in such cases, a patient must be consulted as far as possible. Also, unless a person is unconscious or in a similarly incapacitating condition, therapy cannot be given without the patient's prior approval. The consent must be in writing, where possible, describe the information given to the patient and show that it has been understood.[6]

If therapy is refused by patients, the doctor or other health care practitioner concerned is obliged to inform them of the possible consequences of their decision, but patients can turn down further treatment at any time if doing so is not in breach of provisions in other laws. The decision of patients to refuse or discontinue treatment must be recorded in their medical records and confirm that information was provided about the possible consequences in either event.[7]

Exceptions to the rule that patients' consent must be received for proposed therapy include instances where a patient is either unconscious or unable for some other clinical reason to give consent to urgent treatment. In these cases, approval to go ahead will be taken for granted, unless it is known with certainty that the patient would have refused permission.[8]

Participation of patients in scientific research[9]
The involvement of patients in scientific research is covered by the Rights of Patients Act 1997 and developed in a regulation that took effect two years later. Before formally consenting to take part in such studies, patients must be given details of what is involved, including the risks and benefits that could possibly result. The professionals concerned in the research are also obliged to explain to them that participation can be

declined from the outset or ceased at any time after it has started. It is also prohibited to conduct scientific research on patients without the prior approval of the appointed ethics body or the National Bioethics Committee.

Biological research is not allowed without a prior evaluation of the possible risks on the one hand and benefits on the other. In any event, the interests of the person concerned must take priority over those of science or society itself. Any evaluation by the National Bioethics Committee or the relevant ethics body of a scientific study must have shown that there are no scientific or ethical grounds to oppose its implementation. There are also specific stipulations in the Act covering the examination of clinical records – including biological samples – for scientific purposes. Prior permission to carry out this work must be obtained from the Data Protection Commission, under the Registration and Handling of Personal Data Act 1989, and from either the applicable ethics body or the National Bioethics Committee.

These groups have additional powers to control the work of scientific research connected with health care, and all decisions made by them must respect the terms of Public Administration Act 1993. The Rights of Patients Act also states that pharmacological trials on humans must be in accord with the provisions of Regulation No. 284/1986, which refers to clinical research on medicinal products and guidelines on good clinical practices applying to the European Economic Area (EEA).

Patient confidentiality
Statutory provisions in the Act apply equally to patient confidentiality. Health care professionals are obliged to respect the confidentiality of information about a patient's health, medical condition, diagnosis, prognosis, treatment and other personal data. This professional secrecy continues to apply following the death of a patient, and after the practitioner(s) involved may have taken up a position elsewhere. However, information can be disclosed in critical situations, but only with due regard to the wishes of the deceased person and the interests of others concerned. Where there is doubt, health care personnel can obtain guidance from the Directorate-General of Public Health.[10] (On an associated issue involving confidentiality, patients must be informed if students will be present for training purposes during their treatement presumably so they can say that they do not wish the students to be present.[11]

There are exemptions from these rules. For instance, professional confidentiality does not apply to matters about which a health professional is obliged to report under other legal provisions, such as those in the Child Protection Act 2002. Also, the obligation to secrecy ends once a patient or that person's guardian has consented to the disclosure of information. In cases where a medical practitioner is required to testify in a court of law, the provisions of the Doctors' Act 1988 apply.[12]

Access to clinical records and handling information in them[13]
The handling of patients' information, and access to it, is subject to provisions of the Rights of Patients Act 1997 in more ways than one. Patients' clinical records must be kept at the health care establishment or at the premises of a doctor or another practitioner where they are being maintained. Medical professionals who are in charge of these records are obliged to show all or part of the information to the patients

concerned, or their representatives, if asked to do so. The same right of access must be allowed to official bodies who examine complaints by patients (or their agents) relating to health care received. Provisions in the Information Act 1996 allow a charge to be made for copies of clinical records.

Data contained in medical files that has been supplied by someone other than the patient or clinician concerned must not be shown to the patient without the consent of the person who provided it. If this individual has died, cannot be traced or unjustly refuses to give permission, the Directorate-General of Public Health can be involved. A decision is then made as to whether the patient, or any representative involved, is allowed to see the information.

In cases where a doctor considers that it is not in the interests of patients to be given a copy of their medical records, the replicated material must be sent to the Directorate-General of Public Health without delay. This body will decide during the following eight weeks if a copy of the information can be given to the party asking for it. Should this request be denied, the matter is passed for review to the Minister for Health.

The Act requires that clinical records, by their very nature, must be stored safely, with access restricted to health care practitioners who need to use them. Under the provisions of the Recording and Presentation of Personal Information Act 2000, the Data Protection Commission can authorize access to information in medical records for scientific research. This includes biological samples, but the proviso is that the studies meet the particular conditions written into the Rights of Patients Act 1997. Each time access is allowed, it is subject to conditions considered to be necessary, and the event must also be entered in the records. Patients (or their representatives) are entitled to comment if they believe that information contained in their medical files is incorrect or misleading. In this situation the remarks they make will be attached to these documents.

Additional patients' rights and responsibilities[14]
Provisions in the Act require health care personnel to show respect in their dealings with patients. Only those clinicians directly concerned are permitted to administer treatment and care must be taken that this is given out of sight of those who are not involved. Information about therapy must be accessible only to the medical practitioners concerned.

Patient waiting times and associated issues are covered by the Act. Doctors must give a reason if there is any delay in treating a patient and provide an estimated waiting time of when this will take place. A patient must also be told if it is possible to receive the necessary therapy sooner elsewhere. Where waiting patients are placed in order of priority, the sequence has to be arranged primarily on the basis of clinical need or other similar grounds.

By reason of the Health Service Act 1990, the country is divided into health regions. A patient has a right to choose the most conveniently located doctor and obtain a second opinion about diagnosis, treatment, condition and prognosis. The same entitlements apply with regard to other health care personnel, but patients also have a role to play: they are responsible for the state of their own health as far as it is possible and their fitness will allow.

Support and respect for patients and care of the dying
The Rights of Patients Act has a place for rules concerning patients' admission and discharge. When a person is admitted to a health care establishment, the attending practitioners must introduce themselves and describe their particular fields of expertise. They are also obliged to explain the rules and practices that are in operation and tell the patient who is in charge of the treatment to be given.[15]

Prior to discharge, patients' personal circumstances must be looked into to ensure, as far as possible, that adequate home care or other amenities are provided. On being discharged, patients must be given advice – in writing if requested – on important matters about follow-up, including information about drug dosage, diet, training and exercise. Medical discharge letters and certificates must be issued without undue delay.[16]

Under the Act's provisions, a patient's suffering must be alleviated to the maximum that current health care practice will allow. Those who are being treated in hospital have a right to receive the support of their family, relatives and friends during their stay. Patients and their close relatives are entitled to spiritual, social and religious help during these times.[17]

Care of the dying
The issue of the care and treatment of dying patients is covered by the legislation. Under its provisions, patients have a right to die with dignity. In cases where a patient who is terminally ill explicitly declines further life-prolonging therapy or resuscitation, the doctor concerned must respect that decision. Furthermore, should a dying patient be mentally or physically incapable of making a decision about receiving treatment, the practitioner in charge must try to consult the person's relatives and medical colleagues before deciding to continue or terminate the therapy.[18]

Information on the health and treatment of sick children, and associated issues[19]
The Act contains special rules for sick children. Parents of patients under 16 years of age must be given the same information about their children's health and proposed treatment that an adult patient is entitled to receive under the Act. The children who are to be treated must also be similarly advised about their condition and the planned health care to the extent that their age and maturity will allow them to under-stand. They also have the same right as patients in general to decline any such infor-mation.

Parents who have custody of children under 16 years old can give consent to any necessary therapy required for them. However, the children must be consulted as far as possible, and always if they are over 12 years old. Should the parents not consent to essential treatment for a child in their custody, the doctor responsible, or another clinician, must contact the child welfare authorities, a measure provided for in the Child Protection Act 2002. But if there is no time to take this action because the child is in need of life-saving treatment, the patient's health is the determining factor and the necessary therapy must be started immediately.

Depending on a sick child's state of health, everything possible must be done to enable the patient to develop and enjoy life, despite the illness and treatment being given. Unnecessary tests or operations on children are not permitted and child patients in a health care establishment are entitled to have their parents or other close relatives with them during their stay. In this event, the latter will be accommodated as suitably as possible. Also, the situation permitting, siblings and friends can visit a sick child in hospital. Where a patient is of school age, tuition in keeping with the child's age and state of health must be provided. The care of sick children and the surroundings in which it is taking place must be suited to their age, maturity and condition.

The right to complain
A patient's right to complain is written into the Rights of Patients Act. Patients' complaints about services provided by a health care body must be directed to its central administration; grievances about medical treatment are lodged with the Directorate-General of Public Health or the Committee on Dispute Settlement, as specified in the Health Service Act 1990. Health care personnel are obliged to give guidance to patients or their relatives when they decide to lodge a complaint and give a prompt written reply once a complaint has been received. The management of health care bodies is under an obligation to look into the comments of staff who consider that the rights of patients are being infringed in any way.[20]

Conclusion
It will be seen that Iceland's Rights of Patients Act 1997 is especially detailed in certain areas: patients' right of access to their medical records, children's entitlements before and during the course of treatment, and the prerogatives and responsibilities surrounding biological research on patients. Matters about home care for patients following therapy are also covered, as are the sometimes contentious issues of the right to die with dignity or refuse life-prolonging therapy.

As a whole, the Act provides for a powerful set of patients' rights extending across most of the relevant issues – familiar and otherwise – concerning health care. Indeed, nothing of much relevance seems to have been left out. Thus Iceland's Rights of Patients Act 1997 has a leading place among pieces of advanced legislation on patients' rights in the developed world.

CHAPTER 17

Patient compensation Danish style

A payout in one out of every two claims without breaking the bank? Well, yes

Who says a non-litigious system of patient compensation would be too expensive to run? If the well-established scheme in Denmark is anything to go by, then consider this myth peddled by some in Britain to be well and truly exploded. Even after ten years in business, and a history of paying out in a constantly high proportion of claims, the country's liberal scheme still costs no more than 0.3 per cent of its entire hospital expenditure.

Take the year 2001 as an example. From a total of around 2,500 claims investigated and decided – less a small percentage that were outside the scheme's jurisdiction – compensation was paid in more than 50 per cent of cases.[1] But it was no philanthropic fluke. A similar picture had surfaced in previous years too. Lots of payouts, yet at no crippling cost to the state, is the name of the game. Small wonder, then, that Denmark's politicians seem to be quite pleased with themselves. So, what's the big idea? How do the Danes do it?

The system before the Patient Insurance Act 1992

Before the introduction of the Danish Patient Insurance Act 1992, the prospect of receiving damages for injury caused as a result of medical treatment was based on liability in a non-statutory form known as the *culpa* principle. In line with this precept, clinicians were liable for impairment resulting from their actions only if an adverse outcome was the consequence of their negligence or omission. The system had two interlinked principal objectives. One was to seek to redress damage caused to patients' health by making those responsible liable for their actions. The other aim was to deter medical practitioners from repeating mistakes by making them accountable in this way.[2]

During the 1970s and 1980s it became increasingly clear that a system that imposed upon a patient the burden of proof of a practitioner's negligence, and its connection with injury sustained, was essentially unfair. It also turned out to be virtually impossible for claimants to be awarded damages for 'developmental injury', that is to say, unforeseen subsequent damage to health confirmed to have been a result of the treatment method applied. Not only that: from the cases of claims filed with the insurers of health care establishments, it seemed that the two main aims of the *culpa* principle – redress and its preventive effect on future professional misconduct – were not being realized.[3]

Significant, also, was the fact that the number of claims for damages being made was always low. One explanation put forward for this may be connected with the point that in order to file a claim for compensation it would first be necessary for patients to be aware that injury has occurred, and that it was a result of an act or omission by medical staff.[4]

Except in obvious cases, patients can be unaware of damage affecting their health unless they are notified and told about its cause by the clinician involved or another medical professional. The difficulty then arises that, in providing such information, the practitioner concerned may subsequently be the subject of an action for negligence or professional misconduct by the patient who has been treated.[5]

Objectives of the new legislation

With these considerations in mind, it was decided via the Patient Insurance Act to set up a procedure that would receive the approval of both the hospital service and its medical practitioners. The plan was to introduce a system that would also encourage health care providers to advise patients about their right to claim compensation when damage to their health had occurred following clinician action.[6]

It was strongly felt that the key to achieving this goal lay in the separation of the issue of compensation from the complaints system and two effectively unrelated mechanisms were established for the purpose. As a result, the Patients' Board of Complaints now assesses complaints against medical staff; claims for compensation are dealt with by the Patient Insurance. Each of these bodies is unaware at all times of what the other is doing in cases brought before them.[7]

Such a division of claims from complaints has led to the emergence of a patient counsellor at all hospitals in Denmark. This adviser gives guidance to patients about their rights and prospects about compensation. It is said that the Patient Insurance receives considerable co-operation from medical practitioners and hospitals. Cases of adverse patient outcomes are sometimes reported by the latter even before claims have been lodged.[8]

The results of all these developments are quite startling in another way. An analysis of patient claims against hospitals (with their third party liability schemes) before the Danish Patient Insurance Act coming into force shows that an average of about 250 claims were filed in Denmark each year. By comparison, around 2,800 claims were lodged through the Patient Insurance (formerly Patient Insurance Association) in 2001. In fact, as will be seen later in this chapter, there has progressively been a substantial rise in claims during each of the nine years following the scheme's inauguration. The comparatively low total of filed claims (less than 10 per cent of the current annual level) in pre-Act times also shows that compensation was paid in a very limited number of patient injury cases.[9]

Nor was the other aim of the *culpa* principle – to discourage those involved in patient care from repeating medical errors – especially well served before the introduction of the Patient Insurance Act. In Danish law it is the employer (in this case the hospital authority) and not an individual practitioner who is liable, unless an injury is caused with intent or through gross negligence. As hospital authorities insured against such a risk by taking out third party liability insurance cover, it was the insurer who became liable in a claim. It was considered that this was not the kind of arrangement that would encourage erring members of the medical profession to mend their ways.[10]

The Patient Insurance Act 1992 and its aftermath

As a consequence of this state of affairs and a political trend towards establishing a fairer and more far-reaching system of compensation, the country's legislators looked to neighbouring Nordic countries for a suitable model. The aim was also to initiate a scheme that would provide quicker and easier access to damages than that available through existing law. A publicly regulated patient insurance system was the result, following the introduction of the Patient Insurance Act, which came into force on 1 July 1992.[11]

Thus was formed the multi-faceted Patient Insurance Association (now known as the Patient Insurance), a body made up of conventional insurance organizations and self-insuring hospital authorities who, under the rules, are now the insurers themselves. Claims are examined and decided under the guidance of the body's medical and legal experts, and according to the provisions of the Act. Injury caused to a patient as a result of medical negligence or an intentional act, as well as that brought about by accident in certain circumstances, can be compensated. The procedure is such that the onus of proof by a claimant is less strict and in replacing litigation as a first resort, cases are dealt with more quickly. Cases are handled impartially so that claimants have no need to seek external professional advice or assistance. There is also a public appeals body – the Patient Injury Appeals Board – to which all decisions by the Patient Insurance can be referred for judgement.[12]

Generally speaking, and unlike the schemes operating in some other Nordic countries, the Danish Patient Insurance Act 1992 does not cover patient injury resulting from the actions of medical practitioners in general practice. Nor does it apply to treatment provided in private hospitals and clinics. However, following various major and minor amendments to the Act, a number of clinical procedures taken in private health care now come within its scope in certain situations.[13]

In August 1996 a committee was set up by the Ministry of Health to revise the Patient Insurance Act. One of its proposals was to extend the scope of this legislation to include all forms of patient care in both the public and private sectors. The committee calculated that, once implemented, this added cover would increase the overall compensation bill by around 10 per cent, equivalent to between DKK14.5 and DKK15.5 million (£1,355,000 and £1,448,600 at DKK10.7 to £1).[14] Despite this relatively insubstantial extra cost, the recommendations were yet to be passed into law in early 2004.

A major factor in the compass of the Patient Insurance Act is the requirement for a causal connection between patient injury and the medical procedure applied in any given case. Thus the Act is restricted to examination, treatment, other similar action and to accidents that may occur during the course of such procedures. Damage to a patient resulting from an underlying illness is outside the Act's scope. This means, for example, that infections in open fractures are not covered as it is probable that such infections will not have been caused by treatment provided. Similarly, a patient who dies in hospital from a heart condition that is unconnected with the therapy given at the hospital is also not covered.[15]

The requirement that patient injury must be treatment related means that compensation is not payable under the Patient Insurance Act if the therapy provided has not produced the expected and desired result, or if any discomfort remains following such treatment. Importantly, financial redress is available only for any additional impairment as a result of the therapy received.[16]

There is no allowance in the Act for psychological damage to patients. Among other considerations, legislators decided it would be difficult to assess whether patients' disorders were caused by their psychological illness or as a consequence of the therapy provided. The provisions in the legislation also mean that violation of a patient's rights through a medical practitioner failing to obtain informed consent before treatment cannot be regarded as physical damage. Therefore, it does not entitle such a person to compensation under the Act. Damage to a patient's property is also excluded.[17]

Injury to patients caused by pharmaceuticals is covered by the Patient Insurance Act only if damage is also caused by failure in the use of a particular product. Nonetheless, it is also possible to obtain compensation through the Patient Insurance specifically for the adverse side-effects of drugs under the provisions of another act concerning damages for pharmaceutical injuries.[18]

Conditions for awarding compensation

Once the basic requirements relating to causal connection have been met, any injury that has occurred must also meet certain conditions identified elsewhere in the Patient Insurance Act for compensation to be awarded. It was felt that the introduction of a strict liability element about medical treatment would cause practitioners to stop performing types of therapy having known secondary effects – regardless of whether they were necessary to cure a patient's disorder. The side-effects of the various forms of cancer treatment, for instance, would thus become open to claims for compensation by patients.

The provisions for damages, as laid down in the Act, refer to avoidable and unavoidable or accidental adverse outcomes. Avoidable patient injury is covered if an experienced specialist had acted differently, if defects in – or the failure of – medical equipment had not occurred, or if another treatment procedure had been used instead and the injury would probably have been avoided. Unavoidable or accidental impairment is included when it is rare and too severe for a patient to endure.

These conditions for damages are graded and must be evaluated individually and in sequence, even when a case fulfils several of their requirements. Thus, for example, while a case is being considered under the first of these conditions, it cannot be looked at in the light of the other provisions until it has passed through but failed the first test.[19]

Avoidable injury[20]

The 'specialist rule' provision, which also covers injury as a result of diagnosis that is incorrect or too late, is related to the *culpa* principle previously in force. However, the liability has been extended so that any adverse outcome is measured against that which could have been expected from a top Danish specialist in the relevant field of medicine. This high liability benchmark (*optimus vir*) means that, if a patient's health is damaged because the treatment provided has not followed the best specialist practice, compensation will usually follow.

Put another way, the specialist rule assumes that the best possible expertise is available when treatment or examination takes place in the public hospital service, but the facilities available during any therapy are also taken into account. If, for example, a patient's health is impaired owing to limitations in hospital equipment that are the result of a political priority affecting resources, there is no entitlement to compensation.

A 'total result' argument is not applied when evaluating a case. Any assessment is based on whether the best specialist in the applicable field would, in the same circumstances, have provided a different examination or therapy and as a consequence have avoided injury to the patient involved. In fact, all procedures connected with a course of treatment, including initial examination and subsequent patient supervision and control – and also the clinical judgement involved – are subject to the 'specialist rule' standard. But no consideration is given to knowledge or expertise acquired after an adverse outcome has taken place when assessing an entitlement to compensation.

The specialist rule yardstick is also applied to any type of injury resulting from therapy that has deviated from recognized guidelines and so may entitle a patient to compensation. One such example could refer to an operation for a slipped disc where, because a radioscopy has not been carried out, the procedure is performed to a standard suggesting that there is no slipped disc. In this case the patient concerned will be entitled to compensation for the discomfort caused because the clinical procedure had been discharged at an incorrect level and for any prolongation of the period of illness as a result.

Patient injury caused by erroneous diagnosis is a sub-group of the specialist rule, but it differs from impairment caused by other means in that compensation is often paid because of the further development of a patient's underlying disorder. Treatment omissions are invariably the result of a patient's illness being overlooked despite recognizable symptoms. For instance, if a person with symptoms of cancer is not appropriately examined, therapy can be delayed, leading to a less favourable recovery prognosis. An incorrect diagnosis may also result from a mix-up of laboratory samples, leading to unnecessary procedures such as chemotherapy or radiation treatment, for which compensation can also be paid.

Another provision under avoidable injury is the 'equipment rule'. This entitles a patient to compensation for damage caused by defects in or failure of medical equipment used during the course of treatment. It involves not only items such as measuring apparatus and devices used for administering anaesthetics, but also mechanical implants and prostheses, regardless of whether their purpose is to replace or support a patient's own organs. Nonetheless, injury caused by the failure of biological donor organs is not covered by the provision.

The delimitation relating to the specialist rule means that impairment caused by the incorrect use of equipment is covered by another requirement in the Act, whereas injury resulting from a lack of instrument maintenance or failure is assessed in line with still another provision in this legislation. Damage to a patient's health caused in this way can result in compensation, without an extensive investigation into who had been responsible for the maintenance and smooth-running of the equipment in question.

Examples of equipment failure are if a patient dies because of defects in instruments administering anaesthetics or if a patient suffers injuries from breaking crutches or wheelchair failure. In either case the patient concerned is eligible for compensation.

The equipment rule has also been used for injury caused by the use of a certain identified prosthesis cement. This material had been known to crumble, causing cemented prostheses to come loose, thereby involving a second operation. Avoidable injury is also covered under the 'alternative rule'. This is based on a retrospective evaluation that concludes that an injury to a patient could have been avoided if another equivalent treatment or course of action had been used. For the injury to qualify under the alternative rule, it is a condition that the alternative procedure was available at the time. New types of therapy developed later are not considered acceptable alternatives.

The alternative rule offers patients the prospect of obtaining compensation for impairment caused in a situation where one of two recognized treatment procedures had been followed. In this event, it is a proviso that the injury would in all probability have been avoided if the other method had been adopted. The rule's requirement that an alternative treatment or procedure must also have been considered as equivalent to the therapy given at the time has greatly limited its application. It is taken into account only occasionally in the Patient Insurance decisions each year. The rule is most often applied in orthopaedic surgery, where an alternative treatment may simply involve using a different type of securing material, or choosing between such a product being affixed internally or externally.

The alternative rule is also exercised for injury caused or connected with the treatment of certain types of brain tumour, conditions that can sometimes be managed either through surgery, drug treatment or radiotherapy with equally good results. In such a case, a subsequent assessment involving a patient who has suffered serious damage from, say, radiotherapy could show that it would have been better for the person to have received surgery or drug treatment.

Unavoidable injury[21]
The 'endurability rule' comes into play as a kind of catch-all arrangement in the patient insurance system. Its application may be best defined in negative terms: it applies to treatment injury that could not have been avoided under provisions set out in the Patient Insurance Act. That is, the injury could not have been prevented if a more appropriate therapy, superior equipment, or another equivalent form of treatment or procedure had been used.

The central condition for compensation to be payable under the endurability provision is that the severity of an adverse outcome following treatment must exceed the level that a patient could reasonably be expected to endure. In considering this, the relative acuteness of the injury and the risk of its occurring are taken into account. The impairment must be relatively serious – and being a rare outcome – for compensation to be awarded.

In evaluating the relative seriousness of an injury, an assessment is made of the level of its intensity on the one hand and the gravity of the illness that was treated on the other, including the extent of the therapy and the risks connected with it. The result is that because certain brain, heart and cancer disorders can be especially serious, and their treatment more far-reaching and with a correspondingly high risk of side-effects, compensation is not available. The endurability rule is also invariably applied to treatment-related infections, but it is implemented only if an infection, evaluated by total results, exceeds the level at which a patient is not eligible for compensation.

The acuteness of a patient's underlying illness is assessed by total results. This means damage caused by diagnostic examinations, which subsequently show that the patient had been healthy, will normally come under the definition of relative seriousness and be eligible for compensation. Consideration is also given to the 'rarity' aspect of an injury resulting from treatment. The notion behind the application of this criterion is that the higher the risk of its occurring, the greater the need for a patient to take this into account. Accordingly, adverse outcomes, which occur so frequently that they are accepted as a risk by patients who have agreed to be treated, do not qualify for compensation.

When assessing the rarity of an injury resulting from a medical procedure, risk-increasing factors such as obesity, diabetes and other conditions are taken into consideration. The Patient Insurance uses a rule of thumb measure where a clear-cut injury must have occurred in less than 2 to 3 per cent of patients having a similar disorder, and who have undergone the same treatment, in order to meet the rarity criterion.

Progressive increase in the number of claims filed with the Patient Insurance
The number of claims filed with the Patient Insurance has risen annually from 178 in 1992 to 2,832 during 2001 (see Table 17.1).

Table 17.1 Claims filed, 1992 to 2001

	1992	1993	1994	1995	1996	1997	1998	1999	2000	2001
Total	178	840	1,269	1,658	2,111	2,573	2,405	2,790	2,798	2,832

Source: Patientforsikringen, 2002[22]

In 2001 the Patient Insurance made 2,559 decisions (including those about claims outside the scope of the scheme) in line with the provisions of the Patient Insurance Act.[23] Out of that total, 1,144 patients (45.8 per cent) were entitled to compensation. Statistics of the number of claims paid and reasons for doing so from 1999 to 2001 are shown in tables 17.2a and 17.2b. Figures of the number of claimants not entitled to compensation and outside the scope of the Patient Insurance from 1999 to 2001 are shown in tables 17.3a and 17.3b. (Note: there is a minor, unresolved, discrepancy between the total number of decisions taken by the Patient Insurance in 2001 and the associated aggregate figures shown for the same year in tables 17.2a and 17.3a.)

Table 17.2a Claims paid and reasons for doing so, 1999 to 2001

Decision type[a]	1999	2000	2001
s. 2(1), no. 1 (specialist standard)	415	438	493
s. 2(1), no. 2 (equipment failure)	240	155	34
s. 2(1), no. 3 (alternative technique method)	15	10	22
s. 2(1), no. 4 (reasonability rule)	372	424	500
s. 3(2) (accidents)	11	10	15
s. 4(1) (donors and subjects)	72	95	80
Total	1,125	1,132	1,144

Source: Patientforsikringen, 2002–[24]
[a] With reference to the relevant section of the Patient Insurance Act 1992.

Table 17.2b Percentage of claims paid and those entitled to compensation, 1999 to 2001

Decision type[a]	1999 Total	Comp.	2000 Total	Comp.	2001 Total	Comp.
s. 2(1), no. 1 (specialist standard)	36.9	16.4	38.7	17.5	43.1	19.7
s. 2(1), no. 2 (equipment failure)	21.3	9.5	13.7	6.2	3.0	1.4
s. 2(1), no. 3 (alternative technique method)	1.3	0.6	0.9	0.4	1.9	0.9
s. 2(1), no. 4 (reasonability rule)	33.1	14.7	37.4	16.9	43.7	20.0
s. 3(2) (accidents)	1.0	0.4	0.9	0.4	1.3	0.6
s. 4(1) (donors and subjects)	6.4	2.8	8.4	3.8	7.0	3.2
Total	100	44.4	100	45.2	100	45.8

Source: Patientforsikringen, 2002[24]
[a] With reference to the relevant section of the Patient Insurance Act 1992.

Table 17.3a Claimants not entitled to compensation and outside the scope of the Patient Insurance, 1999 to 2001

	1999	2000	2001
Not entitled to compensation	1,034	1,080	1,065
Outside the scope of the Patient Insurance	290	296	292

Source: Patientforsikringen, 2002[25]

Table 17.3b Percentage of claimants not entitled to compensation and outside the scope of the Patient Insurance, 1999 to 2001

	1999	2000	2001
Not entitled to compensation	44.1	43	42.6
Outside the scope of the Patient Insurance	11.5	11.8	11.6

Source: Patientforsikringen, 2002[25]

Table 17.4 shows how compensation payments have progressively increased from 1 July 1992 to 31 December 2001. In 2001 the total sum awarded – excluding interest – was around DKK205.6 million (£19,214,000 at DKK10.7 to £1).

Table 17.4 Compensation payments, 1992 to 2001[a]

	1992	1993	1994	1995	1996	1997	1998	1999	2000	2001	Total paid
Amount (DKK million)[b]	0.0	5.7	21.8	65.3	83.5	101.0	114.1	127.8	130.0	205.6	854.8

Source: Patientforsikringen, 2002[26]
[a] The population of Denmark in 2004 is about 5.3 million.
[b] Excluding interest.

The corresponding year on year rise in the number of claims received and dealt with has led to escalating administration costs within the Patient Insurance and the Patient Injury Appeals Board. In 1999 this had reached around DKK33.5 million (about £3,131,000). By the end of 2001, the total bill had risen to DKK42.3 million (£3,953,000) for the year.[27]

The Danish Patient Insurance Act contains especially lenient conditions when it comes to paying out damages to donors and healthy subjects (people participating in scientific research). The view is that people who voluntarily help others in this way deserve preferential access to compensation. Injury caused by an accident connected with a patient's treatment and stay in hospital that was not a result of the therapy itself is also covered by the Act. However, in such an event, the assessment of liability is made on the basis of the general liability rule (the *culpa* principle) in Danish law. Accordingly, the right to damages requires that the fault lies with the hospital.[28]

Decisions by the Patient Insurance can be appealed against with the Patient Injury Appeals Board, but appeals must be made within three months of the decision. The Board is a public appeals mechanism, the chairperson of which is a qualified judge. The other members comprise doctors, consumer representatives and those acting for the insured parties. Judgements reached by the Board can, in turn, be appealed against in the High Court within six months of the decision. Under Denmark's act concerning liability in personal injury cases compensation involving all such categories are set at identical levels.[29]

No case for compensation can go to litigation until the Patient Insurance and the Patient Injury Appeals Board have examined the matter and made their decisions. The current average time for a claim to be processed is around seven months, with the complete procedure including paying out compensation usually taking between three and 18 months. It can take several years before a final resolution is reached in complex cases.[30]

Compensation to patients applies only to injury sustained on or after 1 July 1992, the date on which the Patient Insurance Act came into force. Another condition of entitlement (up to 2002) was that the total amount of damages must exceed DKK10,000 (about £935).[31] Table 17.2 shows that in 2001 about 46 per cent of claimants qualified for compensation, but as already stated the true proportion compensated was in excess of 50 per cent, if those cases found to be outside the scope of the Patient Insurance (Table 17.3) are subtracted from the total considered. Indeed, this seemingly rosy picture – from a claimant's perspective – remained much the same for each of the three years between 1999 and 2001.

Conclusion
The principal object of the patient insurance scheme – to provide patient access to compensation for injury caused from medical intervention – seems to have been met since the introduction of Denmark's Patient Insurance Act in 1992. Since then the number of claims has reached a level that has resulted in compensation being paid to more than ten times as many patients as was the case before the Act's inception.[32]

In practice, this works out at one in every two claims being paid, a ratio that seems surprisingly high from any perspective. It could be that the role of the legally led Patient Injuries Appeals Board as a public appeals agency has some significance here. It can't be a bad thing that on average it takes not much more than a few months for compensation to be paid to those who are eligible. (Oh, that the same could be said for the litigation way.)

The initial concerns of Danish politicians, that the costs of a patient insurance scheme such as the one in place would spiral out of control, are now seen to have been groundless. At 0.3 per cent of Denmark's total hospital expenditure[33] it would be difficult to disagree. Denmark's politicians now consider this to be a modest price to pay for greater patient security and the eradication of much of the criticism previously levelled at health care providers and medical practitioners. One question remains to be asked of them: When will the privileges of their insurance and compensation creation be extended to cover the patients of medical practitioners in general practice and those in much of private health care? The answer could be: It's on the horizon.

CHAPTER 18

Patients' legal protection and redress made easy

It is no exaggeration to say that the Finnish system and other Nordic schemes have elements which can be made use of by those who work to develop patients' legal protection within the European Union and, perhaps, even further away.

Martti Mikkonen, Director of Finland's Patient Insurance Centre

The Finns have had a patient compensation system in place for more than half a generation – the Patient Injuries Act was passed in July 1986 and came into force on 1 May 1987. Before this, claims for damages went to litigation and were judged on standard culpability principles. One of the contributing factors to the drafting of the new legislation was the Swedish patient compensation model established in 1975, but the catalyst for and crucial step in the process of change was a report on the issue by Finland's national health services' legal protection committee in 1982.

Other milestones along the road to the Act were the launching of voluntary patient insurance in the private health sector in 1983 and the setting up of the Patient Injuries Board the following year. The voluntary arrangement did not attract sufficient political and commercial unanimity, so it was decided to legislate. With the benefit of hindsight, this move was the most appropriate initiative to have taken to clear the impasse.

The primary aim of the Patient Injuries Act 1986 in its original form was to improve legal safeguards for patients. Another key objective was to withdraw from fault liability as a prerequisite for compensation. But this did not mean that all adverse outcomes following health care or treatment would be compensated; certain categories were left out of the scope of the patient insurance mechanism. This still holds true despite subsequent changes – especially the main amendments among those added in May 1999 – to the original legislation.

Key alterations to the original act[1]

Some of these major adjustments concern compensation for infection injury, unreasonably grave consequences and re-imbursement procedures between insurers. In the latter case, the amended Act allows employment accident and motor insurers, for example, to reimburse directly from patient insurance. The lesser changes to the legislation cover matters involving patient damage following treatment and the statute of limitation. Now, claims for compensation must be made no later than ten years from the date of the health care procedure that led to a patient's injury.

Abandoning the culpability thinking mode in 1987 meant that no blame would be attached to health care professionals and no culprits looked for, since negligence was no longer the criterion for compensation. It was thought that such a move would improve relations among staff and result in greater transparency in their dealings with the community. Moreover, clinicians could focus on their job of treating patients without the fear of litigation.

Loosely, the patient insurance system can be described as an arrangement in between no-fault and malpractice schemes or, perhaps, a combination of the two procedures. This applies especially to treatment injury, an outcome that is assessed in terms of the professional standard of the clinical staff and the adequacy of the treatment in a given situation. For instance, although a clinician is not blamed, the chosen method of treatment and the level of professional performance demonstrated are evaluated.

Where compensation for injury resulting from infection was founded on 'avoidability' in the original legislation, the new law bases this on 'patient tolerance'. The criteria to determine what a patient can tolerate are varied. Was an infection foreseeable? What was the level of injury caused by it? Or what measures were taken to treat the infection? The nature and severity of the original illness or injury that was diagnosed or treated, and the patient's general health, are other considerations.

Case by case judgements are made in order to determine whether an infection injury should have been predicted. The assessments are based on a risk factor of anything above 2 per cent being foreseeable, but considerations such as a patient's illness or injury, or previous operations, are taken into account. Radiation treatment, existing unstable diabetes or other elements that can affect the immune system are also looked at. The amended act no longer considers the origin of an infection to be a basis for compensation, although the time of its occurrence continues to be a determining factor when making awards.

The most acute distinction between the original legislation and the amended one is that compensation for rare and severe infection complications is now more frequently awarded. For instance, infections caused by multi-resistant microbes are more likely to be taken account of, because the consequences are usually severe. Nonetheless, no matter how serious the outcome, the mere severity of an infection is not sufficient justification for compensation if the risks were known beforehand. Moreover, the amended legislation has taken common and minor infections – an infected superficial wound for example – out of the reach of compensation.

There are other changes too. Previously, consideration of unreasonably grave consequences was given only to diagnostic procedures, whereas now it applies to all medical treatment. The prerequisite for compensation is that a patient has suffered a permanent severe illness, injury or loss of life. Furthermore, the outcome must be unreasonable when assessed under the same criteria used for infection injury.

Some fundamental rules are applied in deciding if and how much compensation is to be paid. Any decision about damages can be made only after a disability has been calculated as being permanent. In doing so, Finland's Ministry of Social Affairs and Health classification from 1 to 20 is used to establish the level of disability. Here, class 1 corresponds with 5 per cent and classes 7 to 8 to between 35 and 40 per cent (or severe) disability, respectively.

Although there is no change to the requirement of causal connection between treatment and injury, the law now specifically identifies certain criteria that were previously open to interpretation. For example, the standard of treatment is more precisely defined. When considering whether an outcome could have been avoided, the evaluation is based on the competence of the experienced medical practitioner involved, but top specialist skills are not presumed in the appraisal.

For instance, this high competence benchmark is not applied where a doctor's treatment or examination is centred only on diagnosing an illness, or finding out whether a disorder requires specialist care or examination. Further information received later on any aspect of such an episode will not affect an assessment of whether an experienced practitioner would have acted differently in the circumstances. Nor is compensation affected by disparities between various schools of medicine. In evaluating avoidability, attention is paid to available resources. Experienced professionals are expected to maintain their skills and acquire expertise to carry out new methods of treatment and they are expected to act in an appropriately professional way in all situations.

Provisions of the Patient Injuries Act 1986 and their implementation

The provisions of the Patient Injuries Act 1986 and those in the amended legislation lay down the rules for insurance covering patient injury following health care and treatment in Finland. Similarly, the Act applies to the delivery of prescription drugs. Patient insurance also includes blood, tissue and organ donors and 'healthy persons' (members of the public) voluntarily being examined for purposes serving medical research.[2]

Under the Act, all health and medical care providers must be covered by insurance against liability arising out of their actions. The areas of patient care include hospital treatment, visits to GPs and dentists, eye operations, public health services, medical transportation, sampling, vaccination, blood donation, rehabilitation and physiotherapy. The Act also applies to the actions of public health care professionals and to practice at units within the State health services system.[3]

In certain cases, the law is similarly applied to establishments outside the public sector health care system. A good example of this is where there is a contract between, say, a municipality and a private organization for the provision of home medical care services. This type of service provider is obliged to take out appropriate insurance cover if medical professionals are involved in its work.[4]

Bodily injury, as defined by the Act, refers to any illness, injury or other permanent or temporary weakening of health, or death. However, insurance cover does not include all adverse outcomes following health or medical care. Liability applies only to bodily injury that is likely to have resulted from treatment, and provided that certain criteria are also met. One example of this can refer to aspects of 'treatment injury' where an adverse outcome has occurred from a patient's examination, treatment or other similar action taken or neglected.[5]

The patient insurance scheme will cover such an eventuality only if another experienced medical practitioner would have examined, treated or taken action in another way that probably would have avoided the unfavourable result. But it does not cover cases where, owing to the nature of an illness or injury, it may not have been possible to achieve a good outcome despite the action taken being at a level expected of an experienced professional. Similarly, unavoidable consequences of properly discharged examinations or treatment are not covered, unless the results are unreasonable.[6]

Compensation is paid for equipment-related injury caused by a defect in equipment used in surgery, examination, patient monitoring and other procedures. Damages are also payable for infection received if it originates from an examination, treatment or similar action. Where previously avoidability was a factor, the new law focuses on a patient's tolerance of an injury from infection as a basis for compensation. Therefore an infection qualifies for compensation only if it is more acute than that which a patient can be expected to endure. Nonetheless, the predictability of the infection, the severity of the injury experienced, the nature of the disease or impairment that was being treated and the patient's overall health are all taken into account.[7]

The scope of the Patient Injuries Act extends to other areas that are directly or indirectly part of health care where patients are eligible for compensation. These include incidents where injury has occurred by accident from an examination, treatment or other similar procedure, or from a mishap arising during medical transportation. Injuries received from fire or other similar damage to premises where a patient is being treated, or to the equipment being used for the therapy provided, also qualify.[8]

In addition, compensation is payable when damage to a patient's health has occurred because the wrong prescription drug has been dispensed by a chemist and when a patient suffers injury as a result of medicines that have been unlawfully supplied.[9] But damage caused by pharmaceutical products, correctly prescribed or dispensed, are not covered by patient insurance under the Act. These cases are handled separately and are the domain of the Finnish Pharmaceuticals Insurance Pool.[10] (The issue is described later in this chapter.)

The Patient Injuries Act also covers permanent illness or injury, or the death of a patient caused by examination, treatment or other similar action. In such cases, the outcome and its severity must be considered to be unreasonable when compared with the nature or frequency of the medical condition that was treated, the patient's overall health and the risks involved. As previously stated, a severe outcome is one that falls under classifications 7, 8 or higher in the Ministry of Social Affairs and Health scale of disabilities and handicaps. Only when this criterion has been satisfied, and the permanency of the outcome established, is it possible to judge whether the outcome is unreasonable.[11]

Patient insurance covers medical treatment expenses, other costs arising from an adverse outcome and loss of income or maintenance. It also includes pain and suffering, permanent functional defect or permanent cosmetic damage. If a patient dies, the insurance covers funeral expenses at a reasonable level and a pension for any survivors, assuming such a death has left the latter without an income. Those entitled to a survivor's pension include a widow, widower, minors and anyone under 21 years old who is still receiving formal education.[12]

Compensation for bodily injuries caused by health or medical treatment is paid according to the level of fees charged for such therapy in the public health service. The amount can be adjusted if there are sound medical reasons to consult private health care providers. However, as already explained, patient insurance does not cover minor injury. In 1999 this was defined as incidents involving compensation of less than 1,000 Finnish marks (€167 or £111 at €1.5 to £1). The level is upgraded each year. Any benefits or compensation payable under other laws are deducted from those received from patient insurance.[13]

The Patient Insurance Centre is responsible for all claims handling irrespective of who the insurer is or whether or not the liable party is covered by an in-force patient insurance policy. The claiming process is simple and normally requires no involvement by a lawyer from outside. This is put down to the fact that all health care establishments in Finland have a patients' representative (patient ombudsman) who gives guidance to claimants seeking financial redress.[14]

Claims for compensation are submitted to the Patient Insurance Centre and must be made within three years of the date from which a claimant learned, or should have known, about an injury received. But, if there is a good reason for doing so, compensation can be claimed beyond the deadline up to a maximum of ten years. Decisions by the Centre are given and guidance on how an appeal can be lodged against its judgements. For example, a dissatisfied claimant can ask for a review and if there is sufficient new evidence to support it the case is looked at again. The Centre currently includes twelve member insurers, and is also responsible for paying compensation claims.[15]

A claimant or health care provider who is dissatisfied with a decision by the Patient Insurance Centre can ask the government-appointed Patient Injuries Board to examine the case and provide a written statement. The Board makes no charge for this work and although it only puts forward recommendations the Centre will always accept its opinion. Claimants have the further option of taking a disputed claim to court, in which case standard civil procedure is followed. Local court decisions can be appealed against in the Court of Appeal and ultimately in the Supreme Court, if leave to do so is granted.[16] From 1987 to 1999 the Patient Insurance Centre was sued by an average of 20 claimants a year.[17]

The main compensation route and how it works in practice

In practice the most commonly used avenue for redress is the Patient Injuries Board.[18] This body is appointed by the government for three years at a time and comprises eight members and 16 deputy members, each of whom is proficient in health care affairs. The chairman and vice-chairmen are required to have a masters law degree and at least two of them will have expertise in matters relating to personal injury compensation. The chairman must also have been a judge. Two of the members are specialist doctors and at least one other is a non-medical health care professional. Deputy members have similar credentials.[19]

Members of the Patient Injuries Board and others working for it are responsible for the legality of their actions. The Board's duties include making recommendations about decisions on individual claims at the request of claimants, the Patient Insurance Centre or any health or medical care provider. Similar action by the Board can follow an application from an insurer who is claiming separation of compensation under the Patient Injuries Act. This refers to compensation provided for by other legislation (described later in this chapter) that the insurer has already paid a claimant. When requested, the Board will also issue statements on compensation claims that are being processed in court.[20]

In cases involving certain criteria for determining permanent disability benefits or survivors' pension, claims must first pass through the Patient Injuries Board before the Patient Insurance Centre can make a final decision on them. Should the latter arrive at a decision that differs from the Board's recommendation to the detriment of a claimant, it must attach this advice to its decision.[21] One of the Board's key roles is to harmonize compensation practice in its application to patient injuries and, where required, give general advice to policyholders on claims procedure under the Act. The National Authority for Medicolegal Affairs and the provincial state offices are obliged to assist the Patient Injuries Board in its duties.[22]

Until 2000 the Patient Injuries Board was reviewing between 800 and 1,000 claims annually, nearly 20 per cent of which were resolved in favour of claimants.[23]

The number of actual claims received by the Patient Insurance Centre has risen yearly – a trend that is attributed to an increased awareness resulting from the patients' representative scheme[24] (tables 18.1 and 18.2). Table 18.1 shows the number of annual claims to the Patient Insurance Centre by age group from 1997 to 2000.

Table 18.1 Claims notified to the Patient Insurance Centre by age group, 1997 to 2000

	1997	1998	1999	2000	Total
Age (years)					
Under 1	116	107	163	1,053	1,439
1–9	148	129	127	100	504
10–19	241	242	277	222	982
20–29	530	544	614	499	2,187
30–39	892	856	957	756	3,461
40–49	1,258	1,307	1,256	1,065	4,886
Subtotal, ages 1–49	3,185	3,185	3,394	3,695	13,459
50–64	1,804	1,757	1,990	1,792	7,280
65–74	1,092	1,060	1,080	949	4,181
75–84	588	569	614	525	2,296
85 and over	137	115	137	117	506
Subtotal, ages 50 and over	3,621	3,501	3,821	3,320	14,263
Total	6,806	6,686	7,215	7,015	27,722

Source: Potalusvakuutus (Patient Insurance)[25]

Table 18.2 Claims notified to the Patient Insurance Centre, 1987 to 2000

1987	1988	1989	1990	1991	1992	1993	1994	1995	1996	1997	1998	1999	2000
1,084	2,638	3,107	3,410	4,227	5,168	6,084	6,498	6,973	6,620	6,806	6,686	7,215	7,015

Source: Potalusvakuutus (Patient Insurance)[26]

The Patient Insurance Centre has confirmed that during the period 1987 to 2000 about every third patient insurance claim is paid (Table 18.2). More than two-thirds of these claims covered injury from treatment and a quarter injury from infection. Nearly every second rejected claim was denied on the grounds that injury had been unavoidable. Claims were also rejected in cases where causal connection had not been established. In other instances they were turned down because compensation had been claimed for situations where appropriate care had not delivered the desired outcome.[27]

In 1999 the Patient Insurance Centre paid claims of €15.6 million (about £10,400,000 at €1.5 to £1), of which 91 per cent involved the public sector. Administration costs absorbed €2.9 million (about £1,933,000). The overall total amount of claims paid under patient insurance between 1987 and 1999 was €108.3 million (£72.2 million). In addition to this, the amount reserved for pensions and other benefits due for patient injury was €87.3 million (£58,200,000) for the 13-year period.

Patient insurance premiums written in 1999 were valued at €28.1 million (about £18,733,000), made up of €26.1 million (about £17,400,000) and €2 million (about £1,333,000) from the public and private sectors, respectively.[28]

The scope of the patient insurance scheme

The patient insurance scheme is a non-profit mechanism operating on the principle that the premiums paid by public sector providers equal the total of claims paid plus the cost of administration. A positive spin-off is said to be emerging from the information contained in decisions by the Patient Insurance Centre on accepted claims. This data is being analyzed as part of an ongoing plan of action to enhance quality assurance in health and medical care, and help reduce the incidence of accidents and negligence.[29]

Like the public sector, the patient insurance scheme is compulsory for independent health care professionals who are registered with the National Authority for Medicolegal Affairs and for businesses engaged in health and medical treatment whose practitioners are listed with the Authority. Organizations providing private medical transportation services and pharmacies dispensing prescription drugs must also be covered by the patient insurance system. Failure to insure under the Act will involve an increased premium for the uninsured period. Although, theoretically, this penalty can be up to ten times the standard rate, in reality the charge is three times greater, providing damage to patient health has not occurred. Where this has happened, the premium is raised six-fold by the Patient Insurance Centre. Individuals and businesses engaged in alternative health care are not obliged to be part of the scheme. Their services are covered by professional liability insurance.[30]

All (public-sector) insurance policies for provincial hospital districts and the state are supplied by the Patient Insurance Pool. This covers health and medical care provided by institutions such as hospitals, health centres, nursing homes for the elderly, the fire service and educational establishments specializing in health care. Independent practitioners, institutions and businesses can take out patient cover with other insurers. Private doctors, physiotherapists and other professionals practising as a group under a company title are covered by policies issued in its name. In such cases, with the exception of dentists, there is no need for insurance cover by their respective medical unions.[31]

As previously indicated, under the provisions of the Patient Injuries Act, money collected in insurance premiums from those involved in public and private health care is used for patient compensation and benefits. The size of premiums depends on the risks involved and the latter are classified accordingly. Payments by independent practitioners are set in line with the premium rating criteria applied by individual insurers and usually take the form of a fixed sum. Premiums paid by private businesses and institutions are calculated on the basis of the total payroll.[32]

Insurance for defective pharmaceutical products and the side-effects of dispensed medicines[33]

It has already been stated that damage to patients' health caused by pharmaceutical treatment where medicines have been wrongly prescribed or dispensed is covered by the Patient Injuries Act. However, compensation for injury caused by defective pharmaceutical products is paid under 'pharmaceutical insurance' through the

Finnish Pharmaceuticals Insurance Pool. The same applies to damage caused from the side-effects of dispensed medical preparations where, for example, a patient's allergy is not known.

Pharmaceutical insurance covers:

- medical preparations referred to in the Medicines Act 1987, including blood and blood products used in therapy; all producers, importers and others dealing in pharmaceuticals who are members of the Finnish Co-operative for the Indemnification of Medicines-related Injuries are covered by this class of insurance
- organizations involved in clinical research that are operating under guidelines set by the National Agency for Medicines
- physical diseases or injuries and equivalent mental disorders caused by pharmaceuticals sold or delivered in Finland, including medical expenses and compensation for loss of income or maintenance, pain and suffering, permanent functional defect and permanent cosmetic disfigurement.

It does not cover:

- adverse clinical outcomes that are regarded as being reasonably tolerable and the detrimental consequences of risk-taking procedures considered necessary because of the nature or severity of an illness that has been treated
- injury resulting from the misuse of pharmaceutical products or from some other erroneous action
- treatment from drugs that do not have the expected effect
- costs arising from injury suffered if the amount involved is less than €835 (about £557 at €1.5 to £1) – the minimum amount payable up to 2002.

Claimants are required to contact the Finnish Pharmaceutical Insurance Pool within three years from the date when an injury first became apparent. Every decision made on claims is accompanied by guidance on the alternatives that are open to claimants should they object to the judgement that was reached. In exceptional circumstances compensation can be claimed beyond this deadline but in no more than ten years from the event that led to the injury.

Jurisdiction of the Patient Insurance Centre and how it operates

All organizations writing patient insurance in Finland must be members of the Finnish Patient Insurance Centre. A twelve-member body (in 2002), the Centre is overseen by the Insurance Supervision Authority. The Centre pays compensation in cases where no insurance has been taken out by a health provider and settles claims made to any Finnish insurer that has gone into liquidation, once the company's portfolio and equivalent assets have been transferred to the Centre. In association with the Insurance Supervision Authority, the Centre will also honour claims involving insurers who have closed down but were based elsewhere in the European Union. Effectively, any claimant entitlement from assets in any of these cases is transferred to the Patient Insurance Centre.[34]

Where a claimant does not receive the full compensation due, because an insurer has gone into liquidation or become bankrupt, the policyholder is obliged to pay an additional patient insurance premium. (This does not apply to comparatively small-scale policyholders.) In cases like this, the shortfall is paid jointly by all the insurers involved in patient insurance. The deficit is funded by an annual joint guarantee charge imposed on all these insurance companies. The increased costs that result from this are covered by raising future premiums.[35]

The joint guarantee charge is assessed as a proportion of the value of premiums written – or estimated to be written – by each insurer. The charge is no higher than 2 per cent per annum of the premiums, written or estimated, and must be paid by the due date. Failure to do so results in accrued interest at the rate laid down in the Interest Payment Act 1982. Unpaid joint guarantee charges and accrued interest are collected via debt recovery procedures, without court judgement, in line with the provisions contained in existing legislation.[36]

The Patient Insurance Centre is entitled to receive information from any source considered to be relevant when assessing liability in compensation claims free of charge. This is even when it concerns matters about secrecy or disclosure of personal data otherwise protected by legislation. The right to information also exists if the Centre is faced with the bankruptcy or liquidation of an insurer.[37]

Insurers must notify the Insurance Supervision Authority about the general and special terms and conditions regarding patient insurance one month before they become effective. The Authority can also ask an insurer for a statement detailing the criteria being used to decide the level of insurance premiums and for copies of the documents issued to policyholders. The premiums paid for patient insurance are rated to ensure that the interests of policyholders are safeguarded. Nonetheless, they are required to be in reasonable proportion to the costs arising from the policies that have been underwritten. Regulations by the Insurance Supervision Authority ensure that risks are classified for the purpose of compiling statistics about policies concluded and claims paid. Insurers are obliged to produce all surveys and calculations in a prescribed form.[38]

Where an insurer refuses to issue a patient insurance policy, the Patient Insurance Centre cannot also decline to do so. Policyholders are entitled to terminate a current policy in order to transfer to another insurer. Notice to do so must be given in writing and evidence that a replacement policy has been taken out. Entitlement to compensation for medical and other expenses arising from injury, pain and suffering, defect or other permanent damage under the Act is not dependent on whether a claimant qualifies for redress or benefits on any other grounds because of the same injury.[39]

Compensation for partial loss of income or maintenance or loss of adequate income is paid only to the extent that it exceeds what is payable under another law. However, the Patient Insurance Centre will pay the portion of compensation due under other legislation if a claimant's maintenance is likely to be jeopardized. Any payment to a claimant under another law, or any compensation due in the future from an accepted claim, is deducted from the amount payable under the Patient Injuries Act.[40]

If a claimant is due compensation or benefits because of injury defined under separate legislation, the right to this recompense is transferred to the Patient Insurance Centre – up to the amount already paid out by them. But if a claimant qualifies for compensation or benefits under the Act on the services and aid provided because of disability, such entitlements cannot be made over to the Centre. Where a patient is entitled to compensation from the party who caused an injury or from their employer, the right to this redress is transferred to the party who paid compensation under the Act only if an injury has been caused wilfully or through gross negligence.[41]

Any insurer who has paid compensation for medical or other expenses, reduced income or maintenance, pain or suffering, defect or permanent injury under the Motor Liability Act, the Occupational Accidents Act or the Military Injuries Act is entitled to recover the amount that the injured party would evidently have qualified for under the Patient Injuries Act. As defined in the Insurance Contracts Act, an insurer who has paid compensation to cover medical expenses under a voluntary insurance policy is similarly entitled to recover the portion of compensation that an injured party would have been eligible for under the Patient Injuries Act.[42]

Where compensation due is delayed, the Patient Insurance Centre will pay the overdue amount plus interest allowed for in the Interest Payments Act to cover the period of delay. (This obligation may not apply in certain other situations.) The extra amount is calculated for each day of the delay, but not for the three months following the end of the calendar month in which an injured party made a claim. Up to 2002, any such added settlement of less than €4 (this amount is revised annually) is not paid.[43]

If payment of compensation on time has been unjustifiably delayed by a claimant's actions, the Patient Insurance Centre is not liable to pay any increased amount that reflects a period longer than from the date the hold-up ended. Delays identified in legislative provisions, or those caused by the suspension of relevant public services or other *force majeure* are treated in the same way.[44]

The activities of the Patient Injuries Board are governed by the Insurance Supervision Authority. Its budget is determined annually by the Authority and is financed out of Patient Insurance Centre funds. The Board is entitled to receive, free of charge, any information required for an investigation from public authorities, health and medical care providers or any other relevant sources. A statutory obligation to secrecy is imposed on members, employees and those who are contracted as special advisers both to the Patient Insurance Centre and Patient Injuries Board.[45]

Conclusion

In the concluding piece of his lecture to the 13th World Congress on Medical Law in August 2000, Martti Mikkonen, Director of Finland's Patient Insurance Centre, had this to say about the 'Finnish experience of the Patient Injuries Act in practice'.

Has the law met its targets? Is the system now functioning?

The patient's legal protection has improved a great deal. When the guilt thinking was abandoned, the claims process was simplified and some 2,000 persons' claims are now accepted every year. The cases are investigated with the attending doctors in an open approach and without concealing any relevant facts.

Litigation cases are few and they usually involve the Patient Insurance Centre. Suing individual health care providers for damages has practically ended.

What is important for the policyholders is that the level of damages has been kept within limits generally approved in Finnish tort law. In this setting, we have managed to avoid, at least so far, the negative effects of the American disease.

The different parties to the patient insurance scheme, patients, professional personnel and policyholders are all agreed that the system is a well-functioning arrangement which has gained an established position as an integral part of Finnish welfare. The price paid for the system is low – only €3.4 per every Finn.

It is no exaggeration to say that the Finnish system and other Nordic schemes have elements which can be made use of by those who work to develop patients' legal protection within the European Union, and perhaps even further away.

This summing-up of the patient compensation system in Finland in the wake of the Patient Injuries Act 1986 seems to be borne out by the facts uncovered elsewhere in this chapter. The evidence thus far also appears to confirm the point highlighted about the Danish parallel, that it is possible to manage a patient insurance scheme at low cost – and pay a high proportion of claims into the bargain. The ratio of those paid in Finland may be somewhat lower than that recorded for a couple of other Nordic countries, but at one out of every three claims received it still seems to be comparatively high.

Checks, balances and other key features built into Finland's patient insurance and compensation mechanism are likely to be supporting reasons for its success. It cannot be a bad thing for dissatisfied claimants to be able to get a second opinion that has a good chance of overturning earlier decisions made against them. This happens in 20 per cent of cases that are referred to the Patient Injuries Board – not a prospect to be sniffed at by those with a mind to pursue their claims further.

CHAPTER 19

The rising tide of 'no-fault' schemes

Iceland has joined the cast, with Austria playing a supporting role

Lawyers from the outside don't get much of a look-in in the three other Nordic countries when it comes to claiming damages because of injury from health care. As in Denmark and Finland, the statutory patient compensation schemes introduced in Sweden, Norway and, lately, Iceland all but bar lawyers from being involved. Indeed, the risk of having to pay legal and court fees is non-existent – unless a claimant decides to go to litigation, which is generally an unusual course of action.

There are other advantages. The likelihood of claims through statutory patient compensation schemes being successful appears to be greater than those pursued through litigation. Claims are generally settled more efficiently and speedily via alternative compensation procedures, which have mostly replaced the civil form. On the relatively few occasions that external lawyers and litigation are involved in claims in the Nordic countries, the claimants they represent must usually foot the bill for legal services rendered.

The now mature, no-fault schemes developed in Sweden and Norway seem to be further testimony to their broad approval by the public over litigation, and Iceland converted to the no-fault compensation model in 2001. For its part Austria has adopted a supplementary system that is similar to the Nordic schemes and operates alongside the existing and well-established, although somewhat different, alternative compensation mechanism for patients.

Sweden

Sweden, the prime mover in patient insurance and compensation in their most radical forms, made its debut in no-fault compensation a generation ago. In 1975 the country's first Patient Insurance Act came into force to launch the original model of its patient insurance and compensation mechanism, still known as Patientförsäkringen (PSF). The primary purpose of the innovative new scheme was to make it easier for patients to obtain recompense for injury sustained following health care or treatment given to them.

In 1997 PSF changed from being a voluntary insurance scheme, based on an arrangement between health care providers and the State, to being a statutory compulsory mechanism involving the health service as a whole. The result has been a substantial rise in the number of compensation awards to patients. To put the point in perspective, the total figure for claims paid in 2002 was some 200 times greater than before 1975. The average then was a mere ten cases a year where compensation had been granted; in 2002 around 50 per cent of all cases led to a financial settlement being awarded.[1]

The level of patient compensation is determined according to the personal injury rules of Sweden's existing Tort Damages Act. It covers economic losses, including that of income and costs arising as a result of injury sustained following health care. Non-economic losses such as temporary or permanent pain and suffering are also covered, but compensation is due only once a causal connection between an injury suffered and the health care provided has been established. The crucial factors are whether damage to the patient could have been avoided and that the adverse outcome is not regarded as being normal in the circumstances.[2]

As in other Nordic countries, compensation awarded via Sweden's no-fault procedure is unconnected with any decision made about failure or otherwise by medical staff. Claimants are not required to prove who is to blame.[3] These issues are kept separate and are the jurisdiction of the Medical Responsibility Board (HSAN), an entirely different and unattached regulatory body overseeing complaints concerning health care and medical practitioners.

Similar compensation rules apply to patient injury caused by the side-effects of drugs. In this case, claims for financial redress are the responsibility of the pharmaceutical companies concerned who will have taken out insurance cover for the purpose. However, damage to patients caused as a result of the prescription or administration of drugs outside these regulations and guidelines is covered by insurance protection through Patientförsäkringen.[4]

Where there is dissatisfaction with a decision about compensation, patients or claimants can ask the Patient Claims Panel to intercede. The Panel is an advisory body, which makes recommendations in compensation cases referred to it by patients, health care providers, insurers or a court under the Patient Injury Act 1996, which came into force in July 1997. Until 2002 insurers always accepted what the Panel had proposed they should do and it would appear that the situation remains unchanged in 2004.[5]

The Panel consists of a chairperson, who is a judge by profession, and six other members representing the various interests in patient compensation cases. The services of this body are cost-free to patients who are given the opportunity of having their cases professionally examined before they may consider court proceedings. In 2002 the Panel's conclusions differed from those of the insurers in about 10 per cent of cases.[6]

Patients who are dissatisfied with the Panel's recommendations or an insurer's final decision are at liberty to take civil action in pursuit of their claim for damages. As with the procedures in other countries, litigation in Sweden is a difficult and risky business. Proof must be established that malpractice or neglect of any kind related to a patient's injury has occurred. Furthermore, in the event of an unsuccessful court action claimants face the added prospect of having to pay the legal costs of the defence. Despite these risks, the message from Sweden seems to be that there is an increasing tendency by patients to sue medical practitioners and health care providers.

The payment of patient compensation is unaffected in the few cases where health care establishments may not have taken out insurance cover and are consequently unable to meet the cost of claims. In these circumstances, the Swedish Patient Insurance Association will step in to compensate patients and then claim the amount paid from the hospital or whichever other provider is involved.[7]

Patientförsäkringen, Sweden's patient compensation system, includes a special analysis group, a proportion of whom are medical experts. The role of these professionals is to monitor the development and direction of patient injuries and devise ways of how they can be prevented. Guidelines are based on the evidence revealed and lessons learned from cases dealt with by insurers. PSF's database contains information about all adverse medical incidents. It gives the date of a patient's injury, the employer (county council) concerned, the reason for the treatment and the cause and effect of the damage to the person concerned.[8] Compensation can be awarded for patient injury in all Swedish hospitals, and in primary care.

Norway

With 16 years' experience behind it, Norway's no-fault patient compensation mechanism is well established and continues to develop. The Norwegian compensation system for patients (Norsk Pasientskadeerstatning or NPE) was first discussed in January 1987, and was set up and running the following year. More recently, the jurisdiction of NPE has been enlarged. Under the country's Patient Injury Act, adopted on 15 June 2001 and coming into force on 1 January 2003, the scheme covers all claims relating to health care in the public sector and cases involving private establishments where healthcare is paid for by the public health service.

The application of the country's new Patients' Rights Act, adopted in 1999, provides for further entitlements to the public. It obliges health care providers to refer patients to the compensation scheme when an adverse clinical incident has occurred. Prospective claimants can also obtain advice or assistance from their county's 'patient ombud' (in cases other than those about primary care) before making a claim. This is in addition to the many who already approach NPE directly – both verbally and in writing – before they decide to proceed further. These would-be claimants receive help from a claims handler or an assistant about their case.

The thinking behind the make-up of Norway's statutory independent patient compensation mechanism is two-fold. The scheme provides cost-free access for claimants and a facility that reduces, to a modest level, the need to seek external legal advice or assistance. In cases where patients have appointed lawyers to act for them, NPE will deal directly with their legal representatives.[9] A number of these legal professionals have specialized in patient compensation and, perhaps predictably, maintain that the need for claimants to obtain outside legal representation is greater than NPE tends to suggest.

Norsk Pasientskadeerstatning agrees with this view to the extent that the services of an externally appointed lawyer may be justified in complicated cases. This is especially so when assessing the level of compensation that is to be awarded. In these circumstances, it is in the interests of all parties for NPE to discuss complex issues with the external legal professionals involved rather than with lay persons – as most claimants are bound to be.

Where it is considered necessary for a claimant to receive outside legal advice, the NPE will foot the bill as long as it is justified by the complexity of the case in question. It may even pay less than the full amount of such fees as a condition of the compensation to be awarded. NPE will not accept a claimant's legal fees if there is good reason to believe the appointment of a lawyer to have been an unnecessary measure.[10] (In 2001 a lawyer's fee for two days in court and putting a claimant's case together from scratch was estimated to be the equivalent of between £6,000 and £7,000. The charges are reckoned to be between £6,500 and £7,500 in 2004, although they include VAT, which became payable from about July 2002.)[11]

Nonetheless, NPE has a generally pragmatic approach to the use of external lawyers in compensation claims handled by them. They recognize that there are occasions when such a course of action may be necessary. It seems that there would probably be opposition from the public and judiciary to a patient compensation mechanism that disallowed any outside legal involvement.

In 2000 NPE paid a total of NOK5 million (£427,350 at NOK11.7 to £1) in claimants' lawyers' fees – not a large sum of money by most standards.[12] The corresponding figure for 2003 was NOK11.2 million (around £957,300 at NOK11.7 to £1) including VAT. In the same year NPE paid its own lawyers around NOK3.5 million (around £300,000) in fees.[13] Gratifying though this state of affairs appears to be in terms of fees paid, it is said to contrast sharply with the situation surrounding the patient insurance systems in Denmark and Sweden. In these countries there is said to be a much more rigid attitude to external legal involvement, with the payment of fees being extremely rare.

NPE received more than 18,000 claims for compensation during the period 1 January 1988 (the year the scheme came into existence) to the end of February 2001. From a total of 231 claims in 1988, the annual rate progressively increased in the following nine years, reaching a peak of 2,149 in 1997. The number then reduced slightly to around 2,050 for each of the next two years, before rising again in 2000 to a new high of 2,235 claims. From then on the numbers have remained fairly steady: 2,244 in 2001, 2,584 in 2002 and 2,332 in 2003. The total number of claims lodged with NPE from 1988 to 2003 was 24,948.[14] (To put these statistics into some kind of context, the population of Norway is nearly 4.5 million in 2005.)

Of all claims received between 1988 and 2000 an average of about 37 per cent of claimants were entitled to compensation. The rate fell to 31.7 per cent in 2000, a level that is part of the downward trend registered for the three to four years up to and including that year.[15] The reasons for the drop in successful claims were not clear at the time, but NPE considered that the increasing practice of submitting claims too soon – without due consideration – after alleged medical error has occurred probably indicate that more unjustified claims were being made. Another possible reason given for the reduced number of successful claims was a greater awareness by the public and more frequent use being made of the patient compensation scheme. An average of 35.1 per cent of claimants were entitled to compensation during the extended period 1988 to 2003.[16]

In 2000 NPE paid claims valued at NOK247 million (about £21,111,000) and a total of NOK1.3 billion (about £111,000,000) since the scheme was established in 1988. The average compensation payment was approximately NOK400,000 (about £34,190), a figure that would appear to be high by Norwegian standards. It includes payment for numerous cases involving serious or grave medical mishaps, which are also within NPE's jurisdiction. In 2001 the value of claims paid reduced to NOK218.8 million (around £18,700,000) and rose to NOK245.4 million (about £20,975,000) in 2002 and NOK379.4 million (approximately £32,427,000) in 2003. A total of NOK2.1 billion (about (£180 million) in compensation was paid over the period 1988 to 2003.[17]

This mean settlement level might seem modest when viewed from an international perspective. The comparatively moderate awards may be the result of the fact that all social security payments and those relating, for example, to services (such as home-based support) provided by municipal authorities are subtracted from the compensation paid. This is in keeping with the principle in Norway that nobody is compensated twice.

One of the chief reasons for the success of the Norwegian model given by those who manage NPE is indeed the 'sensible' levels of compensation that are awarded to claimants. It is also considered that a system involving high payments would have become too expensive to run. The same view is said to have been expressed by one or two other nations who have been looking at the no-fault model as something to work on for their own purposes.

A suggestion offered by some advocates of the NPE version to would-be converts is to go for a scheme where a predominance of claimants would be prepared to accept, say, 75 per cent of full compensation in the knowledge that they would not have to face the risks and rigours of a protracted litigation process. Nonetheless, in going for such a system, the advice also is that the door should be left open for those claimants who choose to take the civil route.

Iceland

Iceland's Patient Insurance Act came into force on 1 January 2001. Under certain conditions the new legislation gives patients the right to compensation when physical or mental injury is a result of health care that has been provided, or of a procedure carried out. This includes individuals who participate in medical research or donate tissue, organs, blood or other body matter and suffer harm as a consequence. People who are urgently admitted to a foreign health care establishment and sustain injury through clinical examination or treatment are also entitled to compensation.[18]

Article 24 of the Social Security Act, which was repealed following the Patient Insurance Act, contained a clause about patient insurance, but the consensus over the past few years was that this rule did not properly ensure a patient's right to financial redress. The system was considered to be slow and not 'user-friendly'; for instance, it could be difficult for patients to obtain the necessary medical records from clinicians and hospitals and even when a claim was successful the compensation was low. Under the new compensation scheme, based on those operating in continental Scandinavia and Finland, patients or claimants are not obliged to prove that someone is at fault.[19]

Organizations and others affected by the Patient Insurance Act

All providers of health care and parties otherwise associated with them are liable for damages under the Act.[20] They are:

- hospitals and health centres, whether run by the State, municipalities or other organizations
- other health care establishments regardless of who operate them
- self-employed health service personnel who have been certified for such work by the Minister for Health and Social Security regardless of whether the service they provide is paid for in full by the patient or through sickness insurance in keeping with an agreement with the State Social Security Institute

- the State Social Security Institute, when it concerns patients who urgently need hospitalization in a foreign establishment or other health care organization abroad referred to in the Social Security Act
- medical transport operators.

Health care organizations that are wholly or partially owned by the state and, indirectly, the State Social Security Institute are exempted from the insurance obligations of the other such groups covered by the legislation. Also exempted are establishments operating medical transport for the state, although they can insure against liability along the lines provided for in the Act if they choose to do so.[21] The activities of all these establishments are covered by patient insurance provided by the State Social Security Institute.[22] Responsibility for processing claims, deciding on liability and determining the level of compensation that is to be awarded rests with the Institute.[23] All the parties involved are advised about the decisions that have been reached, and the Institute's conclusions may also be referred to the Social Security Appeals Committee.[24] The other health service providers named in the Act must take out insurance with an insurer who holds an operating licence in Iceland and is responsible for settling claims that are received. Judgements made by insurers on the compensation to be granted can be contested via the conventional civil appeals process.[25]

The scope of the patient compensation scheme where it concerns patients
Compensation is paid for injury suffered in any one of the following circumstances irrespective of whether a person is eligible for damages under tort rules:
- where it is considered that damage to a patient could have been avoided if an examination or treatment had been conducted in the best possible way and was based on current knowledge and experience in the relevant field or, in such cases, if it arises from incorrect diagnosis
- if injury to a patient results from malfunctioning or defective equipment used during examination or therapy or, in such instances, if it is caused by incorrect diagnosis
- when a patient is injured from causes other than that connected with faulty equipment and the examination or treatment is carried out by an establishment covered by the Act, and the incident occurred in such a way that the health care provider would be regarded as being liable for damages under general tort rules
- should subsequent evaluation show that damage to a patient could have been avoided had an alternative and equally suitable form of technique or therapy been used
- when injury has resulted from examination or treatment – including operations conducted for diagnostic purposes – and the damage suffered is from infection or other side-effects greater than that which a patient should reasonably be expected to endure; account is taken of the extent of the impairment, and of the illness and general health of the patient; consideration is also given to the question of whether it is common for injury to result from the type of treatment that was provided and if or to what extent such an outcome could have been anticipated
- when individuals have suffered damage as a possible result of taking part in medical research that is not part of the diagnosis or treatment of an illness

relating to them or donate tissue, organs, blood or other body matter, unless all the indications are that injuries can be traced to another cause but not including the features of a medical product used in procedures carried out.[26] There are other aspects to the patient compensation scheme. For example, compensation may be reduced or cancelled in cases where patients have caused injury to themselves – whether intentionally or through gross negligence on their part.[27] Also, no claim for damages can be made against another party liable under tort law unless the impairment in question has not been fully compensated in line with the requirements of the Act, and then only for the residual amount due.[28]

Furthermore, with the previously mentioned exceptions, compensation is not payable if damage to a patient can be traced to the features of a medical product used in examination or treatment.[29] In another area, where a health service establishment (or its existing or former employees) is liable for damages under tort law, no reimbursement claim can be made against it for payment, unless the injury in question was caused intentionally.[30]

Subject to certain arrangements, the level of compensation to be paid is determined on the basis of tort law.[31] In 2002 damages were awarded if any injury sustained was assessed at ISK50,000 (about £406 at ISK123 to £1) or more.[32] The maximum amount of compensation that could be awarded for a single incident was ISK5 million (about £40,650) but these amounts are adjusted in line with the credit-term index at the start of each year.[33] However, under the Act these financial arrangements do not apply to damage suffered by people possibly taking part in medical experiments, or to donors of organs, tissue, blood and other body matter.[34]

Although 22 claims were received by the State Social Security Institute in 2001, the first (full) year for which the Patient Insurance Act became effective, benefits were paid in only one of these cases. Nine claims were made to insurance companies for cases relating to the private health service sector, but their outcome was not known because the cases had not been completed when this information was received.[35]

Under the Patient Insurance Act 2000, claims for compensation lapse after four years from the time a damaged patient was – or could have been – informed about the injury that was inflicted. In any case claims lapse ten years after the event occurred.[36] The State Social Security Institute is obliged to inform the public about the provisions of the Patient Insurance Act.[37] It also prepares an annual report on the patient patient insurance and compensation scheme in action over the period, which is made accessible to the public.[38]

There is said to be widespread public approval of the Patient Insurance Act and the system that is now in place in its wake. What is not in any doubt is the fact that this legislation has further enhanced patients' rights in Iceland. One of the aims of the patient insurance and compensation mechanism is to reduce the incidence of civil action taken, but it is still too early to tell what impact the scheme is having – or will have – on litigation.

Austria

The compensation system that Austria uses as an alternative to the conventional civil process was set up a number of years ago, but the mechanism is substantially different from and not based on the Nordic no-fault variety. It was established by the various medical bodies (Arztekammer) in each of the country's federal states (Bundeslander) and operates like a legally structured 'court of arbitration'.[39]

The arbitration framework of the Schlichtungstelle is used as a means to resolve disputes between patients and clinicians on matters about health care. In doing so, the object is to arrive at speedy out-of-court financial settlements, thereby avoiding the excessive costs of litigation and adverse publicity that might otherwise arise. The provision of this seemingly quick and efficient way of claiming compensation for clinical failures is considered by some in Austria to have strengthened public confidence in the medical profession.[40]

A judge sits as chairman of the Schlichtungstelle and is assisted by two medical professionals and a jurist who has a wide knowledge and experience of tort law, especially that concerning medical negligence. A representative of the Ombudsman Board for Patients (Patientenawalte), Austria's independent complaints body, is the remaining panel member and acts on behalf of patients. The duty of the Schlichtungstelle is to examine the evidence, without bias, and find out whether or not a clinical failure has occurred. Medical opinions expressed in the process are then discussed before the 'court' with all parties involved. Decisions arrived at as a result, form the basis for any compensation that may be awarded.[41]

The Schlichtungstelle has little formality and is simply structured. There is consequently no need for claimants to appoint a lawyer, although they may do so, if they wish, at their own expense. Otherwise, the process involves no costs for anyone concerned in a case. Compensation awards are comparable to those in similar civil actions.[42] If a decision or settlement by the Schlichtungstelle is rejected, a claimant can take the case to the civil courts, but as in most other countries this can be a lengthy and costly affair.

No-fault supplementary compensation scheme
Nevertheless, there is an additional source of compensation for medical negligence in Austria. During the second half of the 1990s the Austrian Federation and the Austrian Federal States had set up the legal base for a framework to fund and operate a scheme for the purpose. In 1998 Vienna became the first district to implement the new system, with the rest of the country following suit before the turn of the century.

The scheme is managed by special patient ombudsmen and provides a similarly speedy and informal means of claiming compensation as that afforded by the Schlichtungstelle. However, in this arrangement – and akin to the Nordic models – there is no obligation to prove that damage suffered after health care or treatment was a result of medical negligence – whether or not it was the case.[43]

Conclusion
Based on an original Swedish model, it is hardly surprising that there are major affinities in the style and content of the individual Nordic patient compensation systems. It is interesting to find similarities in the high proportions of successful claims arising out of the schemes in Sweden and Norway on the one hand, and Denmark and Finland on the other. With a one in two and one in three chance, respectively, of being awarded compensation, it would be hard to place too much value on the case for claimants in these countries pursuing damages via litigation.

The argument for taking civil action becomes even weaker when one considers that none of the Nordic systems – nor indeed the parallel Austrian system – involves any cost or financial risk to claimants. There are also independent appeals mechanisms for those who are not happy with decisions made about their cases. The greater speed of the process is another advantage of the patient compensation schemes that this handful of countries has devised and established, and the general application of tort law standards suggests that the sums being paid out match those currently obtainable through civil action. It can be no bad thing, also, for claimants not to have to share well-deserved compensation awards with lawyers such as when arrangements of the kind have been made in civil cases contested in the United Kingdom.

The continuing broad approval by the Nordic public of no-fault patient compensation mechanisms suggests that there can be no turning back to the old ways. It's no wonder, then, that the idea seems to be catching on elsewhere. The latest example could be Belgium. In 2002 the Belgian health ministry was in the early stages of discussions about a proposed no fault scheme covering medical accidents. The position in 2005 is that a Belgian government commission is analyzing the financial impact of introducing such a system and is expected to report its findings by the end of the year.[44]

There are always those who will be persuaded to risk civil action in the expectation that they will do better than what may be on offer through an existing alternative means of securing damages. In Sweden, where litigation claims are said to be on the rise, there are indications that this may be the case. Nonetheless, the 'compensation culture' via the civil route, as expressed and evidently mushrooming in the UK where in 2004 there is no alternative – and well established in the USA – has, so far, not taken any meaningful hold in Nordic countries. Perhaps it may not do so to any significant extent for the foreseeable future while specific patient compensation schemes abound that are far removed from the complex, risky and adversarial civil process.

CHAPTER 20

Final thoughts on the crucial issues

There has been no clean sweep of things in the United Kingdom's health service and medical regulation procedures. No out with the old, anachronistic practices and in with the new, enlightened ones that reflect the times. The nation's citizens will continue to have to tolerate arrangements –albeit re-conditioned – that will still be second best to those apparently at the top of the league elsewhere in Europe. Their sustained excoriation of the previous mechanisms and the inequitable outcomes they routinely generated does not appear to have delivered a fitting dividend.

The chosen remedies look like an elaborate sticking plaster fix to some of the most offending parts of the existing procedures, and are likely to be seen as a device to appease powerful vested interests rather than to placate the critics. Complainants will still be unable to have their grievances examined independently as a first resort and professional self-regulation continues uninterrupted because independence was not one of the ingredients in the recipe for reforming medical regulation in the United Kingdom.

The reality is that it continues to be a problem to break the mould whereby grudging, drip-feed allowances towards providing an equitable set of procedures relating to health care are made, rather than actually delivering them. Although there seems not to have been as widespread or forceful a clamour for an alternative form of compensation in clinical negligence cases, the proposals put forward for such a change are revolutionary by comparison, despite the fact that what has been advanced could have been more generous in character.

It is evident that the country's administrators and their advisers have spent much time and money conducting nationwide inquiries, consultations and evaluations to clear the way for change. Yet, in spite of this, the outcome of such action is likely still to be short of a fair deal in meeting the public's concerns about the way complaints relating to health care are investigated and the prospects of being compensated. In reality not much better a result could have been expected, considering the form of the surveys and the composition of those among whom each study was carried out. Thus the combined effect was not exactly a blueprint for a transformation of the status quo; nor perhaps was it intended to be. Not only that, the powers that be did not grasp the opportunity in their analyses to include giving consideration to intro-ducing a set of comprehensive statutory patients' rights to replace the existing arrangement.

What is the difference between an overhauled UK health care complaints system and the best that are on offer elsewhere?
The purpose of the national evaluation of the existing NHS complaints system was 'to provide an evaluation of how the new complaints procedures are operating

across all parts of the NHS…and to meet the information needs of policy makers and managers concerned with the future development of the system'. A further element of the brief was to prepare 'a practical and realistic analysis based as far as possible on the actual experiences of those using and operating the procedure (i.e. complainants and staff respectively)'.[1]

A predictable response resulted from the 4,000 questionnaires circulated to key functionaries connected with or operating the complaints system, as it did from the 315 interviews of complainants, health service staff who had been complained against and NHS personnel otherwise associated with the complaints mechanism. Further meetings by the research team with certain health care focus groups, together with written submissions from an unspecified number of NHS staff and other individuals who had experience of the complaints procedure, were similarly predictable in their outcome. Chapter 2 has given a more detailed account of these findings.

Health service chief executives were found to be in favour of the existing complaints mechanism, with a great majority of them also believing it to be cost-effective. They considered that the 'local resolution' first phase worked particularly well. Complaints managers had a similar view of the system and most judged it to be better than the arrangement it replaced in 1996. There was broad agreement among others operating the complaints procedure (conveners, lay chairs and additional review panel members) that the 'independent review' stage should be more independent, and seen to be so. (Why only *more* independent; why not *completely* independent so as to avoid any misunderstanding by complainants?) Nonetheless, they accepted that complainants did not regard the system as a whole to be independent in practice.

The research also showed that the larger proportion of complainants approached was greatly dissatisfied with the way the procedure worked across the health service. By contrast, and perhaps predictably, NHS staff who had been complained against were mostly content with the system, whereas community health councils in England and Wales (and their counterparts in Scotland and Northern Ireland) with experience of assisting complainants gave a mixed opinion of the mechanism. Patient interest organizations were mostly critical of the complaints procedure, chiefly because it invariably failed to deal satisfactorily with complainants' concerns.

Taking all this into account, it is not surprising that genuinely fundamental reform has not followed the government's national evaluation of the NHS complaints procedure, but improvements involving certain key aspects of the system are in place or in the process of implementation. Arguably the most significant of these changes are centred on the 'independent review' phase. In England this stage of the complaints process has become the responsibility of the Healthcare Commission, a new independent statutory body. The Independent Review Secretariat carries out this function in Wales.

However, it is doubtful whether these various measures will be persuasive enough for the public to believe that the resulting overhauled versions of the NHS complaints procedure will give them appreciably more equity than the one they have replaced. Complainants may continue to feel that a still mostly self-regulated complaints mechanism will be loaded against them – no matter what checks and balances are applied. Also, taking on such a reformed health service complaints system is unlikely to be a much less daunting commitment for them than hitherto.

The chances of a complaint – especially one of a serious nature – being upheld when it is first heard under the new regime will remain uncertain. Despite the proposed checks and balances, this initial 'local resolution' stage will continue to reject or 'resolve' the overwhelming majority of complaints and thus carry on as an effective means of taking cases (whether unjustified, trivial, vexatious or legitimate) out of the system at an early stage. In the comparatively few instances when serious complaints are upheld, the remedial action taken seems likely to persist in only partially reflecting their gravity. It appears probable that complainants will still receive no more than a standard apology and an assurance that measures will be introduced to prevent a recurrence of the error that was the cause of the complaint in question.

The well-established autonomous complaints and medical regulatory mechanisms functioning in each of the five Nordic countries may not be perfect, but they are examples of equitable arrangements for complainants and those whom they are complaining about, which a predominantly self-regulated system like the British models cannot deliver. The perception, at least, is that these systems are not weighted one way or the other.

The way these parallel complaints systems work and some of their in-built attributes were described in Chapter 13. It is worth readdressing a few of the features that reflect the independence and other facets of these other European models:

- Investigators and judges have no existing or previous connection with the health service or medical profession.
- They generally have a high level of legal leadership in the investigations into complaints.
- It is not mandatory for complaints to go through any initial health service procedure before becoming eligible for independent investigation.
- A large percentage of the complaints received by the complaints bodies is usually accepted for detailed formal investigation.
- The proportions that are upheld following such examination are also invariably high.
- Public and private health care are within the ambit of the complaints and regulatory authorities in most Nordic countries.

None of these and other advantages is to be found even in the UK's reformed NHS complaints procedures; nor when any of the health service ombudsmen becomes involved. However, a strong legal element can come into play (in a different way), but only when complaints are ultimately referred to either of the country's two medical regulatory bodies. But the numbers that progress to this stage are comparatively low and are handled within the framework of self-regulation.

Therefore, it is probable that the situation in the UK will continue to compare poorly with that in Nordic countries, even once the reformed complaints and medical regulation procedures begin to mature. The systematically poor conduct of complaints investigators and medical asessors at each of the two phases of the previous NHS complaints procedure – and at Ombudsman level – reported in Chapter 11 may not be exactly replicated in the proposed reformed system. But there can be no guarantee that unacceptable practice of the kind will be sufficiently eradicated in a mechanism that continues to be mostly managed internally by the health service.

Reflecting on patient redress and compensation schemes

The proposals offered by England's chief medical officer in 2003 for a better scheme to redress and compensate patients for clinical negligence in the NHS in England are another matter (Chapter 9). They are bold and radical by customary practice and likely to attract a good level of public approval, but they could nonetheless have been more benevolent in their aims. For example the proposals could have advocated a more all-encompassing, no-fault-based system that would come near to offering the automatic monetary benefits available for other forms of personal injury in the United Kingdom. Such a scheme would have compared well with the advanced systems that operate successfully in some other European countries (see chapters 17 to 19).

Unfortunately a more equitable outcome may have been prevented because of the disproportionate number of collaborators and contributors involved in the initial discussions who represented vested interests. The apparent absence of any representatives from mature, no-fault patient insurance and compensation systems in the discussions could have been another contributing factor in the conclusions that were reached. Why did England's medical officer not include anyone who was experienced in managing such schemes on his committee, or as contributors in his consultation programme?

Still, the proposals have not been finalized so there may yet be a few pleasant surprises, with the reforms turning out to be more far-reaching than previously envisaged. Should this happen increasingly more claimants are likely to turn their backs on the litigation route and thus stem the rising tide of civil medical negligence claims. In changing course, they will avoid getting caught up in an invariably inaccessible and drawn-out procedure that has its fair share of other pitfalls. The devolved administrations should take careful note of whatever turns out to be the alternative English model for patient redress and compensation in setting up their own schemes – if that is what they are planning to do.

Much reform, but not to the extent of independent medical regulation in the UK

While there is no wholesale change to the regulatory bodies for doctors and nurses in the UK, the completed and ongoing reforms to these institutions are striking by past standards. Nonetheless, from the perspective of complainants, the changes seem only to provide a less unfairly devised system of dealing with their allegations than hitherto.

Sir Donald Irvine, past president of the General Medical Council, was more upbeat about the reforms in his foreword to a published review of his regulatory body's work since 1995. He said:

> We are witnessing the fashioning of a new relationship between the medical profession and the public, and an approach to medical regulation to which all major stakeholders must contribute. We can be confident that the changes which government, the medical profession and employers are making will lead to a system of medical regulation which will regain public trust. Within this system a more stream-lined, effective, accountable and vigorously proactive GMC will become the focus for bringing the medical profession and the public together on the professionalism of doctors, their education and their fitness to practise...[2]

His comments could be over-optimistic. For one thing, it is doubtful that institutions of the kind that continue to be financed by the registration fees of the medical professionals whose conduct and practice they regulate will ever succeed in gaining full public confidence. There are likely to be many people not in the business of health care who will say that no amount of reform to the medical regulatory system will gain their confidence while it remains, effectively, in the hands of the profession. Thus the public will probably view the new-look General Medical Council (and the Nursing and Midwifery Council) in the same way. The legitimate question critics may still want to ask is, what makes the British medical profession so special that its members should not be subject to neutrally administered regulation and investigation? As the high-ranking legal spokesperson in a certain independent medical regulatory authority elsewhere in Europe (referred to in Chapter 2) remarked, what are they frightened of?

In early 2003 Dr Ian Bogle, chairman of the British Medical Association, raised the issue of abolishing medical self-regulation in the UK with Sir Graeme Chatto, the incumbent president of the GMC. The question was one of a number he posed to Sir Graeme in the wake of the legislation sanctioning the reforms to the regulatory body, which was reported in the GMC's house newspaper *GMC News*. Dr Bogle remarked:

A few doctors have suggested that it would be cheaper for them if we did away with self-regulation and left the government to do the job instead. What would you say to this?'

The GMC's leader replied:

Whoever regulates doctors will charge them. We prefer to talk about professionally-led regulation in partnership with the public, which we see as the most effective way of protecting the public. Where independent regulation has been removed in other countries [presumably he means the transfer of regulation to government] patients have seen a fall in standards. It would be unhealthy to have a monopoly situation where employers also act as regulators – especially inappropriate in a profession such as medicine, where professional expertise is crucial in setting and maintaining credible standards. The contract between the public and the profession, which we see as the foundation for modern regulation, would be eroded. Doctors would lose ownership of such things as the right to elect members of the profession to the regulator and the ability to establish standards independently of the monopoly employer.[3]

The question and its answer appear a little curious and somewhat flawed. It seems surprising that the 'few doctors' referred to should suggest that the government takes on the role of prospective regulator to replace the GMC. Why the government? Did it not occur to them that a new statutory body, independent of the profession, the health service and the state, might assume this function? It has been shown (in Chapter 13) that several other countries have long possessed such a means of regulating the medical profession.

However, the doctors have a point in suggesting that changing from the present regulatory system would be less costly for them. If the arrangements in Nordic countries are anything to go by it would cost them virtually nothing at all. Medical doctors, dentists and nurses in these countries are not required to pay annual registration fees or any other such payments. They are obliged to pay only a one-off nominal certification charge (for example, €62 – about £41 – in Finland up to 2004, at €1.50 to £1) before being authorized to practise their profession.[4] The fee covers the administration costs involved.

An unhealthy monopoly where the employer (indirectly via the NHS) also acts as regulator could arise if the government were to assume the job of overseeing and controlling the medical profession. But even in this unlikely event it is an exaggeration to say that 'the contract between the public and the profession', which the GMC sees as 'the foundation of modern regulation', would be 'eroded' where otherwise it would not. Indeed, some members of the public may ask what contract the GMC's president is talking about. But, again, why involve the government in the issue – unless it is a kind of red herring to reinforce the case for self-regulation?

Critics may question the right of doctors to elect members of the medical profession to the same body that regulates the way they work and judges their conduct, and they could argue that a regulatory organization with any contentious link with the medical profession is not acceptable. On the other hand, some may see no reason why doctors should not be allowed to take part in such elections provided that the establishment concerned is managed from outside the profession. However, these and other questions considered, there is almost certain to be a consensus among the public that there can be no substitute for a statutory regulatory body (or bodies) that has no material connection with the medical profession.

The implication that the crucial professional expertise needed to set and maintain standards can come only from a GMC in its self-regulated form is overstated by the GMC's president. For instance what is to stop an independent body fulfilling these and all other necessary functions just as well, if not better? The models firmly established in Denmark, Finland, Norway and Sweden are autonomous and operate independently of the medical profession, the health service and government, yet it is clear that their detached position is no bar to performing efficiently. The people administering these institutions will testify that standards have risen since independent medical regulation was established; if it had not the confidence of the public in the system could not have been maintained. Regrettably an opportunity to introduce a similarly equitable and apparently efficient arrangement for regulating the medical profession in the United Kingdom seems to have been deliberately squandered.

Patients' rights – the time to get abreast of the best

It is unfortunate that the provision of comprehensive legal rights for patients and those who represent them in the United Kingdom and the same for the health service and its professionals does not seem to be under consideration. To continue with the apparently loose existing arrangement would seem to ignore the practical and moral justification for change. The case for inclusive legislation is strong for these reasons and because a full and unambiguous set of statutory rights would cost relatively little extra – apart from legal and parliamentary time – to implement.

In its present form the British approach to dealing with patients' rights falls short of the sweeping statutory entitlements that are being provided for in several countries in Europe and elsewhere (see chapters 14, 15 and 16). Not only that, the position of the health service and its professionals are incorporated in these corresponding sets of inclusive legal rights that are available elsewhere. If Israel, Lithuania and Belgium – among the latest converts – are able to confer such entitlements upon their citizens what is stopping the UK's law-makers from doing the same for the British people?

The nominal powers of the UK's health service ombudsmen

It would have been welcomed if in parallel with the evaluation of the NHS complaints procedure the government had arranged for an independent assessment of the work of the Health Service Ombudsman for England and Wales. (It could also have suggested that the other two devolved administrations did the same concerning the operations of their ombudsmen.) Such an appraisal might have uncovered flaws in the workings of the Ombudsman's oganization – including the kind of dubious judgements that seem to be made and other questionable aspects of its work that have been described earlier in this book (chapters 10 and especially 11).

Attention has also been drawn to the previous occupational links with the NHS of numerous key individuals at the Office of the Health Service Ombudsman for England and Wales (Chapter 4). It was suggested that others in this organization could previously have been working in the internally operated complaints system of the NHS, thus raising questions about the reliability of their decision-making. Moreover, it was shown that the previous Northern Ireland Ombudsman had previously been similarly connected with the health service.

As discussed in Chapter 4, although the nation's three ombudsmen have a wide jurisdiction, they have no powers to take action directly, nor can they compel a health service organization to carry out their advice. They can call only for remedial action, which, if accepted, will merely result in an apology from the health service organization concerned and an undertaking by it to remedy the cause of the complaint.

The ombudsmen cannot propose disciplinary or legal action against health service professionals being complained against. Their decisions are final and there is no appeal, except in rare circumstances. Even if appeals were permitted, taking such an action would probably seem a somewhat pointless exercise to complainants in view of the limited powers that are assigned to the UK's ombudsmen. Moreover there is no powerful legal leadership element in investigations carried out by these arbiters of complaints.

It has been shown in Chapter 4 that the only recourse to an unacceptable decision by an ombudsman is judicial review. Yet in the more than 30 years since the Office of the Health Service Ombudsman for mainland Britain was established, judicial review proceedings have never been granted against judgements made by an ombudsman anywhere in the United Kingdom. By contrast, the supporters of hare coursing in one region of the country were allowed such legal action in the appropriate high court in May 2004 to pursue their case.[5] This action concerned a ruling that had forbidden the trapping of hares in the wild for the purpose of letting each animal loose, individually, and then setting a pair of muzzled greyhounds in pursuit of it in the name of sport. A curious distinction many will say.

Is it conceiveable that the Health Service Ombudsmen and those working under their direction are deluded by the special independent status ascribed to them and their organizations? Do they see themselves on a pedestal, above reproach and standing aloof from other complaints examiners, when there are no solid grounds for doing so? Consider the previous occupational links of some of them and what, otherwise, has been revealed about these complaints investigators in Chapter 4. It could be an appropriate time for the nation's administrators to look anew at their role and conduct in the changing climate of health care complaints regulation.

Parting shot

It seems clear from these reflections and conclusions that there is only one redeeming quality about the completed, ongoing or proposed changes to procedures for dealing with complaints about health care in Britain: England's chief medical officer's endorsement of a future patient redress and compensation scheme covering the NHS. The scheme is a concept that comes close to those that are working efficiently in the Nordic countries, but that is where any similarity begins and ends.

The principle of providing full autonomy and independence in the investigation of grievances about the NHS and the medical profession in the United Kingdom has not been accepted by those who have the power to change the system. Despite the most recent public outcry at the spate of health care scandals that surfaced between the mid-1990s and the turn of the century, self-regulated complaints procedures, though modified, continue unabated, and no doubt it is hoped that there will be no similar adverse events on the same scale in future. Meanwhile, the chasm will remain between this kind of anachronistic, still one-sided practice in Britain and the civilized apparent impartiality of the policy followed for years by some other European nations.

But the health service and medical profession in the UK are not alone in being regulated in this broadly undetached style. Institutional self-regulation continues to be a powerful force in numerous other areas of public life. The difference is that, unlike health care, complaints about injury or death that involve other institutions – with certain exceptions such as the police, the armed forces and, in a different way, passenger transportation bodies – are comparatively uncommon.

Perhaps the most interesting example of institutional self-regulation is that relating to the British parliament. In an oblique way it begins with the appointment of the Parliamentary Commissioner for Standards, the officer who looks into breaches of the code of conduct of Members of Parliament (MPs), among other matters.[6] After a recruitment process the candidate is endorsed by the House of Commons Commission (a body of MPs that is responsible for the management of the House) and then put forward for approval by the members of the House of Commons.[7]

After a preliminary inquiry or full investigation into a complaint, the Parliamentary Commissioner for Standards reports the details of the case and conclusions drawn to the Committee on Standards and Privileges – another group of MPs. The latter considers the Commissioner's account; it may carry out further inquiries and then produces its own report. It might also make recommendations to the House of Commons about any further action (including penalties) to be taken against the MP concerned. The Committee on Standards and Privileges publishes its report on the complaint together with the Commissioner's account and evidence. (The Committee issues general guidance to MPs on matters of conduct.) As a result the House of Commons may impose (specified) penalties on the MP concerned. It is responsible for approving any arrangements about the general conduct of MPs.[8] (The House of Lords does not have a standards commissioner. On 31 March 2002 this chamber of the House introduced its own code of conduct containing new rules on registration and declaration of interests, and also advocacy.)[9]

Another example of self-regulation is to be found in The Law Society in its capacity of representing and regulating solicitors in England and Wales. Out of its 105 Council seats, 100 are allocated to solicitor members and five to lay appointees.[10]

However, the Legal Services Ombudsman for England and Wales (who is appointed by the Lord Chancellor under the Courts and Legal Services Act 1990) oversees the handling of complaints against solicitors by The Law Society and those that are dealt with by the regulatory bodies for barristers, licensed conveyancers and other similar professionals.[11]

In other words the Ombudsman will examine the way complaints made about legal professionals have been dealt with by The Law Society. When the Ombudsman considers that a complaint has not been examined properly she is likely to recommend that the Society looks at the case again. This overseer of complaints can widen her inquiry to include the origin of a complaint, but it is unusual for her to take this action. For example, between April and September 2003 the Ombudsman extended her investigation to take in the original complaint in less than one per cent of cases. In such exceptional instances she can make a recommendation against the legal professional concerned. The Legal Services Ombudsman can recommend that compensation is paid for financial loss, distress or inconvenience, or for a combination of all these considerations.[12] (The Scottish Legal Services Ombudsman has a similar role and status.)

In September 2003 it was reported in the national press that the Lord Chancellor had created a post to be taken up by a new Legal Services Complaints Commissioner, whose role would be to examine The Law Society's overall complaints procedure. The Commissioner had been given powers to impose targets on and fine the Society where it failed to meet the set objectives. As an interim measure the Commissioner's duties were to be carried out by the existing Legal Services Ombudsman. The report stated that the government had been threatening to remove The Law Society's self-regulatory powers for some years[13] – which seems to be an example of double standards, considering parliament's not dissimilar system of investigating its own members.

Then there is the Press Complaints Commission, a body that seems to operate a partially self-regulated complaints procedure. The Commission states that its success 'continues to underline the strength of effective and independent self-regulation over any form of legal or statutory control'. In 2004 the Commission comprised 17 members: seven were editors of national and regional newspapers and magazines; ten, including the chairman, were drawn from outside the industry. The Press Complaints Commission is financed by the industry via the Press Standards Board of Finance and judges the conduct of the press media according to a code of practice written by a committee of editors and sanctioned by the Commission.[14]

(In March 2002 the *Daily Mail* reported that Lord Wakeham had relinquished his post as chairman of the Press Complaints Commission and that the Press Standards Board of Finance 'paid tribute' to him, stating: 'The Board wishes to record its appreciation of his outstanding contribution to self-regulation of the press over the past seven years.'[15] The accolade is an oblique example of the kind of doubtful virtue that the key British institutions that continue to practise a form of self-regulation can ascribe to the system. What outstanding contribution can anyone make to self-regulation by a body in this or any other context unless it is to help perpetuate the system itself? The person in charge may be doing a good job but the tribute seems a little extravagant. Approbation of this order would have been more justified had it been directed at someone leading an independent regulatory authority.)

While the police complaints system in England and Wales is generally not from the same mould as the aforesaid complaints mechanisms, it bears some resemblance to the NHS model. Like the position in that procedure, most complaints are investigated (by the police) at local resolution – whether or not a formal investigation is involved – and the majority are resolved at this initial stage. Complainants are asked to give their consent to local resolution being used, and when consent has been received the police must follow the process that has been agreed with the complainant to resolve the issue.[16]

Where complainants are dissatisfied with the way their grievances have been handled by the police they can appeal to the Independent Police Complaints Commission (IPCC). Also, the police service is under a legal obligation to refer certain categories of complaint and incident to the IPCC so that it can decide how the investigation should proceed. A neutral body, the IPCC oversees the police complaints system and succeeded the Police Complaints Authority (PCA) in April 2004. It operates from four regional centres.[17]

An apparently powerful element of the police complaints mechanism is to be found in the composition of the Commission itself. By law, its 18 'commissioners' cannot have worked for a police force and instead are recruited from the legal, health and academic professions and from the voluntary and community secotrs. Teams of investigators, caseworkers and support staff carry out the day to day work of the Commission.[18]

Following appeals from complainants who are discontented with local resolution or when cases are referred to it for some other valid reason there are three main types of investigation[19] in which the IPCC is involved: those supervised by the IPCC, those managed by the IPCC and those conducted wholly by the IPCC.

Police investigations supervised by the IPCC are directed and controlled by an investigating officer from the police approved by the assigned IPCC commissioner who, in certain cases, may appoint such a person from another regional police force. The commissioner's role is to advise the investigating officer and review the progress of the invetigation. Complainants who consider that they have not been adequately informed about the findings of such an investigation or the action that the police propose to take (or not to take) can appeal to the IPCC.

The investigations managed by the IPCC involve the more serious cases of complaint and are carried out by the police with the IPCC in overall charge directing and controlling the process. An IPCC commissioner agrees the remit of the investigation and oversees the way it proceeds. The investigation is led by an investigating officer from the police who is approved by the IPCC commissioner involved and, in some instances, may be drawn from the police force in a different jurisdiction. Investigating officers function under the authority of the relevant IPCC regional director who agrees the form that the investigation is to take and regularly reviews its progress. There is no right of appeal to the IPCC about the outcome of such an investigation.

In instances where investigations are carried out exclusively by the IPCC cases are managed by its own investigators. The investigator who has been appointed reports to the relevant regional director and the case is overseen by an IPCC commissioner. Like the police investigations the IPCC manages, these investigations apply to the most serious types of complaint.

Epilogue

But the practice of institutional self-regulation is not alone in being open to doubt. Even the concept of an independent investigating body in Britain may sometimes be questionable and at odds with its interpretation by those who have established such authorities in other societies. The point has already been made in describing the composition of so-called independent review panels in the UK's 1996 health service complaints procedure. It was also illustrated in drawing attention to the questionable pedigree of certain key personnel in the organizations of the Health Service Ombudsman for England and Wales and Northern Ireland Ombudsman. Outside the ambit of health care, some of the independent inquiries commissioned by successive British governments have also been open to question from the perspective of the existing or previous connections of those who were appointed to lead such investigations and, perhaps, even of their outcome.[20]

A conflict of interest – or even the suspicion of it – arising in any form of investigation purporting to be impartial should be unacceptable in a society that calls itself civilized. It certainly should not be tolerated where it can concern matters of injury or death to patients. Preventing the independent examination of complaints about health care in Britain or anywhere else is indefensible from any perspective, and those with the power to break the cycle know it. Yet the nation's law-makers continue to resist full reform. Perhaps they will change their minds only once their own conduct is subject to independent scrutiny, but that might be a long time for the British public to wait. If evenhandedness is the key axiom in a court of law, the same principle should apply to procedures and tribunals that pass judgement on similarly consequential questions – in this case concerning the health care of the nation's citizens. It's as simple as that.

Preface
1. John Elder, *Who Cares About the Health Victim?*, Chepstow, Klaxon Books, 1998
2. Commissioned by Britain's Department of Health, the evaluation was carried out in 1999 and 2000 and its results and proposals appeared in *NHS Complaints Procedure National Evaluation*, 2001. The Department conducted its own follow-up 'listening exercise', completed in October 2001. The outcome was *NHS Complaints Reform – Making Things Right*, which set out the plans to change the existing system.
3. The Health Committee's inquiry was covered in *Procedures Related to Adverse Clinical Incidents and Outcomes in Medical Care* (Minutes of Evidence), 1999, and the results appeared in the Sixth Report, Vol. 1, Report and Proceedings of the Committee, of a similarly titled document published in November 1999. The Department of Health replied to the Committee in *Memorandum Responding to the Sixth Report of the Health Select Committee (1998–99 Session) on Procedures Related to Adverse Clinical Incidents and Outcome in Medical Care* released in Apr 2000.

Introduction
1. Department of Health, *NHS Complaints Procedure National Evaluation*, London, DoH, Mar 2001

1. A flawed mechansim delivered flawed results
1. Department of Health, *NHS Complaints Procedure*, www.doh.gov.uk/complaints, accessed 3 May 2003; *How to Make a Complaint About the NHS*, www.dh.gov.uk, accessed 10 Aug 2004; *How to Complain About the NHS*, www.dh.gov.uk
2. DoH, *NHS Complaints Procedure*
3. Department of Health, *How to Make a Complaint About the NHS*, www.dh.gov.uk, accessed 10 Aug 2004; Department of Health, *NHS Complaints Reform – Making Things Right*, London, DoH, Feb 2003, s. 3
4. DoH, *NHS Complaints Procedure*, www.doh.gov.uk/complaints/advocacyservice, accessed 6 Dec 2003
5. DoH, *NHS Complaints Procedure*, www.doh.gov.uk/complaints, accessed 3 May 2003
6. Ibid.
7. Ibid.; John Elder, *Who Cares About the Health Victim?*, Chepstow, Klaxon Books, 1998, Chapter 3
8. Ibid.
9. Department of Health, *NHS Complaints 2000–01*, Hospital and Community Health Services, Family Health Services, Summary of main findings, www.doh.gov.uk/nhscomplaints, accessed 1 Feb 2002
10. DoH, *NHS Complaints 2000–01*, Hospital and Community Health Services, Summary of main findings, Table 2, www.doh.gov.uk/nhscomplaints, accessed 19 June 2003
11. Department of Health, *Written Complaints About Hospital and Community Health Services by Service Area, England, 2002–03*, www.performance.dh.gov.uk, accessed 10 Aug 2004; DoH, *NHS Complaints 2000–01*, Written complaints about hospital and community health services, 1996–97 to 2000–01, Table 1, www.doh.gov.uk/nhscomplaints, accessed 1 Feb 2002
12. DoH, *Written Complaints About Hospital and Community Health Services by Service Area, England, 2002–03*, www.performance.doh.gov.uk/hospitalactivity, accessed Aug 2004; DoH, *NHS Complaints 2000–01*, Written complaints about family health services, 1996–97 to 2000–01, Table 13, www.doh.gov.uk/nhscomplaints, accessed Feb 2002
13. DoH, *NHS Complaints 2000–01*, Table 6, www.doh.gov.uk/nhscomplaints, accessed 24

May 2003

14. DoH, *Written Complaints About Hospital and Community Health Services by Service Area, England, 2002–03*
15. Ibid.
16. DoH, *Written Complaints About Hospital and Community Health Services by Service Area, England, 2002–03*
17. ISD Scotland National Statistics, *NHS Trust Complaints – Outcome of Complaints, 2002–03*, www.isdscotland.org, accessed 14 Sep 2004; *Trust Complaints*, Outcome of complaints, 1999–2000 to 2001–02, www.show.scot.nhs.uk/isd, accessed 17 Apr 2003; *Trust Complaints*, Outcome of Complaints, 1998–1999 to 2000–01, www.show.scot.nhs.uk/isd, 17 Apr 2003; *NHS Trust Complaints – Status of Requests for Independent Review*, www.isdscotland.org, accessed 2 Oct 2004
18. ISD Scotland National Statistics, *NHS Trust Complaints – Outcome of Complaints 1998–1999 to 2000–03*, www.isdscotland.org, accessed 2 Oct 2004
19. ISD Scotland National Statistics, *NHS Trusts Complaints – Summary of Issues Raised*, www.isdscotland.org, accessed 2 Oct 2004
20. ISD Scotland National Statistics, *NHS Trust Complaints – Status of Requests for Independent Review*, www.isdscotland, accessed 2 Oct 2004
21. ISD Scotland National Statistics, *NHS Trust Complaints – Summary of Issues Raised*, www.isdscotland.org, accessed 2 Oct 2004
22. ISD Scotland National Statistics, *Primary Care Complaints – by Service 2002–03*, www.isdscotland.org, accessed 19 Sep 2004; *Primary Care Complaints 1999–2000 to 2001–02*, www.show.scot.nhs.uk/isd, accessed 17 Apr 2003; *Primary Care Complaints 1998–99 to 2000–01*, www.show.scot.nhs.uk/isd, accessed 17 Apr 2003
23. ISD Scotland National Statistics, *Primary Care Complaints*, www.isdscotland.org/isd, accessed 18 Sep 2004
24. ISD Scotland National Statistics, *Primary Care Complaints – by Service 2002–03*; *Primary Care Complaints 1998–99 to 2001–02*, www.show.scot.nhs.uk/isd, accessed 17 Apr 2003
25. ISD Scotland National Statistics, *Primary Care Complaints – Independent Review Requests 2002–03*, www.isdscotland.org, accessed 14 Sep 2004; *Primary Care Complaints – Requests for Independent Review, Summary of Issues Raised 1996–97 to 2002–03*, accessed 18 Sep 2004
26. ISD Scotland National Statistics, *Primary Care Complaints – Independent Review Requests 2000–01 to 2002–03*, www.isdscotland.org, accessed 14 Sep 2004; *Primary Care Complaints – Requests for Independent Review 1998–99, 1999–2000*, www.show.scot.nhs.uk/isd, both accessed 17 Apr 2003
27. ISD Scotland National Statistics, *Primary Care Complaints – Requests for Independent Review, Summary of Issues Raised 1998–99 to 2002–03*, www.isdscotland.org, accessed 2 Oct 2004
28. ISD Scotland National Statistics, *NHS Board Complaints – Outcome of Complaints 2000–01 to 2002–03*, www.isdscotland.org, 19 Sep 2004; *NHS Board Complaints – Numbers Received and Response Times, 2000–01 to 2002–03*, www.isdscotland.org, accessed 14 Sep 2004
29. ISD Scotland National Statistics, *NHS Board Complaints – Outcome of Complaints 2000–01 to 2002–03*
30. Ibid.
31. ISD Scotland National Statistics, *NHS Board Complaints – Issues Raised 2002–03*, www.isdscotland.org, accessed 19 Sep 2004
32. Ibid.; ISD Scotland National Statistics, *Health Board/NHS Board Complaints – Summary of Issues Raised 1998–99 to 2001–02*, www.show.scot.nhs.uk/isd, accessed 17 Apr 2003
33. National Assembly for Wales, Health Statistics and Analysis Unit, Statistical Directorate, *Complaints to the NHS in Wales 2001–02* and *Complaints to the NHS in Wales 2002–03*, www.wales.gov.uk/statistics, accessed Jul 2002 and Sep 2003, respectively
34. National Assembly for Wales, Health Statistics and Analysis Unit, Statistical Directorate,

Complaints to the NHS in Wales 2002–03
35. Ibid.
36. Ibid.; *Complaints to the NHS in Wales 2000–01* and *Complaints to the NHS in Wales 2001–02*, www.wales.gov.uk/statistics, Nov 2001 and Jul 2002, respectively
37. National Assembly for Wales, Health Statistics and Analysis Unit, Statistical Directorate, *Complaints to the NHS in Wales 2001–02* and *Complaints to the NHS in Wales 2002–03*
38. Department of Health, Social Services and Public Safety (DoHSSPS), and Department of Health, Information and Analysis Directorate (DoHIAD), Regional Information Branch, information received by fax, 10 Oct 2002
39. Ibid.; Information received by telephone from Department of Health, Social Services and Public Safety, Belfast, 17 Sep 2004
40. DoHSSPS and DoHIAD, information received by fax, 10 Oct 2002
41. Eastern Health and Social Services Board, *Fifth Annual Review of Complaints April 2000–March 2001, Complaints Report 2001–02*; clarification by telephone from EHSSB, May 2003
42. EHSSB, *Complaints Report 2001–02*
43. Ibid.; *Fifth Annual Review of Complaints 2000–01*
44. Ibid.; additional information by telephone, 15 May 2003
45. Ibid.
46. EHSSB, *Complaints Report 2001–02*, Oct 2002
47. EHSSB, *Fifth Annual Review of Complaints 2000–01, Complaints Report 2001–02*
48. Southern Health and Social Services Board, *Annual Report 2000–01, Annual Review of Complaints 2001–02*, received Oct 2002
49. Ibid.
50. Ibid.
51. Ibid.
52. SHSSB, *Annual Review of Complaints 2001–02*
53. Ibid.; *Annual Report 2000–01*
54. Ibid.
55. Western Health and Social Services Board, *Annual Report 2000–01, Annual Report 2001–02*, received May 2003
56. Ibid.
57. Northern Health and Social Services Board, *Complaints Monitoring Report 2000–01* and *Complaints Monitoring Report 2001–02*, received Oct 2002
58. Ibid.
59. NHSSB, *Complaints Monitoring Report 2001–02*
60. Ibid.; *Complaints Monitoring Report 2000–01*
61. NHSSB, *Complaints Monitoring Report 2000–01*

2.   The groundwork on the NHS complaints mechanism has delivered results
1. Department of Health, *NHS Complaints Procedure National Evaluation*, London, DoH, Mar 2001
2. Department of Health, *Reforming the NHS Complaints Procedure: a listening document*, London, DoH, Sep 2001
3. DoH, *NHS Complaints Procedure National Evaluation*, p. 11
4. Ibid., ss. 3.2 to 3.5, p. 15; Department of Health, *NHS Complaints Reform – Making Things Right*, London, DoH, Feb 2003, App. 1, pp. 20–1
5. DoH, *NHS Complaints Procedure National Evaluation*, p. 3
6. Ibid., s. 4.2, Table 4.2, pp. 21–2
7. Ibid.
8. Ibid., s. 4.6, p. 23
9. Ibid.
10. Ibid., s. 4.7, Table 4.5, p. 24
11. Ibid., s. 4.11, p. 25
12. Ibid., ss. 4.16 to 4.18, p. 26

13. Ibid., Table 4.6, p. 27
14. Ibid., s. 4.18, p. 26; Table 4.6, p. 27
15. Ibid., Table 4.6, p. 27
16. Ibid., ss. 3.11 and 3.12, p. 17; Chapter 4, ss. 4.21 and 4.22, p. 27
17. Ibid., Chapter 4, tables 4.7 and 4.8, pp. 28–9
18. Ibid., Table 4.7, p. 28
19. Ibid., Table 4.8, p. 28
20. Ibid., Table 4.9, p. 29
21. Ibid., ss. 4.27 and 4.28, p. 29
22. Ibid., ss. 4.29 and 4.30, p. 30
23. Ibid., Chapter 7, s. 7.46, p. 67
24. Ibid., Chapter 8, s. 8.1, p. 70
25. Ibid., pp. 72–3
26. Ibid., pp. 74–5
27. DoH, *Reforming the NHS Complaints Procedure*
28. DoH, *NHS Complaints Reform – Making Things Right*, App. 1, p. 23
29. Ibid.
30. Ibid., p. 24
31. Ibid.
32. Information on prevailing position received as follows:
    • for England: by fax from Department of Health, Leeds, 8 Jul 2004; Department of Health, Current Guidance, NHS Foundation Trusts, www.dh.gov.uk, accessed 15 Jan 2005
    • for Scotland: by telephone from Department of Health, Edinburgh, 21 Sept 2004; ISD Scotland, Scottish Health Statistics, Review of the NHS Complaints Procedure, www.isdscotland.org, accessed 19 Mar 2005
    • for Wales: in NHS Wales, *Complaints in the NHS – A guide to Handling Complaints in Wales*, 2003; additional details provided by telephone from Independent Review Secretariat, Brecon, 9 Sept 2004
    • for Northern Ireland: by telephone from Department of Health, Social Services and Public Safety, Belfast, 17 Sept 2004
33. Review Committee on NHS Complaints Procedures, *Being Heard: the report of a review committee on NHS Complaints Procedures*, chaired by Professor Alan Wilson, London, Department of Health, 1994
34. Ibid., p. 49
35. DoH, *NHS Complaints Procedure National Evaluation*, Case Studies, 4.13 and 4.14, p. 25
36. DoH, *NHS Complaints Reform – Making Things Right*, App. 2, pp. 25–6
37. Ibid., p. 6
38. Ibid., p. 15
39. Ibid., p. 13
40. DoH, *NHS Complaints Procedure National Evaluation*, p. 22
41. Ibid.

3.   Where and when does the Health Service Ombudsman come in?
1. How to make your complaint, www.ombudsman.org.uk/hse/england/make_complaint.html, accessed 5 Jul 2003; www.ombudsman.org.uk/hse/scotland/make_complaint.html, accessed 5 Jul 2003; and www.ombudsman.org.uk/hse/wales/make_complaint.html, accessed 22 Jun 2004
2. Ibid.
3. Ibid.
4. Putting your complaint to the Ombudsman, www.ombudsman.org.uk/hse/england/putting_complaint.html, accessed 5 Jul 2003; www.ombudsman.org.uk/hse/scotland/putting_complaint.html, accessed 5 Jul 2003; and www.ombudsman.org.uk/hse/wales/putting_complaint.html, accessed 22 Jun 2004
5. What can the Ombudsman investigate?, www.ombudsman.org.uk/ hse/england/

what_can.html, accessed 5 Jul 2003; www.ombudsman.org.uk/ hse/scotland/what_
can.html, accessed 5 Jul 2003; and www.ombudsman.org.uk/ hse/ wales/what_can.html,
accessed 22 Jun 2004

6. Ibid.
7. Matters that the Ombudsman cannot investigate, www.ombudsman.org.uk/hse/england/
matters.html, accessed 5 Jul 2003; www.ombudsman.org.uk/ hse/scotland/matters.html,
accessed 5 Jul 2003; and www.ombudsman.org.uk/ hse/wales/matters.html, accessed 22
Jun 2004
8. Ibid.
9. Ibid.
10. Health Service Ombudsman for England, *Do You Have a Complaint About the Service
you have Received from the NHS?*, booklet received on 12 Jan 2002, p. 4
11. Matters that the Ombudsman Cannot Investigate, www.ombudsman.org.uk, accessed 5
Jul 2003 and 22 Jun 2004
12. What can the Ombudsman investigate?, www.ombudsman.org.uk, accessed 5 Jul 2003
and 22 Jun 2004
13. How Will the Ombudsman Deal With Your Complaint?, www.ombudsman.org.uk/
hse/england/how_deal.html, accessed 5 Jul 2003, www.ombudsman.org.uk/hse/
scotland/how_deal.html, accessed 5 Jul 2003 and www.ombudsman.org.uk/hse/
wales/how_deal.html, accessed 22 Jun 2004; Health Service Ombudsman for England,
Do You Have a Complaint About the Service You Have Received from the NHS?, p. 5
14. How Will the Ombudsman Deal With Your Complaint?, www.ombudsman.org.uk,
accessed 5 Jul 2003 and 22 Jun 2004
15. Ibid.
16. Ibid.
17. Ibid.
18. How To Complain About Us, www.ombudsman.org.uk, accessed 5 Jul 2003 and 22 Jun
2004
19. Matters That The Ombudsman Cannot Investigate, www.ombudsman.org.uk/hse/
scotland/matters.html, accessed 5 Jul 2003
20. Announcement, www.ombudsman.org.uk/hse/scotland/make_complaint.html, accessed
12 Jul 2003
21. Health Service Commissioner for England, Scotland and Wales, *Annual Report
1998–1999*, Chapter 5, fig. 4, p. 34; Health Service Ombudsman, *Annual Report
1999–2000*, www.ombudsman.org.uk/hsc/england
(England) Health Service Ombudsman for England, *Annual Report 2000–2001*, Chapter
2, fig. 4, p. 22; *Annual Report 2001–2002*, Chapter 3, fig. 4; *Annual Report 2002–03*,
Chapter 3, fig. 4; www.ombudsman.org.uk/hsc, accessed 10 Jun 2004
(Scotland) Scottish Health Service Ombudsman, *Annual Report 2000–2001*, Chapter 7,
fig. H2, www.ombudsman.org.uk/shsc, accessed 29 Mar 2003 and Health Service
Ombudsman for Scotland, *Annual Report 2001–2002*, Chapter 6, fig. H2;
www.ombudsman.org.uk/shsc, accessed 7 Apr 2003;
(Wales) Health Service Commissioner for Wales, *Annual Report 2000–2001*, Chapter 6,
fig. 6; *Annual Report 2001–2002*, fig. 6; and *Annual Report 2002–2003*, Chapter 4, fig.
5; www.ombudsman.org.uk/whsc, accessed 10 Jun 2004
22. Health Service Ombudsman, *Annual Report 2002–03*, Chapter 3, fig. 4,
www.ombudsman.org.uk/hsc, accessed 10 Jun 2004
23. Ibid., Chapter 3, fig. 4 and para. 3.17
24. Ibid., Chapter 3, fig. 4, paras 3.18, 3.20 and fig. 7
25. Health Service Ombudsman for Wales, *Annual Report 2002–2003*, Chapter 4, fig. 5 and
para. 4.16, www.ombudsman.org.uk/whsc, accessed 10 Jun 2004
26. Health Service Ombudsman for Scotland, *Annual Report 2001–2002*, Chapter 6, paras
6.12 and 6.13, www.ombudsman.org.uk/shsc, accessed 7 Apr 2003
27. Scottish Public Services Ombudsman, *Annual Report 2002–2003*, Health.
28. Health Service Commissioner for England, Scotland and Wales, *Annual Report*

1998–1999, App. A, p. 41; *Annual Report 1999–2000*, Chapter 5, para. 5.1, www.ombudsman.org.uk/hsc, accessed 1 Feb 2002
(England) Health Service Ombudsman for England, *Annual Report 2000–2001*, Chapter 2, 2.6.1; *Annual Report 2001–2002*, Chapter 3, fig. 4, www.ombudsman.org.uk/hsc, accessed 5 Apr 2003; *Annual Report 2002–03*, Chapter 3, fig. 4, www.ombudsman. org.uk/hsc, accessed 10 Jun 2004
(Scotland) Health Service Ombudsman for Scotland, *Annual Report 2000–2001*, Chapter 7, fig. H2, www.ombudsman.org.uk/shsc, accessed 29 Mar 2003; *Annual Report 2001–2002*, Chapter 6, fig. H2, www.ombudsman.org.uk/shsc, accessed 7 Apr 2003; Scottish Public Services Ombudsman, *Annual Report 2002–2003*, Health
(Wales) Health Service Commissioner for Wales, *Annual Report 2000–2001*, Chapter 6, fig. 6, www.ombudsman.org.uk/whsc, accessed 5 Apr 2003; *Annual Report 2001–2002*, Chapter 6, fig. 6, www.ombudsman.org.uk/whsc, accessed 5 Apr 2003; *Annual Report 2002–2003*, Chapter 4, fig. 5, www.ombudsman.org.uk/whsc, accessed 10 Jun 2004

29. Health Service Ombudsman, *Annual Report 2002–2003*, Chapter 3, fig. 7, www.ombudsman.org.uk/hsc, accessed 10 Jun 2004
(Scotland) Health Service Ombudsman for Scotland, *Annual Report 2000–2001*, Chapter 7, fig. H5, www.ombudsman.org.uk/shsc, accessed 7 Apr 2003; *Annual Report 2001–2002*, Chapter 6, fig. H5; www.ombudsman.org.uk/shsc, accessed 7 Apr 2003; Scottish Public Services Ombudsman, *Annual Report 2002–2003*, Health
(Wales) Health Service Commissioner for Wales, *Annual Report 2000–2001*; *Annual Report 2001–2002*, Chapter 6, fig. 8; www.ombudsman.org.uk/whsc, accessed 5 Apr 2003; *Annual Report 2002–2003*, Chapter 4, Fig. 7, www.ombudsman.org.uk/whsc, accessed 19 Jun 2004

30. Health Service Commissioner, *Annual Report 2002–2003*, Chapter 3, fig. 7, www.ombudsman.org.uk/hsc, accessed 10 Jun 2004

31. Ibid., Chapter 3, s. 3.20

32. Health Service Ombudsman for Scotland, *Annual Report 2001–2002*, Chapter 6, 6.12, www.ombudsman.org.uk/shsc, accessed 7 Apr 2003

33. Health Service Commissioner for Wales, *Annual Report 2001–2002*, Chapter 6, 6.10, www.ombudsman.org.uk/whsc, accessed 5 Apr 2003; Annual Report 2002–2003, Chapter 4, 4.10, www.ombudsman.org.uk/whsc, accessed 10 Jun 2004

34. Re-presented from Northern Ireland Ombudsman, *Annual Report 2000–2001*, s. 1, pp. 10–11

35. Northern Ireland Ombudsman, *Annual Report 2001–2002*, s. 4, p. 105

36. Parliamentary Ombudsman for Northern Ireland and Northern Ireland Commissioner for Complaints, *Annual Report 1998–1999*, s. 4, p. 92; Assembly Ombudsman for Northern Ireland and Northern Ireland Commissioner for Complaints, *Annual Report 1999–2000*, s. 4, p. 92; *Annual Report 2000–2001*, s. 4, p. 136; *Annual Report 2001–2002*, s. 4, p. 100

37. Assembly Ombudsman for Northern Ireland and Northern Ireland Commissioner for Complaints, *Annual Report 2001–2002*, s. 4, p. 105, p. 107

38. Ibid.

39. Parliamentary Ombudsman for Northern Ireland and Northern Ireland Commissioner for Complaints, *Annual Report 1998–1999*, s. 4, p. 92; *Annual Report 1999–2000*, p. 96; Assembly Ombudsman for Northern Ireland and Northern Ireland Commissioner for Complaints, *Annual Report 2000–2001*, s. 4, Table 4.1, p. 142; *Annual Report 2001–2002*, s. 4, Table 4.1, p. 105

40. Assembly Ombudsman and Commissioner for Complaints, *Annual Report 1998–1999*, App. C, p. 103; *Annual Report 1999–2000*, s. 4, App. B, p. 105; *Annual Report 2000–2001*, s. 4, Erratum to App. C, p. 156; and *Annual Report 2001–2002*, App. C, p. 113

41. Health Service Commissioner for England, Scotland and Wales, *Annual Report 1998–1999*, Chapter 1, 1.6, p. 6

42. Jeremy Laurence, 'Patients need justice', *Independent*, 1 Dec 1998

43. Health Service Commissioner for England, Scotland and Wales, *Annual Report 1998–1999*, Chapter 3, 3.2, p. 20
44. Health Service Ombudsman for England, *Annual Report 2000–2001*, Chapter 2, 2.71 and 2.72, pp. 27–8
45. Parliamentary Ombudsman for Northern Ireland and Northern Ireland Commissioner for Complaints, *Annual Report 1998–1999*, p. 2
46. Health Service Commissioner, *Annual Report 2001–2002*, Chapter 1, 1.4, 1.5 and 1.6, www.ombudsman.org.uk/hsc, accessed 29 Mar 2003
47. Ibid, 1.15, www.ombudsman.org.uk/hsc, accessed 29 Mar 2003

4. Is the Health Service Ombudsman really neutral and fair?
1. Information received by telephone from a senior officer of the Office of the Health Service Ombudsman, London, late Sept 1999
2. Information received by telephone from a media contact who had been given this position on secondment by an officer in the Office of the Health Service Ombudsman, London, 2001
3. Office of the Health Service Ombudsman, London, letter, 27 Mar 2001
4. Office of the Health Service Ombudsman, London, letter, 12 Jul 2001
5. Office of the Health Service Ombudsman, London, letter, 26 Jun 2001
6. *Who's Who*, 2003
7. *Who's Who*, 2002
8. Ibid.
9. 10 Downing Street Newsroom, announcement of the appointment of the Parliamentary Commissioner for Administration and Health Service Commissioner for England on 24 Jul 2002, www.number-10.gov.uk/output/Page5705.asp, accessed 21 Feb 2003
10. Office of the Health Service Ombudsman, *A Guide to the Work of the Health Service Ombudsman*, p. 1; Health Service Ombudsman for England, *Do You Have a Complaint About the Service You Have Received from the NHS? How the Health Service Ombudsman can help you*, booklet received 12 Jan 2002, p. 1; Northern Ireland Ombudsman, *What Does the Ombudsman Do?*, folder and complaint form issued by the Northern Ireland Ombudsman, received Feb 2002
11. Health Service Ombudsman for England, *Do You Have a Complaint About the Service You Have Received from the NHS?*; Health Service Ombudsman, www.ombudsman.org.uk/hse/england, accessed 5 Jul 2003; www.scottishombudsman.org.uk, accessed 12 Jul 2003; www.ni-ombudsman.org.uk, accessed 19 Jun 2004
12. Health Service Ombudsman for England, *Do You Have a Complaint About the Service You Have Received from the NHS?*, Jan 2002, p. 1
13. Department of Health, *Complaints – Listening…Acting…Improving, Guidance on Implementation of the NHS Complaints Procedure*, 1996
14. Ibid., Role of the Health Service Ombudsman, 9.4
15. Office of the Health Service Ombudsman, *A Guide to the Work of the Health Service Ombudsman*, Part C, Appeal, para. 45, p. 8, 1996
16. Ibid.
17. Ibid., Appeal, para. 46, p. 8
18. Office of the Health Service Ombudsman, London, letters dated 26 Jun and 12 Jul 2001
19. House of Commons Health Committee, Sixth Report, *Procedures Related to Adverse Clinical Incidents and Outcomes in Medical Care*, p. xl, issued 23 Nov 1999
20. BBC Radio 4, *You and Yours*, 29 Mar 1999
21. House of Commons Health Committee Inquiry, *Procedures Related to Adverse Clinical Incidents and Outcomes in Medical Care*, 8 Jul 1999
22. Office of the Northern Ireland Ombudsman, 'What does the Ombudsman do?' Part 1, public information folder and complaint form
23. Information received by telephone from Office of the Northern Ireland Ombudsman, Feb 2002
24. Ibid.

25. Ibid.
26. Office of the Northern Ireland Ombudsman, 'What does the Ombudsman do?', Part 1
27. Ibid., Part 2
28. Ibid., Parts 1 and 2
29. Ibid., Part 1

5. Reformed medical self-regulation to rule, but will it be OK?
1. Department of Health, *Reform of the General Medical Council*, 'The case for change', p. 4, May 2002
2. Historical details confirmed as accurate by GMC, Jun 2005
3. Updated information from GMC, early 2005
4. General Medical Council, *Referring a Doctor to the GMC: a guide for patients*, Nov 2004, document supplied early 2005; www.gmc-uk.org/register, accessed 16 Apr 2003
5. GMC, *Briefing Sheet*, 'GMC reforms at a glance', supplied 29 Sep 2003; GMC, *Protecting the Public*, 'How are we made up?', www.gmc-uk.org, accessed 16 Apr 2003 and 27 Sep 2003; GMC, *Maintaining Pace: setting the agenda*, 'General Medical Council in 2002', p. 8
6. GMC, *Briefing Sheet*, 29 Sep 2003; Letter from GMC, 6 Nov 2003; GMC, *Protecting the Public*, 'How are we made up?'
7. GMC, *Maintaining Pace*, p. 8; Letter from GMC, 6 Nov 2003, and updated details received since then
8. GMC, *Briefing Sheet*, 'GMC reforms at a glance'; GMC, *Referring a Doctor to the GMC: guidance for members of the medical profession and other healthcare professionals*, booklet, Oct 2002; www.gmc-uk.org/probdocs, accessed 16 Apr 2003
9. GMC, *Referring a Doctor to the GMC*, Oct 2002
10. Ibid.; and updated information from the GMC, early 2005
11. Based on information received from GMC, 3 Jun 2005
12. Ibid.
13. Ibid.
14. GMC, *Referring a Doctor to the GMC*, Nov 2004
15. Ibid.
16. GMC, *The GMC's Fitness to Practise Procedures*, para. 5, document supplied 9 Mar 2005
17. Ibid.
18. GMC, *Referring a Doctor to the GMC*, Oct 2002
19. GMC, *Referring a Doctor to the GMC*, Nov 2004
20. Ibid.
21. Ibid.
22. GMC, *Fitness to Practise Procedures*, para. 10, Mar 2005
23. GMC, *Referring a Doctor to the GMC*, Nov 2004
24. GMC, *Fitness to Practise Procedures*, para. 12, Mar 2005;
25. Ibid., para. 14
26. Ibid., para. 15; GMC, *Referring a Doctor to the GMC*, Nov 2004
27. GMC, *Fitness to Practise Procedures*, paras. 16–18, Mar 2005
28. Ibid., para. 23
29. Ibid., para. 28
30. Ibid., para. 21
31. Ibid., para. 27
32. Ibid., paras. 24 and 25
33. GMC, *Fitness to Practise Procedures*, Oct 2002
34. Ibid.
35. Ibid.
36. Ibid.
37. Ibid.
38. Ibid.
39. Ibid.

40. Ibid.; letter from GMC, 6 Nov 2003; additional information given in 2003
41. GMC, *Fitness to Practise Procedures*, Oct 2002; letter from GMC, 6 Nov 2003
42. GMC, *Fitness to Practise Procedures*, Oct 2002
43. Ibid.; letter from GMC, 6 Nov 2003
44. Ibid.
45. GMC, *Fitness to Practise Statistics for 2003, Annex A – Work of the Screening Section*, 10 Sep 2004
46. GMC, *Annex A – Work of the Screening Section*
47. Ibid.
48. Ibid.
49. Ibid.
50. GMC, *Fitness to Practise Statistics for 2003, Annex B – Work of the Preliminary Proceedings Committee (PPC)*, 10 Sep 2004
51. Ibid.
52. Ibid.
53. Ibid.
54. GMC, *Fitness to Practise Statistics for 2003, Annex C – Work of the Professional Conduct Committee (PCC) in 2003*, 10 Sep 2004
55. Ibid.
56. Ibid.
57. GMC, *Fitness to Practise Statistics for 2003, Annex D – Work of the Health Screeners and the Health Section*, 'Analysis of Health Procedures Activity in 2003', 10 Sep 2004
58. Ibid.
59. Ibid.
60. Ibid.
61. GMC, *Fitness to Practise Statistics for 2003, Annex E – The Work of the Health Committee in 2003*, 'Background', 10 Sep 2004
62. Ibid.
63. GMC, *Fitness to Practise Statistics for 2003, Annex F – Work of the Performance Section in 2003*, 10 Sep 2004
64. Ibid.
65. The Medical Act 1983 (Amendment) Order 2002, Part III – Committees of the Council, para. 5, ss. 2 and 3, www.legislation.hmso.gov.uk, accessed 15 Nov 2003
66. GMC, *The General Medical Council (Fitness to Practise) Rules 2004*, Part II – Investigation of allegations, rule 4
67. Ibid., rules 5 and 6; rule 5 further described and enlarged on in information from GMC, early 2005
68. GMC, *The General Medical Council (Fitness to Practise) Rules 2004*, Part II, rule 8, paras. 1 and 2; GMC, *General Medical Council – Fitness to Practise Procedures*, document supplied 9 Mar 2005
69. GMC, *The General Medical Council (Fitness to Practise) Rules 2004*, Part II, rule 7, para. 1
70. Letter from GMC, 6 Nov 2003
71. Documented information on reformed fitness to practise procedures supplied by GMC in early 2005
72. GMC, *To Agree the Functions and Structure of the Investigation Committee*, Council paper, 15 Oct 2003, received 14 Nov 2003
73. The Medical Act 1983 (Amendment) Order 2002, Part V – Fitness to practise and medical ethics, para. 35C, ss. 1 and 3, www.legislation.hmso.gov.uk, accessed 15 Nov 2003
74. Ibid., para. 35C, s. 2
75. Ibid., para. 35C, ss. 4 and 5
76. Ibid., para. 35C, s. 7
77. Ibid., para. 35C, ss. 5 and 7
78. Ibid., para. 35C, s. 6
79. Written comments and corrections to author's draft from GMC in early 2005

80. GMC, *To Consider Fitness to Practise Reforms – Rules and Guidance*, Discussion and recommendations, 7 Jul 2004, para. 55
81. The Medical Act 1983 (Amendment) Order 2002, Part V – Fitness to practise and medical ethics, para. 35D, s. 2
82. Ibid., para. 35D, s. 3
83. Ibid., para. 35D, s. 4
84. Ibid., para. 35D, ss. 5a–c
85. Ibid., para. 35D, s. 5c
86. Ibid., para. 35D, s. 6
87. Ibid., para. 35D, s. 7
88. Ibid., para. 35D, s. 8
89. Ibid. para. 35D, ss. 9–10
90. Ibid., para. 35D, s. 11–12
91. Ibid., para. 35D, s. 12
92. Ibid., para. 35E, s. 1
93. Ibid. para. 35E, s. 2
94. Ibid., para. 40, ss. 4–5
95. Documented information on reformed fitness to practise procedures supplied by GMC in early 2005
97. GMC, *Annex A – The General Medical Council (Fitness to Practise) Rules 2004*, Part VII – Interim orders, ss. 25 and 26; *Fitness to Practise – Proposed New Rules and Guidance*, A consultation paper, Overview, para. 16, July 2003
97. GMC, *Annex A – Registration Decisions* – draft 7/01/04 (version 2), Arrangement of Procedures, ss. 2, 3 and 4
98. GMC, *Annex B – General Medical Council (Registration Appeals Panels) Rules 2004*, ss. 3 and 7
99. The Medical Act 1983 (Amendment) Order 2002, Part III – Committees of the Council, para. 23; GMC, *Annex B – The General Medical Council (Constitution of Panels) Rules 2004*, rules 3 and 4
100. GMC, *Annex B – The General Medical Council (Constitution of Panels) Rules 2004*, rules 5 and 6
101. GMC, *Annex A – The General Medical Council (Fitness to Practise) Rules 2004*, Part VIII – General, rule 38
102. Ibid., rule 41
103. Ibid., Part I – Preliminaries, rule 3; *Fitness to Practise – Proposed New Rules and Guidance*, Sch. 1, Jul 2003
104. GMC, *Annex A – The General Medical Council (Fitness to Practise) Rules 2004*, Part I, rule 3, Sch. 1 – Performance Assessments, paras. 2 and 3; *Fitness to Practise – Proposed New Rules and Guidance*, Schedules 2 and 3, July 2003
105. GMC, *Annex A – The General Medical Council (Fitness to Practise) Rules 2004*, Sch. 2 – Health Assessments, paras. 1–4; *Fitness to Practise – Proposed New Rules and Guidance*, Sch. 4, July 2003
106. *Annex C, Health Care and Associated Professions, Doctors: The General Medical Council (Legal Assessors) Rules 2004* (SI 2004 No. 2625), ss. 2–5, Explanatory note to Order
107. Information in this paragraph confirmed as being correct by the GMC, June 2005
108. Council for Healthcare Regulatory Excellence, *What We Do*, www.chre.org.uk, accessed 9 Jun 2005
109. Ibid.
110. Ibid.
111. Ibid.
112. Ibid.

Note.
The body of Chapter 5 (generally represented by source notes 2 to 107) in its unedited form was corrected and then confirmed as being accurate by the GMC at the time of writing.

6. A re-named and reformed regulatory body for nursing has emerged
1. Nursing and Midwifery Order 2001, Part II, Article 3, paras. 2 and 7; Part III, Article 8, paras. 5 and 8; Part V, Article 21, para. 1, and Article 22, para. 1; United Kingdom Central Council for Nursing, Midwifery and Health Visiting, *The PREP Handbook*, UKCC, 2001, p. 4
2. Nursing and Midwifery Order 2001, Sch. 1, The Nursing and Midwifery Council and Committees, Part 1, Article 1, paras. 1–3
3. Ibid., Sch. 1, Part 1, Article 8, paras. 1 and 2
4. Ibid., Sch. 1, Part 1, Articles 9 and 10
5. Ibid., Sch. 1, Part 1, Article 11, paras. 1 and 4
6. Ibid., Sch. 1, Part 1, Article 11, para. 3
7. Ibid., Sch. 1, Part 1, Article 15, para. 3
8. Ibid., Sch. 1, Part 1, Article 15, para. 8
9. Ibid., Sch. 1, Part II, Article 18, paras. 1–5
10. UKCC, *UKCC Professional Conduct Annual Report 2000–2001*, p. 4; updated information supplied by NMC, 2004
11. UKCC, *UKCC Professional Conduct Annual Report 2000–2001* (table), p. 4; updated information supplied by NMC, 2003
12. UKCC, *UKCC Professional Conduct Annual Report 2000–2001* (table), p. 5; updated information supplied by NMC, 2003, 2004
13. Nursing and Midwifery Order 2001, Part V, Article 22, paras. 1 and 3
14. Ibid., Sch. 1, Part II, Article 18, para. 6
15. Ibid., Sch. 1, Part II, Article 18, para. 6a–6f
16. Ibid., Sch. 1, Part II, Article 18, paras. 7–11
17. UKCC, *UKCC Professional Conduct Annual Report 2000–2001*, p. 5
18. Nursing and Midwifery Order 2001, Part V, Article 22, paras. 1 and 2; Article 26, para. 6(b)
19. Based on information given and approved by NMC, Aug 2004
20. UKCC, *UKCC Professional Conduct Annual Report 2000–2001*, p. 5; updated information supplied by NMC, 2003, 2004
21. Nursing and Midwifery Order 2001, Part V, Article 27(a)
22. Ibid., Part V, Article 27(b); UKCC, *UKCC Professional Conduct Annual Report 2000–2001*, p. 7
23. Based on data provided and approved by NMC, Aug 2004
24. UKCC, *UKCC Professional Conduct Annual Report 2000–2001*, p. 6; position confirmed by NMC, 2004
25. Information provided by NMC, 2003, 2004
26. UKCC, *UKCC Professional Conduct Annual Report 2000–2001*, Professional Conduct Committee decisions (table), pp. 6–7; updated data from NMC, 2003, 2004
27. Information from NMC, 2004
28. UKCC, *UKCC Professional Conduct Annual Report 2000–2001*, p. 7
29. Information from NMC, 2003, 2004
30. Nursing and Midwifery Order 2001, Part V, Article 33, para. 2(a)
31. UKCC, *UKCC Professional Conduct Annual Report 2000–2001*, p. 7
32. Ibid., p. 8; Nursing and Midwifery Order 2001, Part V, Article 28(a) and (b); information from NMC, 2003
33. UKCC, *UKCC Professional Conduct Annual Report 2000–2001*, p. 8; updated information from NMC, 2003
34. Ibid., p. 8; updated information from NMC, 2003, 2004
35. UKCC, *UKCC Professional Conduct Annual Report 2000–2001*, p. 8
36. Ibid.; additional statistics provided by NMC, 2004
37. Latest statistics from NMC, 2004; UKCC, *UKCC Professional Conduct Annual Report 2000–2001*, table, p. 9
38. UKCC, *UKCC Professional Conduct Annual Report 2000–2001*, p. 9; position further

clarified and updated by NMC, 2004
39. Information from NMC, Aug 2002
40. Nursing and Midwifery Order 2001, Part II, Article 16, paras. 2(a) and 2(b)
41. Ibid., para. 2(c)
42. Ibid., para. 3
43. Ibid., paras. 4 and 5
44. Nursing and Midwifery Order 2001, Part VIII, Article 41 and Article 42, para. 1(a)
45. Ibid., Part V, Article 26, paras. 2a–2d and 5
46. Ibid., Part V, Article 26, paras. 5 and 6
47. Ibid., Part V, Article 29, para. 1
48. Ibid., Part V, Article 29, paras. 3 and 4
49. Ibid., Part V, Article 29, para. 10
50. Ibid., Part V, Article 22, paras. 7 and 8
51. Ibid., Part V, Article 33, paras. 1 and 3
52. Ibid., Part V, Article 33, paras. 4, 5 and 7
53. Ibid., Part V, Article 33, paras. 9–13
54. NMC document, 13 Mar 2003
55. Ibid.
56. Ibid.
57. Nursing and Midwifery Order 2001, Part V, Article 34, paras. 1 and 2
58. Ibid., Part V, Article 34, paras. 5 and 6
59. Ibid., Part V, Article 35, paras. 1–4
60. Ibid., Part V, Article 36, paras. 1–4
61. NMC document, 13 Mar 2003

Note.
The body of Chapter 6 – including that represented by the above source notes in its final but not fully edited form was confirmed as being accurate by the NMC at the time of writing.

7.   No all-inclusive patients' rights legislation in the United Kingdom

1.   Department of Health, *Confidentiality: NHS code of practice*, version 3.5, DoH, 27 Oct 2003, p. 1, paras. 1, 2 and 5, www.doh.gov.uk/ipu/confiden, accessed Dec 2003
2.   Ibid., Foreword; Department of Health, *The Protection and Use of Patient Information: the NHS Confidentiality Code of Practice*, DoH, www.doh.gov.uk/ipu/confiden/protect/index.htm, accessed 9 Oct 2003
3.   Department of Health, *Confidentiality*, version 3.5, p. 1, para. 3; p. 4, para. 11
4.   Ibid., p. 4, paras. 10 and 11
5.   Ibid., p. 4, paras. 12 and 13
6.   Ibid., p. 5, para. 14
7.   Ibid., p. 5, para. 15,
8.   Ibid., p. 5, paras. 16 and 17,
9.   Ibid., p. 5, paras. 18 and 19
10. Ibid., p. 6, para. 21
11. Ibid., p. 7, para. 22
12. Ibid., p. 7, paras. 23 and 24
13. Ibid., p. 7, paras. 25 and 26
14. Ibid., p. 8, para. 27
15. Ibid., p. 9, para. 28
16. Ibid., p. 9, paras. 29–31; p. 14, paras. 32–37
17. Ibid., p. 14, para. 33
18. Ibid., p. 15, para. 38
19. Brief outline of information in NHS Information Authority, *Protecting and Using Confidential Patient Information – A Strategy for the NHS*, www.nhsia.nhs.uk/caldicott/pages/links.asp, accessed 16 Dec 2003, s. 1, p. 1; and s. 8, p. 32,
20. Brief outline of relevant information in Data Protection Act 1998, Chapter 29, Part II,

paras. 7, 8, 10, 13 and 14, www.legislation.hmso.gov.uk/acts 1998, accessed 5 Jan 2004
21. Department of Health, App. A: the Data Protection Act 1998, www.doh.gov.uk/ipu, accessed 2 Jan 2004
22. Department of Health, App. B: the Health Record Access Route, www.doh.gov.uk/ipu, obtained 2 Jan 2004
23. Department of Health, *Good Practice in Consent Implementation Guide: consent to examination or treatment*, p. 3, para. 1
24. Ibid., p. 3
25. Ibid., p. 9, paras. 1 and 2
26. Ibid., p. 9, para. 3
27. Ibid., pp. 9–10, paras. 4 and 5
28. Ibid., p. 11, para. 1
29. Ibid., pp. 11–12, paras. 3, 4 and 5
30. Ibid., p. 12, paras. 6–8; p. 13, para. 9
31. Ibid, Chapter III, pp. 14–16; Chapter IV, pp. 17–19, Chapter V, pp. 20–1; Chapter VI p. 22; Chapter VII, p. 23; and Chapter VIII pp. 24–5
32. DoH, *Good Practice in Consent Implementation Guide*, p. 10, para. 6
33. DoH, *Good Practice in Consent Implementation Guide*, App. A, pp. 27–8
34. Department of Health, *Reference Guide to Consent for Examination or Treatment*, 2001, p. 2, paras. 1 and 3
35. Ibid., para. 3
36. Ibid., para. 2
37. Ibid., para. 4
38. Ibid., pp. 4–25
39. Department of Health, *Consent – What You have a Right to Expect: a guide for adults*, London, DoH, 2001, pp. 2 and 3, www.doh.gov.uk, accessed early 2004
40. Ibid., p. 3
41. Ibid.
42. Ibid., pp. 4 and 7
43. Ibid., p. 4
44. Ibid., p. 4
45. Ibid., p. 5
46. Ibid.
47. Ibid., p. 6
48. Ibid., p. 6
49. Ibid., p. 7
50. Ibid., p. 8
51. Ibid., p. 9
52. Ibid.
53. Ibid., p. 10
54. Ibid., pp. 10–11
55. Department of Health, *Consent – What You have a Right to Expect: a guide for children and young people*, London, DoH, 2001, www.doh.gov.uk, accessed early 2004
56. Ibid., pp. 3–4
57. Ibid., p. 5
58. Ibid., p. 6
59. Ibid., p. 7
60. Ibid., p. 7
61. Ibid., pp. 8–9
62. Ibid., pp. 9–10
63. Department of Health, *Consent – What You have a Right to Expect: a guide for parents*, London, DoH, 2001, www.doh.gov.uk, accessed early 2004, pp. 2–3
64. Ibid., p. 4
65. Ibid., p. 4
66. Ibid., p. 5

67. Ibid., p. 6
68. Ibid., p. 7
69. Ibid., p. 7
70. Ibid., pp. 8–11
71. Department of Health, *Consent – What You have a Right to Expect: a guide for relatives and carers*, London, DoH, 2001, www.doh.gov.uk, accessed early 2001, p. 3
72. Ibid., p. 3
73. Ibid., p. 4
74. Ibid., p. 5
75. Ibid., p. 5
76. Ibid., p. 6
77. Ibid., p. 7
78. Ibid., p. 8
79. Department of Health, *Your Guide to the NHS*, London, DoH, 2001, inside front cover
80. Ibid.
81. *Your Guide to the NHS*, pp. 2–3
82. DoH, *Your Guide to the NHS*
83. Department of Health, *Supporting the Implementation of Patient Advice and Liaison Services (PALS) – Core Standards and Practice Guide*, www.doh.gov.uk, accessed Dec 2003; Department of Health, *NHS Policy and Guidance, Patient Advice and Liaison Services (PALS), Overview*, www.doh.gov.uk, accessed Oct 2003
84. Department of Health, *NHS Complaints Procedure*, Independent complaints advocacy services (ICAS), paras 2 and 4, Department of Health information, www.doh.gov.uk, accessed 6 Dec 2003
85. Commission for Patient and Public Involvement in Health, *CPPIH: About the Commission – What We Do*, para. 1, www.cppih.org, accessed 9 Oct 2003; and *CPPIH: PPI forums – what's new*, para. 1, www.cppih.org, accessed 6 Dec 2003
86. Commission for Patient and Public Involvement in Health, *CPPIH: About the Commission – What We Do*, para. 2, www.cppih.org, accessed 9 Oct 2003; Department of Health, 'What is a patient and public involvement forum?', DoH, 2003, p. 1, www.doh.gov.uk, accessed Dec 2003
87. Department of Health, circular, items 26 and 27: 'Joining a patient and public involvement forum', 2003, p. 5, www.doh.gov.uk, accessed Dec 2003
88. Ibid., Summary of the main points, p. 1
89. Ibid., pp. 1–2; CPPIH, *CPPIH: Local Network Providers – What's New*, para. 2, www.cppih.org, accessed 6 Dec 2003
90. Commission for Patient and Public Involvement in Health, *CPPIH: about the Commission – what we do*, paras. 3 and 4, www.cppih.org, accessed 9 Oct 2003
91. National Patient Safety Agency, *National Patient Safety Agency, About Us*, www.npsa.nhs.uk, accessed 9 Oct 2003
92. Department of Health, *Department of Health: Appraisal, NICE*, www.doh.gov.uk/nice, accessed 26 Jan 2004; National Institute for Clinical Excellence: *Why has NICE been set up?*; *Patient Involvement Unit for NICE: role of PIU in supporting patients and carers*; *Introduction – NICE*, board meetings; *A Short Introduction to the Citizens Council*, all at www.nice.org.uk, accessed 26 Jan 2004 and 22 Jul 2005; National Institute for Health and Clinical Excellence, *About NICE: who we are, patient and public involvement programme*, www.nice.org.uk, accessed 22 July 2005
93. Commission for Health Improvement, www.chi.nhs.uk, accessed 9 Oct 2003; and *About CHI: what is CHI?*, pp. 1–4, www.chi.nhs.uk, accessed 9 Oct 2003
94. Commission for Health Improvement, *CHI – the Future, The Future: CHAI – about CHAI* and *The Future: CHAI – legislation*, www.chi.nhs.uk, accessed 9 Oct 2003; Department of Health, *About the Commission for Social Care Inspection*, www.doh.gov.uk/csci, accessed 9 Oct 2003; Healthcare Commission, *What is the Healthcare Commission and why we exist?*, www.healthcarecommission.org.uk/AboutUs/WhatIsTheHealthcare Commission/fs/en, accessed 14 July 2005

8. **Litigation – still the only game in town for patient compensation in the UK**
1. NHS Litigation Authority, framework document, updated version, ss. 1.1 and 1.2, www.nhsla.com, accessed Jul 2003
2. Ibid., ss. 1.2(i–v)
3. Ibid., ss. 1.4(i and ii)
4. Ibid., ss. 1.3 and 2.2
5. Ibid., s. 1.5; NHS Litigation Authority, letter, 29 Jul 2003
6. NHS Litigation Authority, framework document, s. 2.1
7. Ibid., ss. 2.2(i, v and viii)
8. Ibid., ss. 2.3, 3.2 and 3.3, Annex A
9. NHS Litigation Authority, letter, 29 Jul 2003
10. NHS Litigation Authority, framework document, s. 3.1; NHS Litigation Authority, letter, 29 Jul 2003
11. NHS Litigation Authority, framework document, ss. 4.1, 8.1 and 8.2; *About the NHS Litigation Authority*, key facts, www.nhsla.com, accessed 15 Jul 2003; NHS Litigation Authority, letter, 29 Jul 2003
12. NHS Litigation Authority, *Report and Accounts 2002*, p. 3; *About the NHS Litigation Authority*, www.nhsla.com, accessed 15 Jul 2004
13. NHS Litigation Authority, *Report and Accounts 2002*, p. 3; *About the NHS Litigation Authority*, www.nhsla.com, accessed 15 Jul 2003
14. NHS Litigation Authority, *Report and Accounts 2003*, p. 3
15. Ibid.
16. Ibid.
17. Welsh Risk Pool, 'In brief' and 'History and development', document, 22 Jul 2003
18. Welsh Risk Pool, 'History and development'
19. Welsh Risk Pool, 'History and development'; additional information received by fax from Welsh Risk Pool, 29 Apr 2004
20. Welsh Risk Pool, 'History and development'
21. Ibid.; amended data received by fax from the Welsh Risk Pool, 29 Apr 2004
22. Welsh Risk Pool, 'History and development, Assessing and collecting premiums'; amended and updated information on assessing and collecting premiums received by fax from the Welsh Risk Pool, 29 Apr 2004
23. Welsh Risk Pool, 'Reimbursement of losses'; 'Claims expenditure by year', graph, supplied 22 Jul 2003; updated information received by fax from the Welsh Risk Pool, 29 Apr 2004
24. Scottish Health Service Central Legal Office, letter recived by fax, 24 Jul 2003
25. Ibid., additional information received by fax from the Central Legal Office, 21 Aug 2003
26. Scottish Health Service Central Legal Office, statistical data on patients and clinical damages, information received by fax, 24 Jul 2003
27. Legal Services Commission, *A Practical Guide to Community Legal Service Funding by the Legal Services Commission*, 2003, 'Legal Aid reforms – what has changed?'
28. Ibid., ss. 1.1 and 1.2; corrected or additional information received by fax from the LSC, 26 Aug 2003
29. LSC, *A Practical Guide to Legal Service Funding*, s. 2.4
30. Ibid., s. 1.2; Consumers' Association in alliance with Action for Victims of Medical Accidents, Community Legal Service, *Medical Accidents: your rights if you have been injured during treatment*, information booklet 14, 2003, p. 10
31. Consumers' Association in alliance with Action for Victims of Medical Accidents, CLS, *Medical Accidents*, p. 9; corrected or additional information received by fax from the LSC, 26 Aug 2003
32. LSC, *A Practical Guide to Community Legal Service Funding*, ss. 2.5 and 2.6, 2003
33. Ibid., ss. 2.7 and 2.8
34. Ibid., s. 5.12
35. Ibid., ss. 5.7, 5.8 and 5.9
36. Ibid., s. 5.9, table

37. Ibid., ss. 5.10 and 5.11
38. Ibid., s. 5.11, table
39. Ibid., s. 5.13; corrected or additional information received by fax from Legal Services Commission, 26 Aug 2003
40. Ibid., s. 5.14

9. A patient redress scheme for England has been drawn up
1. Sir Liam Donaldson, *Making Amends – A Consultation Paper Setting Out Proposals for Reforming the Approach to Clinical Negligence in the NHS*, London, Department of Health, 2003, p. 28, para. 19; Department of Health, *Clinical Negligence – What are the Issues and Options for Reform?*, 'Call for ideas', Interested parties who have been sent a letter from Professor Donaldson bringing the document to their attention for comment, list of the 180 individuals, DoH, www.doh.gov.uk/clinicalnegligencereform/appendinterest.htm, accessed 30 Aug 2003
2. *Making Amends*, p. 28, para. 19
3. Ibid., p. 29, para. 20
4. Ibid., p. 117, para. 1
5. Ibid., p. 117, paras. 1 and 2
6. Ibid., pp. 117–18, para. 4
7. Ibid., p. 118, paras. 5–9
8. Ibid., p. 119, para. 10
9. Ibid., Rec. 1
10. Ibid.
11. Ibid.; p. 120
12. Ibid., p. 120
13. Ibid.
14. Ibid.
15. Ibid.
16. Ibid., pp. 120–2, Rec. 2
17. Ibid., p. 122, Recs. 3 and 4
18. Ibid., p. 123, Rec. 5
19. Ibid., pp. 123–4, Rec. 6
20. Ibid., p. 124, Rec. 7
21. Ibid., 1 p. 124, Rec. 8
22. Ibid., p. 124, Rec. 9
23. Ibid., p. 125, Rec. 10
24. Ibid., p. 125, Rec. 11
25. Ibid., pp. 125–6, Rec. 12
26. Ibid., p. 126, Rec. 13
27. Ibid., p. 126, Rec. 14
28. Ibid., pp. 126–7, Rec. 15
29. Ibid., p. 127, Rec. 16
30. Ibid., pp. 127–8, Recs, 17 and 18
31. Ibid., p. 128, Rec. 19
32. *Making Amends*, p. 19
33. Ibid.
34. Ibid., pp. 19–20
35. Ibid., p. 11
36. Ibid., pp. 14 and 111
37. Ibid., p. 15
38. Ibid., pp. 111–12
39. Ibid., pp. 104–5
40. Ibid., p. 105, para. 50
41. Ibid., p. 105, para. 52
42. Ibid, pp. 97–101, paras. 3–30; pp 101–3, paras. 31–44

43. Ibid., p. 105, para. 51
44. Ibid., pp. 111–12, paras. 11–12
45. Ibid., p. 112, paras. 13–14
46. Ibid., p. 113, para. 15
47. Department of Health, *Clinical Negligence – What are the Issues and Options for Reform?*, Annex A, DoH, www.doh.gov.uk/clinicalnegligencereform, accessed 30 Aug 2003
48. Ibid.
49. Ibid., interested parties who have been sent a letter from Professor Liam Donaldson bringing the document to their attention for comment, list of the 180 individuals, published by the Department of Health, on www.doh.gov.uk/clinicalnegligencereform/appendinterest.htm, accessed 30 Aug 2003
50. Department for Work and Pensions, 'Vaccine damage payments' (sections 'Can I get it?' and 'Changes to the Vaccine Damage Payments Act and further claims'), www.dwp.gov.uk, accessed 18 Nov 2004
51. Department for Work and Pensions, 'Vaccine damage payments' (sections 'What is severe disablement?' and 'Changes to the Vaccine Damage Payments Act and further claims')
52. Ibid. (section 'What else should I know?')
53. Ibid. (section 'Can I get it?')
54. Ibid. (section 'What else should I know?'); information or confirmation from DWP, Nov 2004
55. Information from DWP, Nov 2004
56. Ibid.; DWP, 'Vaccine damage payments' (section 'Effects on benefits and tax credits')
57. Jobcentre Plus, 'Industrial Injuries Disablement for an Accident at Work' (section 'About this benefit'), www.jobcentreplus.gov.uk, accessed 18 Nov 2004
58. Jobcentre Plus, 'Industrial Injuries Disablement Benefit (accidents/diseases)' (sections 'Weekly amounts' and 'How do I claim?'), www.jobcentreplus.gov.uk, accessed 18 Nov 2004
59. Jobcentre Plus, 'Industrial Injuries Disablement Benefit for an accident at work' (section 'Other money you may be able to get') and 'Industrial Injuries Disablement Benefit (accidents/diseases)' (section 'How much will I get?'), www.jobcentreplus.gov.uk, accessed 18 Nov 2004
60. Jobcentre Plus, 'Industrial Injuries Benefit for an accident at work' (section 'Other money you may be able to get'), 'Industrial Injuries Disablement Benefit (accidents/diseases)' (sections 'What else should I know?' and 'How much will I get?'), www.jobcentreplus.gov.uk, accessed 18 Nov 2004
61. Criminal Injuries Compensation Authority, *Guide to the Criminal Injuries Compensation Scheme 2001*, Part 1, paras. 8–9, 2003, www.cica.gov.uk, accessed Nov 2004
62. CICA, *Compensation for Victims of Violent Crime*, 'Who should apply for criminal injuries compensation?', 2003
63. Ibid.
64. Ibid., 'We cannot pay compensation in the following circumstances'
65. Ibid., 'Other things which may affect your claim' and 'How do I apply?'
66. Ibid., 'Other things which may affect your claim'
67. Ibid., 'Circumstances before, during and after an incident' and 'Criminal record'
68. Ibid., 'Compensation'
69. CICA, *Guide to the Criminal Injuries Compensation Scheme 2001*, Part 5, C and D, www.cica.gov.uk
70. CICA, *Compensation for Victims of Violent Crime*, 'Compensation', 2003
71. DWP, 'Compensation and social security benefits' (section 'Compensation recovery'), leaflet GL 27, Apr 2004
72. Ibid.

12. Ireland's health service complaints system is under reform

1. Ireland, Department of Health and Children, *Quality and Fairness: a health system for you – Health Strategy 2001*, DoHC, para. 49, Objective 1: The patient is at the centre in the delivery of care, www.doh.ie, accessed 27 Jul 2002
2. Ibid.
3. Ibid.
4. Note re Complaints Procedures in the Health Service, received by fax from Department of Health and Children, Dublin, 10 Jun 2004
5. Explanatory note referring to the Interim Health Service Executive (Establishment) Order 2004, associated with Health (Amendment) Act 2004 (SI 2004 No. 90), The Stationery Office, Dublin, www.doh.ie, accessed 9 Jul 2004
6. Explanatory note referring to the Health (Amendment) Act 2004 (Commencement) Order 2004 (SI 2004 No. 378), The Stationery Office, Dublin, www.doh.ie, accessed 9 Jul 2004
7. Information received by telephone from Department of Health and Children, Dublin, 9 Jul 2004
8. Ireland, DoHC, *Quality and Fairness*, para. 49, Objective 1
9. Ibid., para. 49, Objective 1, and para. 105
10. Ibid., para. 49, Objective 1
11. Ibid., para. 105
12. Information received by telephone from the Department of Health and Children, Dublin, 8 Jul 2004
13. Ireland, DoHC, *Quality and Fairness*, para. 105
14. Information received by telephone from the Department of Health and Children, Dublin, 8 Jul 2004
15. Ireland, DoHC, *Quality and Fairness*, para. 105
16. Ibid.
17. Ireland, DoHC, *Quality and Fairness*, para. 106
18. Ireland, DoHC, *Quality and Fairness*, para. 49, Objective 1
19. Presentation to the Oireachtas Joint Committee on the Strategic Management Initiative, pp. 11–12, 26 Jun 2001, supplied by the Office of the Irish Ombudsman
20. Presentation to the Oireachtas Joint Committee on the Strategic Management Initiative, pp. 12–13
21. Presentation to the Oireachtas Joint Committee on the Strategic Management Initiative, p. 13
22. Eastern Regional Health Authority, Background document, 'Establishment of ERHA marks new departure in delivery of health care', p. 1, para. 1
23. Working group of the Eastern Regional Health Authority, 'Review of complaints procedures protocols and appeals in the region (Summer 2001): the terms of reference for the working group', document issued Sept 2001
24. Ibid., Interim Report, part 1
25. Ibid., Interim Report, part 2
26. Ibid.
27. 'Review of complaints', Interim Report, part 1, Executive Summary, part 3
28. Ibid.
29. Ibid.
30. Ibid.
31. Ibid.
32. Ibid.
33. Ibid.
34. Ibid.
35. Ibid.
36. Ibid.
37. Ibid.
38. Ibid.

39. Ibid.
40. 'Review of complaints', Interim Report, part 4
41. 'Review of complaints', Interim Report, part 5
42. Ibid.
43. 'Review of complaints', Interim Report, part 7; additional data supplied by Eastern Regional Health Authority, fax no. 147, 11 Jun 2004
44. Eastern Regional Health Authority, *People Matter – A Framework for the Enhanced and Effective Handling of Complaints [in the] Eastern Region*, ERHA, 2003; additional data supplied by ERHA, fax no. 147, 11 Jun 2004
45. Waterford Regional Hospital, 'Waterford Regional Hospital complaints procedure: procedures for reporting complaints', 1999
46. Ibid.
47. *Waterford Regional Hospital Complaints Procedure*, Time limit for investigation of complaint, Time limit for replying to complaint, 1999
48. *Waterford Regional Hospital Complaints Procedure*, Time limit for replying to complaint, 1999
49. *Waterford Regional Hospital Complaints Procedure*, Complaints relating to clinical judgement, 1999
50. *Waterford Regional Hospital Complaints Procedure*, Complaints relating [to] judgement, 1999
51. *Waterford Regional Hospital Complaints Procedure*, Verbal complaints, 1999
52. *Waterford Regional Hospital Complaints Procedure*, Written complaints, Dissatisfaction with outcome of written complaint, 1999
53. *Waterford Regional Hospital Complaints Procedure*, Hospital complaints committee, 1999
54. *Waterford Regional Hospital Complaints Procedure*, Appeal, 1999
55. *Waterford Regional Hospital Complaints Procedure*, App., The Patient's Charter, Complaints, 1999
56. Kilkenny Mental Health Services, 'Kilkenny Mental Health Services complaints handling policy and procedures: appeal', document, 14 Feb 2002
57. North Eastern Health Board, *North Eastern Health Board Regional Complaints Procedure: a guide for Health Board Staff*, NEHB, 2001, p. 4
58. Ibid.
59. NEHB, *North Eastern Health Board Regional Complaints Procedure*, p. 5
60. Ibid.
61. Ibid.
62. NEHB, *North Eastern Health Board Regional Complaints Procedure*, p. 6
63. Ibid.
64. Mid-Western Health Board, 'Your voice, shared vision, the Mid-Western Health Board comments and complaints policy: a guide for Health Board staff', feedback, 2002, p. 4
65. Ibid.
66. Ibid.
67. Ibid.
68. Mid-Western Health Board, 'Your voice shared vision', feedback, 2002, p. 5
69. Kevin Murphy, *The Ombudsman Explains the Work of his Office*, document supplied in early 2002, p. 1 (no date)
70. Ibid., pp. 1–2
71. Kevin Murphy, 'Conflict and Accountability: the citizen and the ombudsman', address to the Irish School of Ecumenics, Dublin, Office of the Ombudsman, 2001, p. 11
72. Murphy, *The Ombudsman Explains the Work of his Office*, pp. 1–2
73. Murphy, *The Ombudsman Explains the Work of his Office*, p. 2
74. Ibid.
75. Kevin Murphy, *The Evolving Role of the Irish Ombudsman*, Dublin, Office of the Ombudsman, 2002, p. 6
76. This point confirmed on the telephone by spokesperson in the Office of the Ombudsman, Dublin, Jul 2002

77. Murphy, 'Conflict and Accountability', p. 6
78. *The Ombudsman Explains the Work of his Office*, p. 4, para. 2
79. Ibid., p. 3
80. Ibid., p. 3
81. Ibid., p. 4, para. 1
82. Joint Committee on the Strategic Management Initiative, Dublin, *Second Report of the Joint Oireachtas Committee on the Strategic Management Initiative*, Recs., item 5, pp. 13–14, document released 16 Apr 2002, supplied soon afterwards
83. Information by telephone from Health Service Executive East Coast Complaints and Appeals Office, Dublin, 4 Aug 2005
84. Confirmation by telephone from the Office of the Ombudsman, 2 Aug 2005
85. Department of Health and Children, www.dohc.ie/agencies, accessed 2 Aug 2005
86. Information by telephone from the DoHC, 4 Aug 2005
87. Based on information received by telephone from HSE East Coast Area Complaints and Appeals Office, 4 Aug 2005 and HSE, Naas, Co. Kildare, 5 Aug 2005

13. Independence with legal leadership: the founding principles of Nordic complaints investigations
1. Information by telephone from Sundhedsvæsenets Patientklagenævn (Patients' Board of Complaints), 6 Nov 2002
2. John Elder, *Who Cares About the Health Victim?*, Klaxon Books, 1998, p. 108, from information supplied by Sundhedsvæsenets Patientklagenævn; additional details from Sundhedsvæsenets Patientklagenævn, Nov 2002
3. Information by telephone from Sundhedsvæsenets Patientklagenævn, 6 Nov 2002
4. Synopsis of information from p. 109, *Who Cares About the Health Victim?*, produced from data provided by Sundhedsvæsenets Patientklagenævn who confirmed it as accurate in Nov 2002
5. Letters from Sundhedsvæsenets Patientklagenævn, 1 Feb 2001, 20 Feb 2001; *Who Cares About the Health Victim?*, p. 107, from information supplied by Sundhedsvæsenets Patientklagenævn
6. Letter from Sundhedsvæsenets Patientklagenævn, 30 Oct 2001
7. Letter from Sundhedsvæsenets Patientklagenævn, 20 Feb 2001
8. Letter from Sundhedsvæsenets Patientklagenævn, 30 Oct 2001
9. Statistics received from Sundhedsvæsenets Patientklagenævn (Patients' Board of Complaints), Copenhagen, Denmark, letters dated 20 Feb 2001 and 20 Feb 2002
10. Sundhedsvæsenets Patientklagenævn, 20 Feb 2002
11. Sundhedsvæsenets Patientklagenævn, 6 Nov 2002
12. *Who Cares About the Health Victim?*, p. 107
13. Letter from the Ministry of Social Affairs and Health, Helsinki, Finland, 29 Mar 2001
14. Ibid.
15. Letter from the Ministry of Social Affairs and Health, Helsinki, 8 Apr 2002
16. *Who Cares About the Health Victim?*, pp. 113–14, approved as accurate by the Ministry of Social Affairs and Health, Helsinki
17. Ibid., p. 114
18. Statistics and associated data from the Ministry of Social Affairs and Health, Helsinki, Finland, letter dated 8 Apr 2002
19. Ibid.
20. Ibid.
21. Ibid.
22. Information from Statens Helsetilsyn (Norwegian Board of Health), Oslo, Norway, 28 Jun 2002
23. Ibid.; *Who Cares About the Health Victim?*, 137–8
24. Information from Statens Helsetilysin (Norwegian Board of Health), 28 Jun 2002
25. Ibid.
26. Ibid.

27. Ibid.
28. Ibid.
29. Ibid.
30. Document from Socialstyrelsen (National Board of Health and Welfare), Stockholm, Sweden, Mar 2002
31. Ibid.
32. Ibid.
33. Document from Hälso – och sjukvärdens ansvarsnämnd (Medical Responsibility Board), Stockholm, 5 Nov 2002
34. Ibid.
35. Ibid.; *Fact Sheets on Sweden*, published by the Swedish Institute May 1999, received from Socialstyrelsen, Stockholm, 4 Mar 2002
36. Document provided by Socialstyrelsen, 4 Mar 2002
37. Ibid.
38. Information by telephone from Hälso – och sjukvärdens ansvarsnämnd, 5 Nov 2002
39. Document from Socialstyrelsen, 4 Mar 2002
40. Data sent by Hälso – och sjukvärdens ansvarsnämnd, 23 May and 5 Nov 2002
41. Document from Socialstyrelsen, 4 Mar 2002
42. Ibid.
43. Document from Heilbrigdis – og tryggingamálaráðuneytið (Ministry of Health and Social Security), 24 Jul 2001; additional information provided by the Ministry during subsequent telephone conversation
44. Document from Heilbrigdis – og tryggingamálaráðuneytið, 24 Jul 2001
45. Ibid.
46. Ibid.
47. Ibid.
48. Data received by fax from Heilbrigdis – og tryggingamálaráðuneytið (Ministry of Health and Social Security), 13 Feb 2002
49. Ibid.
50. Ibid.

14. A specific patients' rights Act for Finland and Norway
1. Status and Rights of Patients Act 1992, Chapter 1, s. 2a
2. Ibid., Chapter 2, s. 3
3. Ibid.
4. Ibid.
5. Ibid., Chapter 2, s. 4
6. Ibid.
7. Ibid., Chapter 2, s. 5
8. Ibid.
9. Ibid.
10. Ibid., Chapter 2, s. 6
11. Ibid.
12. Ibid.
13. Ibid.
14. Ibid.
15. Ibid.
16. Ibid., Chapter 2, s. 9
17. Ibid., Chapter 2, ss. 7 and 9
18. Ibid., Chapter 2, s. 9
19. Ibid.
20. Ibid., Chapter 2, s. 8
21. Ibid., Chapter 4, s. 12 (30 Jun 2000/653)
22. Ibid., Chapter 4, s. 13 (30 Jun 2000/653), and Chapter 5, s. 14 (30 Jun 2000/653)
23. Ibid., Chapter 3, s. 10

24. Ibid.
25. Ibid., Chapter 3, s. 11
26. Patients' Rights Act 1999, Chapter 1, s. 1 (1)
27. Ibid., Chapter 2, s. 2(1)
28. Ibid., Chapter 2, ss. 2(2) and 2(3)
29. Ibid., Chapter 2, ss. 2(4) and 2(5)
30. Ibid., Chapter 3, s. 3(1)
31. Ibid., Chapter 3, s. 3(2)
32. Ibid., Chapter 3, s. 3(3)
33. Ibid., Chapter 3, s. 3(4)
34. Ibid., Chapter 3, s. 3(5)
35. Ibid., Chapter 3, s. 3(6)
36. Ibid., Chapter 4, ss. 4(1) and 4(2)
37. Ibid., Chapter 4, s. 4(3)
38. Ibid., Chapter 4, s. 4(4)
39. Ibid., Chapter 4, s. 4(5)
40. Ibid., Chapter 4, s. 4(6)
41. Ibid., Chapter 4, ss. 4(7) and 4(8)
42. Ibid., Chapter 4, s. 4(9)
43. Ibid., Chapter 5, s. 5(1)
44. Ibid., Chapter 5, ss. 5(2) and 5(3)
45. Ibid., Chapter 6, ss. 6(1) to 6(4)
46. Ibid., Chapter 7, ss. 7(1) and 7(5)
47. Ibid., Chapter 7, ss. 7(2), 7(3) and 7(5)
48. Ibid., Chapter 7, ss. 7(4) and 7(6)
49. Ibid., Chapter 8, ss. 8(1) to 8(7)
50. Socialstyrelsen, *Concept of Patients' Rights*, Stockholm, Socialstyrelsen, 18 Sept 2001
51. Health and Medical Services Act 1982 (amended Mar 2000), ss. 2a–2e
52. Ibid., ss. 3, 3c and 4
53. Ibid., s. 3a
54. Ibid.
55. Socialstyrelsen, *Concept of Patients' Rights*

15. Denmark, too, has an array of patients' rights set in stone

1. Patients' Legal Rights and Entitlements Act 1998, Part 2, ss. 6–7
2. Ibid., Part 2, s. 8
3. Ibid., Part 2, s. 9
4. Ibid., Part 2, s. 10
5. Ibid., Part 2, s. 11
6. Ibid., Part 2, ss. 12–13
7. Ibid., Part 3, ss. 14–15
8. Ibid., Part 3, ss. 16–17
9. Ibid., Part 4, ss. 20–1
10. Ibid., Part 5, ss. 23–7
11. Ibid., Part 5, s. 28
12. Ibid., Part 5, ss. 29–31
13. Ibid., Part 6, ss. 33–4

16. How far do patients' rights go in Iceland?

1. Rights of Patients Act 1997, Chapter 1, Article 1
2. Ibid., Article 3
3. Ibid., Article 4
4. Ibid., Chapter 2, Article 5
5. Ibid., Article 6
6. Ibid., Article 7

7. Ibid., Article 8
8. Ibid., Article 9
9. Ibid., Article 10; Regulation on Scientific Research in the Health Sector, no. 552/1999, Articles 4–7
10. Rights of Patients Act 1997, Chapter 3, Article 12
11. Ibid., Chapter 2, Article 11
12. Ibid., Chapter 3, Article 13
13. Ibid., Chapter 4, Articles 14–16
14. Ibid., Chapter 5, Articles 17–21
15. Ibid., Chapter 5, Article 22
16. Ibid.
17. Ibid., Article 23
18. Ibid., Article 24
19. Ibid., Chapter 6, Articles 25–7
20. Ibid., Chapter 7, Article 28

17. Patient compensation Danish style

1. Calculated from statistical data provided by Patientforsikringen (Patient Insurance), Copenhagen, Denmark, 14 Jun 2002
2. Patientforsikringen (Patient Insurance), *The Danish Patient Insurance System*, s.1(1), produced by Patientforsikringen and provided 1 May 2001
3. Ibid.
4. Ibid., s. 10
5. Ibid.
6. Ibid.
7. Ibid.
8. Ibid.
9. Ibid., s. 1(2); updated information from Patientforsikringen, 14 Jun 2002
10. Patientforsikringen, *The Danish Patient Insurance System*, s. 1(3)
11. Ibid., s. 2
12. Ibid.
13. Ibid., s. 3(1)
14. Ibid.
15. Ibid., s. 3(2)
16. Ibid.
17. Ibid., s. 3(3)
18. Ibid., s. 3(4)
19. Ibid., s. 4
20. Ibid., ss. 5(1) to 5(3)
21. Ibid., s. 6(1)
22. Ibid., s. 8; updated statistics from Patientforsikringen, 14 Jun 2002
23. Information from Patientforsikringen, 14 Jun 2002
24. Patientforsikringen, *The Danish Patient Insurance System*, s. 8; updated statistics from Patientforsikringen, 14 Jun 2002
25. Statistics provided by Patientforsikringen, Jun 2002
26. Patientforsikingen, *The Danish Patient Insurance System*, s. 8; updated statistics from Patientforsikringen, 14 Jun 2002
27. Ibid.
28. Patientforsikringen, *The Danish Patient Insurance System*, s. 7
29. Ibid., s. 9; information from Patientforsikringen, 30 Apr 2001
30. Information from Patientforsikringen, 30 Apr 2001
31. Patientforsikringen, *The Danish Patient Insurance System*, s. 3(4)
32. Ibid., s. 10
33. Ibid.

Note.
A very small number of minor alterations to chapter copy called for in the correspondence dated 14 June 2002 from Patientforsikringen, and implemented, are not referred to in the above notes.

18. Patients' legal protection made easy

1. Ministry of Social Affairs and Health, Helsinki, *The Finnish Patient Insurance: major amendments (to the Patient Injuries Act 1986 – in force 1 May 1987) which became law on 1 May 1999*, document supplied 29 Mar 2001
2. Patient Injuries Act 1986, s. 1
3. Patient Injuries Act 1986, s. 4; Marti Mikkonen, 'The Nordic model: Finnish experience of the Patient Injuries Act in practice', abstract of lecture published in 13th World Congress on Medical Law, Aug 2000, *Book of Proceedings II*, p. 793; Finnish Patient Insurance Centre, *Patient Insurance in Finland*, Coverage of patient insurance
4. Finnish Patient Insurance Centre, *Patient Insurance in Finland*, coverage of patient insurance, supplied Mar 2001
5. FPIC, *Patient Insurance in Finland*, Compensation criteria from 1 May 1999
6. Ibid.
7. Ibid.
8. Ibid.
9. Ibid.
10. Ibid.
11. Ibid.
12. FPIC, *Patient Insurance in Finland*, Compensation
13. FPIC, *Patient Insurance in Finland*, Compensation, Co-ordination of benefits
14. Mikkonen, 'The Nordic model'
15. Patient Injuries Act 1986, s. 10
16. FPIC, *Patient Insurance in Finland*, Unsuccessful claims
17. 13th World Congress on Medical Law, Aug 2000, *Book of Proceedings II*, p. 795, 'Redress mechanisms', supplied by Finland's Ministry of Social Affairs and Health, 29 Mar 2001
18. Ibid.
19. Patient Injuries Act 1986, s. 11
20. Ibid., s. 11a
21. Ibid.
22. Ibid.
23. 13th World Congress on Medical Law, 'Redress mechanisms'
24. 13th World Congress on Medical Law, Aug 2000, *Book of Proceedings II*, p. 796, 'Statistics', 20 May 2000, supplied by Finland's Ministry of Social Affairs and Health
25. Document, prepared by Potalusvakuutus (Patient Insurance), 16 Mar 2001 and supplied by Finland's Ministry of Social Affairs and Health, 29 Mar 2001; Mikkonen, 'The Nordic model'
26. Ibid.
27. 13th World Congress on Medical Law, 'Statistics'
28. 13th World Congress on Medical Law, Aug 2000, *Book of Proceedings II*, p. 797, 'Paid claims', and p. 793, 'Liability to insure', supplied by Finland's Ministry of Social Affairs and Health
29. 13th World Congress on Medical Law, 'Paid claims'
30. FPIC, *Patient Insurance in Finland*, Obligation to insure, Failure to insure
31. Ibid., How to insure
32. Ibid., Premium rating
33. Ibid., Injuries caused by pharmaceuticals
34. Patient Injuries Act 1986, s. 5; 13th World Congress on Medical Law, Aug 2000, *Book of Proceedings II*, p. 792, 'Patient Insurance Centre'
35. Patient Injuries Act 1986, ss. 5b and 5c
36. Ibid., s. 5c

37. Ibid., s. 5d
38. Ibid., s. 6
39. Ibid., ss. 7, 7a and 8
40. Ibid., s. 8
41. Ibid., s. 9
42. Ibid., s. 9a
43. Ibid., s. 10a
44. Ibid.
45. Ibid., ss. 11d, 11e and 12

19. The rising tide of no-fault schemes
1. Socialstyrelsen, *Patient Compensation System (Patientforsakringen)*, Stockholm, Socialstyrelsen (National Board of Health and Welfare), 2001, pp. 2–3
2. Ibid., p. 2
3. Ibid.
4. Ibid., p. 3
5. Ibid.
6. Ibid.
7. Patientforsakringen, *Patient Compensation System (Patientforsakringen)*, Socialstyrelsen (National Board of Health and Welfare), Stockholm, Swedish Patient Insurance Association, 2001, p. 3
8. Ibid., pp. 2–3
9. Faxed letter from Norsk Pasientskadeerstatning, Oslo, 9 Mar 2001
10. Ibid.
11. Information received by telephone from from Norsk Pasientskadeerstatning, Oslo, 26 Apr 2004
12. Faxed letter from Norsk Pasientskadeerstatning, Oslo, 1 Nov 2001
13. Information received by telephone from from Norsk Pasientakadeerstatning, Oslo, 26 Apr 2004
14. Faxed letter from Norsk Pasientskadeerstatning, Oslo, 20 Feb 2001; information by telephone from Norsk Pasientskadeerstatning, Oslo, 26 Apr 2004
15. Faxed letter from Norsk Pasientskadeerstatning, Oslo, 20 Feb 2001
16. Information received by telephone from Norsk Pasientskadeerstatning, Oslo, 26 Apr 2004
17. Faxed letter from Norsk Pasientskadeerstatning, Oslo, 20 Feb 2001; information received by telephone from Norsk Pasientskadeerstatning, Oslo, 26 Apr 2004
18. Letter and information from Ministry of Health and Social Security, Reykjavik, on patient insurance and compensation system, 24 Jul 2001; Patient Insurance Act 2000, Articles 1 and 9
19. Letter and information from Ministry of Health and Social Security, Reykjavik, on patient insurance and compensation system, 24 Jul 2001
20. Patient Insurance Act 2000, Article 9
21. Ibid., Article 11
22. Ibid. Articles 13 and 14
23. Ibid., Article 15
24. Ibid., Article 16
25. Ibid., Articles 10 and 12; letter and information from Ministry of Health and Social Security, Reykjavik, on patient insurance and compensation system, 24 Jul 2001
26. Patient Insurance Act 2000, Articles 2, 3 and 4
27. Ibid., Article 6
28. Ibid., Article 7
29. Ibid., Article 3
30. Ibid., Article 8
31. Ibid., Article 5
32. Ibid.
33. Ibid.

34. Ibid., Article 4
35. Letter from Ministry of Health and Social Security, Reykjavik, on claims to the State Social Security Institute, 13 Feb 2002
36. Patient Insurance Act 2000, Article 19
37. Ibid., Article 18
38. Ibid., Article 17
39. Faxed letter from Volksvanwaltschaft (Ombudsman's Board), Vienna, 16 Mar 2001, p. 1, para. 2,
40. Ibid.
41. Ibid., p. 1, para. 3, p. 2, para. 2,
42. Ibid., p. 1, para. 4, p. 2, paras. 3 and 4
43. Faxed letter from Volksvanwaltschaft (Ombudsman's Board), Vienna, 31 Oct 2001; telephone conversation with senior representative of Volksvanwaltschaft (Ombudsman's Board), Vienna, May 2004
44. Information by telephone from Dr Thierry Vansweevelt, professor in tort and medical law, University of Antwerp, Belgium, 3 Jun 2005

20. Final thoughts on the crucial issues

1.   Department of Health, *NHS Complaints Procedure National Evaluation*, 2001, Chapters 1 and 3
2.   General Medical Council, *Changing Times, Changing Cultures: a review of the work of the GMC since 1995*, p. 3, undated but available in 2003
3.   *GMC News*, issue 16, Feb 2003, p. 5,
4.   Information provided by the Ministry of Social Affairs and Health, Helsinki
5.   BBC1, *Countryfile*, reported this case about Northern Ireland on 7 Mar 2004
6.   House of Commons, *House of Commons Guide – Complaints Against a Member of Parliament*, extracts from pamphlet, 2003
7.   Information provided verbally by the Office of the Parliamentary Commissioner for Standards, House of Commons, London, Mar 2004
8.   House of Commons, *House of Commons Guide*
9.   The United Kingdom Parliament, *Standards in Public Life*, Standards of Conduct in the House of Lords, www.parliament.uk/works/standards, accessed 22 Mar 2004
10. *About the Law Society*, www.lawsoc.org.uk/dcs/fourth_tier.asp?section_id, accessed 7 Apr 2004
11. Legal Services Ombudsman, *About the Legal Services Ombudsman: what does the Legal Services Ombudsman do?*, www.olso.org/about.asp, accessed 29 May 2004
12. Legal Services Ombudsman, *What We Do: what will the Ombudsman do if she thinks my complaint was badly handled?* and *How Much Compensation Could I Be Awarded?*, www.olso.org/whatwedo.asp, accessed 29 May 2004
13. Clare Dyer, 'Threat of huge fines on Law Society', *Guardian*, 27 Sept 2003
14. Press Complaints Commission, *About the PCC*, code of practice, www.pcc.org.uk, accessed 27 May 2004
15. 'Wakeham quits Press watchdog', *Daily Mail*, 19 Mar 2002
16. Independent Police Complaints Commission, 'How to make a complaint', 'What happens when I make my complaint?', 'How will my complaint be resolved?', 'Local resolution by the police', www.ipcc.gov.uk, accessed 11 May 2004
17. Ibid.; additional information and clarification from the IPCC, 15 Mar 2005
18. Independent Police Complaints Commission, *IPCC Investigations*, document supplied by the IPCC, 15 Mar 2005
19. Ibid.; telephone clarification and confirmation that all re-presented copy (about the IPCC) was accurate received from IPCC, 21 and 23 Mar 2005
20. For example the reports of the inquiry, *The Decision to go to War in Iraq*, by the House of Commons Foreign Affairs Committee in July 2003, and the subsequent investigation by parliament's Intelligence and Security Committee into aspects of the circumstances leading up to and following the invasion of Iraq provoked accusations of 'whitewash' by

much of the media and public. The findings in January 2004 of the limited British government initiated inquiry by Lord Hutton into the events leading up to the death of Dr David Kelly in July 2003 (associated with the invasion of Iraq), which exonerated all the key players except some at the BBC, seemed to provoke even more widespread accusations of 'whitewash' and onesidedness by the media and public. In July 2004 the more far-reaching and critical *Review of Intelligence on Weapons of Mass Destruction – Report of a Committee of Privy Counsellors*, about the case for attacking Iraq, was produced by an investigating group led by Lord Butler. This was generally considered to be more condemnatory of certain of the main parties involved than the reports of any of the three other investigations about the decision to go to war. Nevertheless, as in the cases of the three earlier reports, none of the individuals in government or its civil and security services who was named in the inquiry resigned their post as a result of it. It seems that nobody was held to be responsible, despite the case for the invasion being 'seriously flawed'. By contrast – and arguably for much less reason – both the chairman and director-general of the BBC and the journalist who was at the centre of events before the death of Dr Kelly resigned their positions after the Hutton Report was published.

Brief credentials of the main figures in the four inquiries are as follows:

- *The Foreign Affairs Committee inquiry*_The chairman of this Labour-dominated committee is Labour MP Donald Anderson, who voted for the attack on Iraq – as presumably did other Labour and Conservative committee members.

- *Parliamentary Intelligence and Security Committee inquiry*_The chair of this committee is Labour MP Ann Taylor, past Secretary to the Treasury (2001–2004) in the Labour government of which she was its Chief Whip (1998–2001). One of the other members of the committee was the Conservative MP Michael Mates, who is also a past government minister.

- *The Hutton inquiry*_Lord Hutton was a high-ranking law officer over many years, in some of which he had previous connections with government. He is a member of parliament's House of Lords.

- *The Butler inquiry*_Cabinet Secretary and Head of the Home Civil Service between 1988 and 1998, Lord Butler served three prime ministers during this period. He also had similar connections with two earlier prime ministers and had been involved with government since the early 1960s. His aides in the investigation were Ann Taylor MP (see above); Sir John Chilcott (extensive involvement in government and connected with security and intelligence services); Michael Mates (recent background already provided); and Lord Inge (member of the House of Lords and a former Chief of the Defence Staff).

The four inquiries are the kinds of exercises that seem to pass for impartial investigations in the eyes of government in the UK – but not, it would appear, in the view of almost anyone else.

BIBLIOGRAPHY

(Publications, documents and website sources)

The list of printed sources of reference or information is presented alphabetically by title under each country. In the case of website addresses this arrangement applies to the abbreviated form of the addressee's name.

Denmark
(Publications and documents)

The Danish Patient Insurance System, Patientforsikringen
Patients' Legal Rights and Entitlements Act 1998, translated into English by Copenhagen Hospital Corporation, 22 Nov 2000

Finland
(Publications and documents)

The Finnish Patient Insurance – major amendments (to the Patient Injuries Act 1986), Patient Insurance Centre
'The Nordic Model: Finnish experience of the Patient Injuries Act in practice', abstract of a lecture published in *Book of Proceedings II,* 13th World Congress on Medical Law, Marti Mikkonen, Aug 2000
Patient Injuries Act 1986, translation in English at the Federation of Finnish Insurance Companies, Oct 2000
Patient Insurance in Finland, Finnish Patient Insurance Centre
Status and Rights of Patients Act 1992, unofficial translation, no. 785/1992

Iceland
(Documents)

Patient Insurance Act 2000
Regulation on Scientific Research in the Health Sector No. 552/199
Rights of Patients Act 1997

Ireland (Republic of)
(Publications and documents)

'Conflict and Accountability: the citizen and the ombudsman', address to the Irish School of Ecumenics by Kevin Murphy, 30 Nov 2001, issued by the Office of the Ombudsman, Dublin
The Evolving role of the Irish Ombudsman, Kevin Murphy, Dublin, Office of the Ombudsman
'Kilkenny Mental Health Services complaints handling policy and procedures: appeal', Kilkenny Mental Health Services, Feb 2002
North Eastern Health Board Regional Complaints Procedure: a guide for Health Board Staff, North Eastern Health Board, Apr 2001
The Ombudsman Explains the Work of his Office, Office of the Ombudsman document, [2002]
People Matter – A Framework for the Enhanced and Effective Handling of Complaints [in the] Eastern Region, Eastern Regional Health Authority, Sep 2003

314

Presentation to the Oireachtas Joint Committee on the Strategic Management Initiative, Irish
    Ombudsman, Jun 2001
Quality and Fairness: a health system for you – Health Strategy 2001, Department of Health
    and Children, issued Nov 2001
'Review of complaints procedures, protocols and appeals in the region', Eastern Regional
    Health Authority, summer 2001
Second Report of the Joint Oireachtas Committee on the Strategic Management, 16 Apr
    2002
'Waterford Regional Hospital complaints procedure', Waterford Regional Hospital, Jul
    1999
'Your voice, shared vision, the Mid-Western Health Board comments and complaints policy:
    a guide for Health Board staff', Mid-Western Health Board, Jul 2002

(*Website*)
www.doh.ie, Department of Health and Children, Dublin

Norway
(*Document*)

Patients' Rights Act 1999

Sweden
(*Publications and documents*)

The Concept of Patients' Rights, Socialstyrelsen, [2001]
Fact Sheets on Sweden (classification FS 76 x V p b), The Health Care System in Sweden,
    Swedish Institute, May 1999
Health and Medical Services Act 1982 (amended in Mar 2000)

United Kingdom
(*Publications and documents*)

About CHI: what is CHI?, *The future: CHAI – Legislation*, *The future: CHAI – About
    CHAI*, Commission for Health Improvement, www.chi.nhs.uk/eng
About the Commission, Commission for Patient and Public Involvement in Health,
    www.cppih.org/about_what.html
About the CSCI, Commission for Social Care Inspection, London, Department of Health,
    www.doh.gov.uk/csci
Annual Report 1999–00 and *Annual Report 2000–01* Assembly Ombudsman for Northern
    Ireland and Northern Ireland Commissioner for Complaints
Annual Report 2001–02 and *Annual Report 2002–03*, Assembly Ombudsman for Northern
    Ireland and Northern Ireland Commissioner for Complaints, www.ni-
    ombudsman.org.uk
Annual Report 1998–99, Health Service Commissioner for England, Scotland and Wales
Annual Report 2000–01 and *Annual Report 2002–03*, Health Service Commissioner for
    Wales, www.ombudsman.org.uk/whsc
Annual Report 1999–00, Health Service Ombudsman for England,
    www.ombudsman.org.uk/hsc
Annual Report 2000–01, Health Service Ombudsman for England
Annual Report 2001–02, Health Service Ombudsman for England,
    www.ombudsman.org.uk/hsc
Annual Report 2002–03, Health Service Ombudsman for England,
    www.ombudsman.org.uk/hsc
Annual Report 1998–99, Parliamentary Ombudsman for Northern Ireland and Northern
    Ireland Commissioner for Complaints

Annual Report 2000–01, Scottish Health Service Ombudsman,
    www.ombudsman.org.uk/shsc
Annual Report 2001–02, Scottish Health Service Ombudsman,
    www.ombudsman.org.uk/shsc
Annual Report 2002–03, Scottish Public Services Ombudsman
Annual Report 2000–01; Southern Health and Social Services Board, Armagh
Annual Report 2000–01 and *Annual Report 2001–02*, Western Health and Social Services
    Board, Londonderry
Annual Review of Complaints 2001–02; Southern Health and Social Services Board,
    Armagh
Appendix A: the Data Protection Act 1998, www.doh.gov.uk/ipu
Appendix B: the Health Record Access Route, www.doh.gov.uk/ipu
Briefing Sheet – GMC reforms at a glance, General Medical Council
Changing Times, Changing Cultures: a review of the work of the GMC since 1995, General
    Medical Council
Clinical Negligence – What are the Issues and Options for Reform?, London, Department of
    Health, www.doh.gov.uk/clinicalnegligencereform
Commission for Health Improvement website, www.chi.nhs.uk
Compensation for Victims of Violent Crime, Criminal Injuries Compensation Authority,
    2003
'Compensation and Social Security Benefits – a basic guide to how social security benefits
    can affect your compensation', Leeds, Department for Work and Pensions, Apr 2004
'Complaints – listening…acting…improving, guidance on implementation of the NHS
    Complaints Procedure', London, Department of Health, Mar 1996
Complaints Monitoring Report 2000–01 and *Complaints Monitoring Report 2001–02*,
    Northern Health and Social Services Board, Ballymena
Complaints Report 2001–02, Eastern Health and Social Services Board, Belfast
Complaints to the NHS in Wales 2000–01, *Complaints to the NHS in Wales 2001–02* and
    Complaints to the NHS in Wales 2002–03, Health Statistics and Analysis Unit,
    Statistical Directorate, National Assembly for Wales, Cardiff,
    www.wales.gov.uk/statistics
Confidentiality: NHS code of practice, version 3.5, London, Department of Health, 27 Oct
    2003, www.doh.gov.uk/ipu/confiden
Consent – What You have a Right to Expect, guides for adults, children and young people,
    parents, relatives and carers, www.doh.gov.uk
Constitution of Panels Rules 2004 (Annex B), General Medical Council
Daily Mail, 'Wakeham quits Press watchdog', 19 Mar 2002
Data Protection Act 1998, www.legislation.hmso.gov.uk/acts1998
Do You Have a Complaint About the Service you have Received from the NHS?, Health
    Service Ombudsman for England, [2001]
Fifth Annual Review of Complaints April 2000–March 2001, Eastern Health and Social
    Services Board, Belfast
Fitness to Practice Procedures, General Medical Council, Oct 2002
Fitness to Practice Proposed New Rules and Guidance – a consultation paper, Jul 2003,
    General Medical Council
Fitness to Practice Reforms: Rules and Guidance – Recommendations, document 4a,
    General Medical Council, 7 Jul 2004
Fitness to Practice Rules 2004 (Annex A), General Medical Council
Fitness to Practice Statistics 2003 (including Annexes A to F), General Medical Council
Forum Support Organisations, Commission for Patient and Public Involvement in Health,
    www.cppih.org/local_new.html
Framework document (updated version), NHS Litigation Authority, Jul 2003
The GMC's Fitness to Practice Procedures (Ref. 07/01/01v14), London, Manchester and
    Edinburgh, General Medical Council
GMC News, General Medical Council, issue 16, Feb 2003,

Good Practice in Consent Implementation Guide: consent to examination or treatment, London, Department of Health, first published Nov 2001

Guardian, Clare Dyer, 'Threat of huge fines on Law Society', 27 Sep 2003

Guide to the Criminal Injuries Compensation Scheme 2001, London and Glasgow, Criminal Injuries Compensation Authority, Jan 2003

A Guide to the Work of the Health Service Ombudsman, Office of the Health Service Commissioner for England, Scotland and Wales, Apr 1996

Handling Complaints: monitoring the NHS complaints procedures. England, financial year 2000–01 (including statistics for 1996–97 to 2000–01), www.doh.gov.uk/nhscomplaints

Health Care and Associated Professions, Doctors: The General Medical Council (Legal Assessors) Rules 2004, (SI 2004 No. 2625), Annex C

House of Commons Guide – Complaints Against a Member of Parliament, Office of the Parliamentary Commissioner for Standards, Dec 2003

How to Complain about the NHS, Department of Health, www.dh.gov.uk/PolicyAndGuidance/OrganisationPolicy/ComplaintsPolicy/NH

How to Make a Complaint about the NHS, Department of Health, www.dh.gov.uk/PolicyAndGuidance/OrganisationPolicy/ComplaintsPolicy/NH

Independent, Jeremy Laurence, 'Patients need justice', 1 Dec 1998

Independent Complaints Advocacy Services (ICAS), London, Department of Health, www.doh.gov.uk/complaintsadvocacyservice.htm

'Industrial Injuries Disablement Benefit for an Accident at Work', (Bl 100A), 4 May 2004, Social Security Office, Jobcentre Plus, Leeds, part of the Department for Work and Pensions, www.jobcentreplus.gov.uk

'Industrial Injuries Disablement Benefit (accidents/diseases)', Jobcentre Plus, Leeds, part of the Department for Work and Pensions, www.jobcentreplus.gov.uk

IPCC Investigations (Ref. COM/8), Independent Police Complaints Commission, London

ISD Scotland – National Statistics, NHS National Services Scotland, Edinburgh, www.isdscotland.org

Making Amends – A Consultation Paper Setting Out Proposals for Reforming the Approach to Clinical Negligence in the NHS, Sir Liam Donaldson, London, Department of Health, Jun 2003

Medical Accidents: your rights if you have been injured during treatment, London, Legal Services Commission, May 2003

The Medical Act 1983 (Amendment) Order 2002 (SI 2002 No. 3135), HMSO, www.legislation.hmso.gov.uk

National Patient Safety Agency – About Us, www.npsa.nhs.uk

NHS Complaints Procedure National Evaluation, London, Department of Health, Mar 2001

NHS Complaints Reform – Making Things Right, London, Department of Health, first published Feb 2003

NHS Complaints Procedure, Department of Health, www.doh.gov.uk/complaints/complaintsleaflet.htm

NICE, Appraisal by Department of Health, www.doh.gov.uk/nice

NICE, Introduction/Background/Why has NICE been set up?/Patient Involvement Unit for NICE, 'A Short Introduction to the Citizens Council', www.nice.org.uk

Northern Ireland Performance Tables (part), 1998–99, 1999–2000 and 2000–2001, Information and Analysis Directorate, Department of Health, Social Services and Public Safety, Belfast

The Nursing and Midwifery Order 2001 (SI 2002 No. 253), HMSO

Patient Advice and Liaison Services (PALS), London, Department of Health, www.doh.gov.uk/patientadviceandliaisonservices

Patient and Public Involvement Forums (PPI Forums), copy of Department of Health letter dated 4 Dec 2003, from www.cppih.org/ppi_new.html

PPI Forums, Commission for Patient and Public Involvement in Health, www.cppih.org/ppi

A Practical Guide to Community Legal Service funding by the Legal Services Commission, London, Legal Services Commission, Apr 2003

The Prep Handbook, United Kingdom Central Council for Nursing, Midwifery and Health Visiting, Jan 2001

Procedures Related to Adverse Clinical Incidents and Outcomes in Medical Care, House of Commons Health Committee Inquiry, 8 Jul 1999

Procedures Related to Adverse Clinical Incidents and Outcomes in Medical Care, Sixth Report, House of Commons Health Committee, issued 23 Nov 1999

Professional Conduct Annual Report 2000–01, United Kingdom Central Council for Nursing, Midwifery and Health Visiting, Nov 2001

Protecting and Using Confidential Patient Information – A Strategy for the NHS, London, Department of Health, www.nhsia.nhs.uk/caldicott/pages/link.asp

The Protection and Use of Patient Information: the NHS confidentiality code of practice, www.doh.gov.uk/ipu/confiden/protect/index

Reference Guide to Consent for Examination or Treatment, London, Department of Health, Aug 2001

Referring a Doctor to the GMC – Guidance for Members of the Medical Profession and other Healthcare Professionals, General Medical Council, Oct 2002

Referring a Doctor to the GMC – A Guide for Patients, General Medical Council, Oct 2002

Referring a Doctor to the GMC – A Guide for Patients (Ref. 07/01/01v14), London, Manchester and Edinburgh, General Medical Council, Nov 2004

Reforming the NHS Complaints Procedure: a listening document, London, Department of Health, Sep 2001

Registration Appeals Panels Rules 2004 (Annex B), General Medical Council

Registration Decisions – draft 7 Jan 2004 (version 2), (Annex A), General Medical Council

Report and Accounts, 2002 and 2003, NHS Litigation Authority

Scottish Health Statistics – NHS Complaints, ISD Scotland, NHS National Services Scotland, Edinburgh, www.isdscotland.org (previous website address: www.show.scot.nhs.uk/isd)

Self-regulation of Professionals in Health Care, London, National Consumer Council, Jun 1999

Standards in Public Life, Standards of Conduct in the House of Lords, The United Kingdom Parliament, www.parliament.uk

Supporting Doctors, Protecting Patients, London, Department of Health, Nov 1999

Supprting the Implementation of Patient Advice and Liaison Services (PALS) – Core Standards and Practice Guide, Department of Health, www.doh.gov.uk/patientadvice-andliaisonservices

Vaccine Damage Payments, Leeds, Department for Work and Pensions, www.dwp.gov.uk

Victims of Crimes of Violence: a guide to the criminal injuries compensation scheme, issue no. 2, Criminal Injuries Compensation Authority, Apr 1999

The Welsh Risk Pool, 22 Jul 2003

What does the Ombudsman do?, Office of the Northern Ireland Ombudsman

Who Cares About the Health Victim?, John Elder, 1998

Who's Who, 2002 and 2003

Written Complaints about Family Health Services by Service Area, England, 2002–03, Department of Health, www.performance.doh.gov.uk

Written Complaints about Hospital and Community Health Services by Service Area, England, 2002–03, Department of Health, www.performance.doh.gov.uk/hospitalac-tivity

Your Guide to the NHS, London, Department of Health, Jan 2001

(*Websites*)

www.chi.nhs.uk, Commission for Health Improvement

www.cica.gov.uk, Criminal Injuries Compensation Authority

www.cppih.org/about_what.html, Commission for Patient and Public Involvement in Health

www.cppih.org/local_new.html, CPPIH
www.cppih.org/ppi, CPPIH
www.dh.gov.uk/PolicyAndGuidance/OrganisationPolicy/ComplaintsPolicy/NH, Department of Health, London
www.doh.gov.uk, Department of Health
www.doh.gov.uk/clinicalnegligencereform, DoH
www.doh.gov.uk/complaints/advocacyservice.htm, DoH
www.doh.gov.uk/complaints/complaintsleaflet.htm, Department of Health, London
www.doh.gov.uk/csci, DoH
www.doh.gov.uk/ipu, DoH
www.doh.gov.uk/ipu/ahr, DoH
www.doh.gov.uk/ipu/confiden, DoH
www.doh.gov.uk/ipu/confiden/protect/index
www.doh.gov.uk/nhscomplaints, DoH
www.doh.gov.uk/nice, DoH
www.doh.gov.uk/patientadviceandliaisonservices, DoH
www.dwp.gov.uk, Department for Work and Pensions
www.ipcc.gov.uk, Independent Police Complaints Commission
www.isdscotland.org (previous website address: www.show.scot.nhs.uk/isd); ISD Scotland, NHS National Services Scotland, Edinburgh
www.jobcentreplus.gov.uk, Jobcentre Plus
www.lawsoc.org.uk, The Law Society
www.legislation.hmso.gov.uk/acts, HMSO
www.nhsia.nhs.uk/caldicott/pages/links.asp, NHS Information Authority
www.nhsla.com, NHS Litigation Authority
www.ni-ombudsman.org.uk, Assembly Ombudsman for Northern Ireland and Northern Ireland Commissioner for Complaints, 2003
www.nice.org.uk, National Institute for Clinical Excellence
www.npsa.nhs.uk, National Patient Safety Agency
www.number-10.gov.uk/output/Page 5705.asp, 10 Downing Street Newsroom
www.olso.org, Office of the Legal Services Ombudsman
www.ombudsman.org.uk/hsc, Health Service Ombudsman for England
www.ombudsman.org.uk/hse/england, Health Service Ombudsman for England
www.ombudsman.org.uk/recruitment, Parliamentary and Health Service Ombudsman
www.ombudsman.org.uk/hse/scotland, Scottish Health Service Ombudsman
www.ombudsman.org.uk/shsc, Scottish Health Service Ombudsman
www.ombudsman.org.uk/whsc, Health Service Commissioner for Wales
www.ni-ombudsman.org.uk, Assembly Ombudsman and Northern Ireland Commissioner for Complaints, 2003
www.parliament.uk, The United Kingdom Parliament
www.pcc.org.uk, Press Complaints Commission
www.performance.doh.gov.uk, DoH
www.performance.doh.gov.uk/hospitalactivity, DoH
www.wales.gov.uk/statistics, Health Statistics and Analysis Unit, Statistical Directorate, National Assembly for Wales, Cardiff

ACHCEW	Association of Community Health Councils for England and Wales
ARC	Assessment Referral Committee
BMA	British Medical Association
CAA	Constant Attendance Allowance
CCB	County Complaints Board, Sweden
CCC	Conduct and Competence Committee
CCO	case co-ordinator
CDF	Clinical Disputes Forum
CEO	chief executive officer
CFA	conditional fee agreement
CHAI	Commission for Healthcare Audit and Inspection
CHC	community health council
CHI	Commission for Health Improvement
CHRE	Council for Healthcare Regulatory Excellence
CICA	Criminal Injuries Compensation Authority
CLO	Central Legal Office
CMO	Chief Medical Officer
CNST	Clinical Negligence Scheme for Trusts
CPP	Committee on Professional Performance
CPPIH	Commission for Patient and Public Involvement in Health
CSCI	Commission for Social Care Inspection
DCA	Department for Constitutional Affairs
DH	Department of Health
DWP	Department for Work and Pensions
ECG	electrocardiogram
EEA	European Economic Area
EHSSB	Eastern Health and Social Services Board, Northern Ireland
ELS	Existing Liabilities Scheme
ERHA	Eastern Regional Health Authority, Republic of Ireland
FAS˙	Foras Aiseanna Saothair (Training and Employment Authority), Republic of Ireland
FHS	family health services
FSO	forum support organization
FTP	fitness to practise
GMC	General Medical Council
GP	general practitioner
HC	Health Committee
HPSS	Health and Personal Social Services, Northern Ireland
HRAIS	Human Rights Information Service
HSAN	Hälso-och sjukvärdens ansvarsnämnd (Medical Responsibility Board), Sweden
HSC	Health Service Commissioner
IC	Investigating Committee
ICAS	Independent Complaints Advocacy Service
INR	International Normalized Ratio
IOC	Interim Orders Committee
IOP	interim orders panel
IPCC	Independent Police Complaints Commission
IRP	independent review panel

IRS	Independent Review Secretariat
LHB	local health board
LSC	Legal Services Commission
LSO	Legal Services Ombudsman
LTPS	Liability to Third Party Scheme
MHAC	Mental Health Act Commission
MOH	medical officer of health, Denmark
NAO	National Audit Office
NCSC	National Care Standards Commission
NHS	National Health Service
NHSIA	NHS Information Authority
NHSLA	National Health Service Litigation Authority
NICE	National Institute for Health and Clinical Excellence; also National Institute for Clinical Excellence
NMC	Nursing and Midwifery Council
NPE	Norsk Pasientskadeerstatning (Norwegian System of Compensation)
NPSA	National Patient Safety Agency
NSF	national service framework
OSC	Overview and Scrutiny Committee
PAG	policy advisory group
PALS	Patient Advice and Liaison Services
PAP	professional advisory panel
PCA	Police Complaints Authority
PCC	Professional Conduct Committee
PCT	primary care trust
PES	Property Expenses Scheme
PIU	patient involvement unit
PPC	Preliminary Proceedings Committee
PPI	patient and public involvement
PPIP	patient and public involvement programme
PSF	Patientförsäkringen (Patient Insurance and Compensation Scheme), Sweden
RHA	regional health authority
SDA	severe disablement allowance
SHA	strategic health authority
SPD	serious deficient performance
SPM	serious professional misconduct
UKCC	United Kingdom Central Council for Nursing, Midwifery and Health Visiting
VDP	vaccine damage payment
WRP	Welsh Risk Pool

Unless otherwise shown all unidentified entries in this index refer to the
United Kingdom

80025 75540